Away for the WEEKEND®
NEW ENGLAND

52 Great Getaways in the
Six New England States
for Every Season of the Year

ELEANOR BERMAN

Revised and Updated

Crown Trade Paperbacks
New York

Acknowledgments

My sincere thanks to the many state and local tourist offices who provided so much helpful information and guidance.

Copyright © 1985, 1988, 1992, 1995 by Eleanor Berman

Published by Crown Trade Paperbacks, 201 East 50th Street, New York, New York 10022. Member of the Crown Publishing Group.

Random House, Inc. New York, Toronto, London, Sydney, Auckland

CROWN TRADE PAPERBACKS and colophon are trademarks of Crown Publishers, Inc.

Manufactured in the United States of America

Maps by Susan Hunt Yule

Library of Congress Cataloging-in-Publication Data
Berman, Eleanor
          Away for the weekend, New England: great getaways in the six New England states for every season of the year/Eleanor Berman.—Rev. and updated.
        p. cm.
              Includes index.
              1. New England—Guidebooks.   I. Title.
        F2.3.B48   1995
917.404'43—dc20   94-41240
                                                                         CIP

ISBN 0-517-88217-5

10 9 8 7 6 5 4 3 2 1

Fourth Revised Edition

Contents

FALL

WINTER

MAPS

INDEX

Introduction

New England has everything: craggy mountains and gentle rolling hills, placid lakes and the surging sea, quaint village greens, and contemporary cities. Whether you want to ski or sail or lie on the beach, soak up culture or escape from civilization, spend a day in chic stores or in virgin woods, you'll find what you are seeking in this rich and remarkable six-state area.

It's almost a problem. In an area so packed with attractions, how can you decide where to start? Should it be the mountains of New Hampshire or Vermont, the beaches of Cape Cod or the rockbound shores of Maine, the "tall ships" at Mystic or the Maritime Museum at Bath?

Away for the Weekend invites you to sample them all, one at a time, as memorable weekend trips. In contrast to most guidebook writers, I have not separated the New England area by states or tried to list all the myriad attractions that each state has to offer. Instead, I have gone by the seasons, picking out some of the very best places and special events to be found throughout the region at different times of the year.

There are a few things you should know from the start. The selections are admittedly personal, limited to locations and events I have visited and enjoyed. Nor is every single sightseeing attraction, lodging, or restaurant in each location included. I've tried instead to pick only the best— places I've either been to myself or had recommended to me by local sources or frequent visitors to each destination. For this fourth edition, many fine, recently opened inns and dining places have been added.

Since New England country inns are one of the particular delights of the region, I've done my best to see and select special inns for each location covered, but keep in mind that this is a guide to destinations and events, not a guide to inns. The lodgings listed here are those convenient for each specific weekend, and in some cases that could mean only motels or hotels. Where there is a choice, I've given the inns, leaving the motel listings to local tourist guides or the Mobil and AAA publications.

In addition to inns, "bed-and-breakfast" establishments have become increasingly popular with travelers. There is sometimes confusion as to what constitutes "bed-and-breakfast." Small inns that serve only breakfast are listed here as inns. Lodgings that are rooms in a private home, with or without a private bath, are what is meant here by "B & B." These can be extremely pleasant places to stay, both because they are economical and because they offer the chance to meet residents and pick up some of the flavor of living in the area. Because it is impossible to mention every individual bed-and-breakfast lodging, I have included a list of areawide registry headquarters at the front of the book.

HOW TO USE THE BOOK

The format for the trips in *Away for the Weekend* assumes that you have a normal two-day weekend to spend, arriving on Friday night and leaving late on Sunday. Fortunately, with easy air travel to cities such as Portland, Maine, and Burlington, Vermont, trips that once were impractical for weekend driving often can now be managed easily. Information regarding air transportation is included for each suggested trip, as well as bus or train information for those who do not have cars or who might prefer not to drive in the unpredictable winter months in New England. There is also a symbol indicating destinations that can be visited conveniently at least in part without a car.

For each trip, there is a suggested itinerary for a two-day stay, with added suggestions to accommodate varying tastes and time schedules. When there is enough to do to warrant a longer stay, a symbol at the start will tell you so. When you do have more than a weekend to spend, you can use these itineraries as a guide to planning a more extensive tour. If, for instance, you are touring the coast of Maine or the mountains of New Hampshire or Vermont, simply consult the maps and index for destinations that make for a convenient route.

Since the trips are arranged by seasons, you can read ahead about special events and reserve before it is too late. Even when the season of a location described is not applicable to your schedule, the lists of sights and accommodations will apply whenever you go.

Because special activities change with the seasons, you may find some destinations listed more than once. In the case of Boston, there is a separate chapter for families who want activities best suited for children. A symbol identifying weekends most likely to appeal to families appears among the indicators at the start of each trip chapter. You are, of course, the best judge of which trips your own children are likely to enjoy.

In many cases, the trips suggested are deliberately out of peak season. The seashore, for example, can be twice as nice in spring or fall, when both crowds and rates are at a minimum.

The symbols that indicate these various categories are:

 = recommended for children

 = accessible at least in part via public transportation

 = recommended for long weekends

As for prices, dollar signs indicate the range for lodging in a double room and dining as follows:

$ = under $70
$$ = $70 to $100
$$$ = $100 to $135
$$$$ = $135 to $200
$$$$$ = over $200

$ = most entrées under $12
$$ = entrées averaging $12 to $20
$$$ = most entrées $20 to $30
$$$$ = over $30 (often prix fixe)

When prices bridge two categories, you will find two symbols. In seafood restaurants, a wide price range usually indicates the cost of lobster dinners, always the most expensive item on the menu. A wide price range for inns may mean that the less expensive rooms do not have private baths. Check with innkeepers to be sure.

When accommodations include meals in their rates, symbols will indicate this:

CP = continental plan (includes breakfast only)
MAP = modified American plan (breakfast and dinner)
AP = American plan (all three meals included)

All of this information is as accurate as could be determined when the manuscript was turned in to the publisher. In the months that elapse between the writing and publication of any book, places sometimes close unexpectedly, and rates can change even before they can be put into print. For this reason, general price categories are used rather than specific rates. It is possible that even these general categories will change over time, with some of the places moving up into a more expensive range. Admissions fees to various attractions will undoubtedly go up as well, and hours sometimes change. So use this book as a guide—generally an accurate one—but *always* check for current prices when you plan your trip. Telephone numbers are included for this purpose.

If you discover that any information here has become seriously inaccurate, or that a place has closed or gone downhill, I hope that you will let me know in care of the publisher so that the entry can be corrected in the future. If you discover places I have missed, or have suggestions for future editions, I hope you'll let me know that as well. Several places have been added or dropped from this edition as a result of suggestions from thoughtful readers.

The maps at the back of the book are simplified to make it easy to see where the suggested destinations are located. They are not reliable guides as road maps, so be sure to have a detailed map in hand before you set out. One way to get an excellent free map of each state in New

England is to write to the travel or tourism office in the various states. These offices offer not only maps but excellent brochures on their states' attractions. Addresses are included at the end of this section, as are telephone numbers for the region's major transportation services.

In most cases, addresses for additional information also are given at the end of each itinerary. Do write well ahead of time, for the more you learn about your destination in advance, the more meaningful and enjoyable your visit will be.

One last warning: It almost goes without saying that when it comes to reservations in small country inns, you must plan well ahead or you will be disappointed. The same is true if you want to visit the shore at the height of the summer season or a ski resort during holiday periods. Most places offer refunds on deposits if you cancel with reasonable notice, so plan ahead—three or four months ahead is none too soon—and have your pick instead of having to settle for leftovers.

Writing this book has been a special pleasure. Having lived and traveled in New England for many years, I began with the impression that I already knew a great deal about the region and its most interesting attractions, but the more I traveled, the more I discovered that I had missed some special places, even in areas I had visited before. And the more territory I covered, the more I appreciated what a remarkable region this really is. I gained a new understanding of my heritage as an American by visiting the places where our nation was born, and new awareness of nature's extraordinary generosity in the beauty that is everywhere in this handful of fortunate states. With each update, I make new discoveries.

I hope *Away for the Weekend* will guide you to the same wonderful discoveries—as well as inspire you to find your own.

STATE TOURIST OFFICES AND REGIONAL TRANSPORTATION COMPANIES

Contact any of these state tourist offices for free maps and literature on attractions throughout their states, as well as for updated bed-and-breakfast registry listings:

Tourism Division
State of Connecticut Department
    of Economic Development
865 Brook Street
Rocky Hill, CT 06067
(800) CT BOUND

Maine Publicity Bureau
PO Box 2300
Hallowell, ME 04347
(207) 623-0363

Massachusetts Office of
    Travel & Tourism
100 Cambridge Street
Boston, MA 02202
(617) 727-3201 or
(800) 447-6277

New Hampshire Office of
  Travel and Tourism
172 Pembroke Road
Box 1856
Concord, NH 03302
(603) 271-2666 or
(800) FUN-IN-NH, Ext. 100

Rhode Island Department of
  Tourism
7 Jackson Walkway
Providence, RI 02903
(401) 277-2601 or
(800) 556-2484

Vermont Travel Division
134 State Street
Montpelier, VT 05602
(802) 828-3236
or

Vermont State Chamber of
  Commerce
Box 37
Montpelier, VT 05601
(802) 223-3443

Reference numbers for major
transportation companies serving
New England:

AMTRAK trains (800) USA-
  RAIL
Bonanza Buses (800) 556-3815
Peter Pan Buses (800) 237-8747
  or (800) 247-8560
Vermont Transit Buses
  (802) 864-6811
Concord Trailways Buses
  (800) 639-3317
Greyhound Buses: Check local
  directories or phone:
  (800) 231-2222

BED-AND-BREAKFAST REGISTRY SERVICES
Covering Several New England States

*Bed & Breakfast/Inns of
New England*
(all states)
128 South Hoop Pole Road
Guilford, CT 06437
(203) 457-0042 or
(800) 582-0853

*New England Hospitality
  Network*
PO Box 3291
Newport, RI 02840
(401) 849-1298
(RI, CT, MA)

*American Country Collection of
  Bed and Breakfasts*
(Western Massachusetts and
  Vermont)
4 Greenwood Lane
Delmar, NY 12054
(518) 439-7001

CONNECTICUT

Nutmeg Bed and Breakfast
PO Box 1117
West Hartford, CT 06107
(203) 236-6698 or
(800) 727-7592

Bed and Breakfast, Ltd.
PO Box 216
New Haven, CT 06513
(203) 469-3260

*Covered Bridge Bed and
    Breakfast*
(Northwest Connecticut)
PO Box 447A
Norfolk, CT 06058
(203) 542-5944

MAINE

Bed and Breakfast of Maine
377 Gray Road
Falmouth, ME 04105
(207) 797-5540

*Bed and Breakfast Down East
    Ltd.*
Macomber Mill Road
Box 547
Eastbrook, ME 04634
(207) 565-3517

MASSACHUSETTS

Berkshire Bed and Breakfast
(Western Massachusetts—
    Berkshires, Sturbridge,
    Springfield, and Pioneer
    Valley)
Main Street
Williamsburg, MA 01096
(413) 268-7244

*Covered Bridge Bed and
    Breakfast*
(some accommodations in the
    Massachusetts Berkshires)
PO Box 447A
Norfolk, CT 06058
(203) 542-5944

Bed and Breakfast Cape Cod
Box 341
West Hyannisport, MA 02672
(508) 775-2772

House Guests
(Cape Cod, Nantucket,
Martha's Vineyard)
PO Box 1881
Orleans, MA 02653
(508) 896-7053 or
(800) 666-HOST

Boston-Cambridge Area
*New England Bed and Breakfast,
    Inc.*
(Boston area)
PO Box 9100, Suite 176
Newton, MA 02159
(617) 244-2112 or
(617) 498-9819

*Bed and Breakfast Cambridge
    and Greater Boston*
PO Box 1344
Cambridge, MA 02238
(617) 576-1492 or
(800) 888-0178

*Bed and Breakfast Associates Bay
    Colony, Ltd.*
PO Box 57166
Babson Park Branch
Boston, MA 02157
(617) 449-5302

Greater Boston Hospitality
PO Box 1142
Brookline, MA 02146
(617) 277-5430

Host Homes of Boston
PO Box 117, Waban Branch
Newton, MA 02168
(617) 244-1308

Bed-and-Breakfast Agency of Boston
47 Commercial Wharf
Boston, MA 02110
(617) 720-3540 or
(800) CITY BNB

NEW HAMPSHIRE

New Hampshire Bed and Breakfast
RFD 3, Box 53
Laconia, NH 03246
(603) 279-8348

RHODE ISLAND

Bed and Breakfast of Rhode Island, Inc.
PO Box 3291
Newport, RI 02840
(401) 849-1298

Newport Bed and Breakfast
44 Everett Street
Newport, RI 02840
(401) 846-0362

VERMONT

Vermont Bed & Breakfast Reservation Service
PO Box One
Fairfield, VT 05455
(802) 827-3827

HIKING INFORMATION

For Appalachian Trail, White Mountains, Monadnocks, and other hiking information throughout New England:

Appalachian Mountain Club
5 Joy Street
Boston, MA 02108
(617) 523-0636

For day hiking in Vermont:

Green Mountain Club
RR1, Box 650
Waterbury Center, VT 05677
(802) 244-7037
(Hiking Center open daily, Memorial Day to Columbus Day, on Route 100, Waterbury Center)

For hiking holidays and inn-to-inn tours:

Vermont Hiking Holidays
Box 750
Bristol, VT 05443
(802) 453-4816

Country Inns Along the Trail
c/o Churchill House
RD 3, Box 3265
Brandon, VT 05733
(802) 247-3300 or
(800) 999-6865

Vermont Walking Tours
Craftsbury Common, VT 05827
(802) 586-7767

Publications:

Backcountry Publications
The Countryman Press
P.O. Box 175
Woodstock, VT 05091
(802) 457-1049

Spring

Overleaf:*The rugged shoreline of Kennebunkport, Maine.*

Sights for All Seasons in Woodstock

When Laurance Rockefeller married Mary Billings, the future of Woodstock, Vermont, was assured.

Mary is the granddaughter of Frederick Billings, an early conservationist and Woodstock native, who went West long enough to make his fortune during the gold rush, then returned to establish a farm that became a model for dairy farmers and environmentalists throughout the state. Many of Vermont's green hills are the results of Billings's reforestation efforts.

Rockefeller was best known as the guiding spirit behind Rockresorts, an organization that also pioneered in conservation by developing resorts that blend with and maximize the natural beauty of their environments.

Since the Rockefellers still use the Billings family home in Woodstock, it was almost inevitable that they would take an interest in the picturesque village, one that has been a favorite resort town since the original Woodstock Inn opened in 1893. The result is one of the most exquisite towns in Vermont, preserved in a manner only Rockefeller millions could manage.

If Woodstock's village green seems somehow to be more perfect than that of other towns, it may be because they've buried the overhead wires to prevent modern technology from marring the Colonial flavor. Most of the homes around the green were in place when General Lafayette passed through the village in 1825. Many have been bought and meticulously restored by the Rockefellers, who lease them out to caring tenants.

The Rockefellers also own the "new" Woodstock Inn, built in 1969, as well as the Suicide Six Ski Resort and the Woodstock Country Club, which boasts a Cross-Country Touring Center, a Robert Trent Jones golf course, and a slew of tennis and paddle tennis courts. Their latest addition is the Woodstock Sports Center, which provides year-round indoor facilities for tennis, racquetball, squash, and swimming. All this is available to inn guests, and for a fee, to anyone in Woodstock.

If that's not enough activity for you, hiking, biking, and riding trails also abound around Woodstock, helping visitors to make the most of the town and its meandering streams, covered bridges, and mountain views. Indeed, there's something for everyone in Woodstock, even if all you want to do is browse through a selection of fine shops.

Though this is truly a town for all seasons, Woodstock is a particularly lovely and welcome destination in the soft green days of spring, that time of year between skiing season and summer when many areas offer little to do.

If you make your headquarters at the Woodstock Inn on the green, you'll be choosing one of New England's classic resorts, traditional in style and surrounded by landscaped gardens. If there is any nip at all in the air, you'll likely be greeted with a welcoming fire in the huge field-stone fireplace that dominates a whole wall of the lobby. The furnishings are country antique, the colors subdued, and the spacious guest rooms are adorned with handsome traditional handwoven covers.

However, this is a resort hotel with over 140 rooms, not a cozy country inn. If something smaller is more your style, there are several lovely antique-filled bed-and-breakfast inns in town, within walking distance of all the shops.

For a warm, country experience, Kedron Valley Inn is the choice, set beside a brook and a spring-fed pond in the horse country of South Woodstock six miles from town. The nearby Kedron Valley Stables offers trail rides, as well as carriage rides through the countryside, a most romantic way to appreciate the back-roads beauty of the area.

For budget-watchers, one of the best values around is the tastefully furnished, antique-filled 1840 Applebutter Inn, a few miles east of town in Taftsville, just off Route 4.

Seeing Woodstock is easy, since everything is clustered within a couple of blocks of the green. More than three dozen historic houses, all still privately owned, can be seen on a walk along Central and Elm streets, which intersect at the green. From Memorial Day on, you can visit one of the loveliest, the Dana House on Elm Street, an 1807 residence that was occupied by family descendants until 1944 when it became the home of the Woodstock Historical Society. It contains a fine collection of period furnishings from 1800 to 1860, as well as many portraits, toys, costumes, and local memorabilia.

The rolling lawn behind the Dana House leads to the banks of the Ottauquechee River and a prime view of the Village Middle Bridge. When it was constructed in 1969 to replace the original, it became the first covered bridge to be built in the state since 1895.

Two other covered bridges are located east and west of town on Route 4. The 1877 Lincoln Bridge, four miles to the west, is the only known remaining wooden example of the Pratt truss, a construction style that was favored later in hundreds of steel bridges across the nation.

Besides the wooden bridges across its river, Woodstock boasts five bronze Paul Revere bells. Four are in church steeples, the fifth is on display on the lawn of the Woodstock Inn. The 1808 Congregational Church on Elm Street houses the oldest.

Be forewarned that dozens of shops will tempt you to detour as you take a stroll through Woodstock. Original work by New England artists is found at Gallery on the Green, and Vermont artists are shown at

Gallery 2, which has one location devoted to fine arts on Central Street, and another exhibiting folk art on Elm Street, just off the green. North Wind Artisans Gallery shows a variety of work by more than 50 Vermont craftspeople. As you stroll, you'll spy more shops selling clothing, jewelry, gifts, and crafts. Almost everyone makes a stop at F. H. Gillingham & Sons, a general store that has been owned by the same family since 1886, to buy country housewares and Vermont specialty foods, including syrup and cheese.

This is also prime antiquing territory with over a dozen shops in and around town, and the handsome Antiques Collaborative at Waterman Place, on Route 4 east near Quechee, a treasure trove with some 30 showrooms filled with collectibles of every kind. For a change in sightseeing pace, visit the Vermont Institute of Natural Science. It offers nature trails on 77 acres and a Raptor Center, a unique living museum housing more than 40 birds of prey.

May 1 marks the annual opening of another Rockefeller project, Billings Farm and Museum. This is a working dairy farm that carries on the raising of prime Jersey cattle begun by Frederick Billings in 1871, plus a series of handsomely restored barns housing exhibits on Vermont family farm life in the 1890s, and some of the best-looking bossys to be seen outside the pages of a storybook. To see sheep and cows grazing against the beautiful backdrop of rolling hills is to see classic rural Vermont at its best.

Demonstrations of skills of a century ago such as rug hooking and braiding, chair caning, and other handwork take place daily. In the barns, you can greet the draft horses and pet the calves in the nursery. The restored and furnished 1890 Farm House includes a basement creamery where you can sample hand-churned butter and see how the house functioned as the hub of the farm operation a century ago. Beginning with traditional plowing early in May, there are special events on many weekends right through Christmas.

In future years, the Billings family home and surrounding woodlands across the road are to become the Marsh-Billings National Historical Park, paying tribute to both Woodstock's and the nation's conservation efforts and traditions.

Having seen the sights and shopped the stores, what else you choose to do in Woodstock depends a lot on the weather and your inclinations. If sports are your choice, the Indoor Center is always ready, the golf course is usually back to playing condition by May, and all-weather tennis courts should be available even earlier.

The Woodstock Inn can furnish you with maps of the most scenic recommended routes for bikers, hikers, or joggers; and horses are available for hire in South Woodstock, offering a pleasant way to see the scenery even during Vermont's notorious spring "mud season."

And there are many scenic side trips to be made by car. One will take you to Quechee to see the gorge and waterfall and visit the riverside shop of glassblower Simon Pierce in a magnificently restored mill. Another road leads to Windsor, a longtime political center of the state with its own parade of historic houses, including the Windsor House, which serves as a Vermont State Crafts Center displaying the work of some 200 state craftspeople. Simon Pearce has established a second glassblowing workshop here.

Still another route takes in the Crowley Cheese Factory and Weston, a thriving little shopping mecca that includes the Original Vermont Country Store and the Weston Playhouse, Vermont's oldest professional theater.

The most memorable side trip out of Woodstock, however, is available from late May, when the buildings are opened at Calvin Coolidge's birthplace, the Plymouth Notch Historic District in the nearby tiny hamlet of Plymouth. Since Coolidge was not one of our more colorful presidents, this trip may not seem a tempting prospect, but it is actually a very special experience. Plymouth Notch has been called a "Yankee Brigadoon," a village virtually unchanged since 1923, when Coolidge was sworn in as president in the family homestead.

At the attractive small Visitors' Center, built of stone and with a Vermont slate roof, you will learn about Coolidge's life, and about the modest frame house where he was raised—the home where his father, a notary public, administered the oath of office when Warren Harding's death cast Vice President Coolidge into the Presidency. The house can be visited, providing a vivid reminder that ours is still a nation where a country boy can rise to greatness.

Within a distance of no more than two city blocks, you can also see the one-room schoolhouse built in 1890, the simple farm homes of Coolidge's family and friends, and the general store once operated by his father. Coolidge Hall, the vaulted room above the general store that was used by the village Grange for weekly dances, served as the 1924 summer White House office. It has been restored with an interpretive exhibit and original furnishings. Presidential gifts of state are displayed in the Visitors' Center and a large collection of early farm implements is exhibited in a late nineteenth-century barn.

Tastings are offered at the the 1890 cheese factory that is still run by the Coolidge family, and you can buy a sample to take home. Six generations of the family are buried in the village cemetery, including the ex-president.

To see the exquisite tiny church built by the townspeople of Plymouth in 1842 and still in use, to feel the continuity of life in this dot of a town, and to stand on the front porch of a humble home rich in mountain views is to understand some of the roots and reasons for our nation's strength.

You'll leave with a new appreciation of "Silent Cal" and empathize with his parting words when he left the White House: "We draw our presidents from the people. I came from them, I wish to be one of them again."

Area Code: 802

DRIVING DIRECTIONS   Woodstock is on U.S. Route 4, reached from north or south via I-91 to I-89 West. It is 148 miles from Boston, 260 miles from New York, and 166 miles from Hartford.

PUBLIC TRANSPORTATION   Nearest air service is at Lebanon, New Hampshire, 15 miles. Amtrak trains serve White River Junction, 14 miles away, and Vermont Transit buses come into Woodstock.

ACCOMMODATIONS *The Woodstock Inn and Resort,* 14 The Green, Woodstock 05091, (800)448-7900 or 457-1100, $$$–$$$$$, MAP available, many money-saving package and sports plans also available • *Kedron Valley Inn,* Route 106, South Woodstock 05071, 457-1473, $$$–$$$$$ MAP • *Jackson House,* Route 4 West, Woodstock 05091, antique-filled 1890s home, $$$–$$$$ CP • *Charleston House,* 21 Pleasant Street, Woodstock 05091, 457-3843, tasteful furnishings, 1835 Greek Revival town house, $$$ CP • *Canterbury House,* 43 Pleasant Street, Woodstock 05091, 457-3077, village Victorian, $$–$$$ CP • *Woodstocker,* 61 River Street, 05091, 457-4432, 1830 village bed-and-breakfast inn, $$–$$$ CP • *Three Church Street,* at that address, Woodstock 05901, comfortable bed and breakfast on the green, tennis and pool, $–$$ CP • *1830 Shiretown Inn,* 31 South Street, Woodstock 05091, 457-1830, small, modest B & B home, $–$$ CP • *Applebutter Inn,* Happy Valley Road (just off Route 4), Taftsville, 05073, 457-4158, $$ CP.

DINING   *The Woodstock Inn* (see above), traditional menu, $$–$$$ • *Kedron Valley Inn* (see above), "nouvelle New England," one of the area's best, $$–$$$ • *The Prince and the Pauper,* 24 Elm Street, 457-1818, charming Colonial atmosphere, continental and nouvelle cuisine, $$–$$$; bistro menu in lounge, $–$$ • *Barnard Inn,* Route 12, Barnard, 234-9961, Swiss chef, historic home, where Woodstockers go for special occasions, $$–$$$ • *Bentley's,* 3 Elm Street, 457-3232, lively, casual, weekend entertainment and dancing, $–$$ • *Spooner's,* Sunset Farm, Route 4 east, 457-4022, informal fare in renovated barn, $–$$ • *The Inn at Wethersfield,* Route 106, Perkinsville (south of Woodstock), 263-9217, a bit of a drive but the food gets raves, prix fixe, $$$$ • Also see Quechee, page 83, and Hanover, pages 233–234.

SIGHTSEEING   *Dana House,* Woodstock Historical Society, 26 Elm Street, Woodstock, 457-1822. Hours: mid-May to late October,

Monday to Saturday, 10 A.M. to 5 P.M.; Sunday, 2 P.M. to 5 P.M.; limited winter hours, best to check. Adults, $3.50; ages 13 to 18, $1; under 13, free • *Billings Farm and Museum,* River Road, Woodstock, 457-2355. Hours: May through October, daily, 10 A.M. to 5 P.M.; November and December, weekends, December 26–31. Adults, $6; children, $3 • *Vermont Institute of Natural Science and Raptor Center,* 457-2779. Hours: May to October, daily, except Tuesday 10 A.M. to 4 P.M.; November to April, also closed Sunday. Adults, $5.00; children, $1 • *Walking Tours of Woodstock,* from Town Information Booth on the Green, 457-1042. Hours: June to October, Monday, Wednesday, and Saturday, 10:30 A.M. $2.50 • *Plymouth Notch Historic District,* Route 100A, Plymouth, 672-3773. Hours: daily, Memorial Day to mid-October, 9:30 A.M. to 5:30 P.M. Adults, $4; under 14, free • *Kedron Valley Stables,* Route 106, PO Box 368, South Woodstock, 457-2734. Trail rides, carriage rides, inn-to-inn riding tours. Call for rates.

INFORMATION Woodstock Area Chamber of Commerce, 18 Central Street, Box 486, Woodstock, VT 05091, 457-3555.

Getting Inspiration in Concord

By the rude bridge that arched the flood,
Their flag to April's breeze unfurled,
Here once the embattled farmers stood,
And fired the shot heard round the world.
                              —Ralph Waldo Emerson

It was on the 19th of April, 1775, that a brave band of farmers in Concord, Massachusetts, fired the fateful shots that started the American Revolution.

The spot and its significance—the bravery of the Minutemen who dared to fire against the mighty British crown—have been movingly marked and preserved to inspire us with patriotism even today, though it's hard to associate the present placid, prosperous little suburban town of Concord with such bloody goings-on.

It's easy, however, to see why the serenity of the town and the natural beauty of its countryside would have attracted a remarkable gathering of American literary giants in Concord nearly a century later. Emerson, who wrote *Nature* here, declared it a "fit" place for a poet, where a walk in the woods had "a breath of immortality in it." Hawthorne and Louisa May Alcott also lived and wrote here, as did Thoreau, whose Walden Pond is just outside of town.

With such an extraordinary blend of history to its credit, Concord is a fascinating place to visit. You actually need to take three separate tours to appreciate all this small town has to offer in the way of military and literary lore and early American architecture—and even then you haven't begun to enjoy the countryside.

Since its greatest fame rests on its pivotal role in the Revolution, it's well to start with a look at the Concord of 1775, a town of 1,600 people, mostly prosperous farmers, who were deeply involved in the movement to gain freedom from the oppression of Great Britain. As a place where Colonial supplies were being stored in anticipation of war, Concord became the target of a British confiscation mission. When General George Gage's troops left Boston for Concord on April 18, Paul Revere spread the alarm on his famous ride.

Drive down Monument Street just beyond the center of town and you'll come to the North Bridge, a reconstruction of the simple wooden bridge where the fateful encounter began. The spot is marked by the famous Minuteman statue, a young American farmer holding gun and plow, created by Daniel Chester French, who is also famed for his Lincoln Memorial statue in Washington. The bridge is now part of Minuteman National Historical Park, and the National Park Service has done its usual informative and tasteful job of bringing historical events to life. The site remains rural. You can cross the bridge and walk the path taken by the soldiers, following the action described on plaques along the way as you head gradually uphill to the Visitors' Center for a panoramic view of the entire scene. In season there are guided tours as well.

Just before the bridge is the Bullet Hole House. The British troops fired a shot at the owner. The bullet hole may still be seen in the shed. The home is now a private residence.

There are many other noteworthy remains of the events of that April 19, and of early Revolutionary activities in Concord. You can see Colonel Barrett's farm, where a cache of arms was hidden, the target of the British army's mission to Concord. At Monument Square you can climb to the top of the Old Burying Ground, where members of several Revolutionary families rest, and see beyond it to the ridge that runs to Meriam's Corner, from which the patriots followed the retreat of the British on the road below.

Minuteman Park actually stretches all the way from Concord to Lexington, along Route 2A, the road the British followed on their way from an early-morning skirmish on Lexington Green and again on the way back to Boston following the Concord battle, when further fighting took place all along the route. The Battle Road Visitors' Center on Route 2A just outside Lexington has its own exhibit room, and a movie and orientation program. If you want to follow the entire sequence of events on April 19, you'll want to include not only the park but the town of Lexington, another pleasant Colonial site with its own share of historic buildings.

But if you have just a weekend, you may prefer to stick to Concord, and by now you're probably ready for a lunch break at the Colonial Inn, a 1716 landmark right on the green in the center of town, and another storage site for Colonial arms. As you munch your Colonial chicken pie or Boston scrod, you'll actually be starting your literary tour of Concord. Thoreau's family lived in the old part of the inn when it was still a private home; after the inn began taking in lodgers, it became known as Thoreau House.

You should also have noted another important literary spot, the home of Reverend William Emerson, Ralph Waldo's grandfather. The house, known as The Old Manse, was so close to the North Bridge that the Reverend actually watched the battle of Concord from an upstairs window. Descendants of the Emerson family lived here for 169 years, except for a period from 1842 to 1845 when Nathaniel Hawthorne and his bride, Sophia Peabody, rented the house. It was here that Hawthorne wrote *Mosses from an Old Manse.*

Hawthorne moved away to Salem but returned to Concord in 1852 to the home known as the Wayside, where he remained for the rest of his life. There's an orientation program and a half-hour tour there to tell you about him and the Wayside's other interesting residents.

The Alcott family also stayed at the Wayside while their home was being completed, but it was The Orchard House, where they lived for 20 years, that became the setting for *Little Women.* The tour here includes many of Louisa's mementos, including the costumes used by the Alcott girls when they gave their famous plays. Outside is the School of Philosophy—founded by Bronson Alcott and Ralph Waldo Emerson, the two leaders of the American Transcendentalist movement—where great thinkers of the day studied and spoke.

Emerson's own home, where he moved in 1835 with his wife, Lydian, and remained until his death in 1882, is known simply as Emerson House. The guides will show you a collection of many of his books, personal effects, and furniture.

Thoreau, the only one of the resident writers who was a native son, loved the town, and once wrote: "I have never got over my surprise that I should have been born into the most estimable place in all the world. . . ."

The Thoreau Lyceum, headquarters of the Thoreau Society, is an institution devoted to the preservation of Thoreau's ideals. It contains much of his memorabilia, and has a replica of his famous Walden Pond cabin on the grounds. There are changing exhibits here, as well as a research library and a book and gift shop. Thoreau's wilderness outpost, Walden Pond, is now part of a state recreational reserve, a busy place enjoyed by boaters, swimmers, and fisherman. Take a walk down the nature trail to the lovely pond and the stones that mark the site of the real cabin, and you can see why the spot inspired Mr. Thoreau.

Both Thoreau and Bronson Alcott spent time in the Old Jail in town, when they refused to pay poll tax as a way to protest government-supported slavery. The incident was the inspiration for Thoreau's famous essay, "On Civil Disobedience."

You'll learn still more about Concord's extraordinary group of writers at the lovely 1873 Concord Library, which houses their manuscripts as well as a statue of Emerson and busts of the others by Daniel Chester French. The contents of Emerson's study and the furnishings of Thoreau's Walden House are on display at the Concord Museum, where the tour also includes a series of period rooms that provide an introduction to Concord history.

All of Concord's writers are buried on the Author's Ridge in Sleepy Hollow Cemetery, just above the town.

If all those sights are becoming overwhelming, take a shopping break downtown. Concord these days is basically an upscale suburban town, and most of the shops on Main and Walden are geared more toward local residents than tourists, but you'll find a variety of galleries and gift shops, toys and teddy bears, as well as conservative clothing stores. More shops are found around the old train station on Sudbury Road, and Thoreau and Belknap streets. Don't overlook the excellent gift shops at the Concord Museum, The Old Manse, Orchard House, and the Thoreau Lyceum.

On Sunday, you might want to spend part of the morning on the architectural walking tour described in a brochure published by the Concord Chamber of Commerce. It is available at the information booth on Heywood Street and at other locations around town. It will lead you down Monument, Liberty, and Main streets and along Lowell and Lexington roads, along brick sidewalks bordering the green and gravel paths just out of the town center, past lovely historic homes and white-spired Colonial churches dating from the early 1700s to the mid-1850s.

One, the 1750 home of Jonathan Ball, now houses the Concord Art Association, which holds regular exhibits. Another only-in-Concord attraction is the Grapevine Cottage, former home of Ephraim Walls Bull, who planted the wild grapes that eventually developed into the ubiquitous Concord grape. A plaque marks his accomplishment, and you can still see a grape arbor by the side of the house.

Finally, you can take your pick of places to get back to nature. There's Walden Pond preserve, as well as the Great Meadows National Wildlife Refuge, whose Concord location is reached from Monsen Road, off Route 72. This is a great place for walking nature trails and spotting a great diversity of birds. Many waterfowl nest in the refuge's wetlands.

Or, if you'd rather glide along in a canoe, as Emerson and Thoreau once did, head for South Bridge Boat House in Concord and paddle your way along Concord's three rivers: the Concord, Sudbury, and Assabet.

If you have young children with you, take the ten-mile drive to the headquarters of the Massachusetts Audubon Society at Drumlin Farm in Lincoln, a 220-acre farm with lots of friendly barnyard animals as well as walking and hiking trails and a picnic area. Special programs for families, from sheep shearing to guided nature walks, are held on Saturday and Sunday at 11:00 A.M. and 2:00 P.M.

It's especially fun to make this trip around Patriot's Day on April 19, when both Concord and Lexington offer early-morning reenactments and other festivities to mark the date. The events, which change from year to year, are sometimes scheduled on a weekend rather than the actual day, so it's best to check with both chambers of commerce for the current year's schedule.

Concord is probably at its most beautiful in mid-May, when its fine Colonial homes are set off by the pinks, purples, and whites of flowering trees. But whenever you make the trip, you're almost sure to find the town a treasure trove of history, as well as a chance to emulate Thoreau and get back, at least a bit, to nature.

Area Code: 508

DRIVING DIRECTIONS   Concord is on Route 2, reached from I-495 or Route 128. Route 2A, the Battle Road, leads from Lexington to Concord. It is 25 miles from Boston, 248 miles from New York, and 138 miles from Hartford.

PUBLIC TRANSPORTATION   For many residents, Concord is a commuter outpost for Boston, so there is frequent train service from North Station. Phone 227-5070 for information. Many of the sights are within walking distance of the center of town.

ACCOMMODATIONS   *Hawthorne Inn,* 462 Lexington Road, Concord 01742, 369-5610, a lovely 1870 home; but with just five rooms, so reserve early; $$–$$$$ • *Colonel Roger Brown House,* 1694 Main Street, Concord 01742, 369-1305 or (800) 292-1369, restored 1775 Colonial, $–$$ • *Colonial Inn,* Monument Square, Concord 01742, 369-9200, prize location on the green, rooms in old inn or new motel wing, $$–$$$ • *North Bridge Inn,* 21 Monument Street, Concord 01742, 371-0014, blend of inn ambience and hotel amenities, near town center, $$$–$$$$ CP • *Longfellow's Wayside Inn,* off Route 20, Sudbury 01776, 443-1776, a 1702 Colonial beautifully restored by the Ford Foundation and operated by a nonprofit trust—a charmer with just ten rooms, so reserve well ahead, $$ CP • *Anderson Wheeler Homestead,* 154 Fitchburg Turnpike (Route 117), Concord 01742, 369-3756, 1890s farmhouse overlooking the Sudbury River, 3 miles from Concord center, $ CP.

DINING *Aigo Bistro,* 84 Thoreau Street, Concord, 371-1333, a touch of Provence, highly praised, $$ • *Colonial Inn* (see above), $$ • *Walden Station,* 24 Walden Street, Concord, 371-2233, varied menu, restored firehouse, $–$$ • *Papa Razzi,* 768 Elm Street, Concord, 371-0030, family-style Italian, pizza, $–$$ • *Willow Pond Kitchen,* 745 Lexington Road, Concord, 369-6529, roadhouse, nothing fancy, but good, homey food at good, homey prices, $ • *Longfellow's Wayside Inn* (see above); very popular, so reserve early, $$–$$$ • *Chez Claude,* Route 2A, Acton, 263-3325, popular French restaurant, $$–$$$ • *Le Lyonnais,* 416 Great Road, Route 2A, Acton, 263-9068, also highly rated for traditional French fare, $$–$$$ • *Ciao,* 452 Great Road (Route 2A), Acton, 263-6161, northern Italian, interesting stained-glass decor, $$ • *Le Bellecoeur,* 10 Muzzey Street, Lexington, 861-9400, formal dining room, $$–$$$, or light fare in the café, $.

SIGHTSEEING *Minute Man National Historical Park,* North Bridge Visitor Center, 174 Liberty Street, Concord, 369-6993. Hours: daily, 9 A.M. to 5:30 P.M. year-round. Free • *Battle Road Visitor Center,* off Route 2A, Lexington, 862-7753. Hours: mid-April to November, daily, 9 A.M. to 5:30 P.M. Free • *The Wayside,* 455 Lexington Road (Route 2A), 369-6975. Hours: April to October, Friday to Tuesday, 10:30 A.M. to 5 P.M.; hours sometimes vary, so best to call. Adults, $3; under 16, free • *The Old Manse,* Monument Street at the Old North Bridge, 369-3909. Hours: Mid-April through October, Wednesday to Monday, 10 A.M. to 5 P.M., except Sundays, from 1 P.M. Adults, $4.50; ages 6 to 12, $2.50 • *Orchard House,* 399 Lexington Road (Route 2A), 369-4118. Hours: April through October, Monday to Saturday, 10 A.M. to 4:30 P.M., Sunday from 1 P.M.; November to March, Monday to Friday, 11 A.M. to 3 P.M., Saturday, 10 A.M. to 4:30 P.M., Sunday 1 P.M. to 4:30 P.M. Closed January 1–15. Adults, $4.50; students, $4; ages 6 to 12, $3. • *Emerson House,* 28 Cambridge Turnpike at Lexington Road (Route 2A), 369-2236. Hours: mid-April through October, Thursday to Saturday, 10 A.M. to 4:30 P.M., Sunday from 2 P.M. Adults, $3.50; ages 7 to 17, $2.50 • *Thoreau Lyceum,* 156 Belknap Street, 369-5912. Hours: April through December, Monday to Saturday, 10 A.M. to 5 P.M., Sunday from 2 P.M.; January 1 to February 15, Thursday to Saturday, 10 A.M. to 5 P.M., Sunday from 2 P.M.; February 16 to March 31, Tuesday to Saturday, 10 A.M. to 5 P.M., Sunday from 2 P.M. Adults, $2; students, $1.50; grades 1 to 8, $0.50 • *Concord Museum,* 200 Lexington Road, 369-9609. Hours: guided tours, April to December, Monday to Saturday, 10 A.M. to 5 P.M., Sunday from 1 P.M., January to March, to 4 P.M. Adults, $5; students, $3; under 15, $2 • *Concord Free Public Library,* 129 Main Street at Sudbury Road, 371-6240. Hours: Monday to Thursday, 9 A.M. to 9 P.M., Friday to 6 P.M., September to June, Saturday also, 9 A.M. to 5 P.M.; October to May, Sunday also, 2 P.M. to 5 P.M. Free • *Walden Pond State Reservation,* 915 Walden Street (Route

126 at Route 2), 369-3254. Hours: daily until dark. $2.00 parking fee, charged April to October • *Drumlin Farm,* S. Great Road (Route 117, 1/2 mile east of Route 126), Lincoln, 259-9807. Hours: Tuesday to Sunday, 9 A.M. to 5 P.M. Adults, $6; ages 3 to 15, $4 • *Great Meadows National Wildlife Refuge,* Weir Hill Road (north off Lincoln Road), Sudbury, 443-4661. Hours: grounds open daily, dawn to dusk. Visitor Center open daily, 8 A.M. to 4:30 P.M., except closed holidays and weekends in winter. Additional trails and observation towers in Concord, Monsen Road (off Route 62, 1 mile northeast of Concord center). Free.

INFORMATION Concord Chamber of Commerce, 2 Lexington Road, Concord, MA 01742, 369-3120.

Herbs and History in Connecticut

Adelma Grenier Simmons is a performer. Audiences are rapt when she talks about the herbs she grows at Caprilands, her 50-acre farm in Coventry, Connecticut. And when she tells you that herbs such as sage preserve a person's youth, you're likely to become a believer, seeing the energy and charm of the grandmotherly Mrs. Simmons.

Caprilands visitors not only learn about herbs and their uses and tour the 31 gardens on the property, they are treated to one of Mrs. Simmons's legendary five-course luncheons, served in her eighteenth-century farmhouse and flavored with her home-grown seasonings. It's a very special day, and one that leaves you ready to explore Connecticut's "quiet corner" as well as the town of Norwich, where you can discover some Colonial history and a thoroughly modern inn and health spa.

A visit to Caprilands begins at 11:00 A.M. with one of Mrs. Simmons's colorful introductions to herbs, delivered in a Colonial barn whose rafters are festooned with drying bunches of lavender and other fragrant plants. Her herbal lore, the result of half a lifetime of study, is both factual and fanciful. In the spring, she concentrates on teaching how to plan and plant your own garden, with a lecture spiced with humor and legends.

She may tell you, for example, that silver rosemary is good for the mind and memory, so it is a good thing to plant "in case you have need of that. It's also good for making tea," Mrs. Simmons adds, "and if that doesn't work, you can wash your dog's hair with it."

Occasionally, an assistant may fill in for Mrs. Simmons, taking care to give the same light touch to the talk.

Visitors may stroll the gardens at will. Touches of the Simmons wit and whimsy abound. There's a heart-shaped Bride's Garden, a Silver Garden planted only with silvery plants, and a Shakespeare Garden filled with the herbs mentioned by the Bard. The latest addition is an identification garden. In all there are 300 herb varieties.

For lunch, guests are seated at long tables crammed into the three main floor rooms of the farmhouse. Hostesses circulate from room to room answering questions, but they won't give away the recipes or reveal what herbs you are tasting until the meal is over.

"Then it's too late." Mrs. Simmons chuckles. After lunch, she can usually be found in the bookshop, autographing some of her more than two dozen recipe books.

Guests are free to wander once again through the gardens or to browse in the heavenly scented gift shop in the restored barn, which features, among other things, Caprilands herbs that have been dried and packaged. There is also a most attractive greenhouse gallery with herb plants, seeds, and hanging baskets for sale.

From Coventry, the weekend can move in two directions, depending on whether spa sophistication or country escape is your pleasure. Or you can try to take in a bit of both.

For country, head north on Silver Street to Route 44 east and into the unspoiled northeast corner of the state, an area of wooded hills and bucolic back roads, with clear streams for fishing or canoeing, and village greens ringed by homes dating back to Colonial days. The area is divided into "hill towns" and "mill towns," the latter developed in the lower areas along the Quinebaug River. Most of the inns are in the lovely rural villages on the hilltops.

For one of the prettiest of the hill towns, turn north on Route 169 (you'll quickly see why it has been declared a Scenic Highway) to Woodstock—not the famous one but a Connecticut country cousin—a village of stone walls and historic houses that date to 1686.

There is no Main Street as such here, just clusters of homes and occasional shops. About midway through the town on the crest of a long ridge is Woodstock Hill, where huge old trees shade handsome country houses spanning a couple of centuries in architecture. One that stands out is Roseland Cottage, a bright pink Gothic-style house built in 1864 for a wealthy gentleman named Bowen, a New York newspaper publisher, who installed the best of everything, right down to a private bowling alley. The house and gardens and barns, owned and operated by the Society for the Preservation of New England Antiquities, are open to visitors.

Woodstock is hardly a shopping mecca, but it does offers its own small group of shops near the intersection of Route 169 and Route 171. In addition to a sampling of local crafts at Scranton's Shops, there is the Irish Crystal Company with beautiful imported lead crystal and the Livery Shops with gifts and antiques. Windy Acres has dried and silk flowers as well as fresh blooms, and the Christmas Barn and Shop has 12 rooms of gifts, candles, tree decorations, and fabric. A mile off 169 on Woodstock Road in East Woodstock is Brunarhan's, a furniture showroom where handcrafted pieces in pine and oak are available.

The gracious Inn at Woodstock Hill, set on 14 acres, is a recommended stop for lodging or dinner. Lord Thompson Manor is another excellent choice, a stately 30-room beauty on 40 acres in nearby Thompson, a picturesque hamlet with stately trees and fine old homes, where the Vernon Stiles Inn has been serving meals to travelers since 1814. There are many historic small bed-and-breakfast homes in these unspoiled villages, especially in Pomfret, a lovely town that is home to a prestigious prep school.

The best way to appreciate the back-roads beauty of this area is simply to drive from town to town. There are historic buildings worth a look in many of the villages along the way. Of special interest are the Prudence Crandall Museum in Canterbury, home of New England's first school for black girls; the 1890 Brayton Grist Mill with two exhibits in Pomfret; and the Jonathan Trumbull House in Lebanon, the fine 1740 home of Connecticut's Revolutionary War governor.

And there are some unexpected attractions as well. The Quinebaug Valley Hatchery near Plainfield is one of the Northeast's largest and most modern trout hatcheries, producing 500,000 to 600,000 brown and rainbow trout annually. It offers viewing ponds, not to mention great fishing.

Buell's Greenhouses in Eastford is a major national mail-order source for gloxinias and African violets. Thousands of these plants are on display—140,000 African violets alone.

Farther south on Route 169, is the town of Brooklyn, another of those out-of-the-way discoveries off the tourist paths. Brooklyn's New England Center of Contemporary Arts is a charming rustic gallery with changing exhibits of work by recognized living artists. There is usually an artist in residence to talk about his or her work. The Golden Lamb Buttery is a unique dinner stop, offering gourmet fare in a farm setting. Come early for a free hayride through the fields, or to sit on the deck watching the ponies, donkeys, and horses graze.

If you want to get out and walk in the countryside, there are 11 state parks and forests in the area and another half-dozen preserves offering miles of hiking trails. Quaddick Park on East Putnam Road has canoe rentals as well. A full listing of outdoor options is provided in the free Quiet Corner guides.

A more sophisticated scene awaits in Norwich, a small city reached by continuing south on Route 169 or driving about half an hour south on Route 32 from Coventry. The airy, elegant Norwich Inn looks more California than Connecticut. A separate building on the grounds houses a luxurious spa where you can work off your luncheon calories, then be massaged and pampered to your heart's content. Even if you don't stay here, the excellent dining room is worth a visit.

The present town of Norwich may not look too promising at first glance, but the riverfront is acquiring a fresh new look, and there is a surprising amount of history to be found here. This was one of the 12 largest cities in the colonies in 1776, and one Christopher Leffingwell was a major reason. The industrious Mr. Leffingwell established not only the first paper mill in Connecticut, but also a stocking factory, a pottery works, chocolate and fulling mills, a clothier's shop, and a dye house. He was major supplier to the Continental Army.

His home, the chief sightseeing attraction in Norwich, was also an inn that was visited by many dignitaries, and is today one of the outstanding remaining Colonial dwellings in the state.

The two-story structure is actually two homes brought together with an addition at the rear, with sections dating from 1675 to 1765. The interior has been authentically restored and beautifully furnished by the Society of the Founders of Norwich. Among its highlights is the George Washington Parlor, named in honor of a visit here by the general in 1776.

While you are in Norwich, step into the Slater Memorial Museum for a surprise—full-size plaster casts of Greek, Roman, and Renaissance sculpture masterpieces, including *Winged Victory, Venus de Milo,* Michelangelo's *Pietà,* and dozens more. The museum is connected to an art school, and students draw from the models. For visitors, it is the next best thing to a European museum tour.

Golfers may prefer to forget all this and take advantage of the course next door to the Norwich Inn. For warm days there is a delightful outdoor terrace next to the pool with views of the greens.

Country lover or spa sophisticate, if you plan an herb-flavored weekend, remember that reservations are a necessity at Caprilands, and the earlier the better, since Mrs. Simmons is something of a local legend. She tells her guests that caraway is believed to bring those who eat it back to the place where they tasted it. It isn't known whether she laces her luncheon dishes with this herb, but guests here do tend to return and to bring their friends—and the 50 seats in the house fill up in a hurry.

Area Code: 203

DRIVING DIRECTIONS   Caprilands is on Silver Street, the first left after you pass the intersection of Route 31 South. To go directly to Caprilands from Hartford, the best route is I-84, going northeast. From Boston, go west on the Mass Pike (I-90) until it merges with I-84. Take the Rockville-Coventry exit off I-84 (Route 31 south), turn left on

Route 44, and then take the second right onto Silver Street. Coventry is about 70 miles from Boston, 140 from New York, and 30 miles southeast of Hartford. Norwich is on Route 32 southeast of Coventry; Woodstock is to the northeast via Routes 44 and 169.

ACCOMMODATIONS   *The Inn at Woodstock Hill,* 94 Plaine Hill Road and Route 169, Woodstock 06267, 928-0528, $$–$$$ CP • *Lord Thompson Manor,* Route 200, Thompson 06277, 923-3886, $$–$$$ CP • *Norwich Inn,* 607 West Thames Street, Route 32, Norwich 06360, 886-2401, $$$–$$$$ • **Pleasant smaller B & Bs in historic homes:** *Ebenezer Stoddard House,* Route 171 and Perrin Road, West Woodstock 06267, 974-2552, $$ CP • *Karinn,* Route 169, Pomfret 06250, 928-5492, antiques, fireplaces, $$, CP • *Samuel Watson House,* Route 193 and the Common, Thompson 06277, 923-2491, $–$$ CP.

DINING   *The Golden Lamb Buttery,* Hillandale Farm, Bush Hill Road, Brooklyn, 774-4423, exceptional, open June to December, prix fixe, $$$$$ • *The Harvest at Bald Hill,* Routes 169 and 171, South Woodstock, 974-2240, pleasant, excellent continental menu and notable wine list, $$–$$$ • *The Inn at Woodstock Hill* (see above), continental, $$–$$$ • *Vernon Stiles Inn,* Route 200, Thompson, 923-9571, charming nineteenth-century tavern, $$ • *Norwich Inn* (see above), noted nouvelle cuisine, delicious spa menu, $$–$$$ • For lunch, try the *Vanilla Bean Café,* 450 Deerfield Road, Pomfret, 928-1562, a restored barn, $.

SIGHTSEEING   *Caprilands Herb Farm,* 534 Silver Street, Coventry, 742-7244. Visits to gardens and gift shops are free. Lecture and luncheon, April through December, $18 (check for any recent price change), reservations essential • *Roseland Cottage,* Route 169 on the Common, Woodstock, 928-4074. Hours: Memorial Day to Labor Day, Wednesday to Sunday, noon to 5 P.M.; Labor Day to mid-October, Friday to Sunday, noon to 5 P.M. Adults, $4; ages 5 to 12, $2 • *Brayton Grist Mill,* Mashamoquet Brook State Park, Route 44, Pomfret. Hours: May to September, Saturday and Sunday, 2 P.M. to 5 P.M. Donation • *New England Center for Contemporary Art,* Route 169, Brooklyn, 774-8899, May to November, Wednesday to Sunday, 1 P.M. to 5 P.M. Free • *Jonathan Trumbull House,* Route 1 (off Route 87), Lebanon, 642-6100. Hours: May 15 to October 15, Tuesday to Saturday, 1 P.M. to 5 P.M.; hours may vary, so best to call. Adults, $2; children under 12, free • *Prudence Crandall Museum,* Routes 14 and 169, Canterbury, 546-9916. Hours: Wednesday to Sunday, 10 A.M. to 4:30 P.M. Closed December 15 to January 15. Adults, $2; ages 5 to 18, $1 • *Leffingwell Inn,* 348 Washington Street, Norwich, 889-9440. Hours: Tuesday to Saturday, 10 A.M. to noon and 2 P.M. to 4 P.M.; Sunday, 2 P.M. to 4 P.M.; winter hours, weekends only. Adults $3; children, $1 • *Slater Memor-*

ial Museum and Converse Art Gallery, 108 Crescent Street, Norwich, 887-2506. Hours: September to June, Monday to Friday, 9 A.M. to 4 P.M., weekends from 1 P.M.; July and August, Tuesday to Sunday, 1 P.M. to 4 P.M. Free • *Quinebaug Valley Trout Hatchery,* Cady Lane, Central Village, 564-7542. Hours: daily, 10 A.M. to 4 P.M. Free. Fishing permit, $1 • *Buell's Greenhouses,* Weeks Road, Eastford, 974-0263. Hours: Monday to Saturday, 8 A.M. to 5 P.M.

INFORMATION Northeast Connecticut Visitors District, PO Box 598, Putnam, CT 06260, 928-1228 • Norwich Chamber of Commerce, 35 Main Street, Norwich, CT 06360, 887-1647.

Rites of Spring on Nantucket

Spring comes late to Nantucket, bursting in at last near the end of April in a rush of blue skies, golden forsythia, and millions of bright yellow daffodils—an estimated three million at last count.

Weather-weary islanders celebrate the long-awaited end of winter gray with their own special spring rite, a Daffodil Festival, which fills the town with golden blooms and features a parade of antique cars and a tailgate picnic that have become island traditions. The weekend has grown to include an annual Basket Show by the Artists' Association, an annual house tour and entertainment by Morris dancers. Though it's a local party, everyone is welcome, and there are few more gala ways to usher in the season.

Preseason visitors to the island are rewarded with a glimpse of a Nantucket that is often obscured by the boatloads of summer tourists. In the mild and breezy sunshine of springtime, Nantucket town is not a bustling resort at all, but a quiet and beautiful small town of 7,000, where everyone offers a friendly hello. Cobbled streets and sea captains' mansions become not backdrop for the beach, but the focal point of delightful walks into the past.

This is, after all, the historic island outpost, 30 miles out at sea, that was once the third largest city in Massachusetts, sending brave seamen to the far corners of the globe for the whale oil that lighted the lamps of the world. And weathered shingled cottages still mark the original farming settlement in the 1600s and the austere Quaker era of the early 1700s that preceded the prosperous whaling days.

Both simple cottages and stately homes remain, perfectly preserved by a turn of fate that seemed disastrous 140 years ago. A destructive business district fire in 1846, coupled with the discovery of kerosene and the resulting dwindling demand for whale oil that followed in the

1850s, sent Nantucket into an economic decline that lasted for years. Hard times meant that no one could afford to "modernize," so while the rest of the mainland was changing, Nantucket remained untouched, becoming America's largest living Colonial town.

Toward the end of the last century, visitors discovered that this beach-rimmed island was also a perfect vacation spot. New hotels went up, and islanders began to open their shingled houses to paying guests.

But world wars and the Depression slowed things, and the island's real renaissance did not come until the 1960s. It began with one man, Walter Beinecke, a wealthy summer resident who formed a corporation named Sherburne, after Nantucket's first settlement, to rescue and renovate the decaying wharves. Sherburne went on to acquire large portions of island real estate and to take over and renovate some of the better hotels.

Though Sherburne has sold its holdings, the development movement goes on—too much so to suit many who loved the island as it was. Strict ordinances have been passed to see that nothing spoils the island's remarkably preserved past. All new construction must conform to the simple shingled architecture of the original homes, so the church steeples and lighthouses remain the tallest structures on Nantucket.

A good place to learn about some of the people and events of Nantucket's rich past is the Thomas Macy Warehouse on Straight Wharf, where exhibits trace the island's development from whaling to summering. The warehouse is one of 13 sites maintained by the Nantucket Historical Association, all open to the public with one moderately priced admission pass. These include the wonderful Whaling Museum; the Old Mill, which still grinds corn; the Old Gaol; the Quaker Meeting House; and the 1686 Jethro Coffin House, the oldest building on the island, re-restored after being struck by lightning in 1987.

But if the day is fine, there's no more pleasant way to explore than on a walking tour of the town, starting on Main Street. It is interesting to note that the cobblestones that seem so picturesque today were put down originally for very practical reasons—to keep heavy whale-oil drays from sinking into the mud.

The walking tour takes you past the Pacific Club, whose membership was limited to shipmasters who had whaled in the Pacific, and brings you to the corner of Main and Fair, where R. H. Macy of retailing fame gave up his first storekeeping job with his father to go whaling, then became a forty-niner in search of gold, which he found when he eventually headed for New York to found the store we know today.

Continuing on to upper Main, you pass the brick mansions of the ship-owning Coffin family, aboard whose vessel, *Charles and Mary,* Herman Melville once went to sea. The Coffins were responsible for planting the stately elms on Main Street as well as bringing back and planting the pines, larches, and heather that have spread across the island landscape.

A few doors down on Walnut Lane is the Nathaniel Macy House, built in 1723, and now open to the public. Next comes one of the most fascinating sections of any street in New England: 12 magnificent whaling mansions built by various members of the Coffin and Star-buck families, testaments to Nantucket's wealth and taste. The three Starbuck brick-columned mansions that stand in a row have been the subject of countless snapshots.

Wherever you walk, you'll run into more fascinating history, and more historic homes that are now open to let you share it more intimately.

There's the house where Maria Mitchell, the most famous early female astronomer, was born, and various residences and monuments to the Folger family, including a memorial to Abiah Folger, wife of Josiah Franklin and mother of Benjamin Franklin. Facing Main on Pleasant, the Hadwen House, a Historical Association Property, has a beautiful 1850s-style garden in the rear that is maintained for the public by the Nantucket Garden Club.

Walk far enough in any direction and you're back to the ever-present sea that made Nantucket what it was in the past—as well as the popular spot it is today. Early in the year you can have the endless beaches to yourself, and while spring temperatures aren't normally warm enough for swimming, they are frequently perfect for beach-combing and tanning in blissful solitude.

Biking is another ideal spring pastime, taking you away from the cobblestones to wide-open vistas of cranberry bogs and low-lying moors of bayberry and scrub pine, which are the scenes that give Nantucket its faraway feel.

If you come for the Daffodil Festival, when you arrive you'll find Nantucket's cobbled Main Street festooned with yellow flowers in every store window and doorway, bountiful and original arrangements devised to compete for the coveted judges' blue ribbons for best window displays.

Prizes are awarded for contestants in Saturday morning's antique auto parade as well. The procession of classic cars from Model As to MGs parades past bystanders on Main Street; many of the occupants come in vintage costumes that match the ages of the cars.

The best part of the day comes when everyone follows the procession of contestants down the daffodil-lined road to the picturesque fishing village of 'Sconset for a tailgate picnic party that just may be the most elegant event of its kind anywhere. Prizes are the lure once again, this time for the most artistic food display, and you'll see everything from a picnic for Raggedy Ann and Andy to a caviar-and-champagne feast served to diners on velvet-seated gilt chairs brought along for the occasion. All the spreads are lavishly laden with daffodils, as are many of the diners. At one year's event, even a dog arrived wearing a yellow bonnet to mark the day.

The picnic ends before three o'clock, leaving time for a walk along 'Sconset's magnificent beach and through the twisting lanes of one-time fisherman's shanties that are now charming summer cottages or, if you prefer, a look at the shops in Nantucket village. There are a few T-shirt shops, but on the whole, very few geegaw souvenirs are to be found here. Most of the shops carry quality merchandise, much of it handmade, and browsing is a pleasure. Antiquers will find plenty of temptation—more than two dozen shops all around town.

One special place to watch for is Nantucket Looms at the foot of Main Street, with its hand-loomed mohair scarves and other lovely woolens. The Spectrum on Main is a cooperative showing fine crafts, and Nantucket Folkworks on Broad Street features folk art by New England artists. You'll find examples of the island's best-known craft, Nantucket Lighthouse baskets, in many stores around town. Each hand-painted ivory top is different, and since the price tags run into the hundreds, if you plan to indulge, you ought to have the fun of choosing from a full selection. The Golden Basket on Main and at Straight Wharf, the Lightship Shop on East Chestnut Street, and Nantucket Basket Works on Daves Street are among the many places to look.

If you have time on Sunday, there are plenty of museums and historic houses to visit. The Peter Foulger Museum, with its mixed memorabilia of Old Nantucket, and the famous Whaling Museum are both of special interest.

Sunday is also the start of the two-day annual Daffodil Show sponsored by the Nantucket Garden Club in cooperation with the American Daffodil Society. You needn't be a flower worshiper to appreciate the unusual varieties and handsome arrangements.

The first show in 1974 was the start of the island's daffodil mania. The Nantucket Garden Club set a goal of planting one million daffodil bulbs; eager islanders and naturalization have tripled the count, and the show lasts from March to May. Why daffodils and not tulips? Because while the island's deer population loves tulip bulbs, it seems that they don't care for daffodils.

The festival weekend, incidentally, has chalked up an admirable record of above-average weather, usually sending happy visitors home with an early tan.

Off-season lodgings used to be sparse on Nantucket, but since the Daffodil Festival has begun to attract visitors, many hotels and inns open early. Many of the ship captains' homes and shingled cottages that abound here are now bed-and-breakfast inns, making for snug havens. Off-season prices are way down, good news on an island where it is hard to find moderate rates in midsummer.

Nantucket is distinguished among summer resorts for the large number of fine restaurants, and more of these are now open for the festivities as well. The Boarding House, American Seasons, 21 Federal, The Second Story, Le Languedoc, Obadiah's, DeMarco, and India

House are among the island's best. Newer restaurants getting good reviews include Cioppino's and Black-Eyed Susan's, a tiny café with creative ethnic fare at very fair prices.

There's a happy spirit of anticipation in the air in springtime Nantucket. Like the local homeowners, who can be seen putting fresh coats of paint on the shutters, shopkeepers and hotel and restaurant operators are busy sprucing up after the long winter. Hammers and paintbrushes are in evidence everywhere, and on Main Street, merchants are busily arranging new stock, awaiting the coming rush of summer customers.

There are some who love off-season Nantucket best in the fall, after the summer people have left, but though the island is handsome in its autumn hues, there's a feeling of renewal in the spring that is missing in the winding-down days at season's end. From its daffodil-strewn roadsides to downtown's winding lanes, Nantucket has just come alive, and it is a guaranteed spring tonic for early birds.

Area Code: 508

DRIVING DIRECTIONS *Nantucket Steamship Authority,* PO Box 284, Woods Hole, MA 02543, 477-8600, runs boats to the island from Hyannis year-round for both cars and passengers. The trip takes approximately 2¼ hours. Hy-Line, Pier 1, Ocean Street Docks, Hyannis, MA 02601, 775-7185, has service for passengers from Hyannis only during warm months. Both provide parking facilities if you want to leave your car. Island parking is not a problem in spring, but cars really are not necessary on Nantucket. Most of the activity centers within town, which is easily walkable. Bike rentals are plentiful, and you can rent a car or hire a taxi for a day's exploring. Hyannis is just over 80 miles from Boston, 271 miles from New York, and 187 miles from Hartford.

PUBLIC TRANSPORTATION Several airlines service Nantucket from Boston, New York, Baltimore, Philadelphia, New Bedford, Hyannis, and Martha's Vineyard; check Chamber of Commerce for a current list. Bonanza (800-556-3815) offers bus service to Hyannis from New York, Providence, and Boston. Plymouth & Brockton buses also run between Logan Airport, Boston, and Hyannis (746-0378).

ACCOMMODATIONS Rates are for summer; prices are considerably less out of season. Check to be sure that all your intended Nantucket destinations are open off-season. *Jared Coffin House,* 29 Broad Street, 02554, 228-2405, restored 1845 sea captain's mansion, elegant, $$$–$$$$ • *Harbor House,* South Beach Street, 02554, 228-1500, attractive resort complex with rooms in main house or cottages, pool, $$$$$ • *The White Elephant and the Breakers,* Easton Street, PO Box 359, Nantucket 02554, elegant resort hotels, $$$$$ • *Four Chimneys,* 38 Orange Street, 02554, 228-1912, stately 1835 captain's mansion, spacious and gracious, $$$–$$$$ • *Roberts House,* 11 India Street, 02554, 228-9009, 1880 home, fireplaces, large rooms, canopy beds, $$$–$$$$; same owners maintain the attractive *Meeting House* adjacent to the inn, same rates • *Ships Inn,* 13 Fair Street, 02554, 228-0040, tiny charming captain's home, $$$ CP • *Carlisle House Inn,* 26 N. Water Street, 02554, 228-0720, tasteful, antique-filled eighteenth-century home, $$–$$$$ CP • *Corner House,* 49 Centre Street, 02554, 228-1530, cozy 1790 home, screened porch and patio, $$–$$$$ CP • *Cliff Lodge,* 9 Cliff Road, 02554, 228-9480, 1771 sea captain's home, light and airy, harbor views from the roof walk, $$$–$$$$ CP • *Fair Winds,* 29 Cliff Road, 02554, 228-1998, farther up the hill, water views from many guest rooms, $$$$ CP • *Fair Gardens,* 27 Fair Street, 02554, 228-4258, cozy shingled guest house with lovely garden, $$$–$$$$ CP • *Sherburne Inn,* 10 Gay Street, 02554, 228-4425, attractively decorated, stately nineteenth-century home, $$$–$$$$ CP • *Martin House Inn,* 61 Centre Street, 02554, 228-0678, attractive, good value, $$–$$$$.

DINING Opening dates vary year to year; it's best to check. Most are small, so reserve ahead in season. • *21 Federal Street,* 21 Federal Street, 228-2121, among the best in town, $$$ • *Straight Wharf Restaurant,* Straight Wharf, 228-4499, regional American, chic, $$$–$$$$ • *The Second Story,* 1 South Beach Street, 228-3471, eclectic, creative menus, $$$. • *DeMarco,* 9 India Street, 228-1836, excellent (and expensive) northern Italian, $$$–$$$$ • *India House,* 37 India Street, 228-9043, choice of light or formal dining in a historic house, $$–$$$$ • *The Boarding House,* 12 Federal Street, 228-9622, charming cellar café, $$–$$$ • *The Club Car,* 1 Main Street, 228-1101, dinner in a most elegant diner, $$$–$$$$ • *Le Languedoc,* 24 Broad Street, 228-2552, excellent, sophisticated menu, $$$; café downstairs, $$ • *American Seasons,* 80 Centre Street, 228-7111, charming setting, choice of American regional dishes, $$–$$$ • *The Woodbox,* 29 Fair Street, 228-0587, 1709 inn, beams, fireplace, $$$ • *Cioppino's,* 20 Broad Street, excellent seafood, $$$ • *Obadiah's,* 2 India Street, 228-4430, seafood, cozy, reasonable, $$ • *Quaker House,* Centre and Chestnut streets, 228-9156, good value for four-course dinners, $$$ • *Black-Eyed Susan's,* 10 Indian Street, phone unlisted, join the line for creative, economical ethnic dishes, $$ • *Easy Street Café,* Easy Street and Steamboat Wharf, 228-5824, informal, shore dinners, lobster, good chowder, $$ • *Arno's,* 41 Main Street, 228-7001, old standby with new owners, casual, reasonable, $–$$ • *Atlantic Café,* 15 South Water Street, 228-0570, casual, popular, $–$$ • *Cap'n Toby's Chowder*

House, Straight Wharf, 228-0836, try the fried clams, $–$$ • *The Brotherhood,* 23 Broad Street, is the local favorite for overstuffed sandwiches, inexpensive dinners, chowder, $. After dinner, you can dance to a rock band at the *Rose and Crown,* 23 South Main Street, hear quiet music at the *Atlantic Café* (see above) and a pianist at *The Club Car* bar (see above). Summer visitors also see pages 150–151; *Topper's* and *Chanticleer,* the island's two premier dining places, are not open for daffodil season.

RESERVATION SERVICES Nantucket Accommodations, Box 217, Nantucket, MA 02554, 228-9559 • Nantucket & Martha's Vineyard Reservations, Box 1322, Vineyard Haven, MA 02568, 693-7200.

SIGHTSEEING *Historic Nantucket Properties,* maintained by Nantucket Historical Association, 2 Union Street, 228-1894. Hours: in season, daily, 10 A.M. to 5 P.M., off-season as posted. Visitor's passes— good for all of the following and more—are available at all locations. Adults, $8; ages 5 to 14, $4 • *Whaling Museum,* Broad Street at head of Steamboat Wharf, individual admission, $4; children, $2 • *Thomas Macy Warehouse,* Straight Wharf, individual admission, $3; children, $2 • *Jethro Coffin House* (oldest house), Sunset Hill off West Chester Street, individual admission, $3; children, $2 • *Old Mill,* Mill Hill, Prospect Street, individual admission, $2; children, $1 • *Hadwen House,* 96 Main Street, individual admission, $2; children, $1 • *Fair Street Museum,* Fair Street, individual admission, $4; children, $2 • *Peter Foulger Museum,* Broad Street, individual admission, $4; children, $2.

BIKE RENTALS *Cook's Cycle Shop,* 6 South Beach Street, 228-0800 • *Nantucket Bike Shops,* Steamboat Wharf and Straight Wharf, 228-1999 • *Young's Bicycle Shop,* Steamboat Wharf, 228-1151.

INFORMATION Nantucket Island Chamber of Commerce, 48 Main Street, Nantucket MA 02554, 228-1700.

Admiring the Miracle in Providence

You are cordially invited to visit Providence, Rhode Island, to see a miracle in progress. That isn't exaggeration. For anyone who knew the city in the old days, the recent changes are nothing short of miraculous.

As late as the 1960s, this city was in serious decline. The old industrial base was run-down, merchants were leaving downtown for the shopping malls, the population was dwindling, and much of the city's fine stock of historic older homes had turned into slums.

Today Providence is in the midst of a remarkable turnaround. It began with the transformation of neighborhoods, in one of the nation's most lauded restoration campaigns. The work in progress is a rejuvenated downtown. This is more than urban renewal: It is a complete remapping of the heart of the city, in which parking decks that had long covered over branches of the Providence River were ripped up and the waterway allowed to follow its scenic course through the center of town.

The domed State House building still presides over Providence from its hilltop perch, but below everything is changing. At this writing, a new railroad station has been built and the old Beaux Arts station grandly restored; a restaurant and office complex are planned for it. The Capital Center project is rising below the station, with new tenants filling the office buildings and bringing jobs with them. A new convention center opened in 1993, attracting a posh new Westin Hotel to the city. And instead of moving out, stores are coming in. A major department store will be an anchor of Providence Place, a $300 million mall, office, and hotel project to be built not far from the State House lawn. By the time you read this, many of these plans may be reality.

Along with the vibrant physical changes, there has been a restaurant revolution that has food critics singing the city's praises, all the more reason why Providence merits a weekend to discover how a city can transform itself.

An ideal choice is the first weekend in June, the date of the annual Festival of Historic Houses sponsored by the Providence Preservation Society. For this one weekend only, visitors are able to go inside some of the exceptional private homes and gardens of the College Hill Historic District, the area where the miracle began.

The district, which lies between the Brown University campus and downtown, was the earliest settlement in the state and the first center of the city. It is widely recognized as one of the most notable collections of early American homes in the country, one that is even more remarkable because these houses have been continually lived in for more than 200 years.

Yet, like Providence itself, College Hill was in trouble. Many of the older homes were in decay and were being torn down to make room for the expansion of Brown's campus. The group that formed to preserve College Hill faced a formidable task, but today its efforts are a model of what can be accomplished when a community cares about preserving its heritage.

On Benefit Street, the core of the restoration efforts, there are now more than 100 handsomely restored historic houses. The street has been dubbed "A Mile of History," where taking a stroll is like stepping back to the eighteenth and early nineteenth centuries. The Nightingale-Brown House, built in 1792, is the neighborhood showplace, one of the largest eighteenth-century wooden structures in the country. Like many of the privately owned homes, it is sometimes open to the public on this special weekend to help raise funds for continuing preservation efforts, which have now spread to many other city neighborhoods.

The festivities usually begin on Friday night with a candlelight tour along Benefit Street or other streets in National Historic Districts. Changing areas are chosen for the House and Garden Tour on Saturday afternoon, and on Sunday afternoon a Preservation Trolley Tour takes in a selection of historic neighborhoods around the city. Talks on various aspects of perservation fill out the schedule.

Typically, a dozen private residences open for the candlelight tour. Their carefully restored exteriors present fine examples of Federal, Greek Revival, and early Victorian detailing, while the interiors are both traditional and contemporary.

To add to the pleasures of the weekend, try to snag one of the rooms at the Old Court, a small inn perfectly located on Benefit Street. More accommodations on College Hill are available through Bed-and-Breakfast of Rhode Island, see page xi. Closer to downtown, the State House Inn offers period furnishings in an 1887 setting. The restored Omni Biltmore Hotel, a landmark, usually offers special rates for house-touring visitors.

The array of architecture on College Hill includes not only residences but house museums, churches, and grand mansions adapted for use as offices. Some of the mansions date back to the China-trade era following the American Revolution, the time when many Providence traders made their millions. The area borders the historic Brown University campus, so visitors can also view the school's handsome quadrangles and stately buildings. In many ways Brown's emergence as one of the most sought-after Ivy League colleges has paralleled the reblooming of its neighborhood.

Brown deserves a return visit for a closer look. Campus highlights include the 1770 University Hall, the John Hay and Rockefeller Libraries, and Wriston Quadrangle. The David Winton Bell Gallery in the List Art Building, across from the main gate, presents changing art exhibits that are often worthwhile. Art exhibits are found also at the Providence Art Club, studios and galleries in two eighteenth-century houses off nearby Benefit Street.

The city's finest art collections, however, belong to the highly regarded Rhode Island School of Design (universally known as RISD or "rizz-dee"), whose campus lies just below Brown. RISD's five-story museum on Benefit Street is first-rate, with everything from Oriental art to French Impressionists in its collection. The Pendleton House next door was the nation's first example of an "American Wing," and is devoted to early American furniture and decorative arts.

Another RISD gallery is the Woods-Gerry, situated in a nineteenth-century Federal mansion, which displays the work of talented faculty, students, and alumni of the school. Many of them are world leaders in the designing arts. The gallery is on Prospect Street, which boasts other splendid mansions, most of them still private residences.

While you are in Providence, you may want to learn more about its founder, Roger Williams, one of the great champions of modern democracy, who planned the town as a model of religious tolerance. The Roger Williams National Memorial is in a park on North Main, the site of his original settlement. A slide show describes his life and the development of the site.

The First Baptist Meeting House on North Main, with a Christopher Wren–inspired, 185-foot steeple, was founded by Williams and his followers in 1638, with this building actually constructed in 1775. Step in to see the massive Waterford crystal chandelier inside.

A statue of Williams stands at his burial place on Prospect Terrace, a photographer's favorite spot for its panoramic view of the city and the countryside beyond. If you have children along, you'll also want to visit the Roger Williams Park three miles south of the city for its zoo and children's nature center. The Victorian park offers 430 acres of woods, waterways, and winding drives, a Japanese garden, and a classic carousel. The zoo recently gained an African Plains exhibit, and also features a tropical rain forest pavilion and a glass-sided habitat where polar bears swim.

One of the best features of a weekend in Providence is that the city is truly, as the brochures promise, a "walkable city," and most of the sights can be covered easily on foot. Pick up the self-guiding map, "A Stroll Through Providence," at the Convention and Visitors Bureau near the railroad station. These days there are pleasant discoveries literally waiting at almost every turn.

Noteworthy stops in town include the Rhode Island State House, modeled after the U.S. Capitol; the John Brown House, which John Quincy Adams called "the most magnificent and elegant private mansion that I have ever seen on this continent"; the gloriously restored 1878 City Hall; the 1707 home and garden of Governor Stephen Hopkins, a signer of the Declaration of Independence; the Museum of Rhode Island History at Aldrich House, the former residence of U.S. Senator Nelson W. Aldrich; and the Providence Athenaeum, an 1838 Doric structure that was one of America's first libraries as well as the place where Edgar Allan Poe courted Sarah Helen Whitman, a resident of Benefit Street.

Near downtown at 65 Weybosset Street, look for the Providence Arcade, an 1828 covered shopping street that looks like an enormous Greek temple. Said to be the country's first indoor shopping mall, it is filled with boutiques and cafés, and makes for a pleasant stroll. Interesting boutiques and galleries are also found on South Main Street, a block down the hill from Benefit Street. Many are housed in restored Colonial buildings.

Another part of Providence that should not be overlooked is the Federal Hill area, this city's thriving "Little Italy." Past the arch spanning Atwells Avenue, the streets feature Old World street lamps and fountains, plus a wealth of good eating.

But traditional Italian is just the start of the excellent dining that has become one of the city's recent claims to fame. The couple who put Providence on the culinary map are George Germon and Johanne Killeen, husband and wife, who both graduated from RISD. Their creative Italian dishes at Al Forno have gained national praise. The list of other notable dining places continues to grow.

After dinner, you might want to see the latest offering by the highly regarded Trinity Rep theater company, now in its fourth decade as one of the nation's leading regional repertory troupes.

Long an industrial town in the shadow of its worldlier neighbor, Boston, Providence has rescued the treasures of its rich past and come into its own as a livable and charming city. For those who knew the city only in the past, it is a transformation worth discovering.

Area Code: 401

DRIVING DIRECTIONS   From north or south take I-95, from west take Route 44 or Route 6, from east take I-195 to the center of Providence. It is 49 miles from Boston, 185 miles from New York, and 75 miles from Hartford.

PUBLIC TRANSPORTATION   Amtrak trains, most major airlines, and Greyhound and Bonanza buses serve Providence. Bonanza provides frequent service to Boston's Logan Airport.

ACCOMMODATIONS   *The Old Court,* 144 Benefit Street, Providence 02903, 751-2002, 1863 home turned B & B in the historic district, $$$ CP • *State House Inn,* 43 Jewett Street, Providence 02908, 785-1235, restored 1887 structure, $$ CP • *Westin Hotel,* 1 West Exchange Street, Providence 02903, 598-8000, indoor pool and spa, $$$–$$$$ • *Omni Biltmore Hotel,* Kennedy Plaza, Providence 02903, 421-0700, $$$. Inquire about weekend packages, particularly for the Festival of Historic Houses • *Marriott Providence,* Charles and Orem streets, Providence 02904, 272-2400, $$$$ • *Days Hotel,* 220 India Street, Providence 02903, 272-5577, $$–$$$ • *Holiday Inn Downtown,* 21 Atwells Avenue, Providence 02903, 831-3900, $$–$$$ • *Johnson & Wales Inn,* Routes 114A and 44, Seekonk, MA 02771, (508) 336-8700, $–$$ CP.

DINING *Al Forno,* 577 South Main Street, 273-9760, $$–$$$ • *Angels,* 125 North Main Street, 273-0210, $$–$$$ • *Capital Grille,* One Cookson Place, 521-5600, $$–$$$ • *Hemenway's Seafood Grill,* 1 Old Stone Square, 351-8570, $$–$$$ • *Pot au Feu,* 44 Custom House Street, 273-8953, formal dining room, $$–$$$; downstairs bistro, $$ • *Blue Point Oyster Bar,* 99 North Main Street, 272-6145, $$ • *New Rivers,* 7 Steeple Street, 751-0350, electic contemporary menus, delightful setting, $$–$$$ • *In-Prov Citta Divina,* Kennedy Plaza, 351-8770, eclectic Italian, $$–$$$ • *Pizzico,* 762 Hope Street, 421-4114, Italian bistro, highly recommended locally, $$ • *Rue de L'Espoir,* 99 Hope Street, 751-8890, international menus, interesting decor, $$ • *Adesso,* 161 Cushing Street, 521-0770, California-style grill, innovative pastas, $$$ • *Gatehouse Grill,* 4 Richmond Square, 521-5229, Provençal cuisine, water views, live jazz on weekends, $$–$$$ • *Ristorante Antico-Toscano,* 245 Atwells Avenue, 274-4232, fine Tuscan fare in Little Italy, $$ • *The Blue Grotto,* Atwells Avenue, 272-9030, another Little Italy favorite, $$ • *L'Epicureo,* 238 Atwells Avenue, 454-8430, elegant dining, evolved from longtime local market, $$$ • *Down City Diner,* 151 Weybosset Street, 331-9217, trendy spot for good, reasonable food, $–$$ • *The Hot Club,* 575 South Water Street, 861-9007, $ • *l'Elizabeth,* 285 South Main Street, 621-9113, Victorian decor, popular for cocktails and desserts, $ • *Leon's on the Westside,* 166 Broadway, 273-1055, favorite for breakfast, Sunday brunch, $$.

SIGHTSEEING *Providence Festival of Historic Houses,* early June. For current ticket prices and schedule, contact Providence Preservation Society, 21 Meeting Street, Providence 02903, 831-7440 • *Rhode Island School of Design Museum of Art,* 224 Benefit Street, 454-6500. Hours: September 1 to June 15, Tuesday to Saturday, 10:30 A.M. to 5 P.M. except Thursday, noon to 8 P.M., Sundays, 2 P.M. to 5 P.M.; rest of year, Wednesday to Saturday, noon to 5 P.M. Adults, $2; ages 5 to 18 and students, $0.50; free admission on Saturday • *Woods-Gerry Gallery,* 62 Prospect Street, 331-3511. Hours: During school year, daily except Tuesday, 11 A.M. to 4 P.M., Sunday from 2 P.M.; June and July, Monday to Friday, 11 A.M. to 4 P.M. Free • *Providence Art Club,* 11 Thomas Street at Benefit Street, 331-1114. Hours: September to June, Monday to Friday, 10 A.M. to 4 P.M., Saturday, noon to 3 P.M., Sunday, 3 P.M. to 5 P.M.; closed weekends July and August. Free • *Brown University,* tours from Admissions Office, Corliss Bracket House, Prospect and Angell streets, 863-2378. Hours: Monday to Friday, hourly except noon, 10 A.M. to 4 P.M.; Saturday, mid-September to mid-December only, 10 A.M. to noon • *David Winton Bell Gallery,* 64 College Street, in List Art Center, 863-2932. Hours: late August to early June, Monday to Friday, 11 A.M. to 4 P.M.; weekends from 1 P.M. Free • *John Brown House,* 52 Power Street at Benefit Street, 311-8575. Hours: March 1 to December 31, guided tours Tuesday to Saturday, 11 A.M. to 4 P.M., Sunday from 1 P.M. Adults, $5.50; under 17, $2 • *Roger Williams National Memorial,* 282 North Main Street, 528-5385. Hours: daily, 8 A.M. to 4:30 P.M. Free • *First Baptist Church,* 75 North Main at Waterman, 454-3418. Hours: guided tours Sunday, at 9:30 A.M. in July and August, at noon rest of year. Church is open Monday to Friday, 9:30 A.M. to 3:30 P.M. Free • *Rhode Island State Capitol,* Smith Street, 277-2357. Hours: Monday to Friday, 8:30 A.M. to 4:30 P.M., tours from 9:30 A.M. to 3:30 P.M. Free • *Providence Athenaeum,* 251 Benefit Street, 421-6970. Hours: Monday to Friday, 8:30 A.M. to 5:30 P.M., Wednesday to 8:30 P.M., Saturday, 9:30 A.M. to 5:30 P.M.; closed Saturday in summer. Free • *Governor Stephen Hopkins House,* Benefit and Hopkins streets, 884-8337. Hours: April to December, Wednesday and Saturday, 1 P.M. to 4 P.M. Free • *Roger Williams Park,* Elmwood Avenue, 785-3510. Hours: Park open daily, 7 A.M. to 9 P.M. Free. *Roger Williams Park Zoo,* daily, 9 A.M. to 5 P.M. in summer, shorter hours off-season—best to check. Adults, $3.50; children, $1.50.

INFORMATION Greater Providence Convention and Visitors Bureau, 30 Exchange Terrace, Providence, RI 02903, 274-1636. Hours: Monday to Friday, 8:30 A.M. to 5 P.M.

A Whale of a Time on Cape Ann

Some places watch for the first robin or the first signs of green on the trees. On Cape Ann, the arrival of spring means just one thing: The whales are back.

"The other cape," as some call it, is the lesser-known northern Massachusetts strip eight miles out to sea that inspired onetime summer resident T. S. Eliot to write about "those who are in ships/whose business has to do with fish."

This is fishing country, all right, especially Gloucester, where some 150 million pounds of fish come in each year, the biggest catch of any port on the East Coast.

But fish aren't the whole story, by any means. Gloucester shares its cape with Rockport, an artists' town whose boulder-strewn seven-mile coastline, harbor full of sailboats, and picturesque cove packed with shops and galleries bring out both lovers of beauty and thousands of strolling summer shoppers.

In spring, it's the beauty that takes precedence—and it's also spring when Cape Ann takes on the title of "Whale Watching Capital of the World." Sign on for a cruise and sign up at one of the lovely inns in the area, and you're ready for a rare weekend. If you're a chamber-music buff, make it in June and you'll be able to attend the annual Rockport Chamber Music Festival as well. The fine Gloucester Stage Company, which offers plays at its headquarters in an old warehouse, is also well worth a visit.

Just like clockwork every year, humpback, minke, finback, and right whales return here to the offshore feeding grounds of Jeffreys Ledge and Stellwagen Bank. They put on quite a show, especially the humpbacks. These showoffs breach the surface, flinging the entire lengths of their 50-foot, 40-ton bodies into the air, and then crash down with mammoth bellyflops, sending shock waves in all directions. They slap their flippers and bang their massive tails, and they blow clouds of bubbles into the air.

All this takes place within clear sight of the whale-watching boats. There are several ships to choose from, all about equal by most accounts. You may have more trouble deciding among the many nice places to stay in the area. One excellent choice is Sea Crest Manor, an antique-filled home once owned by a governor of Massachusetts. Set away from the town off Route 127A, with a view of the sea from its second-floor sundeck, it's the sort of civilized place where tea is served at 4:00 P.M. each day. Not far away, directly on the water, is the Captain's House, a friendly guest house with an unbeatable view.

The Yankee Clipper is a complex of three handsome Colonial houses, two of them on the curving lawn that runs right down to the water. The rooms vary, with the more traditional furnishings in the Bullfinch House across the road. The owners of the Yankee Clipper also run the Ralph Waldo Emerson Inn. Both are on Route 127 North in the area known as Pigeon Cove, and both have pools for guests' use in warmer weather. Old Farm Inn is a 1799 farmhouse on five acres on Pigeon Cove, with warm country ambience, a caring hostess, and paths to the coastline. The Inn on Cove Hill is an attractive eighteenth-century home in town, done in informal country style; the rates are very reasonable.

A personal favorite is the Eden Pines Inn, a simple clapboard Colonial perched smack on the water on a secluded road away from town, off Route 127A in the direction of Gloucester. This is an airy, summery hideaway with spectacular views from the oversize rooms.

Rockport was never a major early trading port like some of its coastal neighbors, because its broad harbor was unprotected from the elements until a breakwater was built at the turn of this century. It was named for the granite beds in the surrounding hills, which became the chief industry of the town. The quarries attracted a large colony of Scandinavians, who served as stonecutters.

As the Scandinavians were arriving, so were the artists, attracted by the combination of Cape Ann's rugged coastline and woodland beauty. The terrain and its luminous light has been a magnet for painters and sculptors since the early eighteenth century, when Fitz Hugh Lane first began capturing the scene from a granite studio atop Duncan's Point in Gloucester. The Cape Ann Historical Museum has a comprehensive collection of his work. Winslow Homer also painted here.

As often happens when artists congregate in scenic spots, summer visitors followed. Gloucester maintained its fishing fleet, but with the completion of a major highway into town in the 1950s, tourism became Rockport's major industry. Even though the town is being developed rapidly and can be uncomfortably packed in the center on a summer day, it retains much of its salty charm.

Most visitors head directly for Bearskin Neck, a spit of land extending out to sea and lined with fishing shacks now transformed into shops of every imaginable kind. You'll need no guide—just join the throngs and make the rounds of the stores and their scrimshaw, hand-blown glassware, pewter, leather, T-shirts, crafts, and clothing.

Take note of one of the shanties on an extension of Bearskin Neck, known as Motif Number One because it has been painted by so many area artists. The Rockport Art Association, housed in a restored tavern on Main Street, is the year-round center of the current art scene, which continues to flourish even though the subject matter has diminished since the shacks and ships' riggings gave way to shops and ice-cream stands. There are a number of interesting art galleries here, as well.

And there is more art to be seen in Gloucester, where the North Shore Art Association has its summer headquarters and spacious gallery. You will pass them on the way to the Rocky Neck Art Colony in East Gloucester, said to be the oldest art colony in the country; here you can watch artists at work as well as visit galleries and dine in picturesque restaurants.

From Gloucester, it's a lovely ride to the Beauport Museum way out on the water on Eastern Point Boulevard. This 26-room mansion, the home of Henry Davis Sleeper, a prominent antiques collector and interior designer of the 1920s, is a feast of decorative arts, with each room dedicated to a particular decor, from Oriental to Paul Revere.

Hammond Castle Museum in Magnolia is an unusual find in these simple seafaring environs. Mr. Hammond, it seems, was so taken with what he saw in Europe that he decided to build his own castle at home, complete with drawbridge and filled with Roman, medieval, and Renaissance pieces. The Great Hall here is worthy of a cathedral, with magnificent stained-glass windows at either end, a huge fifteenth-century fireplace, and an 8,600-pipe organ rising eight stories high.

You could easily fill two days viewing the whales, the shops, and the museums, but do leave some time to appreciate the rich natural beauty of the area. Take a walk south of town to the end of Atlantic Avenue and the Headlands, dramatic outcroppings of rock where you can look out to sea and back at the harbor and homes. Then drive to Pigeon Hill at the end of Landmark Lane, a small park atop one of the highest elevations around, for a soaring view. This is the site of the annual Midsummer's Day celebration, held by the local Swedish community in mid-June, an event that features a maypole, costumes, music, and dancing.

Turn off Route 127 just before Old Farm Inn for Halibut Point, Cape Ann's farthest reach out to sea, a 69-acre state park at the northern end of the peninsula, with its own boulder-rimmed shoreline view, reached via a path through the woods.

The Eastern Point Sanctuary in East Gloucester is prime hiker's territory, with many guided walks from the Coast Guard lighthouse. And then there are the beaches, two of them in town, more off Route 127A between Rockport and Gloucester. In between it all, you can feast on the freshest seafood to be found, everything from local cod and haddock to good old New England lobster. Make a note that Rockport is dry, so you'll have to bring your own wine for dinner.

With that exception, Cape Ann serves everything you need for a seaworthy weekend—with whales as an unbeatable main course.

Area Code: 508

DRIVING DIRECTIONS   Cape Ann is on Route 127, off Route 128, on the north shore of Massachusetts, 38 miles north of Boston, 246 miles from New York, and 136 miles from Hartford.

PUBLIC TRANSPORTATION   Regular train service to Rockport and Gloucester from Boston's North Station, 617-227-5070. It's possible to manage in the center of Rockport without a car.

ACCOMMODATIONS   *Seacrest Manor,* 131 Marmion Way, Rockport 01966, 546-2211, $$–$$$ CP • *The Captain's House,* 109 Marmion Way, Rockport 01966, 546-3825, $$ CP • *Yankee Clipper Inn,* 96 Granite Street, Route 127, Pigeon Cove, Rockport 01966, 546-3407, $$–$$$$ CP; $$$$–$$$$$ MAP • *Ralph Waldo Emerson Inn,* Phillips Avenue, Route 127, Pigeon Cove, Rockport 01966, 546-6321, $$–$$$ • *The Inn on Cove Hill,* 37 Mt. Pleasant Street, Rockport 01966, 546-2701, $–$$ CP • *Addison Choate Inn,* 49 Broadway, Rockport 01966, 546-7543, $$ CP • *Old Farm Inn,* 291 Granite Street, Pigeon Cove, Rockport 01966, 546-3237, $$–$$$ CP • *Eden Pines Inn,* Eden Road, Rockport 01966, 546-2505, $$–$$$ CP • *Sally Webster Inn,* 34 Mt. Pleasant Street, Rockport 01966, 546-9251, small, inviting decor, $–$$ CP • **Motels with ocean views, pools:** *Twin Light Manor,* Atlantic Road, Gloucester 01930, 283-7500, $$$–$$$$; *Bass Rocks Ocean Inn,* Atlantic Avenue, Gloucester 01930, 283-7600, $$–$$$; *Cape Ann Motor Inn,* 33 Rockport Road, Gloucester 01930, 281-2900, $$–$$$.

DINING   *The Greenery,* 15 Dock Square, Rockport, 546-9593, salads, seafood, pasta, on the harbor, $–$$ • *My Place By-the-Sea,* 72 Bearskin Neck, Rockport, 546-9667, water views, light and regular menu, $$ • *The Glass Verandah,* Yankee Clipper Inn (see above), sophisticated seafood specialties, $$–$$$ • *Peg Leg,* Beach Street, Rockport, 546-3038, informal, old favorite, $–$$ • *Sea Level Café,* 14 Bearksin Neck, Rockport, 546-2180, nautical decor, water views, $–$$ • *The Seaside,* 21 Dock Square, Rockport, 546-3905, informal spot for chowder, fried clams, etc., $–$$ • *Brackett's Ocean View,* 29 Main Street, Rockport, 546-2797, good family choice, $ • *The Lobster Pool at Folly Cove,* 332 Granite Street (Route 127), Rockport, 546-7808, deck on the bay, $–$$$ • *White Rainbow,* 65 Main Street, Gloucester, 281-0017, 1830 landmark, special, excellent continental cuisine, $$–$$$; also café menu, $–$$ • *Bistro,* 2 Main Street, Gloucester, 281-8055, French country ambience, gourmet fare, $$ • *The Square Café,* 197 East Main Street, Gloucester, 281-3951, small café near the North Shore Art Association and Rocky Neck, excellent reviews, $$ • *Evie's Rudder,* 73 Rocky Neck Avenue, East Gloucester, 283-7967, seafood, picturesque waterfront views, $$–$$$ • *The Studio,* Rocky Neck Avenue, East Gloucester, 283-4123, another prime setting for seafood, big deck overlooking the harbor, $$ • For clams, drive to Essex on Ipswich Bay, where some say the fried clam was invented, and where *Woodman's,* Main Street, on the Causeway, 768-6451, is a local institution that fans say is worth the mob scene. Also excellent is *Tom Shea's,* 122 Main Street, 768-6931, right across the road.

SIGHTSEEING   Whale watching off Cape Ann, usually half-day cruises, average $21. Contact any of the following for current schedules and prices (all are zip code 01930): *Cape Ann Whale Watch,* Main Street, Rose's Wharf, Gloucester, 283-5110 or (800) 877-5110; *Capt. Bill & Son's Whale Watching,* 9 Traverse Street, Gloucester, 283-6995 or (800) 33-WHALE; *Yankee Whale Watch,* Cape Ann Marina, Gloucester, 283-0313; *Seven Seas Whale Watch,* Seven Seas Wharf, Gloucester, 283-1776 or (800) 283-1776; *Yankee Whale Watch,* 75 West Essex Avenue, Gloucester, 283-0313 or (800) 942-5464 • *Rockport Chamber Music Festival,* PO Box 312, Rockport 01966, 546-7391. Concerts by Manhattan String Quartet and others on weekends in June at Hibbard Gallery of Rockport Art Association. Write or phone for current season dates and prices • *Cape Ann Historical Association Museum,* 27 Pleasant Street, Gloucester, 283-0455. Hours: year-round except February, Tuesday through Saturday, 10 A.M. to 5 P.M. Adults, $3.50; children, $2 • *Rockport Art Association,* 12 Main Street, 546-6604. Hours: Monday to Saturday, 9:30 A.M. to 5 P.M., Sunday 1 P.M. to 5 P.M. Free • *Gloucester Stage Company,* 267 East Main Street, Gloucester, 281-4099. Hours: mid-May to October and December; phone for current schedule and ticket prices • *North Shore Arts*

Association, 197 East Main Street, Gloucester, 283-1857. Hours: early June to September, Monday to Saturday, 10 A.M. to 5:30 P.M., Sunday 1 P.M. to 5:30 P.M. Free • *Beauport,* 75 Eastern Point Boulevard, Gloucester, 283-0800. Hours: mid-May to mid-September, Monday to Friday, 10 A.M. to 4 P.M.; mid-September to mid-October, also Saturday and Sunday, 1 P.M. to 4 P.M. Adults $5; children, $2.50 • *Hammond Castle Museum,* 80 Hesperus Avenue, Gloucester, 283-7673. Hours: June to October, daily, 10 A.M. to 5 P.M.; rest of year, Thursday, Friday, Sunday, 1 P.M. to 4 P.M., Saturday, 10 A.M. to 4 P.M. Adults, $6; ages 6 to 12, $3.50.

INFORMATION   Cape Ann Chamber of Commerce, 33 Commercial Street, Gloucester, MA 01930, 283-1601 or (800) 321-0133; Rockport Chamber of Commerce, Route 127, Box 67, Rockport, MA 01966, 546-6575.

The Three Bs: A Maine Education

The time is 3:00 A.M. on a chilly spring night, a good time to be snuggled in bed under a New England patchwork quilt. So why are all those cars still out in a parking lot in Freeport, Maine?

They belong to sportsmen, savvy shoppers, insomniacs, tourists, and the just plain curious from every part of the country, part of some 3½ million people who stop day and night, year-round, at one of America's shopping phenomenons, L.L. Bean, the nation's only 24-hour-a-day, seven-day-a-week retail store.

Mr. Bean's enterprise has developed into a major tourist attraction and a Maine institution, one that has transformed Freeport into a shopping mecca. Two nearby neighbors, Bowdoin College in Brunswick and the Maritime Museum in Bath, are also longstanding institutions, each reflecting another facet of the state. Put the Bs together for a weekend that is a pleasure-filled Maine education.

Leon Leonwood Bean never dreamed what lay ahead in 1912 when his intense dislike for cold, wet feet led him to create a new kind of hunting shoe with leather uppers on rubber overshoe bottoms. Armed with a mailing list of Maine hunting license holders, he advertised that with his new product their feet would be "properly dressed for hunting bear or moose." He guaranteed "perfect satisfaction in every way," a promise that proved expensive when 90 of the first 100 pairs sold were returned with their bottoms separated from the boots.

But Bean was true to his word. He gave refunds, borrowed more money, perfected his product, and started mailing out more catalogs; this time, things went well. Under Bean's grandson, Leon Gorman, the company now does a whopping $870 million in annual sales.

Today's mammoth store, decorated with granite paths, pine beams, and an 8,500-gallon indoor pond stocked with trout, has been described as "a cross between Bloomingdale's and a forest glen." You'll find everything for the outdoors, from canoes to clothing. Across the road is a factory store stocked with irregulars and markdowns at bargain prices.

Bargains, in fact, have become the watchword in Freeport, as some 150 discount stores have opened to take advantage of the crowds drawn to Bean.

It makes for mammoth traffic jams, almost obscuring the fact that Freeport is a fine old New England town. Starting in mid-May, you can leave the crowds behind for the picturesque harbor at South Freeport and enjoy delicious lobster and the best lobster roll I've tasted in Maine at the Harraseeket Lunch and Lobster Company.

Freeport's handsome Harraseeket Inn puts you within walking distance of L.L. Bean, and more bed-and-breakfast inns are opening all the time, but you may find the atmosphere more peaceful if you make your headquarters in nearby Brunswick or Bath.

Brunswick is a town filled with fine homes—and history. Much of it centers on Bowdoin College, Maine's proudest educational institution, whose heritage goes back to 1794 and whose alumni list includes the likes of Henry Wadsworth Longfellow, Nathaniel Hawthorne, Admirals Peary and MacMillan, and President Franklin Pierce.

Free campus tours are given from late May through August, but you can easily stroll the handsome 40-building campus and see the main sights on your own. Bowdoin's museums merit some time.

The Walker Art Building collections span the centuries and the globe, but most notable are the American paintings such as Gilbert Stuart's portrait of Thomas Jefferson, and other portraits by Copley and Eakins. There are many Gilbert Stuarts, including a portrait of James Bowdoin III, son of the Massachusetts governor for whom the school was named, who commissioned a number of works and then bequeathed his art to Bowdoin in 1811, giving it one of the earliest college art collections in America.

Bowdoin's second museum, the Peary-MacMillan Arctic Museum, honors the exploits of two adventurous alumni explorers, who were the first to reach the North Pole. If you've ever wondered what it took to make this historic trip, here is the place to find out. The museum features nearly life-size, painted cutout figures of Peary and MacMillan in Eskimo dress, and interesting artifacts from the expedition, including the odometer, telescope, and navigational instruments they used. Stuffed polar bears and walruses give some notion of the animals they found on their journey, and another section of exhibits details the life of the inhabitants of the Arctic in the first half of this century, their clothes, tools, carvings, and paintings.

Both the college and the area between Federal and Maine streets are Historic Districts, and a walking tour will reward you with a look at some of the finest of the remaining homes. Among the beauties are 63 Federal Street, the home of Harriet Beecher Stowe, and 25 Federal, the residence of Longfellow and his wife when he taught at Bowdoin in 1829. Lincoln Street is lined with Greek Revival homes, unchanged since they were built in the 1840s. One exception is the house at No. 3, a 1772 structure that was moved here and altered. It is considered the oldest home in the village.

Park Row homes date from 1798 to the mid-1800s, with the Italianate brick double house at 159-161 Park Row deserving special note. Guided tours from the Pejepscot Historical Society Museum, No. 159, take you through the building next door, the Skolfield-Whittier House, furnished just as beautifully as it was in 1863. Also of interest is 6-8 College Street, a onetime station on the underground railroad that shielded slaves en route to Canada. Number 26 College Street was the boyhood home of Pulitzer Prize-winning poet Robert Peter Tristram Coffin.

Finally, Civil War buffs should note the 226 Maine Street home of General Joshua L. Chamberlain, who was also a governor of Maine and president of Bowdoin. It is now a museum with many original furnishings and memorabilia tracing Chamberlain's life, including Civil War relics.

If you return in summer, the Bowdoin campus is the setting for the Maine State Music Theater, presenting Broadway musicals, and a Summer Music Festival of chamber concerts at the First Parish Church. Many more events take place at Brunswick's Thomas Point Beach, including the annual Maine Festival featuring state performing artists and craftsmen, a Bluegrass Festival, and the Maine Highland Games.

In spring, the pleasant contrast of a few peaceful hours in Brunswick and the bustling shops in Freeport makes for a full and varied day—and leaves time for further exploration in Bath on Sunday. Bath and boats have been synonymous ever since the first 30-ton vessel, the *Virginia,* was launched here in 1607. More than 4,000 other ships have followed since.

The sign over the gates of the Bath Iron Works, proclaiming that "Through these gates pass the world's best shipbuilders," is no idle boast for a company that celebrated its 110th birthday in 1994 and has many current employees who come from a long line of shipbuilding ancestors. Bath boats, from sleek racing yachts to military vessels, have long been noted all over the world for their fine craftsmanship. During World War II, 82 U.S. destroyers were built here, more than were built by the entire empire of Japan. The Iron Works still makes commercial boats and boats for the U.S. Navy.

The Maine Maritime Museum celebrates this long seafaring heritage in a living museum complex that also includes an internship program that helps keep the art of building wooden boats alive. In warm weather, you can see several parts of the Maritime Museum by boat along the Kennebec River.

Park at the Visitors' Center at the Percy and Small Shipyard, beyond the Iron Works on Washington Street, and begin by touring the only surviving shipyard in America where large wooden sailing vessels were constructed. One, the six-masted *Wyoming,* was the largest wooden sailboat ever built in the United States.

Signs in the buildings and shops explain the steps in creating a boat, from laying out patterns and cutting frames to sailmaking and caulking. Guides are available to take you through, but if you choose to tour on your own and you have any questions about the shipbuilding process, they'll be answered by the bright young apprentices who work in the Apprentice Shop, learning the intricacies of constructing traditional Maine wooden crafts. The 18-month training program is partially supported by the sale of their boats. You can also see the actual construction of some of the old boats that are now in the process of restoration.

If the museum boat *Hardy II* is running, hop aboard; otherwise, drive back to town to reach the Sewall House, an 1844 columned and shuttered mansion that contains the furnishings and memorabilia of the wealthy Sewall family as well as ships' models and a history of the Bath Iron Works. Among the models is a 12-foot mahogany-and-brass replica of J. P. Morgan's 343-foot yacht, *Corsair,* built by the Iron Works in 1930.

A few blocks down Washington Street at the Winter Street Center, there are three floors of old photos, logs, and dioramas telling the story of Bath's maritime history, and an exhibit showing a century of Maine steamboats.

The walk along Washington puts you in the heart of Bath's historic district, past Federal, Greek, Gothic Revival, and Italianate mansions once owned by wealthy shipbuilders and sea captains.

Besides the mansions, have a look at the restored nineteenth-century Front Street, with its brick sidewalks and old-fashioned lampposts, starting with the attractive City Park. The statue in the pond is appropriately known as *Spirit of the Sea.* At the top of Front Street is City Hall and the Old Customs House, and Waterfront Park will give you a view of the river. If the weather is mild, Popham Beach and Reid State Park, two of Maine's best white-sand beaches, are nearby. You can also visit the fishermen's coves of Orr's and Bailey Islands, see the thousands of migratory birds and waterfowl that congregate at Merrymeeting Bay, visit the Swan Island State Park Wildlife Area, or hike through Morse Mountain's coastal wilderness. Between museum, town, and surroundings, you can easily fill a full day in Bath.

End the day with a Maine seafood dinner and you've completed your three Bs tour, perhaps with a bonus B to take home—all those bargains you picked up in Freeport.

And in case you want one last shot, remember that L.L. Bean will be open no matter how late you linger over dessert.

Area Code: 207

DRIVING DIRECTIONS   Freeport is on I-95, 20 miles north of Portland. It is 125 miles from Boston, 335 miles from New York, and 225 miles from Hartford. Follow U.S. Route 1 north for Brunswick and Bath.

PUBLIC TRANSPORTATION   Greyhound Bus service to Brunswick; nearest air service is Portland.

ACCOMMODATIONS *Harraseeket Inn,* 162 Main Street, Freeport 04032, 865-9377, luxury inn, $$–$$$$ CP • *Isaac Randall House,* Independence Drive, Freeport 04032, 865-9295 or (800) 865-9295, wooded setting, walking distance to shops, $$–$$$ CP • *Captain Daniel Stone Inn,* 10 Water Street, Brunswick 04011, 725-9898, attractive and comfortable small hotel, $$–$$$$ CP • *The Stowe House,* 63 Federal Street, Brunswick 04011, 725-5543, motel rooms attached to 1807 Federal home of Harriet Beecher Stowe, $–$$ • *Brunswick Bed and Breakfast,* 165 Park Row, Brunswick 04011, 729-4914, pleasant home near the college, $–$$ CP • *Harpswell Inn,* 141 Lookout Point Road, Harpswell (peninsula adjoining Brunswick) 04079, 833-5509, on a quiet cove by the sea, $$ • *The Inn at Bath,* 969 Washington Street, Bath 04530, 443-4294, done with great taste, $$–$$$ CP • *1024 Washington,* at that address, Bath 04530, 443-5202, handsome Victorian, $–$$ CP • *Packard House,* 45 Pearl Street, Bath 04530, 443-6069, 1790 home in town's historic district, $–$$ CP • *Elizabeth's Bed 'n Breakfast,* 360 Front Street, Bath 04530, 443-1146, 1820 home on the river, $ CP • *Fairhaven Inn,* North Bath Road, Bath 04530, 443-4391, country setting, good value, $–$$ CP.

DINING *Jameson Tavern,* 115 Main Street, Freeport, 865-4196, Colonial home, $$ • *Harraseeket Lunch and Lobster Company,* South Freeport harbor, 865-4823, lobster pound on the docks, usually open from mid-May, super, $–$$ • *Fiddlehead Farm,* 15 Independence Drive, Freeport, 865-0466, cozy farmhouse, good food, $$–$$$ • *The Great Impasta,* 42 Maine Street, Brunswick, 729-5858, tasty northern Italian, good value, $–$$ • *The Stowe House* (see above), beams and hanging plants, salad bar, $–$$ • *Richard's,* 115 Main Street, Brunswick, 729-9673, German-American, $$ • *The Omelette Shop*

Café, 111 Maine Street, Brunswick, 729-1319, for breakfast or lunch, burgers, too, $ • *Cook's Lobster House,* 833-6641, and the *Original Log Cabin,* 833-5546, both on Route 24 on Bailey Island, are informal places to savor Maine lobster dinners, both $–$$$ • *Jack Baker's Oceanview Restaurant,* Route 24, Bailey Island, 833-5366, a bit more ambience with your seafood, $–$$$ • *Kristina's,* 160 Center Street, Bath, 442-8577, eclectic menu, attractive dining room, $–$$ • *Holbrook's Lobster Wharf and Snack Bar,* Cundy's Harbor Road, Cundy's Harbor, 725-5697, favorite informal spot on the docks, seasonal, $–$$ • *The Osprey,* Robinhood Center, Riggs Cove off Route 127, Georgetown, 371-2530, nautical decor, fine American menu, open from mid-May, $$–$$$ • *New Meadows Inn,* Bath Road, West Bath, 443-3921, shore dinners, lobster, $–$$$.

SIGHTSEEING   *Maine Maritime Museum,* 243 Washington Street, Bath, 443-1316. Hours: daily, 9:30 A.M. to 5 P.M. Adults, $6; children, $2.50; boat cruises, $6 • *Bowdoin College,* Brunswick, 725-3000. Guided tours from the Moulton Union Building, late May to late August, 9 A.M. to 4 P.M. Free • *Bowdoin Museum of Art,* Walker Art Building, September to June, Tuesday to Saturday, 10 A.M. to 5 P.M., Sunday, 2 P.M. to 5 P.M. Free • *Peary-MacMillan Arctic Museum,* Hubbard Hall, same hours as Museum of Art. Free • *Pejepscot Historical Society Museum,* 159 Park Row, 729-6606. Hours: Monday to Friday, 10 A.M. to 3 P.M., first Saturday each month, 1 P.M. to 4 P.M. Free. The society also maintains the *Skolfield-Whittier House,* 161 Park Row. Hours: Memorial Day to Labor Day, same hours as above. Adults, $4; ages 6 to 12, $2; and the *Joshua L. Chamberlain Museum,* 226 Maine Street. Hours: Memorial Day to Labor Day, by appointment. Adults, $2; children, $1. Combined visit to all museums: Adults, $5; children, $2.

INFORMATION   Freeport Merchants Association, Box 451, Freeport, ME 04032, 865-1212; Chamber of Commerce of the Bath-Brunswick Area, 59 Pleasant Street, Brunswick, 725-8797.

Antiquing in Old Connecticut

Nobody knows quite how it happens. First one antiques shop springs up, then another, and before you know it a whole town is wall-to-wall antiques.

There are a few such towns in New England—Sheffield, Massachusetts, and Searsport, Maine, among them—but none with choicer shops or scenery to offer than the historic town of Woodbury, Connecticut. Woodbury has become the "antiques capital" of the state, and in combination with its beautiful Colonial neighbor, Washington, it is a prime weekender's destination.

You'll need no guidebook to find the shops—Woodbury's long Main Street along Route 6 is filled with them. They range from American Federal period furnishings at David Dunton to rustic Canadian pieces at Monique Shay to country French at Country Loft. British Country Antiques offers lots of pine and oak, painted armoires, and other English specialties; Gerald Murphy has a nice mix of American and English country and formal; and Grass Roots offers a variety of dealers and moods. The names may change as shops change hands, but the variety and quality of stores is constant.

The "most beautiful shop in Woodbury" award goes to Mill House, located a few miles outside town on Route 6. The main shop, a seventeenth-century gristmill, and several outbuildings along the Nonewaug River hold a vast variety of eighteenth-century English and French furniture and accessories.

Between the Main Street shops you'll spy more Woodbury trademarks: the white spires of no fewer than four fine New England churches, and the 1754 Curtis House, the oldest hostelry in the state. Woodbury is also filled with early Colonial homes, the most notable being the Glebe House, which dates from the late 1600s and is credited as the birthplace of the American Episcopal Church. The lovely garden is the only one in America created by Gertrude Jekyll, the great English garden writer and designer considered one of the most important women ever to work in the field of horticulture. Her 1927 plan, not used at that time, was found and carried out in 1987 and the blooms have grown lovelier each year.

When you've exhausted the shops or your spending money, follow Route 47 about eight miles north to Washington to discover one of the prettiest New England villages in this or any state. The home of two prestigious prep schools, Washington is a haven of old homes and old money. The big village green, dominated by the tall Congregational church and surrounded by glistening white Colonial homes set off with dark shutters, is all but perfect. Even the drugstore here is tucked into a Colonial home.

Though this is a very private town, there is enough to see and do to keep you happily occupied. The Gunn Museum on the green is filled with memorabilia from Washington homes, including fine collections of clothing, dolls, textiles, and tools displayed in life-size vignettes.

The most unusual of Washington's sights takes you back even farther than Colonial times. The Institute for American Indian Studies promises and delivers "10,000 years in Quinnetukut" (Connecticut). The recently enlarged museum, one of the few devoted to early Indian life in this part of the country, aims to become a major center where the histories and cultures of New England's Native American populations can be shared. It is expanding and improving by the year. "As We

Tell Our Stories," a fine exhibit, features tapes of actual Algonkian people interpreting their own history, including the memories of tribal elders. Other displays tell about some of the important elements in the lives of early natives—deer that furnished clothing, corn for nourishment, clay to make pots, baskets and wampum that were used for trade. One gallery is devoted to changing exhibits, including contemporary Indian art.

Outdoors is a reconstructed Algonkian village, a typical Indian encampment of the 1600s, with both reed- and bark-covered wigwams and a longhouse where a chief might have lived.

Films and other programs are scheduled for Saturday and Sunday afternoons, and there is an excellent gift shop.

Other local shops are clustered in Washington Depot, just a couple of miles away on Route 47. English and French antiques, as well as home accessories and a kitchen shop can be found at Washington House, and an exceptional selection of furniture and accessories awaits at The Tulip Tree. The Hickory Stick Bookstore also makes for fine browsing. The Pantry in Washington Depot is a highly recommended stop for lunch. They also serve afternoon tea and make up elegant picnic lunches.

You have a choice of interesting places to stay in this area. If Colonial is your style, Woodbury offers the Merryvale Bed and Breakfast, an antique-filled 1789 home still boasting its original wide oak floorboards and fireplaces, and the Curtis House, a best bet for budget-watchers. It's a modest place, where you can sleep in a four-poster bed and dine in Early American surroundings.

A few miles to the south in Southbury, the Harrison Inn has modern and attractive resort facilities, including indoor and outdoor swimming, tennis, and golf.

If you are up for a splurge, consider the Mayflower Inn in Washington, one of the poshest (and priciest) lodgings in Connecticut. Opened in 1992 after a restoration reputed to have cost $15 million, this is the very model of a country hotel, done with exquisite taste. The traditional gray shingle architecture of the original inn and several added buildings is known as "American Shingle Style," and it reflects New England, but the furnishings inside would be quite at home in the English countryside. The main sitting room is like a page from *House Beautiful,* with its velveteen upholstery and cozy clutter.

None of the 25 guest rooms are alike. They are decorated in fine prints with coordinated stripes and solids and with lovely antiques. There are canopy beds, sleigh beds, and country iron headboards; some rooms have fireplaces, others bay windows. All the rooms have a small library and exquisite accessories such as alarm clocks of English leather and Spode plates on the nightstand.

If you can't stay here, come for dinner. The food is excellent and the inn is worth seeing.

More tempting choices are found above Washington at Lake Waramaug in New Preston, where Boulders is the best of several excellent
inns around the lake. New Preston itself is developing into a quaint
and busy shopping enclave offering antiques, art, and a variety of other
wares.

You might spend Sunday just checking out the sights of the shops
you missed or getting back to nature in the 95 acres of Lake Waramaug
State Park or the Flanders Nature Center in Woodbury, a 1,000-acre
sanctuary with many lovely nature trails. Or you can continue either
antiquing or gazing at prize Connecticut architecture in two lovely
towns nearby: Kent and Litchfield.

To get to Kent via a magnificent back-country drive, route yourself
from Washington south to New Milford on Route 109 uphill and
downhill past white farms, red barns, stone walls, and split-rail fences.
Signs reading FARM FRESH EGGS FOR SALE may tempt you to detour. At
The Egg and I, country sausages, hams, and pork are the house specialties, and visitors are invited to tour the farm.

At Route 7, turn north and pass through the little town of Gay-
lordsville, where you may choose to stop again for the antiques stores.
The Bittersweet Shop, a cooperative of 14 dealers, has everything from
furniture to paintings to quilts.

In Kent there are many antiques shops on or near Route 7, and other
places to explore as well—the Kent Art Association gallery, the
restored railroad station now known as Kent Station Square, and a
complex behind it with an art gallery in an old railroad car and an
antiques shop housing 15 dealers.

You'll see Kent Falls State Park right on Route 7 as you come into
town, and if you want to stretch your legs, the easy trail up beside the
falls will reward you with a series of scenic views, complete with roaring sound effects. Another very special stop in Kent is the Sloane-
Stanley Museum, the late artist Eric Sloane's collection of handcrafted
Early American wooden tools, which are truly works of art.

If you prefer architecture to antiques, follow Route 109 north from
Washington to Route 63 and Litchfield, a town that is on every list of
the "most beautiful towns in America." Litchfield is considered by
many to be the finest unrestored, unspoiled Colonial town in New
England. This is a town for walking, and it's easy to see the sights
since the magnificent homes are concentrated on two long blocks,
North and South streets, off the green.

Tapping Reeve opened the nation's first law school here in his
superb 1773 home with his brother-in-law, Aaron Burr, as his first
pupil. Eventually, the pupils outgrew the house and a school building
was erected in 1784. John C. Calhoun was a student here, lodging in
the rectory next door and planting some of the elms that remain along
the street.

Farther down the street is the 1736 home where Ethan Allen, Revolutionary War leader of the fabled Green Mountain Boys, is believed to have been born. Other significant buildings include the onetime residence of Oliver Wolcott, Jr., now the town library, and the obligatory structure boasting "George Washington slept here," in this case the Elisha Sheldon Tavern.

The Historical Society recently renovated its fine quarters on the corner of South Street, and a stop will tell you a lot about Litchfield's development. You'll learn, for example, that this was also home to the Sarah Pierce Academy, the nation's first academy for women, conveniently located for socializing with Mr. Reeve's law students.

Litchfield has a growing number of art galleries, including the gallery of Frank Federico, who has won many awards. For dining, the West Street Grill, a stylish bistro on the green, gets critics' raves for its innovative menu.

Outside of town are two expert glass artists, Tony Carretta and Larry LiVolsi, who invite visitors into their studios to watch them create beautiful sculptures of glass.

If the day is fine, you may prefer to forget the shops and head for the White Memorial Foundation, the state's largest nature center and wildlife preserve, with almost every kind of outdoor activity plus Bantam Lake, 11 ponds, and the Bantam River. There are 35 miles of trails and a unique bird-watching facility as well as nature exhibits in the Conservation Center.

Another magnificent strolling place is Topsmead State Forest, a former estate whose grounds and gardens are now open to the public for hiking and picnicking with fabulous views of the Litchfield hills.

You need not be a real flower fancier to appreciate Litchfield's White Flower Farm. May and June are the peak bloom months for the eight acres of exotic display gardens in a nursery that is one of the nation's outstanding breeding grounds for perennial plants. Besides the gardens, there are 1,200 varieties of flowers in 20 acres of growing fields. Delphiniums are a specialty, as are tuberous begonias.

It is less than 25 miles between any two points in this area— Litchfield to Kent or either town from Woodbury or Washington—so you'll find it easy to spend several days in this beautiful section of old Connecticut, enjoying the wealth of sights. But if you never manage to tear yourself away from Woodbury and the shops, you needn't apologize. You won't be the first to have fallen prey to the lures of the antiques capital of Connecticut.

Area Code: 203

DRIVING DIRECTIONS   Woodbury is on Route 6, west of Waterbury, at Exit 155 of I-84. It is about 140 miles from Boston, 85 miles from New York, and 45 miles from Hartford.

PUBLIC TRANSPORTATION   Bonanza buses to Southbury, New Milford, or Kent.

ACCOMMODATIONS   Ask about weekend and winter packages • *Heritage Inn,* Village Green, Heritage Road, Southbury 06488, 264-8200 or 800-932-3466, $$–$$$ • *Curtis House,* Main Street, Woodbury 06798, 263-2101, $–$$ CP • *Merryvale Bed & Breakfast,* 1204 Main Street South, Woodbury 06798, 266-0800, $$ CP • *Mayflower Inn,* Route 47, Washington 06793, 868-9466, $$$$$ • *Boulders Inn,* Route 45, New Preston 06777, 868-0541, $$$$$ MAP • *Hopkins Inn,* Hopkins Road, New Preston 06777, 868-7295, open May to October, $–$$ • *Inn on Lake Waramaug,* New Preston 06777, 868-0563, mini-resort, rooms are in lodge, not the old inn, $$$$$ MAP • *The Country Goose,* Route 7, Kent 06757, 927-4746, eighteenth-century Colonial, $$–$$$ CP • *Chaucer House,* 88 North Main Street, Route 7, Kent 06757, 927-4858, small Colonial inn within walking distance of shops and Bonanza bus stop, $$ CP • *Mavis,* 230 Kent Cornwall Road, Route 7, Kent 06757, 1860 Greek Revival home, Victorian roses and ruffles, $$ CP • *Constitution Oak Farm,* 36 Beardsley Road, Kent 06757, 354-6495, a working farm in the country, $–$$ CP • *Fife 'n Drum,* Route 7, Kent 06757, 927-3509, attractive rooms in lodge adjoining restaurant, $$–$$$.

DINING   *Carole Peck's Good News Café,* 694 Main Street South, Route 6, Woodbury, 266-4663, admired local chef, modern American food, art gallery, music on weekends, $$–$$$ • *Curtis House* (see above), $$–$$$ • *Fritz's,* 10 Sherman Hill Road, Route 6, Woodbury, 263-3036, German specialties, $$ • *The Olive Tree,* Routes 6 and 64, Woodbury, 263-4555, continental with a Greek flair, $$ • *Mayflower Inn* (see above), $$–$$$ • *Bacci's,* 900 Main Street South, Southbury, 262-1250, northern Italian, attractive, $$ • *Heritage Inn* (see above), good bet for Sunday brunch, $$–$$$ • *Hopkins Inn* (see above), Austrian owner and menu, excellent, $$ • *Boulders Inn* (see above), attractive decor and setting, varied menu, $$–$$$ • *Le Bon Coin,* Route 202, New Preston, 868-7763, exceptional French bistro, $$$ • *Doc's,* Route 45, New Preston, 868-9415, Italian, informal, gourmet pizzas, $–$$ • *The Café,* Route 45, New Preston, 868-1787, $$–$$$ • *West Street Grill,* 43 West Street, Litchfield, 567-3885, $$–$$$ • *Toll Gate Inn,* Route 202, Litchfield, 567-4545, 1745 landmark, fine dining room, $$–$$$ • *Maison LeBlanc,* Route 7, New Milford, 354-9931, fine French, $$–$$$ • *Fife 'n Drum* (see above), known for its piano bar, $$–$$$ • **For lunch, tea, or a picnic to go:** *The Pantry,* Titus Square, Washington Depot, 868-0258.

SIGHTSEEING   *Glebe House,* Hollow Road, off Route 6, Woodbury, 263-2855. Hours: April to November, daily, except Tuesday, 1 P.M.

to 5 P.M. Admission, $2 • *Institute for American Indian Studies,* Curtis Road, off Route 199, Washington, 868-0518. Hours: Monday to Saturday, 10 A.M. to 5 P.M., Sunday from noon. Adults, $4; children, $2 • *Flanders Nature Center,* Flanders Road, off Route 6, Woodbury, 263-3711. Hours: trails open daily, dawn to dusk • *Gunn Historical Museum,* on the Green, Washington, 868-7756. Hours: Thursday to Saturday, noon to 4 P.M. Free • *Sloane Stanley Museum,* Route 7, Kent, 927-3849. Hours: mid-May to October, Wednesday to Sunday, 10 A.M. to 4:30 P.M. Adults, $3; children, $1.50 • *Litchfield Historical Society Museum,* South Street, on the Green, 567-4501. Hours: April to mid-November, Tuesday to Saturday, 11 A.M. to 5 P.M., Sunday from 1 P.M. Adults, $2; under 16, free; includes admission to *Tapping Reeve House and Law School,* South Street, Litchfield, 567-4501. Hours: mid-May to mid-October, Tuesday to Saturday, 11 A.M. to 5 P.M., Sunday from 1 P.M. Adults, $2; children, free • *White Flower Farm,* Route 63 south, Litchfield, 567-8789. Hours: April to October, weekdays, 10 A.M. to 5 P.M., weekends, 9 A.M. to 5:30 P.M. Free • *White Memorial Foundation Center,* Route 202, Litchfield, 567-0857. Hours: grounds open daily; free. Museum open year-round, Tuesday to Saturday, 9 A.M. to 5 P.M., Sunday from 11 A.M. Adults, $1.50; children, $0.75. • *Topsmead State Park,* Buell Road off East Litchfield Road (Route 118), Litchfield, 845-0226. Daylight hours. Free • **Litchfield Glass artists (best to phone before stopping by):** *Tony Carretta,* 513 Maple Street, The Milton Barn, Litchfield, 567-4851; *Larry LiVolsi,* Lorenz Studio and Gallery, Route 109, Lakeside, 567-4280. Free.

INFORMATION Litchfield Hills Travel Council, PO Box 968, Litchfield, CT 06759, 567-4506.

Greeting Spring in Sandwich

The oldest town on Cape Cod is just about the loveliest.

There are few places anywhere that can match the quiet charm and serenity of Sandwich. Beach-bound traffic tends to pass this historic village by, leaving it to those who like meandering down Colonial lanes, sitting beside a millpond, antiquing, or exploring gardens and fascinating little-heralded museums, one of them featuring a collection of famous Sandwich glass.

If you fit the bill, you'll find this special town at its very best late in May, when the wide lawns are still wearing fresh coats of green, and gracious homes and spired New England churches are framed by pastel clouds of crabapple, laurel, and dogwood blossoms. That's the time, too, when thousands of prize rhododendrons begin their annual seasonal spectacular at Heritage Plantation, a remarkable combination 76-acre showplace garden and museum complex.

Sandwich is also within easy reach of Sandy Neck, a 6½-mile barrier beach that is the most extensive conservation area outside the National Seashore, a world of gulls and dunes and marsh-side blueberry patches. So if the weather is right, you can add sunbathing and nature walks to your agenda.

There are two kinds of lodging right in the center of old Sandwich, the landmark Dan'l Webster Inn on Main Street or small bed-and-breakfast inns. The original historic inn, dating from 1692, is long gone, but the current Dan'l Webster is most attractive, though be forewarned that it often attracts tour groups for lunch. Choicest and quietest rooms are in the new wing or the recently restored historic houses next door and across the street. Ask for a wing room looking out at the garden, or if you want to splurge a bit, the handsome suites with fireplaces in the Fessenden House.

Of the bed-and-breakfast inns, the Captain Ezra Nye House, a 1792 home right across the street from the inn, is a top choice, and so is the elegant Victorian Isiah Jones Homestead down the block. Six Water Street has a winning location right on the shoreline of Shawme Pond, and Wingscorton Farm Inn, a beautifully furnished 1758 Colonial off Route 6A, has acres of lawn and is a short walk to a private beach. For a room with a water view, Bay Beach is the place.

You'll probably want to begin your stay just by taking a walk and enjoying the graceful ambience of the town, with its central green and millpond.

Sandwich was founded in 1637 by ten men from Saugus, Massachusetts, who made their way to the top of Cape Cod and established a settlement they named after Sandwich, England. There are still many monuments to attest to this long history. The columned Sandwich Town Hall dates all the way back, and the Dexter Grist Mill on Shawme Pond near the center of town is a restoration of the mill that operated here in 1640. Next door is the restored Hoxie House, one of the oldest homes on the Cape. It is open to the public in summer.

One of the local prides is the exquisite Wren-style steeple of the First Church of Christ, containing what is said to be the oldest church bell in America, dating to 1675.

Sandwich is only a village, so you'll have no problem finding your way along the central arteries, Main and Water streets, or onto the side roads with their handsome homes. You'll find many worthwhile detours along the way.

Near the old mill and also on the pond is the Thornton Burgess Museum, dedicated to the author of the "Peter Cottontail" stories, who grew up in Sandwich. Web-footed creatures of all kinds stroll the lawns here, and you can visit Peter's own house.

One of the most historic buildings in town is the 1638 First Parish

Meetinghouse, which currently houses the Yesteryears Doll Museum. The dolls are the private collection of Mr. and Mrs. Ronald Thomas of Sandwich, who created the museum to house their lifetime of acquisitions, most of them rare dolls from Germany and Japan. There are dollhouses furnished in period style, miniatures, and other interesting toys on display as well. The gift shop is chock full of dolls, doll clothing, and accessories.

The main attraction in town for most people is around the corner at the Sandwich Glass Museum, where several rooms handsomely display a comprehensive collection of the renowned glassware that was made here from 1825 to 1888. Even if the name "Sandwich glass" means little to you, you'll recognize the "lacy" designs developed here, which continue to influence our glassware patterns today. Though the museum seems small at first glance, it takes at least an hour to follow properly the interesting development of pressed glass, which proceeded from this factory's first experiments at mass production, to the ornate pieces and glowing colors that were eventually produced by midcentury.

Among the more famous Sandwich pieces on exhibit are dolphin candlesticks in translucent and opaque colors, and the high-quality cut and engraved pieces that were made in the late 1860s and 1870s when the Sandwich operation could no longer compete with larger factories, and turned back to elegant hand-blown glassware.

This museum is a "sleeper," more interesting than you might have expected, and it may well leave you with a new interest in the craft of glassmaking. Don't be surprised if you are inspired to pick up a paperweight or some other unusual glass souvenir at the sales desk on your way out.

If you've taken your time, taken in the sights, and taken time for a leisurely lunch at the Dan'l Webster Inn, you may need no further activity for a pleasant Saturday than to browse the half-dozen antique stores, the art gallery, and the handful of tasteful gift shops in town, almost all near the middle of the village. Antique buffs will want to note the annual Cape Cod Antique Dealers Association show and sale, held in early June at Heritage Plantation.

If you want to complete all the sights, take a brief driving tour to Old Cemetery Point, the town's first burying ground, dating back to 1683; the site of the original glass factory at Jarves and Factory streets; and the old Quaker Meetinghouse and Graveyard, circa 1810, at Gilman and Spring Hill Road in East Sandwich. Also in East Sandwich, off Chipman Road, you can see the Thornton Burgess Briarpath, the original Peter Cottontail country, where there are now walking trails to let you follow in Peter's footsteps.

One other pleasant excursion is aboard the Cape Cod Scenic Railroad, a vintage train that runs from Sandwich to Hyannis, a 1¾-hour jaunt.

With the sights checked off and a good night's sleep, you'll be fresh for the new barrage of attractions awaiting at Heritage Plantation. This amazing complex is dedicated to the memory of Josiah K. Lilly, Jr., described in the plantation brochure as "one of the most distinguished and unassuming twentieth-century American collectors."

What did Mr. Lilly collect? Name it. There are four separate buildings filled to the brim with his antique guns and military memorabilia and miniatures, vintage automobiles, paintings and American folk art, tools, crafts, and Currier and Ives lithographs. The museum buildings themselves are attractions. The car collection is housed in a round barn inspired by the Shaker structure in Hancock, Massachusetts. The Military Museum is in a hand-hewn building held together by oaken pins and hand-wrought iron, a reproduction of a Revolutionary-period structure called the Temple in New Windsor, New York. The Arts and Crafts gallery, overlooking Upper Shawme Lake, features a real old-fashioned 1912 carousel, still in perfect order to give visitors a nostalgic ride.

Just so as not to miss anything in the way of Americana, there's also a working windmill transplanted from the nearby town of Orleans. And there are various galleries that feature changing art exhibits as well.

As if all that weren't enough, the Lilly family has located Heritage Plantation on the former estate of Charles O. Dexter, who gained distinction for hybridizing the now-famous Dexter rhododendrons. The annual blooming of thousands of rhododendrons and other flowering evergreens in May and June is an unforgettable spectacle. There are many other flower gardens, a daylily garden featuring 550 varieties, picnic grounds, a café, and several quiet nature trails on the grounds as well.

Bring along a picnic, and Heritage Plantation can easily occupy your whole day on Sunday. Or you might choose to end your weekend by taking an afternoon drive east on Route 6A, the old King's Highway that goes through the Cape's attractive North Shore towns. Since the water is colder and the beaches not quite as bountiful as on the southern side of the peninsula, Route 6A has escaped the awful commercial buildup that has all but spoiled Route 28 across the way. The shaded drive through some of the old Colonial settlements such as Barnstable, Yarmouth, Dennis, and Brewster is scenic anytime, but without the summer traffic, you can really appreciate the lovely old homes along the way, many of them now housing antiques and crafts shops or converted into attractive inns.

If you drive straight through to Orleans and the intersection with the Mid-Cape Highway, the drive will take under an hour; if you stop to browse, it can take half a day. In the center of each town, you'll see a turnoff to the harbor and the beach, the chance to take a stroll or have a seafood dinner before you head home.

If you've given up on Cape Cod and its traffic and hassles, a springtime visit to Sandwich and its neighbors may change your mind. With history intact and without summer crowds, it is easy to see why so many people fell in love with the Cape in the first place.

Area Code: 508

DRIVING DIRECTIONS   Sandwich is the first town on the Cape after crossing the Sagamore Bridge, reached via the Mid-Cape Highway, Route 6, or Route 6A. It is 45 miles from Boston, 255 miles from New York, and 145 miles from Hartford.

ACCOMMODATIONS   *Dan'l Webster Inn,* 149 Main Street, Sandwich 02563, 888-3622, $$$–$$$$ (ask about MAP and weekend plans) • *Captain Ezra Nye House,* 152 Main Street, Sandwich 02563 (800) 388-2278 or 888-6142, $–$$ CP • *Isiah Jones Homestead,* 165 Main Street, Sandwich 02563, 888-9115 $$–$$$ CP • *Wingscorton Farm Inn,* 11 Wing Boulevard (off Route 6A), East Sandwich 02537, 888-0534, $$$ CP • *Six Water Street,* at that address, Sandwich 02563, 888-6808, $$ CP • *The Summer House,* 158 Main Street, Sandwich 02563, 888-4991, modestly priced 1835 B & B, $ CP • *Bay Beach,* 1-3 Bay Beach Lane, PO Box 151, Sandwich 02563, 888-8813, excellent motel-style bed-and-breakfast inn on the water, $$$–$$$$ CP • Some mid-Cape inns worth noting are the elegant *Wedgewood Inn,* 83 Main Street, Route 6A, Yarmouth Port 02675, 362-5157, $$$ CP; *Isaiah Clark House,* 1187 Old King's Highway, Brewster 02631, 896-2223, $$–$$$ CP; and the delightful *Isiah Hall Bed and Breakfast Inn,* 152 Whig Street, Dennis 02638, 385-9928 or (800) 736-0160, off on a quiet road within walking distance of beach, $$–$$$ CP.

DINING   *Dan'l Webster Inn* (see above), $$–$$$ • *Beehive Tavern,* 406 Route 6A, Sandwich, 833-1184, casual dining, $–$$ • *Marshland,* Route 6A, Sandwich, 888-9284, casual spot for all three meals, $ • *Captain's Table,* 14 Gallo Road, 888-8440, $–$$ and *Horizon's,* 98 Town Neck Road, 888-6166, are informal places on the water in Sandwich, both $–$$ • **The following restaurants, all considered among the Cape's finest, are on or near Route 6A within a half hour's drive from Sandwich:** *Chillingsworth,* Route 6A, Brewster, 896-3640, prix fixe, $$$$$; café menu $$; *Bramble Inn,* Route 6A, Brewster, 896-7644, prix fixe $$$$; *High Brewster,* 964 Satucket Road, Brewster, 896-3636, $$$$; • **Less pricey recommendations:** *Mattakeese Wharf,* Barnstable Harbor, 362-4511, seafood with a view, $–$$$; *Gina's by the Sea,* 134 Taunton Avenue, Dennis, 385-3213, $$; *Brewster Fish House,* 2208 Main Street, 896-7867, $$; *Abbicci,* 43 Main Street, Yarmouth Port, 362-3501, $$–$$$.

SIGHTSEEING *Heritage Plantation of Sandwich,* Grove and Pine streets, 888-3300. Hours: mid-May to mid-October, daily, 10 A.M. to 5 P.M. Adults, $7; ages 6 to 18, $3.50 • *Sandwich Glass Museum,* 129 Main Street, 888-0251. Hours: April 1 to October 31, daily, 9:30 A.M. to 4:30 P.M.; November, December, February, March, Wednesday to Sunday, 9:30 A.M. to 4 P.M. Closed January. Adults, $3; under 12, $0.50 • *Yesteryears Doll and Miniature Museum,* Main and River streets, 888-1711. Hours: May 15 through October, Monday to Saturday, 10 A.M. to 4 P.M. Adults, $3; children, $1.50 • *Cape Cod Scenic Railroad,* PO Box 7, South Carver 02366, 771-3788; Tuesday, Wednesday, Thursday, Saturday, and Sunday, June through October; weekends only in May, November, December. Runs between Hyannis and Sandwich. Phone for current schedule and rates.

INFORMATION Cape Cod Chamber of Commerce, Routes 6 and 132, Hyannis, MA 02601, 362-3225.

 # Surprising City by the Sea: Portland, Maine

"I have this friend," the Portland native was telling us, "that everybody thought was crazy. Years ago he started buying wrecked-up buildings near the waterfront. People laughed at him and asked what on earth he was going to do with those old buildings."

The punch line, of course, is that the friend is now a millionaire. The redevelopment of the waterfront, now a bustling area of attractive shops and restaurants known as the Old Port Exchange, led the way to a remarkable renaissance in Portland, Maine. It is a development that would have been hard to predict by anyone who knew the city a couple of decades ago.

Now young professionals from throughout New England are moving to this city that native Henry Wadsworth Longfellow once described as "the beautiful town that is seated by the sea." Portland is turning into an increasingly sophisticated and appealing place to live in and to visit, with a thriving arts community, a magnificent art museum designed by I. M. Pei, and some of the best food to be found north of Boston.

But it remains true that the first thing you notice in Portland is not buildings, but water. The city is on a peninsula with views of deep blue sea on three sides, the vistas made more dramatic because Portland is situated on a high crest of land. The proximity to shoreline, boat cruises, and the nearby rocky cliffs below Maine's most photographed and painted landmark, Portland Head Lighthouse, make visiting this city a double pleasure.

That the rebirth of Portland should have taken so long despite its fortunate location reflects how far the city had lagged. Once a prosperous shipping and shipbuilding port and the capital of Maine, it developed early in its history into a major center for importing molasses from the West Indies. The port continued to flourish until a devastating July 4 blaze in 1866 destroyed 1,800 buildings and left 10,000 people homeless. Though the city rebuilt quickly with the sturdy stone Victorian structures still evident today, it suffered a more serious setback later in this century when the port declined, partly because of the opening of the St. Lawrence Seaway.

In time, the deserted buildings near the harbor became havens for artists and craftspeople, who could get them for rock-bottom rents. They formed an Old Port Association hoping to tempt browsers, stringing up their own lights and shoveling their own streets to make things more enticing, since the city no longer provided such services to the decaying area. That was the start of the recent revival, abetted by the Maine Way urban renewal program.

Meanwhile, downtown Portland underwent its own facelift. Today Congress Street, the main business thoroughfare, has been spruced up with brick sidewalks, old-fashioned street lamps, and a cleaning job that removed a century of grime from the old facades. New buildings abound, and Monument Square at the corner of Congress and Middle is now a plaza where colorful food carts offer everything from bagels to health food. Lunchtime entertainment adds to its lure as a local gathering place.

The liveliest activity in town is centered in the Old Port, between Monument Square and the wharves on Commercial Street. Here's where young people gather in trendy cafés and tourists shop the many offbeat stores—dozens of them—selling everything from pottery to antiques to clothing. The area continues to grow as more blighted blocks are restored, and it has become a showcase for craftspeople from throughout northern New England.

Even with all these changes, Portland remains at heart a small city (population 65,000)—an inviting place where you can easily walk to all the sights.

The old face of Portland, part dowdy, part Old World charm, is still very much in evidence among the new buildings on Congress; a walking tour is an architecture buff's delight and a good place to begin your look at the city. The Convention and Visitors Bureau will supply you with free printed tours for different parts of the city. The Congress Street guide points up the contrasts now to be found on this street whose history spans more than two centuries.

At 425 Congress you'll find the Wadsworth-Longfellow House,

circa 1785, crammed between stores and banks. The hostess-guided tour of the boyhood home of the famed poet and his family is a detour not to be missed by anyone interested in American literature or history. Further on, the Federal-era First Parish Church is neighbor to the newer Casco Bank Building, and Beaux Arts and Queen Anne structures adjoin the ultramodern library—an unconventional yet somehow congenial blending of styles.

Switching over to the Old Port Exchange guide, you'll learn about the city's ups and downs as a shipping center, and the filling of land in the 1850s to form Commercial Street, which soon was lined with wharves and warehouses. Most of the major structures dating from the 1866 rebuilding are on Middle, Exchange, and Fore streets, which offer another field day for architecture buffs. Custom House Wharf, home of Boone's, a local seafood landmark, and the departure point of the Casco Bay Line boat rides, hasn't been prettied up as much as the rest of the neighborhood, and gives you an idea of what the entire area looked like not so long ago.

You'll probably not need the printed guide to notice one of the most intriguing new additions, the trompe l'oeil mural by Portland artist Chris Denison at Exchange and Middle, transforming a blank brick wall into what looks for all the world like a period building. The open corner in front of the mural now serves as a gathering spot where informal summer concerts are held.

There's no question that you'll be tempted to interrupt your building-gazing to look into the shops here, so allow plenty of time. Among the many crafts shops, look out for the Maine Potters Market at 376 Fore Street, a cooperative displaying the work of a dozen of the state's artisans. A bounty of art galleries and antiques shops beckon as well in the Old Port and on Congress. Shipwreck & Cargo on Commercial Street may be of special interest for its marine antiques, hardware, and salvage, which sometimes yields rich finds for decorators and renovators. Names and owners do change, so check the current list of local antiques stores, available in most of the shops.

Between the landmarks and the looking, you can while away a very pleasant day in Portland, but before your energy flags, part of your day should be saved for the glorious Portland Art Museum. One prize permanent display here is the collection of Winslow Homers donated by Charles Shipman Payson, the same patron who was principally responsible for the $11.6 million building. Joan Whitney Payson's collection including works by Chagall, Degas, Gauguin, Monet, Picasso, and other masters has also been installed here.

In addition, there are works by other artists associated with Maine or Maine subjects, such as John Singer Sargent, Stuart Davis, and Edward Hopper, part of the growing State of Maine Collection. While the museum's own collection builds, it is working hard to bring in visiting shows of high caliber.

Perhaps the most stunning work of art here is the building itself, done in red brick and in shapes emphasizing circles, squares, and arches deliberately planned to work with the traditional architecture of the city and the adjoining original museum landmark buildings of the 1900s. It is rightfully one of Portland's prides.

If time permits, fans of the Victorian period will want to make a stop at the Victoria Mansion, an elaborate example of the most ornate styles of the era.

When hunger pangs strike, you're surrounded by tempting possibilities in Portland, and there is evening entertainment for every taste, from jazz in the Old Port to the Portland Symphony. Check also for performances by the Portland Ballet, the Portland Lyric Theater, and the Portland Stage Company. If you want really late entertainment or you have insomnia, remember that L.L. Bean is open all night in Freeport, just 15 minutes away.

Come Sunday, you might choose either to head for the wharf and board a cruise boat or take a driving tour to see some of the city's prime water views. With planning, you can even manage both.

For the views, follow Congress Street east past the Portland Observatory and Monjoy Hill (once the site of a tent city of burnt-out survivors of the 1866 fire) to the Eastern Promenade overlooking Casco Bay. The homes here are bordered by a breezy park with benches where you can enjoy the sights, and in the warmer months the Observatory, a historic signal tower, can be climbed for an even more panoramic perspective.

Fort Allen Park boasts a cannon straight from the USS *Constitution,* and the Eastern Cemetery, near Monjoy Hill on Congress and Washington, is a fascinating site dating back to 1639 that is full of centuries-old headstones embellished with angels and curlicues. The Western Promenade, another neighborhood of lovely homes, offers its own special view. On a good day you can see the White Mountains.

Back in town, follow State Street across the bridge to South Portland and watch for further Route 77 signs to Cape Elizabeth. (Turn left at the first school if the sign is missing, as it was recently.) It will take you to Fort Williams Park and the famous Portland Head Lighthouse, built for George Washington in 1791 and even more imposing on its steep rocky perch than all those countless photos can convey. The museum in the former housekeepers' quarters tell the fascinating history of the lighthouse.

Farther on is Two Lights State Park, with 40 acres on the shore, and the Two Lights Lobster Shack, a prime stop for lobster or clams at picnic tables with ocean views. If the weather is conducive to beach-combing, drive farther on Route 77 to Crescent Neck Beach State Park or Higgins Beach or Scarborough Beach State Park in Scarborough. At Ferry Beach, off Route 207 in Prouts Neck, you can view the community whose rugged cliffs were the inspiration for many of

Winslow Homer's works. The artist's studio remains here, much the way he left it, though it is not open to the public.

You can have your driving tour and still get back to Portland in plenty of time for an afternoon or sunset cruise from the wharf and a final seafood dinner—a fitting close to a visit to a city by the sea.

Area Code: 207

DRIVING DIRECTIONS I-95 and U.S. Route 1 both lead into downtown Portland, located on the southern Maine coast 109 miles north of Boston, 322 miles from New York, and 212 miles from Hartford.

PUBLIC TRANSPORTATION Portland is served by Delta, US Air, United, and Continental airlines, and Greyhound and Concord Trailways buses. Downtown is easily manageable without a car.

ACCOMMODATIONS Within walking distance of downtown sights are: *Portland Regency,* 20 Milk Street, Portland 04101, 774-4200 or (800) 727-3436, restored armory building in Old Port, $$–$$$ • *Sonesta Hotel,* 157 High Street, Portland 04101, 775-5411, gracious landmark, $$–$$$ • *Holiday Inn By the Bay,* 88 Spring Street, Portland 04101, 775-2311, $$$ • **Inn alternatives in restored town houses:** *Inn at Park Spring,* 135 Spring Street, Portland 04101, 774-1059, $$ CP • *Pomegranate Inn,* 49 Neal Street, 772-1006 or (800) 356-0408, Portland 04102, $$ CP • *Inn on Carleton,* 46 Carleton Street, Portland 04102, $–$$ CP • *West End Inn,* 146 Pine Street, 772-1377, $$ CP • *Inn by the Sea,* 40 Bowery Beach Road, Cape Elizabeth 04107, 799-3134 or (800) 888-4287, mini-resort on the ocean, tennis, pool, $$$$–$$$$$ • **Budget buys:** *Days Inn,* 738 Main Street, Portland 04106, 774-5891, $–$$ • *Susse Chalet Motor Lodge,* 340 Park Avenue, Portland 04102, 871-0611, $. Many more hotels and motels south of town near the Maine Mall and the airport; write to Visitors Bureau (address below) for a complete list.

DINING In a city that now is bursting with restaurants, here are some recommendations by the natives. **For seafood:** *Street and Co,* 33 Wharf Street, 775-0887, $$–$$$; *Snow Squall,* 18 Ocean Street, South Portland, 799-2232, $$; *Newick's,* 740 Broadway, South Portland, 799-3090, $–$$$; *Channel Crossing,* 431 Front Street, South Portland, 799-5552, big open-air patio on the waterfront, $$; *The Galley at Handy Boatyard,* 215 Foreside Road, Route 88, Falmouth, 781-4262, $$–$$$; *Drydock,* 84 Commercial Street, 774-3550, on the waterfront in the Old Port, raw bar, $$, also excellent for lunch, $; *DiMillo's Floating Restaurant,* Long Wharf, 772-2216, seafood with atmosphere, though many locals consider this for tourists only, $$–$$$ • **For Italian:** *The Roma Café,* 769 Congress, 773-9873, $$; *Village Café,* 112 Newbury Street, 772-5320, home cooking, huge portions, reasonable, $–$$ • **For Chinese:** *Hu Shang,* 29 Exchange, 773-0300, among the most popular places in town, $ • **Miscellaneous:** *Alberta's,* 21 Pleasant Street, 774-5408, interesting, offbeat dishes, Bohemian atmosphere, $$; *Café Always,* 47 Middle Street, 774-9399, innovative menu, $$; *The Madd Apple Café,* 24 Forest Avenue, 772-6606, barbecue and southern specialties, $–$$; *Back Bay Grill,* 65 Portland Street, 772-8833, art deco mood, sophisticated food, $$–$$$; *Hugo's Portland Bistro,* 88 Middle Street, 774-8538, international dishes, lively, $–$$; *David's,* 164 Middle Street, Portland, 773-4340, $–$$; *Katahdin,* Spring and High streets, 774-1740, funky, good home cooking, reasonable, $; *F. Parker Reidy's,* 83 Exchange Street, 773-4731, restored Victorian bank, steaks and late-night activity, $–$$ • **Breakfast:** *Christine's Dream,* 41 Middle Street, 774-2972, $ • **Informal lunch or dinner:** *Gritty McDuff's Brew Pub,* 396 Fore Street, 772-BREW, the local micro-brewery, with pub fare, fish and chips, chile, etc., $ • **Finally, for lobster:** *The Roma Café* (see above) usually offers seasonal bargain twin lobster specials, and if the weather is fine, it's hard to beat *Two Lights Lobster Shack,* at the entrance to Two Lights State Park, Cape Elizabeth, 799-1677. (Note: They stop steaming lobster at 8 P.M.) Prices vary with the season's catch.

SIGHTSEEING *Wadsworth-Longfellow House,* 484-489 Congress Street, 879-0427. Hours: June to Columbus Day, Tuesday to Saturday, 10 A.M. to 4 P.M. Adults, $3; under 12, $1 • *Portland Museum of Art,* 7 Congress Street, 775-6148. Hours: Tuesday to Saturday, 10 A.M. to 5 P.M., Sunday from noon, Thursday until 9 P.M. Adults, $4; 6 to 18, $1 • *Victoria Mansion,* 109 Danforth Street, 772-4841. Hours: Memorial Day to Labor Day, Tuesday to Saturday, 10 A.M. to 4 P.M., Sunday from 1 P.M. to 5 P.M.. Adults, $4; under 18, $1.50 • *Portland Observatory,* 138 Congress Street, 774-5561. Hours: July and August, Wednesday, Thursday, Sunday, 1 P.M. to 5 P.M., Friday and Saturday 10 A.M. to 5 P.M.; in June, September, October, Friday to Sunday, 1 P.M. to 5 P.M. Adults, $1.50; under age 13, $0.50 • *Museum at Portland Head Light,* Fort Williams Park, 1000 Shore Road, Cape Elizabeth, 799-2661. Hours: June 1 to October 31, daily, 10 A.M. to 4 P.M., guided tours at 11 A.M. and 2 P.M.; April, May, November, December, weekends only. Adults, $2; children, $1 • **Boat trips:** *Casco Bay Lines,* Custom House Wharf, 774-7871; *Bay View Cruises,* Long Wharf, 761-0496, each offers a variety of cruises several times daily, including sunset and evening sails, call for specifics; *Odyssey,* whale-watching cruises, phone 775-0727 for information; *MS Scotia Prince,* International Terminal (800) 341-7540 or (800) 482-0955 in Maine, leaves Portland nightly for Nova Scotia, with 22- and 46-hour mini-cruises available. Phone for current schedules and prices.

INFORMATION   Greater Portland Convention and Visitors Bureau, 305 Commercial Street, Portland, ME 04101, 772-5800.

Crafts Spectacular in the Pioneer Valley

You can hardly find a good orrery nowadays.

In case you don't know, an *orrery* is a mechanical reproduction of the solar system, named for Charles Boyle, the fourth Earl of Cork and Orrery, who had the first known such contrivance made in about 1710.

Handmade orrerys are sold at the Craftfair of the American Crafts Council in West Springfield, Massachusetts—unbelievably intricate devices with enough gears to make three separate clocks. This just goes to prove that there's very little you can't find at this Super Bowl of crafts shows, a gathering of America's top craftspeople in a spectacular event that is one of the largest of its kind in the country.

It is an appropriate location, since Springfield is part of the Pioneer Valley, a region that has grown into a crafts center in its own right. More than 1,500 artists and craftspeople live in the region, drawn by the combination of natural beauty and the rich cultural life supplied by five area colleges—Amherst, Mount Holyoke, the University of Massachusetts, Hampshire, and Smith. Northhampton, the home of Smith College, is the lively center of things, a town filled with galleries, fine turn-of-the-century architecture, and a growing number of good restaurants.

Springfield's Craftfair will occupy a good part of a day. Some 600 artisans take part, selected from almost four times that many who apply to the show's jury of master craftsmakers and store buyers. The artisans include potters, tin, gold, iron, and silversmiths, candle molders, glassblowers, basket weavers, leather cutters, quilters, zither makers, wood carvers, weavers, and creators of orrerys and other wares so diverse as to defy description.

The event was originally held in outdoor tents in Rhinebeck, New York, but by 1984 the crowds had grown so large that a move was necessary, and the big Eastern States Exposition Center in West Springfield won the prize. It is bigger than ever now, with sales in the millions, and thousands turning out for the three-day event.

The displays offer everything from a ceramic toothbrush holder to a handmade rolling pin, from casseroles and canisters to large sculptures and exquisite furniture, with price tags anywhere from $25 to $25,000. In fact, if there is anything to complain about, it is the huge number of displays. Don't buy until you've covered everything; the perfect choice may be just around the corner.

There will be plenty of food stands to refuel your energy along the way, plus the traditional tavern and New England wine gardens on the center's grounds, which are also the annual site of the largest fall fair in New England.

When you've had your fill of browsing, you'll find plenty more to see and do in the Springfield area. This old New England town has recently spruced up its historic downtown around Court Square, a charming urban park, and is quite a pleasant place for a stroll and a bit of sightseeing.

You don't have to be a sports lover to enjoy Springfield's most colorful attraction, the Basketball Hall of Fame. The museum celebrates the sport that was born at Springfield College back in 1891. The lively exhibits are planned to get spectators involved in the game.

Visitors enter past a Basketball Fountain, a cascade of baskets tumbling from a 40-foot ceiling. Besides a host of exhibits—including Bob Lanier's gilded size 22 sneakers—you can see a movie that puts you smack in center court in the middle of the action, walk through an archway made of multicolored regulation sneakers, pass through a room hung with 300 colorful college jerseys, and even try your hand at shooting from a moving sidewalk facing a battery of baskets. The game's great players and coaches are enshrined in the Honors Court, with medallions and a brief history of each career. They are also featured in action in exciting, lifelike stroboscopic photo images that illustrate the dynamics and grace of the sport.

Other highlights include a look at how uniforms and equipment have changed over the years and a peek at what it is like inside an actual locker room, with displays of the locker contents of some of today's superstars.

On the more cultural side, head for the complex at State and Chestnut streets known as The Quadrangle, where four museums are clustered around a green. The George Walter Vincent Smith Art Museum offers European and Oriental decorative arts, the Connecticut Valley Historical Museum features period rooms and antiques plus collections of glass, pewter, and silver, and the Museum of Fine Arts has paintings and sculpture by American and European artists. The Science Museum features an African and a dinosaur hall, an aquarium, and a planetarium along with nature exhibits.

The Springfield Armory, the inspiration for Longfellow's poem, *The Arsenal at Springfield,* is a National Historic Site, with a unique collection of small arms through the centuries. And if you want to stroll an urban pocket of choice Victoriana, walk over to Mattoon Street, two blocks east of Main. The tree-shaded, cobblestone block with its old-fashioned streetlights also has been listed on the National Register of Historic Places.

Springfield has its share of hotels and motels, in the city or in West Springfield, convenient to the Craftfair, but you might well prefer to move on to the Pioneer Valley and the charming small towns that are home to its well-known "Five Colleges." Not the least of the reasons to be here is the variety of restaurants, from old New England to trendy ethnic.

You also get a cross section of architecture on these handsome campuses. In Amherst, there's Amherst College, with its traditional halls of ivy and picture-book green, plus the mammoth modern University of Massachusetts and the rustic buildings of Hampshire College. Old and new manage to mix nicely along the quadrangles of Smith in Northampton and Mount Holyoke in South Hadley. Both of these fine women's colleges, along with Amherst, offer excellent art galleries on campus.

Northampton's Main Street is the place for gallery hopping as well as admiring architecture. Listed on the National Register of Historic Places, the street offers a sampling of Victorian styles. The library holds memorabilia of former resident Calvin Coolidge. Up the hill at the top of Main Street, Smith campus highlights include a stroll along Paradise Pond, a stop to see the rare plants at the Lyman Plant House, and a look into the Museum of Art for works by Picasso, Degas, Seurat, and other masters.

One unique attraction on Main Street is the Words and Pictures Museum, a project of the locally based creators of the Ninja Turtles. It features sequential art, comic books, and graphic novels. You can become a comic book artist yourself, playing with the words and pictures that tell your story, or step over the frame of a comic to become part of the action.

Neighboring towns have their own attractions. Deerfield, just a few miles north of Northampton, is one of the loveliest old New England towns, and offers a dozen beautifully furnished museum-homes. See page 192 for more details. The 1813 Dickinson Homestead in Amherst, where Emily Dickinson was born and lived most of her life, will surely interest those who admire her poetry.

For shopping, Northampton is definitely the place. Thorne's Marketplace at 150 Main is a period department store transformed into boutiques and restaurants without losing the curved stairways, high tin ceilings, and shining wood floors of the original building. There are four antiques shops within a few yards of each other on Market Street, including the multidealer Antique Center of Northampton.

But fine crafts are the real lure in this artisans' haven, and more than a dozen galleries beckon to show off their work. Two choice stops are Pinch Pottery, 179 Main, where Leslie Ferrin's creative ceramics are featured, and the Don Muller Gallery, 40 Main, with a spectrum of crafts. Even the contemporary showcases here are handmade. The rest of the galleries include everything from handwoven contemporary rugs to American Indian art to hand-blown goblets.

It's a weekend to send you home with a new appreciation of the fine craftspeople who are keeping the artistry of American handcrafts alive and well. And if you don't return with an original souvenir, it certainly won't be for lack of choice. You might even turn out to be the first on your block with an orrery.

Area Code: 413

DRIVING DIRECTIONS Springfield can be reached via I-91 from north or south and from east or west via the Massachusetts Turnpike, I-90. The Eastern States Exposition Center is off I-91 at Exit 3. Northampton is 20 miles farther north off I-91. Springfield is about 90 miles from Boston, 150 miles from New York, and 26 miles from Hartford.

PUBLIC TRANSPORTATION Amtrak serves Springfield and may be offering special fares to the Craftfair with bus shuttle service from the station. Several major airlines fly into Bradley International Airport, which serves Hartford-Springfield; Greyhound, Peter Pan, and Vermont Transit provide bus service.

ACCOMMODATIONS *Ramada West Springfield,* 1080 Riverdale Street, West Springfield 01089, 733-8652, $$$ • *Days Inn,* 437 Riverdale Street, West Springfield 01089, 785-5365, $–$$ • *Marriott Hotel,* 1500 Main Street, Springfield 01115, 781-7111, $$$–$$$$ • *Sheraton Springfield Monarch Place,* 1 Monarch Place, Springfield 01104, 781-1010, $$$–$$$$ • *Lord Jeffrey Inn,* on the Common, Amherst 01002, 253-2576, the classic college inn, $$–$$$ • *Allen House Inn,* 599 Main Street, Amherst 02002, 253-5000, elegant 1886 Victorian with period furnishings, $$ CP • *Hotel Northampton,* 36 King Street, Northampton 01060, 584-3100, refurbished 1927 town landmark, centrally located, $$–$$$$ • *Autumn Inn,* 259 Elm Street, Northampton 01060, 584-7660, pleasant motel near Smith campus, $$. See also Deerfield, page 197.

DINING *Old Storrowton Tavern,* 1305 Memorial Avenue, Eastern States Exposition Grounds, Exposition Road off Route 147, West Springfield, 732-4188, 1795 tavern, $$–$$$ • *Hofbrauhaus,* 1105 Main Street, West Springfield, 737-4905, long-established German, Old World atmosphere, $$–$$$ • *Student Prince and Fort,* 8 Fort Street, 734-7475, German, with interesting collection of beer steins, $$

• *Monte Carlo,* 1020 Memorial Avenue, West Springfield, 734-6431, convenient Italian, opposite Eastern States Exposition grounds, $–$$$ • *Tavern Inn Restaurant,* 91 West Gardner Street, Springfield, 781-2882, near the Basketball Hall of Fame, sports decor, $ • *Eastside Grill,* 19 Strong Avenue, Northampton, 586-3347, Cajun specialties, very popular, $–$$ • *Spoleto,* 50 Main Street, Northampton, 586-6313, creative Italian, $–$$ • *Wiggins Tavern,* Hotel Northampton (see above), 200-year-old tavern, New England specialties, $$–$$$ • *The Depot,* 125A Pleasant Street, Northampton, 586-5366, stylishly renovated train station, varied menu, $–$$ • *Spaghetti Freddy's,* next to the Depot, 586-5366, good pasta at good prices, $–$$ • *Fitzwilly's,* 23 Main Street, 584-8666, local gathering spot, $–$$ • *India House,* 45 State Street, Northampton, 586-6344, tandoori specialties, $ • *Paul and Elizabeth's,* 150 Main Street in Thorne's Market, 584-4832, local vegetarian favorite, $–$$ • *La Cazuela,* 7 Old South Street, 586-0400, Mexican and Southwestern dishes, $–$$ • *Green Street Café,* 64 Green Street, 586-5650, European flavor, lunch and dinner, $–$$ • *North Star,* 25 West Street, Northampton, 586-9409, seafood, $–$$ • *The Northampton Brewery,* 11 Brewster Court, Northampton, 584-4176, brew-pub, very popular, $–$$ • *Yankee Pedlar Inn,* 1866 Northampton Street, Holyoke, 532-9494, Colonial ambience, longtime favorite in the area, $$ • *The Log Cabin,* Route 141, Easthampton Road, Holyoke, 536-7700, rustic setting and fine views, $$ • *Lord Jeffrey Inn* (see above), $$$ • *Judie's,* 51 North Pleasant Street, Amherst, 253-3491, pleasant, informal, good for lunch or dinner, $–$$ • *Seasons,* 529 Belchertown Road (Route 9), Amherst, 253-9909, airy former barn, country views, eclectic menu, $$ • *Windows on the Common,* 25 College Street, South Hadley, 534-8222, formal dining or light fare at Fedora's Tavern, $–$$. For a light lunch, try *The Black Sheep Deli,* 79 Main Street, Amherst, or, in Northampton, the *Country Deli & Café* or the *Coolidge Park Café* in the Hotel Northampton. See also Deerfield, page 197.

SIGHTSEEING *American Craft Council Craftfair,* Eastern States Exposition Center, West Springfield, 736-3003, usually mid-June, for current dates and rates, contact American Craft Enterprises, 21 South Eltings Corner Road, Highland, NY 12528 (914) 883-6100. • *Basketball Hall of Fame,* 1150 West Columbus Avenue, 781-6500. Hours: daily, 9 A.M. to 5 P.M., July to Labor Day, to 6 P.M. Adults, $7; ages 8 to 15, $4 • *Springfield Library and Museums,* the Quadrangle, State and Chestnut streets, 739-3871, four museums. Hours: Thursday to Sunday, noon to 4 P.M. Adults, $3; ages 6 to 18, $1; free to all on Friday • *Springfield Armory National Historic Site,* One Armory Square, 734-8551. Hours: Memorial Day to Labor Day, daily, 10 A.M. to 5 P.M., closed Monday rest of year. Free • *Mead Art Gallery,* Amherst College, 542-2335. Hours: weekends 1 P.M. to 5 P.M., weekdays, 10 A.M. to

4:30 P.M. Free • *Smith College Museum of Art,* Elm Street, Northampton, 585-2760. Hours: Tuesday to Saturday, noon to 5 P.M., Sunday 2 P.M. to 5 P.M. (hours change, best to confirm). Free • *Words and Pictures Museum,* 244 Main Street, Northampton, 586-8545. Hours: Tuesday to Sunday, noon to 5 P.M. Free • *Historic Deerfield,* PO Box 321, Deerfield, MA 10342, 774-5581. Hours: daily 9:30 A.M. to 4:30 P.M. Adults, $10; children, $5 • *Dickinson Homestead,* 280 Main Street, Amherst, 542-8161. Hours: May to October, Wednesday through Saturday, tours offered every 45 minutes from 1:30 P.M. to 3:45 P.M. March through April, and November to mid-December, Wednesday and Saturday only, $3.

INFORMATION   Greater Springfield Convention and Visitors' Bureau, 34 Boland Way, Springfield, MA 01103, 787-1548 or (800) 723-1548.

Savoring the Shore in Connecticut

Early in June, when ringing cheers send off the annual Yale-Harvard regatta on the Thames River in New London, the oarsmen will be following the same historic river route that once took clipper ships out to sea.

Connecticut's upper shoreline, the focal point for much of the state's early history, is a three-century treasury of seafaring lore from the days of masted schooners to today's nuclear submarines.

But despite its salty attractions and the presence of Mystic Seaport, America's prime maritime destination, much of the 40-mile shore area north of New Haven has remained unspoiled. Quaint Old Lyme still owes as much of its flavor to its Colonial heritage as to its proximity to the sea. And such nautical lures as New London's Coast Guard Academy and Stonington's lighthouse and fishing fleet remain delightfully overlooked by tourist crowds.

Cruising the shore by land is a perfect outing for early June, when the old Ivy League rowing rivalry is replayed as it has been for well over 100 years.

Typically, crew races are scheduled for three starting times between 11:00 A.M. and 12:30 P.M., and spectators can cheer on the Crimson or the Blue from riverside viewing areas along the four-mile course. For those wishing a closer look at the excitement, there is an observation boat, offering brunch and Dixieland entertainment as well as a better view. Other festivities take place all day along the New London pier, the scene of many special events throughout the spring and summer.

The pier and its activity are signs of a city fighting hard to recoup some of its illustrious past as a wealthy whaling outpost. While New London has lost the glory of its early days, there are some interesting sights to be seen here and a new science center is rising on the waterfront. A walking tour might well start at the city's pride, its lovingly restored nineteenth-century train station, designed by Henry Hobson Richardson, the architect of Boston's Trinity Church. The station stands opposite the pier, convenient for those who want to connect to ferries for Block Island or Fishers Island.

Nearby is the restored schoolhouse named for native son Nathan Hale, who taught here prior to enlisting in George Washington's army. It was moved to be accessible to visitors.

Also near the waterfront is a statue of another notable town resident, playwright Eugene O'Neill, shown here as a young boy. The Dutch Tavern, O'Neill's favorite bar, is on Green Street, just off Captain's Walk, New London's main street. His boyhood home, Monte Cristo Cottage, has been restored, and tours are available weekdays or by appointment. In summer, the Eugene O'Neill Theater Center in nearby Waterford presents play readings by promising new authors.

Next door to the O'Neill Center is Harkness Memorial Park, a 234-acre waterfront estate that hosts Summer Music, a wonderful program of classical and popular music with big name performers. You can order tickets in the sheltered tent or sit on the lawn and enjoy a picnic under the stars. A picnic buffet is served on the grounds, but must be ordered in advance.

Some of New London's other sights include the 1930s Customs House, whose front door was once part of the frigate *Constitution;* the Shaw Mansion, U.S. naval headquarters for Connecticut during the Revolutionary War, and four columned whaling-merchants' mansions known collectively as Whale Oil Row.

As you proceed south from Whale Oil Row, you'll come to Hempstead Street, with several fine old homes including one of Connecticut's oldest, the 1678 Hempsted House, the only home that escaped the town's burning by the British in 1781.

New London's U.S. Coast Guard Academy, a cluster of handsome, traditional red-brick buildings on 100 acres high above the Thames, has inviting grounds, a well-endowed museum, and a multimedia center at river's edge that gives a comprehensive picture of the Coast Guard's role in our nation's history. The academy holds colorful formal dress parades in spring and fall; check for current dates.

There is a bonus for visitors when the *Eagle* is in port. The 295-foot square-rigger that led the nation's Bicentennial parade of tall ships is a magnificent floating classroom for cadets each summer. When not at sea, it is usually at home in New London, available for free tours of the deck and the quarters of officers and crew.

Near the academy on Mohegan Avenue is the campus of Connecticut College and the Lyman Allyn Art Museum, named in memory of a famous sea captain. It contains art, antiques, and a wonderful collection of dollhouses, dolls, and toys. The Deshon-Allyn House, a Federal-style whaling captain's home, is part of the museum complex.

Also on the campus is the Connecticut Arboretum, a particularly fine nature preserve, which offers 445 acres with hiking trails.

A favorite New London attraction in summer is Ocean Beach Park, a family beach with boardwalk games and rides. The imaginative Children's Museum of Southeastern Connecticut in Niantic, below New London, is another pleaser, filled with hands-on exhibits, learning, and fun for everyone from toddlers to preteens.

Groton, just across the Thames from New London, is the home of the U.S. Navy submarine base, the largest of its kind in the world, providing yet another perspective on America's maritime traditions. The world's first nuclear submarine, the 320-foot *Nautilus,* was launched here in 1954. At the USS Nautilus Memorial at the base you can trace the progress of submarines from early days to the nuclear age and board that first nuclear-powered sub. Working periscopes, an authentic control room, and mini-theaters are part of the exhibits.

Fort Griswold State Park in Groton marks some of the town's older historic moments. The site of an important Revolutionary War battle in 1781, the Memorial Tower and statue on a hill overlooking the Thames make an impressive picture. There is a small museum at the base of the tower, and the view from the top is worth every step of the climb.

New London and Groton can take one day or two, depending on your interest in nautical affairs. If you have never been to Mystic Seaport Museum, you really need another whole day for the feast of sights here: majestic wooden sailing vessels, a complete nineteenth-century village with working shops, museum buildings filled with rare boats, models of ships, figureheads, scrimshaw, marine art, and a please-touch children's museum filled with toys a sea captain's youngsters might have enjoyed.

There is much to see and do in Mystic, including a visit to the delightful penguin pavilion at the Mystic Aquarium. You may very well decide to save it for a weekend all its own.

In any event, do not omit the little towns beyond Mystic. Noank, jutting out into the west side of the Mystic River, offers spectacular views of Fishers Island Sound. The fine homes recall a time when this was a center for shipbuilding and lobstering. Later, it was an art colony, and galleries still display the work of local artists. Abbott's Lobster in the Rough here is a longtime summer favorite on the shore.

Stonington, a tiny hamlet beyond Mystic at the very edge of the shoreline, is for many the favorite destination on the shore. This wonderfully picturesque town has a Greek Revival center, a green surrounded by spired white churches, narrow streets lined with eighteenth- and nineteenth-century sea captains' homes, and a lighthouse dating to 1823 that houses a museum of village history. The view of Long Island Sound from the tower on a clear day is not to be missed.

Stonington's harbor is still crowded with working fishing boats, with many of the fishermen tracing their ancestry back to whalemen recruited in the Azores in the 1830s. Their old tradition of the blessing of the fleet continues here with a colorful ceremony in late June or early July.

North Stonington offers a unique dining opportunity, the chance to watch authentically costumed cooks preparing dinner over the open hearth at Randall's Ordinary. Their Colonial cookery is delicious, and the dinner is worth the drive. Guest rooms in the house and the restored barn are equally authentic, though they may be a bit spare for some tastes.

Should you be feeling lucky, you can head further inland from North Stonington for a change of pace at the Foxwoods High Stakes Bingo and Casino. You'll be amazed at the lavish facilities tucked away in the countryside in Ledyard on the Mashantucket Pequot reservation. There's even a Las Vegas–style theater where big name entertainers appear.

New London's best lodging is the Lighthouse Inn, the Victorian mansion of steel baron Charles S. Guthrie, near Ocean Beach Park. It has been renovated into an elegant enclave just a block from a private beach. Rich paneling and a carved spiral staircase lead to lavish guest rooms, including four huge front bedrooms with canopy beds and water views. There are rooms in an adjacent carriage house as well, and an excellent dining room. In town, the Radisson Hotel offers modern quarters within a short walk of the pier, and there is a Victorian bed-and-breakfast inn a short drive from the town's center.

If a Colonial inn is more to your taste, there are two good bets in Old Lyme, just a few miles down the shore, worthy stops for dinner as well as overnight. Whether you select the Bee and Thistle, an informal yellow Colonial house, or the Old Lyme Inn, an 1850s mansion with an elegant French menu, you will find yourself in a very special town whose entire wide, shaded Main Street has been declared a National Historic District.

One of the finest residences on the street was the home of a pioneering American art colony. The columned Georgian mansion is known as Florence Griswold Museum for "Miss Florence," who housed, fed, and nurtured a group of American Impressionist painters including Willard Metcalf and Childe Hassam, who developed the so-called ideal Lyme landscape that brought much attention to the area.

The house, now a National Historic Landmark, serves as headquarters for the Lyme Historical Society and contains paintings and panels left by the early artists, as well as collections of china, tools, and toys, and furnished period rooms, such as the front parlor, circa 1830. The famed dining room is lined with a double row of painted panels and furnished as it was when the artists took their meals there in the early part of this century.

The Old Lyme Art Association next door was founded in 1914 as a showcase for the many artists who continued to be attracted to the town, and it remains a prestigious gallery.

Another inviting lodging option a few miles down the coast is the Saybrook Point Inn in Old Saybrook, a stylish 62-room resort on the water with a spa and an indoor pool.

At the least, opt for lunch at the dock in Old Saybrook, watching the boats come and go. If all that nautical atmosphere makes you want to go farther out to sea, you'll find several options in the area, including shipping out on one of the windjammers, replicas of two-masted nineteenth-century schooners, that sail out of Mystic regularly for one-, two-, or five-day cruises.

Area Code: 203

DRIVING DIRECTIONS   All of the towns mentioned are on I-95, north of New Haven. New London is 113 miles from Boston, 125 miles from New York, and 45 miles from Hartford.

PUBLIC TRANSPORTATION   Amtrak goes to New London, Old Saybrook, and Mystic, but you'll need a rental car to get around once you arrive.

ACCOMMODATIONS   _Lighthouse Inn,_ 6 Guthrie Place (off Pequot at Lower Boulevard, one-half mile east of Ocean Beach Park), New London 06320, 443-8411, $$–$$$ CP • _Radisson Hotel,_ 35 Governor Winthrop Boulevard and Union Street, New London 06320, 443-7000, indoor pool, $$–$$$ • _Queen Anne Inn,_ 265 Williams Street, New London 06320, 447-2600, Victorian B & B, $$$ CP (with afternoon tea) • _Gold Star Inn,_ 156 Kings Highway, Groton 06340, 446-0660, pleasant motel, indoor pool, $$ • _Bee and Thistle Inn,_ 100 Lyme Street, Old Lyme 06371, 434-1667, $$–$$$ • _Old Lyme Inn,_ 85 Lyme Street, Old Lyme 06371, 434-2600, $$–$$$ CP • _Saybrook Point Inn,_ 2 Bridge Street, Old Saybrook 06475, 395-2000, $$$–$$$$, ask about weekend packages. See page 228 for Mystic.

DINING   _Lighthouse Inn_ (see above), elegant, with water views, $$–$$$ • _Ye Olde Tavern,_ 345 Bank Street, 442-0353, New London, maritime decor, steak and seafood, $$–$$$ • _The Gondelier,_ 92 Huntington Street, New London, 447-1781, Italian, $$ • _Two Sisters Deli_

on Bank Street is the favorite spot for lunch in New London, $ •
Diana, 970 Fashion Plaza, Poquonnock Road, Groton, 449-8468,
change of pace, Lebanese decor and menu, $$ • *Randall's Ordinary,*
Route 2, North Stonington, 599-4540, authentic Colonial fireplace
cookery. Be sure to reserve ahead; there is only one seating nightly,
prix fixe, $$$$ • *Bee and Thistle Inn* (see above), $$–$$$ • *Old Lyme
Inn* (see above), $$$–$$$$ • *Saybrook Point Inn* (see above), $$–$$$ •
Dock & Dine, Saybrook Point, Old Saybrook, 388-4665, unbeatable
water views, outdoor terrace in warm weather, $$–$$$. Also see Mys-
tic, page 229.

SIGHTSEEING *Yale-Harvard Regatta,* early June. Contact the
tourism district office listed below for dates and current information on
special events. • *U.S. Coast Guard Academy,* Mohegan Avenue, New
London, 444-8270. Hours: Visitors' Pavilion open May to October,
daily, 10 A.M. to 5 P.M. Museum open May to October, 8 A.M. to 4 P.M.
weekdays, and to 5 P.M. weekends and holidays. • *Eagle* ship tours,
Friday, Saturday, Sunday, 1 P.M. to 4 P.M., whenever the ship is in port.
Free. Write or call the academy for the *Eagle's* schedule, cadet dress
parades, and Coast Guard Band concerts. • *Shaw Mansion,* 305 Bank
Street, New London, 443-1209. Hours: Wednesday to Friday, 1 P.M. to
4 P.M. Saturday 10 A.M. to 4 P.M. Adults, $2; children, $0.50 • *Nathan
Hale Schoolhouse,* Union Plaza, New London, 443-8331. By appoint-
ment. Free • *Hempsted House,* 11 Hempstead Street, New London,
247-8996. Hours: Tuesday to Sunday, 1 P.M. to 5 P.M. Adults, $3; under
18, $2 • *Ocean Beach Park,* Ocean Avenue, New London, 447-3031.
Hours: Memorial Day to Labor Day, daily, 9 A.M. to 6 P.M. Parking:
weekdays, $7; weekends, $9. Walk-in fees: nonresident adults and
children, $2 • *Harkness Memorial State Park,* Route 213, Waterford,
443-5725. Hours: mansion open daily, Memorial Day to Labor Day, 10
A.M. to 5 P.M.; grounds open all year. Parking, summer weekdays, resi-
dents, $4; nonresidents, $5; weekends, residents, $4, nonresidents, $8;
rest of year, free. Summer Music Concert information: 442-9199 •
Connecticut College Arboretum, Connecticut College Campus,
Williams Street, New London, 439-2140. Hours: daily during daylight
hours. Free • *Lyman Allyn Art Museum,* 625 Williams Street (near col-
lege), New London, 443-2545. Hours: Tuesday, Thursday, Friday, and
Sunday, 1 P.M. to 5 P.M., Wednesday, 12:30 P.M. to 9 P.M., Saturday, 11
A.M. to 5 P.M. Admission, $3 • *Monte Cristo Cottage,* 325 Pequot
Avenue, New London, 443-0051. Hours: early April to mid-December,
Monday to Friday, 1 P.M. to 4 P.M., and by appointment. Adults, $3;
children, $1 • *USS Nautilus Memorial and Submarine Force Library
and Museum,* U.S. Naval Submarine Base, Route 12, Groton, 449-
3174. Hours: April 15 to October 14, Wednesday to Monday, 9 A.M. to
5 P.M., Tuesday 1 P.M. to 5 P.M.; rest of year, Wednesday to Monday, 9
A.M. to 4 P.M., closed Tuesday. Free • *Ft. Griswold State Park,* Monu-

ment and Park avenues, Groton, 445-1729. Hours: open daily, dawn to dusk • *Groton Monument and Monument House,* Memorial Day to Labor Day, daily, 10 A.M. to 5 P.M.; Labor Day to mid-October, weekends only. Free • *Children's Museum of Southeastern Connecticut,* 409 Main Street, Niantic, 691-1255. Hours: Monday and Wednesday to Saturday, 9:30 A.M. to 4:30 P.M., Sunday 1 P.M. to 5 P.M. Admission, $2.50 • *Mystic Seaport,* 75 Greenmanville Avenue, Mystic, 572-5315. Hours: daily, 9 A.M. to 5 P.M., late June to Labor Day to 8 P.M. Adults, $15; children 6 to 12, $7.50 • *Mystic Marinelife Aquarium,* 55 Coogan Boulevard, Mystic, 572-5955. Hours: July 1 to Labor Day, daily, 9:00 A.M. to 5:30 P.M., rest of year to 4:30 P.M. Adults, $9; children, $5.50 • **Boat trips:** Check current schedules and rates. *Captain John's Sportfishing Center,* 15 First Street, Waterford, 443-7259, deep-sea fishing and whale watching; *Project Oceanology,* Avery Point, Groton (800) 364-8472, educational cruises aboard the Enviro-Lab; *Voyager Cruises,* Steamboat Wharf, Mystic, 536-0416, sailing excursions; *Steamboat Sabino* and schooner *Brilliant,* Mystic Seaport, 572-5315; *Mystic Whaler* and *Mystic Clipper,* 7 Holmes Street, Mystic, 536-4218, windjammer cruises.

INFORMATION Southeastern Connecticut Tourism District, PO Box 89, 27 Masonic Street, New London, CT 06320, 444-2206.

Exploring Blooming Boston

Boston keeps getting better. From the cobbled streets of Beacon Hill to the gleaming marble of Copley Place, from the Victorian boulevards of Back Bay to the bustling waterfront, this is a town that has retained the best of the old while keeping up with the new in a blend of vivacious harmony few cities can match.

No city offers more diversity. Some of 350-year-old Boston remains a citadel of conservatism—quiet charm and tradition, perfectly preserved red-brick town houses, fifth-generation Brahmins, tea at 4:00 P.M., and swan boats gliding on the lake in the Public Garden as they have since 1877.

Yet today's Boston is also nonstop action—sculls and sailboats on the Charles, joggers and skaters on the Esplanade, crowds converging on the food stalls in Quincy Market, shoppers nudging to get at the bargains in Filene's Basement.

It is the city of culture—of a world-renowned symphony and Museum of Fine Arts—and a maelstrom of rabid Red Sox and Celtics fans, Irish and Italian politicos, marathoners, camera-toting tourists, schoolchildren walking the red line of the Freedom Trail, plus thousands of young people who attend 150 area colleges and universities, giving the city eternal youth.

You can't really begin to know this complex city in a weekend, but you can sample its multiple pleasures more easily than you might imagine, because central Boston is essentially a compact, walkable area where a little foot power can take you a long way. Cars are only a nuisance, since the traffic is crowded and confusing.

So "pahk your cah," as the Bostonians really do say, stop at the Boston Common information booths on Tremont Street or the Prudential Center to arm yourself with a city map and information, and plan a walking tour of the neighborhoods that will show you the fascinating facets of this urban gem. If your foot power lags, just board the "T," the efficient, easy-to-use subway system, or one of the sightseeing trolleys that make continuous loops of the city, letting you get off and reboard as often as you wish.

Boston Common, the oldest public park in America, is a beautiful introduction to the city's sights. In spring it is resplendent with magnolias in bloom.

You might begin by following Tremont Street west from the information booths, turning left on Park Street to Beacon Street and the State House at the top of that bastion of old Boston, Beacon Hill. Samuel Adams laid the cornerstone for Charles Bulfinch's gold-domed architectural masterpiece.

To appreciate the ambience of the Hill, you need only stroll the cobbled, gaslit streets lined with rows of fine brick town houses with gleaming brass door knockers, overflowing flower boxes, and finely detailed ironwork. Take Joy Street and go left on Mt. Vernon to reach the perfect hushed pocket of the past called Louisburg Square. You can visit the inside of a typical upper-class home of the past at the Nichols House on Mt. Vernon Street.

A left turn on Pinckney behind Louisburg Square and a walk downhill will bring you to Charles Street, a choice row of antiques shops, cafés, and coffee houses leading back to Beacon.

The corner of Beacon and Charles streets is of special note, both as the departure point for the British on their fateful expedition to Lexington and Concord and as the very spot where Officer O'Malley held up traffic to make way for the eight ducklings of Mrs. Mallard on their way to the Public Garden in Robert McCloskey's timeless children's tale. A detour to see the garden in its springtime prime, with a ride on the famous swan boats on the pond, is highly recommended. A sculpture commemorates the famous ducklings.

Walk right two blocks on Beacon beside the garden to Arlington and across the Arthur Fiedler Memorial Bridge to reach the Esplanade and pause to watch the activity on the Charles River and the promenade beside it. The Hatch Memorial Shell is the site of summer serenades by the Boston Pops Orchestra, and the space around it is a spot favored by joggers, skaters, and people watchers. You can see the domes of MIT just across the Charles in Cambridge, the town that is also the home of the splendid Harvard campus.

From here you can tour another handsome side of Boston by returning past Beacon to Marlborough or Commonwealth and turning right to follow the eight alphabetical streets from Arlington to Hereford through the Back Bay.

Boston was a lot hillier before the Back Bay was developed. Henry James once used the word "odiferous" to describe this 450-acre oozy swampland, which later was filled with soil leveled off from some of the hills. What emerged over a period of some 125 years was a model of nineteenth-century architecture in a green setting by Frederick Law Olmsted. Commonwealth, a parade of stately stone Victorian row houses with a wide grassy mall in the center, is the grandest street. Marlborough is simpler and greener, and some like it even better.

The alphabetical streets stop past Hereford at Massachusetts Avenue. A couple of blocks beyond is Kenmore Square, a gathering place for students from Boston University, which runs farther southwest along the river. To the east, near a park called the Fenway and the better-known Fenway Park, home to Boston's beloved Red Sox, are Simmons and Northeastern colleges. The Boston Museum of Fine Arts, which houses one of the nation's outstanding collections of French Impressionist and American art, is in the same neighborhood. The Manets in the Impressionist Gallery are fabulous. Emerson College occupies some of the town houses on Beacon, closer to the Public Garden, though it is scheduled at some point to move to a suburban campus.

On the other side of Commonwealth Avenue are Newbury and Boylston, traditional shopping streets. At Boylston and Hereford, you'll come to the Prudential Center, built over what was once the Boston trainyard and is now the Massachusetts Turnpike. There is shopping here, also, including department stores. The Prudential Tower Skywalk offers a stunning 360-degree view of the city.

The "Pru" is now connected by overpass to the Hynes Convention Center and across busy Huntington Avenue to Copley Place and its lineup of posh stores. Walk through the Copley Place arcade and out through the Westin Hotel lobby and you will emerge on Copley Square, another city landmark, surrounded by the Boston Public Library, Trinity Church, and one of the city's grande-dame hotels, the Copley Plaza. Don't fail to stop in the Public Library to see the art treasures and the glorious courtyard in this Beaux Arts treasure by the renowned architectural firm of McKim, Mead, and White. There is another soaring city view to be had at the top of the John Hancock Tower off Copley Square.

From Copley Square, follow Dartmouth Street west two blocks to

Newbury for the best of the shops and galleries, stretching four blocks back to the Public Garden at Arlington. The Louis of Boston store in the former Museum of Natural History is among the local landmarks, and their café is a chic stop for lunch. There are also many sidewalk cafés on Newbury to provide a resting place for weary sightseers. Mirabelle, Sonsie, and the Armani Express are popular spots for those who want to see and be seen, by night as well as by day.

At the corner of Newbury and Arlington, opposite the Public Garden, is the Ritz Carlton, a Boston landmark since 1927. You can't see why the Ritz has so many loyal patrons from the tiny, understated lobby, but you will understand if you treat yourself to a weekend and enjoy the kind of attentive Old World service that is a rarity today. At the least, come for afternoon tea or the legendary lavish Sunday brunch, or for dancing on the roof terrace.

The Ritz now shares honors as Boston's best with the Four Seasons, located around the corner on Boylston Street and also facing the Public Garden. Newer and more lavish, this is the city's only five-diamond establishment, and it offers every luxury from an indoor pool to free morning limousine service to downtown. Their Aujourd'hui restaurant is one of the city's best.

This is more than enough to fill a wonderful day, with stops at the many shops and sights along the way, but the Downtown Crossing must be squeezed in on Saturday if you want to have a look at another Boston institution, Filene's Basement. It is a 15-minute walk or just a hop if you board "the T" at Arlington and Boylston. Get off at Park Street, turn right when you emerge, and cross Tremont to Winter Street and the stores. Filene's and Jordan Marsh are both one block away on the corner, where Winter and Summer streets intersect with Washington—a pedestrians-only crossing that is the busiest intersection in New England. The scene is further enlivened by colorful wooden pushcarts filled with all kinds of wares and by impromptu entertainment by street musicians. Lafayette Place, an enclosed shopping area next to Jordan Marsh, adds to the crowds.

The famous Filene's bargain basement is nothing like the clones that have appeared in other cities. It is frequently a madhouse. The longer merchandise remains, the lower the markdown; aficionados watch the action day by day like brokers on Wall Street, waiting for the perfect moment to buy. On any given day, a new batch of bargains may arrive—anything from designer clothing to Oriental rugs—to be fought over by eager customers. There are no dressing rooms, but that doesn't stop anyone from trying on the merchandise. Even if you don't want to participate, it is definitely a major only-in-Boston sight.

On Washington Street to the right of all this shopping activity is the "combat zone," Boston's adult entertainment district. Go left on Washington, and at the corner of School Street you will run right into history: the Old South Meeting House, a center of pre-Revolutionary agitation; the Old Corner Bookstore, once a gathering place for Emerson, Hawthorne, and other literary greats; the old City Hall and the Old State House, the seat of Colonial government.

Less than a block away on the left is the Government Center, a curving red brick plaza and its showpiece, the Boston City Hall. When it was completed in the late 1960s and early 1970s, some considered the center controversial for its modernity; others find that it blends pleasingly with its historic neighbors. You be the judge.

You can combine this last group of historic sites with a leisurely look at the waterfront and the North End on Sunday, either by following the orderly red lines of the Freedom Trail—the road marking events leading up to the American Revolution—or by making your own way and watching for the sights. On your own, start back to the Government Center. A walk down the steps and across the street will bring you to Faneuil Hall, site of many town meetings at which impassioned patriots planned their fight for liberty.

Beyond is the Faneuil Hall Marketplace, composed of three long buildings. You can literally eat your way through the domed Quincy Market in the center, which is filled with a heavenly assortment of food stands offering just about every edible you can imagine. The food market is flanked by cafés and the North and South Market buildings, with dozens of shops plus lots of pushcart wares, a flower market, and the Haymarket, an open-air produce exchange. All of this occurs in a festive setting of cobbled walks, bright banners, and clowns, mimes, and musicians that attracts more than a million people a month. You'll find plenty of places here for a pleasant brunch, or you can do-it-yourself at the various food stands.

There are many things to see and do on the booming Boston waterfront, including the fun-filled New England Aquarium and cruises in the harbor. For more details on some of the harbor attractions and other city sights, see "Bringing the Kids to Boston," page 219.

To complete a look at the city, you'll want to proceed beyond Quincy Market via a pedestrian tunnel under the Fitzgerald Expressway at Hanover Street and into the North End, Boston's "Little Italy." (The expressway will be disappearing in the next few years in a major redevelopment plan, the $5 billion Central Artery Project that will include an eight- to ten-lane underground expressway and a four-lane tunnel connecting directly to Logan Airport; meanwhile, expect extensive construction.)

There is a European feeling to the North End's old residential area of brick houses and narrow streets, and dozens of tempting stops in Italian bakeries, coffee shops, and restaurants. A few blocks from the start of Hanover Street, a right on Richmond will bring you to the Paul Revere House, and a few blocks farther is the Old North Church, the city's oldest, where lanterns in the steeple were the signal for Revere's famous ride.

If you follow the Freedom Trail all the way to Charlestown, you can board "Old Ironsides," otherwise known as the USS *Constitution,* the oldest commissioned warship afloat in the world, and wind up at the site of Bunker Hill, the first battle of the Revolution, marked by a 220-foot monument with a stunning view of the city from the top. Going from the Old North Church to Bunker Hill will add 2½ miles to your route.

Having seen most of central Boston, you still haven't explored its cultural treasures, such as the Museum of Fine Arts, the exceptional Isabella Gardner Museum set in a virtual palazzo, the excellent Museum of Science, and the special architecture of the Christian Science Center. Nor have you visited the very moving Kennedy Memorial Library Museum on Dorchester Bay or had the unforgettable experience of hearing the fanatic fans at Fenway Park or paid a visit to Cambridge. And one weekend can't begin to take in all the nighttime attractions—theater, ballet at the handsomely restored Wang Center for the Performing Arts, symphony and opera, sports, and all the other forms of music and entertainment that a city full of sophisticates and college people regularly attracts.

There is always something more to do in Boston, and in recent years, something new to see almost every time you go back. But top among its pleasures is the activity that never palls no matter how many times it is repeated—strolling the neighborhoods that preserve the past in a blooming contemporary city.

Area Code: 617

DRIVING DIRECTIONS   From north or south, take I-93/3 or I-95; also from the north, Route 1, 1A, or 128. From the west, take I-90, the Massachusetts Turnpike, or Route 2, 9, or 20. Boston is 98 miles from Hartford and 208 miles from New York.

PUBLIC TRANSPORTATION   Boston can be reached by Amtrak, most major bus lines, and most airlines. Cars are only a nuisance in the city. Cabs, subways, a water ferry, and shuttle buses serve the airport, and the downtown transit system is excellent.

ACCOMMODATIONS   So many possibilities, so few low prices! Almost all hotels do offer weekend packages at reduced rates. This is a selective listing in descending order of price. When you inquire about current packages, find out whether parking is included—parking can cost $20 a day! • The luxury choices, all $$$$$: *Ritz Carlton,* 15 Arlington Street, 02117, 536-5700 or (800) 225-7620, still the epitome of Boston graciousness • *Four Seasons Hotel,* 200 Boylston Street, 02116, 338-4400 or (800) 332-3442, elegant top choice, admirable service, health club and pool • *Le Meridien,* 250 Franklin Street, 02110, 451-1900, stunning hotel in old Federal Reserve Bank building • **On the waterfront:** *Bostonian,* Faneuil Hall Marketplace, 02109, 523-3600 or (800) 343-0922, tasteful, recommended • *Boston Harbor Hotel,* 70 Rowes Wharf, 02110, 439-7000 or (800) 752-7577, posh, formal, great views • *Marriott Long Wharf,* 296 State Street, 02109, 227-0800, striking contemporary • **Back Bay:** *Copley Plaza,* 138 St. James Avenue, Copley Square, 02116, 267-5300 or (800) 826-7539, nicely restored landmark, sometimes busy with conventions, $$$$–$$$$$ • *Colonnade,* 120 Huntington Avenue, 02116, 424-7000, small, low-key, elegant, $$$$$ • *Boston Park Plaza,* 64 Arlington Street at Park Plaza, 02117, 426-2000 or (800) 225-2008, big, convenient, good weekend packages, $$$$ • **Other choices:** *Copley Square,* 47 Huntington Avenue, 02116, 536-9000 or (800) 225-7062, $$$–$$$$ • *Lenox Hotel,* 710 Boylston Street, 536-5300 or (800) 225-7676, $$$$–$$$$$ • *Tremont House,* 275 Tremont Street, 02116, 426-1400, $$$ • *Howard Johnson* has three city locations, not great but with reasonable weekend packages: *57 Park Plaza Hotel,* 200 Stuart Street, 02116, 482-1800, $$–$$$$; *Howard Johnson Motor Lodge Fenway,* 1271 Boylston Street, 267-8300, $$–$$$; and *Howard Johnson Kenmore Square,* 575 Commonwealth Avenue, 267-3100, $$–$$$ • *Newbury Guest House,* 261 Newbury Street, 02116, 437-7666 or (800) 437-7668, town houses converted to inn, modest but good price and location, $$–$$$ CP • Really limited budgets call for motels in outlying areas, such as *Susse Chalet Inn Boston/Neponset,* 800 Morrissey Boulevard, Neponset, 287-9100, $; *Days Inn-Newton,* 399 Grove Street, Newton, 02162, $$–$$$; or *American Youth Hostels,* 12 Hemenway Street, 536-9455, dorm accommodations, $. **Bed-and-breakfast reservation services:** Many choices in Boston; see full listing pages x and xi.

DINING **A group of Boston hotels are among the city's best dining places, all $$$–$$$$** • *Aujourd'hui,* Four Seasons Hotel (see above); *Ritz Carlton Dining Room* (see above), famous Sunday brunch; also *The Roof* at the Ritz Carlton, dinner and dancing, $$$–$$$$ plus entertainment charge; *Julien,* Le Meridien (see above); *Seasons,* Bostonian Hotel (see above); *Rowe's Wharf,* Boston Harbor Hotel (see above) • **Headquarters for Boston's best-known chefs:** Jasper White at *Jasper's,* 240 Commercial Street, 523-1126, $$– $$$$$; and Lydia Shire, at *Biba,* 272 Boylston Street, 426-7878, $$$–$$$$; Shire's newest venture is *Pignoli,* 79 Park Plaza, 338-7500, $$–$$$ • **More of the best:** *L'Espalier,* 30 Gloucester Street, 262-3023, romantic, prix fixe, $$$$$ • *Maison Robert,* 45 School Street, 227-3370, French menu in Old City Hall, $$$–$$$$, also café with outdoor terrace, prix fixe, $$ and $$$ • *Hamersley's Bistro,* 553 Tremont Street, 423-2700, "nouvelle American," very popular, $$–$$$$ • *Locke Ober,* 4 Winter Street,

542-1340, Old World institution since 1875, $$$–$$$$ • *Capital Grille,* 359 Newbury Street, 262-8900, handsome steakhouse, $$–$$$ • *Emporio Armani Express,* 214 Newbury Street, 437-0909, chic, $$–$$$ • *Mirabelle,* 85 Newbury Street, 859-4848, elegant café, $$–$$$ • *Sonsie,* 327 Newbury Street, 351-2500, café-bistro, eclectic menu, $$–$$$ • **Less pricey**: *Another Season,* 97 Mount Vernon Street, 367-0880, romantic Back Bay café, $$–$$$ • *Ristorante Toscano,* 421 Charles Street, 723-4090, fine northern Italian, $$–$$$ • *Hungry I,* 71½ Charles Street, 227-3524, French, intimate, $$–$$$ • *St. Botolph,* 99 St. Botolph Street, 266-3030, hidden town house gem, American menu, $$–$$$ • *Rocco's,* 5 Charles Street, South Boston, 723-6800, avant-garde café, very popular, $–$$$ • *Skipjack's,* 199 Clarendon Street, 536-3500, casual, good seafood, $$ • *Papa Razzi,* 271 Dartmouth Street, 536-6560, gourmet pizza to Italian dinners, $–$$ • *Blue Diner,* 150 Kneeland Street, 338-4639, wide-ranging menu, open all night, $–$$ • *Blue Wave,* 142 Berkeley Street, 424-6664, cheerful, noisy, cheap, $ • **North End Italian choices**: *Felicia's,* 145A Richmond, 523-9885, old-timer, $–$$ • *Mama Maria's,* 3 North Square at Little Prince Street, 523-0077, elegant new look in the area, $$$ • *Pomodoro,* 319 Hanover Street, 867-4348, creative menus, $$ • *Giacomo's,* 35 Hanover, 523-9026, open kitchen, grill specialties, $$ • **For cappuccino, gelati, etc.:** *Café Paradiso,* 255 Hanover Street, 742-1768; *Caffe Vittoria,* 296 Hanover Street, 227-7606 • (This gentrifying neighborhood attracts a hip, young crowd) **South End choices:** *St. Cloud,* 557 Tremont Street, 353-0202, New American menu, $$ • *Jae's Café and Grill,* 520 Columbus Avenue, South End, 421-9405, excellent Asian specialties, $–$$; *Claremont Café,* 535 Columbus Avenue, South End, 247-9001, informal bistro, $–$$; *Icarus,* 3 Appleton Street, 426-1790, innovative American cuisine, live jazz, $$ • **Some long-time institutions**: *Legal Seafoods,* Copley Place and two locations on Stuart Street behind Park Plaza Hotel (see above), almost too popular—be prepared for a long wait, $$–$$$ • *Durgin Park,* 340 North Market Street, Faneuil Hall Marketplace, 227-2038, roast beef and baked beans family-style in hectic but historic surroundings, $$ (don't go to the one on Copley Place—it's not the same experience) • *Union Oyster House,* 41 Union Street, 227-2038, oldest in the city, fine chowder, $$–$$$ • **Good budget choices:** *Omonia,* 75 South Charles Street, 426-4310, Greek, $ • *Piccola Venezia,* 63 Salem Street, North End, 523-9802, $ • *Jacob Wirth,* 33-37 Stuart Street (across from the Wang Center), 338-8536, no-frills German, same spot since 1868, $–$$ • *No Name,* 15 Boston Fish Pier, 338-7539, good prices for fresh seafood, go early to avoid long lines, $ • *Boston Beer Works,* 61 Brookline Avenue near Kenmore Square, 536-BEER, attractive lively brew-pub, $–$$ • **For lunch:** *Isabella Gardner Museum* (see under Sightseeing), a superb setting for lunch, terrace in warm weather, $ (no museum admission required) • The most romantic spot in town for dancing and a city view is the *Customs House Lounge, Bay Tower Room,* 60 State Street, 723-1666. Skip the expensive dinner; come for drinks and the view.

Several top local favorites are out of the city center; those with a car may want to try the following: *Olives,* 10 City Square, Charlestown, 242-1999, raves for Mediterranean fare and gourmet pizzas, $$–$$$ • *Figs,* 67 Main Street, Charlestown, 242-2229, another winner for pasta and pizza, $–$$ • *Elephant Walk,* 70 Union Square, Somerville, 623-9939, French and Cambodian food, $–$$ • *Providence,* 1223 Beacon Street, Brookline, 232-0300, dramatic decor, varied menu, $$–$$$ • *Dali,* 415 Washington Street, Somerville, 661-3254, Spanish, tapas, $–$$. See also family dining, page 223, and Cambridge, page 280.

SIGHTSEEING *Boston National Historical Park Visitors Center,* 15 State Street, 242-5642. Hours: daily, June to August, Monday to Friday, 8 A.M. to 6 P.M., Saturday and Sunday, 9 A.M. to 6 P.M.; rest of year to 5 P.M. Information on the Freedom Trail—free ranger-led, 90-minute guided walking tours offered regularly; check current schedule • *Old State House,* 206 Washington Street at State Street, 720-3290. Hours: April to October, daily, 9:30 A.M. to 5 P.M.; rest of year, Monday to Friday, 10 A.M. to 4 P.M., Saturday, 9:30 A.M. to 5 P.M., Sunday, 11 A.M. to 5 P.M. Adults, $2; ages 6 to 18, $0.75 • *State House,* Beacon and Park streets, 727-3676. Hours: Monday to Friday, 9 A.M. to 5 P.M. Guided tours: 10 A.M. to 4 P.M. Free • *Nichols House Museum,* 55 Mt. Vernon Street, 227-6993. Hours: May to October, Tuesday to Saturday, noon to 5 P.M.; February to April and November and December, Monday, Wednesday, and Saturday, noon to 5 P.M. Admission, $4 • *Prudential Center Skywalk,* 800 Boylston Street, 236-3318. Hours: Monday to Saturday, 10 A.M. to 10 P.M., Sunday, noon to 10 P.M. Adults, $2.75; ages 5 to 15, $1.75 • *John Hancock Observatory,* St. James Avenue and Trinity Place, 572-6429. Hours: May to October, Monday to Saturday, 9 A.M. to 10 P.M., Sunday, 10 A.M. to 10 P.M.; rest of year, daily, noon to 10 P.M. Adults, $3; ages 5 to 15, $2.25 • *Museum of Fine Arts,* 465 Huntington Avenue, 267-9300. Hours: Tuesday to Sunday, 10 A.M. to 4:45 P.M., Wednesday to 9:45 P.M.; Thursday and Friday, west wing only to 9:45 P.M. Adults, $8; ages 6 to 17, $3.50; pay what you wish on Wednesday, 4:45 P.M. to 9:45 P.M. • *Isabella Stewart Gardner Museum,* 280 The Fenway, 566-1401. Hours: Tuesday to Sunday, 11 A.M. to 5 P.M. Adults, $6; students, $3; under 12, free • *John Fitzgerald Kennedy Library Museum,* I-93 south, Exit 17 at Columbia Point, Dorchester, 929-4523. Hours: daily, 9 A.M. to 5 P.M. Adults, $6; students, $4; children, $2 • *Paul Revere House,* 19 North Square, 523-2338. Hours: April 15 to October 31, daily, 9:30 A.M. to 4:15 P.M.; rest of year, closed Monday. Adults, $2.50; ages 5 to 17, $1 • *USS Constitution,* Charlestown Navy Yard (part of Boston National Historical Park), Charlestown, 241-9078. Hours: ship tours daily, 9:30 A.M. to 3:50 P.M. Free • *USS Constitution*

Museum, 426-1812. Hours: daily 9 A.M. to 5 P.M.; to 6 P.M. from late June to Labor Day; to 4 P.M. January to March. Adults, $3; ages 6 to 16, $1.50 • *Boston Harbor Cruises,* daily sightseeing cruises, 227-4321. Phone for current schedules and prices. Walking tours: *Boston By Foot,* 367-2345, May to October; phone for current offerings • *Beantown Trolley,* 236-2148; ninety-minute narrated tours. Riders may get off at any stops and reboard later. Adults, $16; ages 5 to 11, $5.00; under 5, free. See more Boston attractions, page 223.

ENTERTAINMENT *Bostix Ticket Booth,* Faneuil Hall Marketplace, 723-5181, half-price theater, music, and dance tickets on day of performance. Hours: Tuesday to Saturday, 11 A.M. to 6 P.M., Sunday noon to 4 P.M.

INFORMATION Boston Common Visitor Information Booth, Tremont Street and Prudential Center Visitors' Center, both open daily, 9 A.M. to 5 P.M. For written information, contact Greater Boston Convention and Tourist Bureau, Prudential Plaza, PO Box 490, Boston, MA 02199, 536-4100 or (800) 888-5515.

Summer

Overleaf: *Boating in Newport, Rhode Island. Photograph by John T. Hopf, courtesy of Newport County Chamber of Commerce.*

Flying High in Quechee

Summer arrives with a whoosh in Quechee, Vermont.

For more than a decade now, by 6:00 P.M. on the Friday of the third weekend in June, the village green is crowded with people waiting to see the season's most colorful send-off.

By then, the green already has been transformed into a patchwork of striped and star-spangled giant balloons, waiting to soar on the favorable evening breeze. One by one, the balloons are filled with flaming gusts of hot air. First they grow big and round, then stand erect, and eventually sail aloft to the loud cheers of admiring bystanders.

It was an inspired idea to stage an annual balloon festival in this classic New England green. Colorful hot-air balloons astride the wind always cause people to gaze with pleasure and a bit of envy, but there is something special about the combination of the bright soaring balloons and pastoral hills and farms that makes it well worthwhile to make the trip to Quechee—and to bring along several rolls of film.

Since the winds are also right at 6:00 A.M., early risers can see the spectacle repeated on Saturday. Even those who watch the Friday night liftoff are likely to return on Saturday morning to get another angle with their cameras or to watch their favorite balloon make a new ascent. And in case they still miss the perfect shot, there's always Saturday night and Sunday morning to try, try again.

If you become curious about what it takes to get the balloons aloft or how they ever get down again, the festival program will fill you in on everything—riding the wind and handling propane tanks, tether ropes, and burners—so you'll learn just how it's done.

Between launchings, the green is filled with down-home music and entertainment, dozens of crafts booths, and food stands, all adding further to the air of gaiety inspired by the balloons. The smell of barbecued chicken on the outdoor grills may well tempt you to stay here for lunch or return for an economical outdoor dinner.

The festival takes place in a tiny town that is photogenic even without benefit of balloons. Quechee is best known for the river gorge that can be seen on Route 4 outside of town on the way to Woodstock. Not all visitors make the detour into the village, where the Ottauquechee River provides the town with a scenic natural backdrop of swirling downhill rapids and a waterfall.

To miss Quechee means missing a fascinating mill restoration, historic homes, some fine country inns, and a tasteful, tucked-away condominium community that provides all kinds of recreational facilities. Concerts and Saturday afternoon polo matches are other Quechee summertime lures.

If you stay at the Quechee Inn at Marshland Farm, you'll be within walking distance of the green but safely away from the crowds. The two-story inn was the 1793 home of Col. Joseph Marsh and one of Vermont's most distinguished families, whose members included a governor, a university president, and a U.S. ambassador to Italy. The brick-floored, timbered living room, equipped with a bar, offers a comfortable sitting area; there's a pleasant outdoor terrace and lawn for sunning, and an attractive Colonial-style dining room.

Bikes, canoe rentals, and a fly-fishing school are available right at the inn, and guests also have access to the clubhouse, pools, a sandy lake beach, children's recreation area, golf course, and tennis, squash, and racquetball courts of the Quechee Lakes resort community on 5,000 acres of woods and meadows in the nearby hills. It's also possible to rent one of the attractive condominiums here and move in for the weekend.

Another quite elegant little lodging is the Parker House Inn, a handsome Victorian house in the village, recently redone with flair. Also right in town is the Country Garden Inn, a very attractive small bed-and-breakfast home with nice gardens, where breakfast is served in a sunny solarium. Both these inns provide guest privileges at Quechee Lakes.

The Quechee Bed & Breakfast Inn is another attractive choice, though it is on Route 4 rather than in town. It will please antiquers who want to spend time at the lavish three-story Antiques Collaborative just across the road in Waterman Place, a stylish little complex that also offers change of dining pace at Rosalita's Southwestern Bar & Grill.

Another happy choice off Route 4 is the Sugar Pine Farm, a new bed-and-breakfast inn built to look like a traditional farmhouse and beautifully furnished with country pieces and folk art.

The prime sightseeing attraction in town is the workshop and gallery of glassblower Simon Pearce, an Irishman who took over the old red-brick woolen mills on the dam in Quechee and harnessed the hydroelectric power to provide energy for his glass furnace. Pearce and his workers still make every piece painstakingly by hand, and the public is welcome to watch them at their labors, as well as to inspect the hydroelectric plant.

The showroom and shop are stunning, with great arched windows looking out on the river. In addition to Pearce glassware, pottery, and handwoven Irish woolens, a few antiques are for sale. Bargain hunters can also find reduced prices on some of the Pearce glasses and pitchers, though the price for "seconds" of such meticulously made items is still high. There is also an excellent restaurant where you can have lunch or dinner with a river view.

Farther west on Route 4, heading toward Woodstock, you'll find Scotland by the Yard, which offers tartan and tweed fabrics and handsome woolen clothing and sweaters. Continue into Woodstock and you'll have your fill of shops and restaurants. For more on Woodstock see pages 3–8.

If you need further diversions, you can see polo played every Saturday at the Quechee Polo Club. For evening activity, take a drive across the Connecticut River to Hanover, New Hampshire, where something is probably happening at Dartmouth's Hopkins Center.

Add the sporting possibilities and the color of the balloons to the peace of the countryside around Quechee, and you need little more to lift the summer season to a soaring start.

Area Code: 802

DRIVING DIRECTIONS   Quechee is located four miles from I-89 on Route 4, midway between Woodstock and White River Junction, Vermont. It is about 143 miles from Boston, 255 miles from New York, and 161 miles from Hartford.

PUBLIC TRANSPORTATION   Air service to Lebanon, New Hampshire, 7½ miles: Amtrak to White River Junction, 7 miles.

ACCOMMODATIONS   *The Quechee Inn at Marshland Farm,* Clubhouse Road, Quechee 05059, 295-3133, $$$$ MAP • *Quechee Lakes Rental Corporation,* Box 85, Quechee 05059, 205-7525, $$$$ • *Parker House Inn,* Quechee Village 05059, 295-6077, attractive small Victorian inn, $$–$$$ CP • *Country Garden Inn,* 37 Main Street, Quechee 05059 (800) 859-4191, $$ CP • *Quechee Bed & Breakfast Inn,* Quechee 05059, 295-1776, 1795 Colonial home, $$–$$$ CP • *Sugar Pine Farm,* Route 4, Quechee 05059, 295-1266, $$ CP • *Applebutter Inn,* Happy Valley Road (just off Route 4), Taftsville 05073, 457-4158, lovely small inn just a few miles from Quechee, $$ CP. Also see Woodstock on page 7 and Hanover on pages 233–234 for additional lodging and dining suggestions.

DINING   *The Quechee Inn at Marshland Farm* (see above), pleasant atmosphere, $$–$$$ • *Parker House Inn* (see above), on the formal side, $$–$$$ • *Simon Pearce Restaurant,* The Mill, Quechee, lunch, $, dinner, $$ • *Rosalita's Southwestern Bar & Grill,* Route 4, Waterman Place, Quechee, 295-1600, $–$$.

SIGHTSEEING   *Quechee Balloon Festival,* Village Green, Quechee, usually late June, sponsored by Quechee Chamber of Commerce. Admission, $2 • Call for schedules, information.

INFORMATION   Quechee Chamber of Commerce, PO Box 106, Quechee, VT 05059, 295-7900.

A Summer Fling in Connecticut

Come early July each year, a steady procession of cars can be seen bypassing beach and barbecue to head for a park in Norwalk, Connecticut.

Their destination? The Round Hill Scottish Games, a colorful summer tradition that features more than 700 contestants, from seven to seventy, taking part in the piping, dancing, and sporting competitions that have been part of Scottish tradition for as long as anyone can remember.

Traditionally held near the Fourth of July holiday, it's not the usual Independence Day festivity, nor is this suburban commuter territory in Fairfield County an area you might ordinarily choose for a getaway destination. Yet it offers all the elements for a uniquely pleasant outing, with both beach and wooded beauty at hand, plus good shopping, summer theater, and a number of excellent restaurants nearby. If you know where to look, you may even find some old New England atmosphere here in the suburbs.

The games, which draw well over 10,000 spectators each year, are patterned after the famed Highland Games in Scotland. The event originated early in the century in nearby Greenwich when a group of Scottish emigrants from the area joined forces to provide an occasion to wear their native Highland dress and preserve a bit of their heritage for their children. Proceeds in the early years were used to help other newly arrived Scots in this country.

Word of the occasion spread, the participants began to multiply, and the spectacle became such an attraction that the Round Hill Scottish Games Association was formed in 1923 to oversee the event and disperse the profits to a number of charities. The location has been moved several times to accommodate ever-growing crowds.

There are three categories of events taking place all at once, giving something of the feeling of watching a three-ring circus. Athletic games such as track events and soccer are climaxed by the incredible "tossing of the caber."

A caber looks much like a telephone pole, measuring 16 feet in length and weighing over 150 pounds. Legend has it that caber tossing dates back to the days before bridges were built, when brawny Scottish lads made their way across the waters by uprooting a tree and tossing it across the stream as a walkway. Today, heaving the heavy pole is a feat to try even the halest, and many contestants find they can hardly *lift* the caber, much less toss it anywhere. Their feeble efforts are greeted by hoots of laughter from the high-spirited holiday crowd.

Yet each year a few stout lads emerge who seem to have inherited the prowess of their ancestors, and a husky contender inevitably comes forward to give the king-size missile a prodigious toss that sets off wild cheering from the sidelines.

While the sportsmen are having at each other, more than a hundred dancers are competing in another area of the grounds. The dancers, gaily decked out in plaid knee socks, kilts, tunics, and caps, are judged by their skill in executing the carefully prescribed steps of dances such as the highland fling, the sailor's hornpipe, and the sword dance. The littlest contestants begin in the morning, followed by big brothers and sisters, and finally the adults. Many spectators seem to remain mesmerized for hours watching the graceful dancers perform their nimble steps.

To give stamina to the bystanders, refreshment stands are strategically placed, serving regional fare such as Scottish meat pies or fish and chips as well as an all-American menu of hot dogs and Cokes. There are souvenir stands as well, with tiny plaid tams for the tots, Celtic jewelry and other crafts, and a selection of beautiful wool tartan plaids of the clans, for sale by the yard.

Last and far from least of the events is the bagpipe competition, with pipers and drummers in full regalia performing individually as well as in groups. The bagpipe bands in their colorful plaids come from all over the Northeast and as far away as Canada and Bermuda.

The pipers and bands march one by one to perform the specified categories of music: a march, a reel, a strathspey, and the tongue-twisting piobaireachd. Then, when the judging is done and the winner declared, the musicians mass for one last spectacular parade across the grounds, an unforgettable finale of sound and color.

For those who are making a weekend of it, Norwalk has some unexpected pleasures to offer. Silvermine Tavern here is no longer the stagecoach stop it was in 1767, but an inn with great Early American charm in a picture-book location overlooking a waterfall and a duck-dotted pond. Be sure to ask for one of the three choicest rooms—the ones that have balconies overlooking the falls. Even if you don't stay here, do have at least one meal—not so much for the food as for the cozy, low-ceilinged dining room filled with antique tools and the deck overlooking the ducks and geese on the pond. It's a perfect choice for Sunday brunch, a generous buffet spread.

The Silvermine section of Norwalk, a pre-Revolutionary township settled beside the Silvermine River, is picturesque country. It emerged as a noted artists' colony when sculptor Solon Borglum set up a studio here in 1895 and other artists soon followed suit. In 1922, a group got together to buy land and an old barn just across from the tavern and formed the Silvermine Guild of Artists. It is both school and gallery, with changing exhibits and a permanent section of original art and handcrafts for sale, many at reasonable prices. Silvermine Guild is also the scene of a summertime chamber music series.

The main part of Norwalk is also quite old, dating to 1649, but other than the village green you wouldn't know it today, since a British assault during the Revolutionary War all but wiped out the town. However, there are a couple of ancient cemeteries remaining for grave-rubbing buffs, one on Gregory Boulevard dating back to 1652.

South Norwalk, a formerly run-down area now known locally as SoNo, has had a facelift that includes brick sidewalks and antique street lamps. Washington Street, the two-block heart of the area, features many interesting shops for browsing, as well as some excellent dining. After dinner, you may want to check the schedule at the SoNo Theater, which features film classics.

The major sightseeing attraction in SoNo is the Maritime Center, located in a restored nineteenth-century factory building on five acres of Norwalk waterfront. This is part aquarium, part giant-screen IMAX Theater, and part Maritime Hall, the latter a lively look at the ecology and maritime history of Long Island Sound, told with hands-on exhibits, electronic games, and displays of classic boats. The aquarium is small in scale but includes some fascinating creatures such as stingrays and sharks, and has unique features such as a video camera that zooms for a close-up of creatures living underwater and a "touch tank" where you can handle starfish and other denizens of the sea. Harbor seals cavort in a tank that allows them to swim indoors or out.

A special pleasure is boarding the museum boat for a 30-minute cruise to serene Sheffield Island, where you can tour a tiny 1868 lighthouse. If you bring a picnic lunch, you can stay a while and enjoy feeling away from it all, then board a later boat back.

Quite a different South Norwalk attraction is the New England Brewing Company, makers of Atlantic Amber and other brands. It is at once a pub, brewery, and mini-brewery museum, where free tours of the brewing process are offered.

Another sightseeing gem in the center of Norwalk is the Lockwood-Mathews Mansion. Legrand Lockwood was a poor boy who lived out the fantasy of becoming rich and returning to show off for the hometown folks. A quarter of a century before the Vanderbilts and Astors began building their opulent "cottages" in Newport, Lockwood came back to his native Norwalk to build a 60-room mansion the likes of which had never been seen in this area. For the then-exorbitant sum of $2 million, he brought in European architects to create sweeping staircases, a three-story skylit octagonal rotunda, frescoes, inlaid woods and marbles, carved cherubs and nymphs, and such revolutionary modern devices as a hot-air furnace, hot and cold running water, and 14 full baths. A children's theater was tucked away under the eaves; wine cellars and two bowling alleys were built in the basement. In 1873 the *New York Sun* pronounced Mr. Lockwood's dream house "perhaps the most perfect and elegant mansion in America."

Though it later came on hard times, the mansion was saved by a group of local preservationists and the restoration became a community project supported by many volunteers and the Norwalk Junior League. It is well on the way back to its former magnificence, and well worth a visit.

Norwalk's final claim to fame is bargain shopping. On West Avenue, not far from the mansion, is Loehmann's, the well-known women's fashion outlet, and farther down the street is Decker's, a haven for men. Gant shirts here sell for half the price at department stores, and there are many other quality labels as well. The side wall is usually stacked with Shetland or cashmere sweaters at excellent prices. Decker's also has women's sweaters and shirts.

Other outlet stores are measly, but the big bargain outlet these days is on East Avenue (Exit 16 off the Connecticut Turnpike, south of the turnpike), where many dealers have come together in one location, with all manner of wares for sale at savings.

Antiquing is another favorite pastime in these parts. Head north on Route 7 beyond the Merritt Parkway and go beyond the newer shopping centers to the road that used to be known as "antique row." Watch on the right for the sign to Cannondale Village, a onetime railroad crossing that has been restored into a shopping complex. Detour on Route 33 for country scenery, and a visit to Ridgefield, a delightful Colonial town with an avant-garde art museum, a Revolutionary War tavern for touring, and some excellent restaurants. It's a good plan to time your arrival to include lunch or dinner.

If chic boutiques are more to your taste than antique shops, you may prefer to make your way to Westport, Norwalk's eastern neighbor on Long Island Sound. It is home to countless advertising and entertainment biggies, and has interesting shops to explore along its two-block Main Street as well as in small complexes running for several miles along U.S. Route 1, known in town as State Street.

Westport lodgings are more expensive, but they are choice. One possibility is a former country club on the Sound, The Inn at Long Shore, now part of a town recreational center with attractive Colonial-decor guest rooms upstairs in the clubhouse and tennis courts and a golf course right outside the door. Or if you want to splurge, the tiny Cotswold Inn, tucked away on a side street near the center of town, is an elegant establishment in gracious Old World style. The newest luxury lodging in town is the Inn at National Hall, an elegant rebirth of a venerable building on the banks of the Saugatuck River near the center of town.

If you don't want to miss out on the beaching most people associate with a summer weekend, you can visit Westport's Sherwood Island, a state park with more than a mile and a half of sandy beach on the Sound and facilities for cookouts and picnicking. Though it shares the pebbles that plague sound beaches, it is one of the best on the Connecticut shore.

Any of the back roads off Route 33 in Westport heading north to the Merritt Parkway will take you into magnificent wooded residential sections that are a sightseeing tour in themselves, and if you want to get a little closer to nature, Westport's Nature Center has wooded trails through a 53-acre sanctuary.

Come evening, Westport has more than its share of fine dining, and this is also the home of one of America's oldest summer theaters, the Westport Country Playhouse, where you'll most likely find the biggest names among the performers out on the summer circuit. And free concerts from jazz to rock to symphony are scheduled almost every summer night at the Levitt Pavilion on the banks of the Saugatuck River near the middle of town.

What with beaching, browsing, and the sophisticated cuisine these wealthy commuter communities enjoy, you're likely to find that your days in Fairfield County will whiz by. Taken together with the Scottish Games and annual Fourth of July fireworks at Norwalk's Calf Pasture Beach, it makes for a sparkling summer weekend.

Area Code: 203

DRIVING DIRECTIONS Norwalk and Westport are reached via I-95, the Connecticut Turnpike, or Route 15, the Merritt Parkway. Norwalk is 160 miles from Boston, 50 miles from New York, and 60 miles from Hartford.

PUBLIC TRANSPORTATION Metro North train service to Norwalk and Westport.

ACCOMMODATIONS *The Inn at Long Shore,* 260 Campo Road South, Westport 06880, 226-3316, $$$ • *Cotswold Inn,* 76 Myrtle Avenue, Westport 06880, 226-3766, $$$$–$$$$$ • *Inn at National Hall,* 2 Post Road West, Westport 06880, 221-1351, $$$$–$$$$$ CP • *Silvermine Tavern,* Silvermine and Perry avenues, Norwalk 06850, 847-4558, $$, CP • *Norwalk Inn,* 99 East Avenue, Norwalk 06851, 838-5531, more motel than inn, but centrally located and reasonable, $–$$ • *Courtyard by Marriott,* 474 Main Avenue, Route 7, Norwalk 06851, 849-9111 or (800) 321-2211, $–$$.

DINING In Westport, trendy restaurants tend to change quickly. Here are those in favor at press time: *Sole E Luna,* 25 Powers Court, Westport, 222-2827, much lauded northern Italian, $$ • *Restaurant Zanghi,* 2 Post Road West, Westport, 221-7572, attractive setting, eclectic and excellent menu, $$ • *Pompano Grill,* 1460 Post Road East, Westport, 259-1160, continental, seafood, and grill specialties, $$–$$$ • *Café Christina,* 1 Main Street, Westport, 221-7950, friendly European café in the old library, $$–$$$ • *Meeting Street Grill,* 1563

Post Road East, Westport, 256-3309, American fare, $$–$$$ • *Da Pietro's,* 36 Riverside Avenue, Westport, 454-1213, northern Italian and country French, $$$ • *Spazzi,* 1229 Post Road, Fairfield, 256-1629, popular and trendy Italian in the town just beyond Westport, $$ • **Old-timers that have stood the test of time in Westport:** *Chez Pierre,* 146 Main Street, Westport, 227-5295, French café, $$$ • *Allen's Clam & Lobster House,* 191 Hills Point Road, Westport, 226-4411, $$–$$$ • *Le Chambord,* 1572 Post Road East, Westport, 255-2654, formal French, $$$–$$$$ • **SoNo choices** (once again, the trendier places tend to change): *Pasta Nostra,* 116 Washington Street, South Norwalk, 854-9700, tiny and usually packed for excellent pasta, $$–$$$ • *La Provence,* 86 Washington Street, South Norwalk, 855-8958, charming French café, $$ • *Amberjack's Coastal Grill,* 99 Washington Street, 853-4332, dining in a former bank, seafood is a specialty, $$ • *Rattlesnake,* 2 South Main Street, 852-1716, southwestern grill, wait till you see the bar—it's shaped like a snake! $–$$ • *New England Brewing Company,* 13 Marshall Street, 866-1339, brewpub and brewing museum, free tours of brewery, $–$$ • **Other Norwalk choices:** *Miche Mache,* 18 South Main Street, Norwalk, 838-8605, much lauded New American, $$ • *Maria's Trattoria,* 172 Main Street, 847-5166, popular Italian café, gets crowded, $–$$ • *Apulia,* 70 North Main Street, 852-1168, southern Italian, same owners as Maria's but less hectic, $–$$ • *Meson Galicia,* 10 Wall Street, 866-8800, attractive café in old trolley barn building, well-prepared Spanish specialties, $$–$$$ • *Silvermine Tavern* (see above), $$–$$$ • **Two Ridgefield winners:** *Stonehenge,* Route 7, Ridgefield, 438-6511, attractive setting, fine dining, $$$, or prix fixe, $$$$$ • *The Inn at Ridgefield,* 20 West Lane, Ridgefield, 438-8282, Colonial decor, nouvelle menu, $$$, or prix-fixe menu, $$$$$.

SIGHTSEEING *Round Hill Scottish Games,* Cranbury Park, Norwalk, 854-7806. Annual event, usually weekend of the Fourth of July, starting at 9 A.M. and continuing all day. Adults, $6; ages 6 to 15, $4. Phone for current dates and information • *Maritime Center of Norwalk,* North Water Street, 852-0700. Hours: daily, 10 A.M. to 5 P.M., to 6 P.M. in summer. Admission for Maritime Hall and Aquarium: adults, $7.50; children, $6.50; IMAX theater, adults, $6; children, $4.50; combination ticket, adults, $11.75; children, $9.50. Boat cruises: phone for schedules, rates • *Lockwood Mathews Mansion Museum,* 295 West Avenue, Norwalk, 838-1434. Hours: March to mid-December, Tuesday to Friday, 11 A.M. to 3 P.M., Sunday, 1 P.M. to 4 P.M.; summer months, also Saturday, 1 P.M. to 4 P.M. Adults, $5; students, $3; under 12, free • *Silvermine Guild of Artists,* 1037 Silvermine Road, New Canaan, 966-5617. Hours: Wednesday to Saturday, 11 A.M. to 5 P.M., Sunday from noon. Donation • *Nature Center for Environmental Activities,* 10 Woodside Lane, Westport, 227-7253. Hours: Monday to

Saturday, 9 A.M. to 5 P.M.; Sunday, 1 P.M. to 4 P.M., closed holidays. Adults, $1; under 14, $0.50 • *Westport Country Playhouse,* 25 Powers Court, Westport, 227-4177. Check current season's offerings • *Levitt Pavilion for the Performing Arts,* Jesup Road, Westport, 226-7600. Phone for current listing of free summer programs.

INFORMATION   Coastal Fairfield County Convention & Visitors Bureau, 297 West Avenue, Norwalk, CT 06850, 854-7825 or (800) 866-7925. Tourism Information Center located at I-95, exits 15S/14N.

Scenery by the Sea in Ogunquit

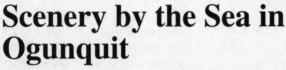

Families love Ogunquit. So do singles, lovers of the opposite and the same sex, photographers, artists, nature seekers, theatergoers, week-enders without cars, teenagers, toddlers, and great-grandparents.

When you see the powdery three-mile stretch of beach curving into a backdrop of rugged cliffs, you'll know instantly why Ogunquit draws such a mélange of fans. The site the Indians called "Beautiful Place by the Sea" is aptly named, and the bountiful beach is a special treasure in Maine, a state whose rockbound coastline yields few such open spaces.

The beach alone explains why Ogunquit has been a popular vacation haven for 100 years, ever since a bridge was built in 1888 across the river that once divided the shore from the town. But Ogunquit has also made the most of its cliffs, topping them with a magnificent winding path called the Marginal Way, which meanders in and out of the bayberries and brush for a scenic mile of strolling, with unparalled views of the crashing sea beyond. It is a walk that never palls no matter how many times it is repeated.

Follow the Marginal Way to its end and you come to another facet of this delightful town. Perkins Cove is a picturesque little harbor that was discovered more than half a century ago by artists and crafts-people. Now the onetime fishermen's shanties are filled with shops, restaurants, and galleries.

The Ogunquit Playhouse on Route 1 is another longtime resident, a mainstay on the summer circuit since 1933. And to further add to Ogunquit's special pleasures, you don't need a car here—in fact, you're almost better off without one, since parking spaces are at a premium and weekend traffic is a pain. Almost everything is walkable, and should your energy flag, all you need do is hop aboard one of the town's old-fashioned trolley buses, which make the rounds from 8:00 A.M. to midnight during the season.

It's hardly a surprise to learn that the beach is busy on weekends, particularly near the most popular entry at Beach Street, where there are snack bars and dressing rooms. Both the footbridge at Ocean Street off U.S. Route 1 north of the village and the Moody Beach Entrance on Ocean Avenue via Bourne Avenue are less congested. Happily, however, if you are willing to walk a bit, no matter where you enter you can still find plenty of space to plant your blanket and sit back to people-watch, a particularly colorful pastime given the mix of beachgoers.

You hardly need an itinerary for Ogunquit. When you've had enough sun (or if the unthinkable happens and it rains), just head down Shore Road to Perkins Cove, checking out the crafts and clothes along the way. Candles, cuddly stuffed animals, custom-designed jewelry, and hand-blown glass are among the varied offerings in the slew of shops in town.

There are many art galleries to choose from, including the Ogunquit Art Association Gallery and the Barn Gallery, which offers concerts, films, and lectures as well as exhibits. The Ogunquit Museum of American Art is exceptional, a handsome building of stone and wood with many windows to bring in the view of the rocky cove and meadows outside, and a lovely sculpture garden and lawns that make the most of the setting. The five galleries include works by Reginald Marsh and Charles Burchfield.

Antiquers will want to visit The Blacksmith's Mall on Main Street (Route 1), which opened in 1994 with over 50 antiques-and-collectibles dealers, while bargain hunters shoulds head to the outlet malls to the north in Wells or to the south in Kittery. Families will enjoy River Lily Farm, where visitors can pick their own fruits, flowers, and vegetables and enjoy hayrides on the farm. And should you have a yen to get out to sea, Finestkind offers lobstering trips, sightseeing cruises, and sailing trips from Perkins Cove.

Where to stay in Ogunquit really depends on your personal preferences and pocketbook, for there's everything from guest house to motel to low-key resorts, all convenient to the beach. On the upscale end of things, Hartwell House has beautifully furnished rooms. Many in the main house have French doors leading to private balconies. The pretty Trellis House is among my favorites of the smaller B & B inns because of the convenient yet quiet location on a lane just off busy Shore Road.

Among the many dining options, Arrows is the current gourmet choice. If you are thinking about Maine lobster, head for the Ogunquit Lobster Pound, where you pick your own dinner to be cooked on the coals outdoors.

You might prefer to be able to visit during the week when the many

Boston families who flock here on Saturday and Sunday have returned home, but somehow Ogunquit is a town that even weekend crowds can't spoil. Walking the expanses of beach or contemplating the waves from the Marginal Way, the rest of the world recedes before the splendor of this "Beautiful Place by the Sea."

Area Code: 207

DRIVING DIRECTIONS   Take I-95 to U.S. Route 1 or simply follow Route 1, which becomes Main Street in Ogunquit. Ogunquit is 70 miles north of Boston, 40 miles south of Portland, 275 miles from New York, and 170 miles from Hartford.

PUBLIC TRANSPORTATION   Air service to Portland, about 30 minutes north of, and Portsmouth, 20 minutes south of Ogunquit. Amtrak serves Wells, which is about 10 minutes north of Ogunquit. During the season, the Coastal Connection—a local bus service—connects Kittery, York, Ogunquit, Wells, Kennebunkport, and Kennebunk; phone 282-5408 for information.

ACCOMMODATIONS   Ogunquit zip codes all 03907. **A few choice picks among dozens are:** *Hartwell House,* 110 Shore Road, Ogunquit, 646-7210, $$$–$$$$ CP; *Trellis House,* 2 Beachmere Place, Ogunquit, 646-7909, $$$ CP; *Puffin Inn,* 233 U.S. Route 1, 646-5496, charming decor, though on busy road—ask for a room facing the rear, $$ CP • *The Morning Dove,* 30 Bourne Lane, 646-3891, 1860s home, gardens, ask for Grandma's Attic, $–$$$ CP • *The Ogunquit House,* 7 King's Highway, 646-2967, restored 1880 schoolhouse, cottages, $$ CP • **Motel-resorts on the water:** *Sparhawk,* Shore Road, 646-5562, tennis, pool, $$$$ CP; *Norseman Motor Inn,* Ogunquit Beach, 646-7024, directly on the beach, $$$–$$$$; *Sea Chambers,* 37 Shore Road, 646-9311, tennis, pool, $$$–$$$$ CP; *The Aspinquid,* Beach Street, 646-7072, motel units and efficiencies, tennis, pool, $$–$$$$$; *Cliff House,* Bald Head Cliff, Shore Road, 646-5124, classic resort recently remodeled, motel-type rooms, spectacular view, but far from town, $$$–$$$$.

DINING   *Arrows,* Berwick Road, Ogunquit, 361-1100, sophisticated cuisine in a 1765 farmhouse, $$$–$$$$ • *Barnacle Billy's,* Perkins Cove, 646-5575, informal, nautical, outdoor deck, $–$$$ • *Hurricane,* Oarweed Lane, Perkins Cove, 646-6348, trendy favorite, $$$ • *Cove Garden,* Shore Road, 646-3509, picturesque setting on the water, Italian menu, $$ • *Jonathan's,* 2 Bourne Lane, 646-4777, gardens, an aquarium, wide-ranging menu, entertainment, popular concerts upstairs,

$–$$ • *Clay Hill Farm*, Agamenticus Road, 361- 2272, gracious country setting (car essential), $$–$$$ • *Poor Richard's Tavern*, Shore Road, 646-4722, country inn decor, New England fare, $$ • *The Old Village Inn*, 30 Main Street, 646-7088, seafood, continental menu, perennial favorite in one of the town's oldest buildings, circa 1833, $$ • *Diane's*, 111 Shore Road, 646-9703, continental, quaint atmosphere, $–$$ • *Ogunquit Lobster Pound*, Route 1, 646-2516, $–$$$ • *Gypsy Sweethearts*, 18 Shore Road, 646-7021, creative dishes, reasonably priced, $$; also known for breakfast, $.

SIGHTSEEING   *The Ogunquit Museum of American Art,* Shore Road at Narrow Cove, 646-4909. Hours: July through September, Monday to Saturday, 10:30 A.M. to 5 P.M., Sunday from 2 P.M. Donation • *Barn Gallery,* Shore Road and Bourne Lane, 646-5370. Hours: June to Columbus Day, Monday to Saturday, 10 A.M. to 5 P.M., Sunday from 2 P.M. Gallery free. Ask for film and concert schedules. • *Finestkind,* Barnacle Billy's Dock, Perkins Cove, 646-5227, variety of cruises, phone for current schedules, rates.

INFORMATION   Ogunquit Chamber of Commerce, Box 2289, Ogunquit, ME 03907, 646-2939. Information Bureau: 646-5533.

On Top of the World at Mt. Washington

The first scientists who set out to measure Mt. Washington back in 1784 calculated that the peak was some 10,000 feet high. They were a wee bit off the mark—the actual height is 6,288 feet—but it's easy to understand their error.

The White Mountains of New Hampshire, the highest in the Northeast, have a majesty beyond their actual measure. Unlike the soft green mountains next door in Vermont, these are rugged granite peaks, stark and grand, and the view from Mt. Washington, the highest of them all, was aptly described by P. T. Barnum as "the second greatest show on earth."

Ever since one Darby Field became the first to climb Mt. Washington back in 1642, adventurers have found the mountain an irresistible lure. Scores of hikers take up the challenge or head for some of the other magnificent trails in the surrounding Presidential Range—Mts. Adams, Jefferson, Monroe, and Eisenhower, to name a few—New England's prime hiking territory. Many hikers stay in the Appalachian

Mountain Club Lodge at Pinkham Notch or take advantage of the club's many guided walks and workshops.

But you needn't be an alpine climber to enjoy the Mt. Washington Valley. Since the first carriage roads were cut through the mountain passes in the early nineteenth century, increasing numbers of people have come every year just to be inspired by the views. Painters such as Thomas Cole and writers like John Greenleaf Whittier were among the early visitors.

These days you can scale the mountain by railway or by car as well as on foot, browse in scores of outlets, and enjoy a number of fine inns—all enhanced by the ever-present mountain views.

When it comes to settings, there are few hotels anywhere to rival the Mt. Washington, built in 1902, with no expense spared to make it one of the nation's premier resorts. Though the hotel has had some financial troubles in recent years, first-time visitors are still awed by the unforgettable image of the giant, gleaming white, twin-towered, red-roofed hotel, set against the mountains like a fairy-tale palace. There are two golf courses with breathtaking mountain views, 12 clay tennis courts, lovely bridle paths, pools, and playgrounds—everything for a well-rounded vacation.

If old-fashioned grandeur is not your style, there are alternatives for almost every taste. Since these mountains are so special, my favorite places are those that let you gaze at them. These lodgings come both grand and modest. The White Mountains Hotel is a new resort but built with a gracious old look, and it has an unbeatable location right at the base of Cathedral Ledge. The vistas from the dining room and the golf course are fantastic. Snowvillage Inn is off by itself on a hilltop. It has the feel of an Alpine resort, serene and informal, and with a grand perspective of the Presidentials. The Darby Field Inn, named for that pioneering climber, is a cozy farmhouse set by itself on Bald Hill, 1,000 feet above the valley.

Outside Jackson, one of the loveliest villages in the area, Nordic Village offers spacious condominiums; ask for the top level for the best views. In the town, on the way to Black Mountain, is Paisley and Parsley, a tastefully decorated bed-and-breakfast home, with picture-book vistas from the picture window.

And then there is Notchland Inn, set by itself at the entrance to Crawford Notch, an old granite-and-timber home with a parlor designed by Gustav Stickley, a founder of the arts and crafts movement. It is nicely renovated with lots of fireplaces and pleasant sitting areas. The owners have horses and a couple of llamas on the extensive grounds, as well as 8,000 feet of Saco River frontage, two prize swimming holes, and a hot tub in a gazebo by the pond.

Some equally appealing but more down-to-earth lodging choices are listed at the end of this chapter.

The first order of business for most Mt. Washington visitors is simply to see the scenery, and Routes 16 and 302, which intersect in North Conway, lead to the best of it.

Wait for the clearest and calmest of days before you head for Mt. Washington itself. Bring along a sweater because the summit tends to be windy and foggy much of the time. In fact, it is said that the highest wind ever recorded, 231 miles per hour, was measured at the weather station here.

The eight-mile auto toll road to the top, reached off Route 16 above Jackson, is the quick way up, with beauty filling every mile as you pass through lush greenery and wildflowers on your way above the timberline to the stark granite peak. You can do it in your own car, with an audio cassette tour that comes with the price of admission, or take a van for a guided tour.

Allow about three hours for the 3½-mile round-trip ride on the steam-powered Cog Railway, the world's first mountain-climbing railway, built in 1869. It takes off from Route 302, east of Twin Mountain, and chugs its way slowly up a right-of-way with plenty of steep grades to take your breath away. If you want an aerial view of things, the gondola at Wildcat Mountain at Pinkham Notch will fill the bill.

Down in the valley, the most dramatic scenery is at the various "notches," the passes between the mountains. A hike, however short, is strongly recommended. You can pick up trail maps and information at the Appalachian Club headquarters on Route 16, Pinkham Notch, and at Crawford Notch State Park headquarters on Route 302, near the Mt. Washington Hotel.

Crawford Notch is where White Mountains tourism began—and according to legend, it is where the Presidentials acquired their names. Soon after the first carriage road went through, the region's most noted climber, innkeeper Ethan Allen Crawford, led a hiking party bearing a barrel of rum to Mt. Washington's bare and windy summit. There, raising their mugs in turn to surrounding peaks, they named the mountains as they toasted America's Presidents. A marker shows the site of Crawford's inn, now vanished along with most of the other big turn-of-the-century wooden hotels.

If you are looking for a picnic spot, Echo Lake State Park near North Conway offers swimming and picnic grounds along with a scenic road to Cathedral Ledge and a panoramic look at the mountains and the Saco River Valley. There are two easy hikes here with rewarding vistas. Diana's Bath is a half-mile path leading along waterfalls. It is reached from the parking area off West Side Road, just north of North Conway. The Black Top path is found at the top of Hurricane Mountain Road, a scenic drive in itself. It is an unde-manding walk along the summit, with wonderful views.

Canoers should note that Saco Bound on Route 302 in Center Conway specializes in canoeing and kayaking and offers rentals as well as lessons and guided canoe and raft trips on the river.

When you are ready for more worldly pursuits, you'll find North Conway a lively center for the region. You can hardly call it unspoiled, but it manages to remain a pleasant town despite a main street that is a mélange of motels, shops, fast-food stops, and restaurants. Art galleries, antiques, a quilt shop, jewelry artisans, Scottish and Irish sweater shops, and clothing boutiques are all part of the eclectic mix.

The east end of town has become nirvana for bargain hunters, with more than 100 manufacturers' outlets. They include Anne Klein, Polo/Ralph Lauren, L.L. Bean, Donna Karan, Liz Claiborne, Patagonia, and Timberland, to drop just a few brand names. People grumble about the traffic jams, but there are savings to be had here, and the shops certainly take care of the problem of what to do on a rainy day. If you pick up a good local map, you'll find that you can avoid some Main Street traffic by taking parallel roads.

The valley is rich in activities as well as scenery in the summer. The Mt. Washington Valley Theater Company offers productions throughout the season in North Conway. The annual Arts Jubilee, usually July 4 through August, brings free concerts and entertainment, and arts-and-crafts shows featuring local crafters are regular events throughout the region.

If the kids are along, you can take them to the water slide at Attitash and to Heritage New Hampshire, a sound-and-light journey depicting everything from a voyage from England in 1690 to a train ride through Crawford Notch in 1910. From Heritage they'll probably beg you into Story Land next door, where there are rides and life-size depictions of children's stories. Neither attraction is cheap, and neither is a must—just a way to keep everyone occupied should you need activities for restless small fry.

A final not-to-be-missed attraction won't cost you a cent. The Kancamagus Highway, Route 112 between Conway and Lincoln, runs for 32 magnificent miles right through the heart of the White Mountain National Forest. Named a National Scenic Byway, it is one of the region's real treasures, created by the U.S. Forest Service to provide both scenery and access to beautiful wilderness through picnic areas and hiking trails. You'll see waterfalls like Lower Falls, Rocky Gorge, and Sabbaday Falls from the road; the small beaches near Lower Falls and the pool above Rocky Gorge are popular swimming places should the day be fine.

If you want to stretch your legs, detour for Champney Falls, a pleasant hour's walk from the trailhead off the highway.

You can take the highway around the mountains to see some of the wonders on the other side, such as Franconia Notch with its famous Flume and the Old Man of the Mountain.

Or maybe just save Kancamagus for a last drive and go home savoring some of the best scenery New England has to offer.

Area Code: 603

DRIVING DIRECTIONS   North Conway, the center of activity in the Mount Washington Valley, is at the intersection of Routes 16 and 302. Coming from the south, take I-93 north to Route 3 east to Route 302 or take I-95 to Route 16 north. From east or west, take Route 302. North Conway is 140 miles from Boston, 350 miles from New York, and 245 miles from Hartford.

PUBLIC TRANSPORTATION   Concord Trailways bus service to Conway and Jackson, air service to Portsmouth (1½ hours) or Manchester (2 hours), New Hampshire, or Portland, Maine, 1½ hours.

ACCOMMODATIONS   For mountain views: *Mt. Washington Hotel,* Bretton Woods 03575, 278-1000 or (800) 258-0330 outside New Hampshire), $$$$–$$$$$ MAP; *White Mountains Hotel and Resort,* at Hale's Location off West Village Road, North Conway 03860, 356-7100 or (800) 533-6301, $$–$$$$; *Snowvillage Inn,* Snowville 03849, 447-2818 or (800) 447-4345, $$–$$$ CP or $$$–$$$$ MAP; *Darby Field Inn,* Bald Hill, Conway 03818, 447-2181 or (800) 426-4147, $$–$$$ CP or $$$–$$$$$ MAP; *Nordic Village,* Route 16, Jackson 03846, 383-9101 or (800) 472-5207, spacious units with kitchens are a good value, ask for higher condo units for best views, $$–$$$$; *Paisley and Parsley,* Box 572, Route 16B, Jackson 03846, 383-0859, $–$$$ CP; *Notchland Inn,* Hart's Location (off Route 302), Bartlett 03812, 374-6131, $$$$ MAP • **Other good choices:** *Stonehurst Manor,* Box 1900, North Conway 03860, 356-3113 or (800) 525-9100, gracious estate, $$–$$$, $$$–$$$$ MAP; *Christmas Farm Inn,* Box 176, Jackson 03846, 383-4313, $$–$$$ or $$$–$$$$ MAP; *Inn at Thorn Hill,* Jackson 03846, 383-4242, gracious home with excellent dining room, $$$$–$$$$$ MAP; *Wentworth Resort Hotel,* Jackson 03846, 383-9700, old-time resort, golf and tennis, recently refurbished, $–$$$ • **Good values:** *Forest Inn,* Route 16A, PO Box 37, Intervale 03845, 356-0772, homey and welcoming inn away from traffic, 25 wooded acres with trails, $–$$ CP; *Buttonwood Inn,* Mt. Surprise Road, PO Box 3297, North Conway 03860, 356-2625, B & B convenient to town but tucked on five private acres, $–$$$ CP • *Cranmore Mt. Lodge,* Kearsage Road, North Conway 03860, 447-2181, modest country inn with modernized barn, pool, tennis, hiking trails, $$ CP, $$$ MAP; *Village House,* PO Box 359, Jackson 03846, 383-6666, comfortable village inn, pool and tennis, many weekend packages, $–$$ CP • **Budget choices:** *Nereledge Inn,* River Road, North Conway 03860, 356-2831, headquarters for rock climbing and fly-fishing instruction, $–$$ CP; *Cranmore Inn,* Kearsage Street, PO Box 1349, North Conway 03860, 356-5502, pool, walking distance to town, $–$$ CP • **Away from it all:** *Philbrook Farm Inn,* North Road, Shelburne 03581, 466-3831, old-fashioned farm setting, hiking, swimming, riding, $$$ MAP; *Stafford's in the Field Inn,* Chocorua 03817, 323-7766, simple farm ambience, sophisticated fare, $$$$–$$$$$ MAP • For more small inns, write for the pamphlet "Country Inns in the White Mountains," P.O. Box 2025, North Conway, NH 03860, 356-9460 or (800) 562-1300.

DINING *The 1785 Inn,* Route 16, North Conway, 356-9025, exceptional food and setting, $$–$$$ • *The Bernerhof,* Route 302, Glen, 383-4414, excellent Swiss fare, $$–$$$ • *Inn at Thorn Hill* (see above), prix fixe, $$$$ • *Dana Place Inn,* Route 16, Jackson, 383-6822, sophisticated menu, $$–$$$ • *Thompson House Eatery* (T.H.E.), Routes 16 and 16A, Jackson, 383-9341, farmhouse setting, inventive menu, $–$$ • *Wildcat Inn & Tavern,* Jackson Village, 383-4245, rustic charm, good food and prices, $–$$ • *Christmas Farm Inn* (see above), American menu, $$ • *Darby Field Inn* (see above), continental menu, $$–$$$ • *Mt. Washington Hotel* (see above), prix fixe, $$$$$ • *Ledges,* White Mountains Hotel (see above), good value, great views, $$ • *Scottish Lion,* U.S. 302, North Conway, 356-6381, Scottish decor, English-Scottish specialties, $–$$ • *Stonehurst Manor* (see above), pasta to paella, $–$$$ • *Notchland Inn* (see above), prix-fixe five-course dinners, $$$ • *Stafford's in the Field Inn* (see above), take a country drive for a legendary dinner, reservations essential, prix fixe, $$$. Lively informal dining: *Horsefeathers,* Main Street, North Conway, 356-2687, $–$$; *Red Parka Pub,* Route 302, Glen, 383-4344, $–$$.

SIGHTSEEING *Appalachian Mountain Club* (AMC), Pinkham Notch Camp, 466-2727, evening programs, workshops, guided hikes. Call for current schedules • *Mt. Washington Cog Railway,* Route 302, Twin Mountain, 846-5404 or (800) 922-8825. Hours: late July to Labor Day, hourly, 8:00 A.M. to 4 P.M.; late June to late July, daily 9 A.M. to 4 P.M., September to early October, 9 A.M. to 2 P.M.; early May to late June, runs as needed, hours may vary, so best to check; reservations advised. Adults, $35; children, $24 • *Mt. Washington Auto Road,* Route 16, Pinkham Notch, 466-3988. Hours: mid-May to late October, daily, 7:30 A.M. to 6 P.M., weather permitting. Car and driver, $14; each additional adult passenger, $5; children, $3; under 5, free; guided tour, adults, $17, children, $10 • *Wildcat Mountain Gondola,* Route 16, Pinkham Notch, Jackson, 466-3326. Hours: July 4 to Columbus Day, daily, 10 A.M. to 4:15 P.M.; late May to July 4, weekends only. Adults, single ride, $8; children, $4 • *Attitash Alpine Slide,* Route 302, Bartlett, 374-2368. Hours: daily in summer, 10 A.M. to 6 P.M.; early June and September to mid-October, weekends, 10 A.M. to 5 P.M. Rides, $6; ages 6 to 12, $4 • *Heritage New Hampshire,* Route 16, Glen, 378-9776. Hours: May to mid-October, daily, 9 A.M. to 6 P.M.;

mid-May to mid-June and Labor Day to mid-October, 9 A.M. to 5 P.M. Adults, $7.50; ages 8 to 12, $4.50 • *Story Land,* Route 16, Glen, 383-4293. Hours: mid-June to Labor Day, daily, 9 A.M. to 6 P.M.; September through Columbus Day, weekends only, 10 A.M. to 5 P.M. $14 admission for all.

INFORMATION   Mt. Washington Valley Chamber of Commerce, Route 16, PO Box 2300, North Conway, NH 03860, 356-5701 or (800) 367-3364. The Chamber of Commerce offers free room reservation service.

Looking for the Real York

Pick your favorite York—historic village, beach resort, yachting port, or rocky Maine peninsula.

Until a few years ago, each one was a separate village, known respectively as York Village, York Beach, York Harbor, and Cape Neddick. Though officially they've been combined into a single community, it is still commonly called "The Yorks," plural because each part has such a distinct personality. Together, they offer a mini-sampler of the Maine coast.

For history buffs, York Village is the chief lure. The onetime Indian settlement of Agamenticus has the distinction of being not only the oldest surviving English settlement in Maine, dating back to 1624, but America's first chartered city, established in 1642. Its name at that time was Gorgeana, after Sir Ferdinando Gorges, an English soldier and mariner who was then proprietor of the Province of Maine.

It was given the name York and reduced to mere township when it was seized by Massachusetts along with the whole Province of Maine in 1652. In spite of frequent Indian attacks threatening its existence in the 1600s, York survived and by the eighteenth century had become a prosperous provincial capital and an important way station between Portsmouth and points east. Its wharves and warehouses bustled with treasures from the lucrative West Indies trade.

One of the warehouses on the York River was owned by John Hancock, the well-known signer of the Declaration of Independence. It has been restored and is now maintained by the Society for the Preservation of Historic Landmarks as a museum displaying tools of Colonial times as well as ship models and other relics of York's seafaring days.

As York diminished in commercial importance, it gained new prominence late in the nineteenth century as a seaside resort. Many wealthy easterners, including one Samuel Clemens (better known as Mark

Twain), bought up the fine Colonial residences of the village as summer homes. A number of the historic houses in town never changed hands, however, and even today are still occupied by descendants of their builders, making York Village something of a living museum with an unusual sense of its past and a determination to preserve it.

More than half a dozen buildings in the village now comprise Historic York and are open to the public. One of most fascinating is the 1719 Old Gaol, one of the oldest remaining public buildings in the country. Stone dungeons with walls three feet thick and separate cells for criminals, women lawbreakers, and debtors were actually part of the gaoler's home. Kids love poking through the cells and peeking through the window in the children's bedroom, where the prisoners were passed their meals. Almost everyone poses outside in the pillory, sticking head and arms through the openings where minor offenders were held in public view as punishment for their misdeeds.

Another interesting stop is the 1742 Emerson-Wilcox House, which has served as home, tavern, and post office over its long history. Now it offers period rooms, a chimney passage, and some exquisite eighteenth-century crewel bed hangings.

Other stops with tales of the past to tell are the 1745 Old Schoolhouse, where children learned navigation, bookkeeping, and surveying along with their three Rs; and Jefferd's Tavern, where weary stagecoach passengers found refreshments after their dusty ride in the late 1700s. The tavern is now the visitor center for the Old York Historical Society.

Over the course of the summer you can see all kinds of Colonial crafts demonstrations in Historic York's properties, including the making of candles, clothing, soap, cheese, and natural dyes. Fishermen's crafts such as net tying and crafting lobster traps are shown at the Hancock Wharf, and demonstrations of cooking on the open hearth are given.

The town walking tour will take you to all of these attractions and more—the restored Elizabeth Perkins House, the Old Burying Ground, the green, handsome private homes, and a couple of fine New England churches. Stop at the town information booth on Route 1 for the walking-tour pamphlet and summer schedule of special events.

Route 1 also has a couple of interesting shopping stops, such as the York Antiques Gallery, where many dealers display their wares, and the Woods to Goods store, a unique outlet for carved ships, toys, and frames made by inmates in Maine prisons—some very fine work sold at reasonable prices.

If York Village has the monopoly on local history, Nubble Light on Cape Neddick takes the prize for scenery. From the south, follow Route 1A past Long Sands Beach to Nubble Road; from the north take Route 1A to Broadway to reach the lighthouse that is one of Maine's most photographed landmarks. You'll understand why when you see its site—a spectacular rocky promontory over the sea—which epitomizes this coast's special character.

Continuing on Route 1A north past Short Sands beach, you'll find Cape Neddick harbor, fed by York's second river, the Cape Neddick. The small beach at the river's mouth is sheltered, a good place for small children or picnickers.

York Beach, with its two main town beaches, is most likely to appeal if you like a lot of action and people around, or perhaps if you have children, especially teenagers. The town of York Beach is filled with tourist shops, food stands, and an amusement park. It won't appeal to all tastes, but it does offer the advantage of varied activities within walking distance of lodgings, so it's easy for you and your teens to go off in different directions.

There are lots of reasonably priced Victorian rooming houses in this area, and a growing number of attractive bed-and-breakfast homes throughout the villages, but the choicest lodgings in York are in the remaining section, York Harbor.

This is boating territory, and the picturesque harbor is filled with crafts of all kinds, from sleek yachts to fishermen's dories. The inns make the most of the scene. At Dockside Guest Quarters, you can sit on the porch and watch skippers navigating around the tricky 90-degree turn where the York River comes into the sea. The Maine House here dates from the late 1800s and retains the flavor of a sea captain's home, filled with model sailboats, paintings of clipper ships, and scrimshaw, and with bookcases lined with books on lighthouses and sailing. Five rooms are in the house, the rest in pine cottages along the shore, done in rustic-nautical decor.

Edwards' Harborside Inn has a sunporch overlooking the harbor, where you can see the lobster boats setting out; and Stage Neck Inn, on a spit at the entrance to the harbor, is surrounded by water on all sides. The latter is a full-scale resort with tennis, boating, and an 18-hole golf course. York Harbor Inn lacks the direct water view, but makes up for it with a lot of Early American charm. The best news is that all these inns are reasonably priced by today's standards.

York Harbor has its own beach, pebbly but more peaceful than the others. It's here that you'll find the start of a mile-long cliff walk beside the sea that is one of the most pleasant strolls to be found anywhere on the coast. Go to the beach end of Harbor Beach Road, on the left just after a weathered building that is part of a private swim club, and left again along a boardwalk parallel to the beach for the beginning of this path hugging the shore. There are outcroppings of rock to scramble on, and a magnificent view of the waves spewing foam against the cliff on one side, with wildflowers, evergreens, and handsome seaside homes on the other, and the muted sounds of the buoy bell in the distance.

Eventually the path ends at a rocky beach just short of Cow Beach Point. You can head back here or pick your way onward until you reach a sheltered rocky beach adjacent to Norwood Farms Road, which leads back to Route 1A.

What with beach and boats and all the Yorks to explore, you may not need further activities; but if you have a long weekend, there's a lot to see and do just south of York in Kittery and then just over the bridge in Portsmouth, New Hampshire, only 12 miles away.

Kittery's Fort Clary State Memorial, with its restored hexagonal blockhouse and view across to Nubble Light, is high on the list. The Kittery Naval Museum and a number of historic homes are also of interest in this once-wealthy shipbuilding town, including the exquisite Lady Pepperell House and John Bray House, the oldest dwelling in Maine. Kittery's current big attraction is a slew of outlet stores for bargain shoppers—they stretch for miles along Route 1.

Portsmouth deserves at least half a day for Strawbery Banke, an outdoor museum of 30 buildings representing Early American life in a seacoast village. Some of the buildings are fully restored and furnished; others hold exhibits.

Unlike other restorations that re-create only the early settlement, this village portrays.life as it has changed over the years, a fascinating approach. The Drisco House, for example, is furnished on one side as it might have looked in 1790, on the other as it would have been in the 1950s. Furnishings in other homes range from the 1770s to 1908. The newest addition opened in 1994, the Abbott Corner Store and Kitchen, revives the 1940s, including the ration stamps needed to buy products during World War II, which probably seems like ancient history to the schoolchildren touring the complex. This village from the past also ties itself firmly to the present by giving working space to contemporary craftspeople in some of its historic houses.

Other interesting exhibits reveal the construction techniques of the eighteenth century, and the architectural analysis that goes in the process of restoration.

There are many more fine homes to be seen in Portsmouth, one of them the former residence of naval hero John Paul Jones, and a wealth of interesting shops to explore. Portsmouth harbor cruises and outings aboard the *Viking Sun* to the Isle of Shoals and Star Island are also highly recommended. There are nightly dinner cruises, too, and weekend evening cruises with dancing and entertainment.

None of these will ease the task of selecting your favorite York—but they may just add to your conclusion that Maine's southernmost coastal resort has multiple reasons for a visit.

Area Code: 207

DRIVING DIRECTIONS   York is on Route 1A, off U.S. Route 1 on the southern coast of Maine; take the York exit of I-95, the Maine Turnpike. It is 62 miles from Boston, 267 miles from New York, and 157 miles from Hartford.

PUBLIC TRANSPORTATION Air and Greyhound bus service to nearby Portsmouth, New Hampshire. Limousine service is available from Boston and Portland airports.

ACCOMMODATIONS Note that most lodgings are closed in winter. *Dockside Guest Quarters,* PO Box 205, York Harbor 03909, 363-2868, $$ CP • *Edwards' Harborside Inn,* Stage Neck Road, PO Box 866, York Harbor 03911, 363-3037, $$–$$$ CP • *York Harbor Inn,* Route 1A, PO Box 574, York Harbor 03911, 363-5119 or (800) 343-3869, $$–$$$ CP • *Stage Neck Inn,* PO Box 97, York Harbor 03911, 363-3850 or (800) 222-3238, $$$–$$$$ • *Hutchins House,* 209 Organug Road, York 03909, 363-3058, lovely home with exceptional location on the York River, open weekends only, $$ CP • *Riverbank Cottage,* 11 Harmon Park Road, York Harbor 03911, 363-8333, charm, quiet location, harbor views, $–$$ CP • *Canterbury House,* Route 1A, York Harbor 03911, 363-3505, Victorian home overlooking the harbor, choice of continental breakfast, $–$$, or full breakfast, $–$$$ • *Bell Buoy,* 570 York Street, Route 1A, York Harbor, 03911, 363-7164, pleasant Victorian in a quiet setting, $$ CP • *Willows Inn,* Long Beach Avenue, York Beach 03910, 363-8800, Victorian home on the beach, $$–$$$ CP • Many more unpretentious, moderately priced Victorian guest houses are lined up across from the beach, on Long Beach Avenue; ask the Chamber of Commerce for complete list.

DINING *Cape Neddick Inn and Gallery,* Route 1, Cape Neddick, 363-2899 a best bet, $$–$$$ • *Dockside Dining Room* (see above), $–$$ • *York Harbor Inn* (see above), ocean views, $$–$$$ • *Lighthouse Restaurant,* Nubble Road, 363-4054, unbeatable location, seafood with panoramic views, $–$$$ • *One Fish, Two Fish,* Route 1, York Corner, 363-8196, simple decor, good fresh seafood, $$ • *Chef Mimmo's,* Route 1A, York Beach, 363-3807, very good Italian food in an unlikely location—the middle of the action at York Beach, crowded, $$ • *Fazio's,* 38 Woodbridge Road, York, 363-1718, locally recommended Italian, $–$$; also connected to La Stella pizzeria, $ • **For lobster lovers:** *Cape Neddick Lobster Pound,* Route 1A, 363-5471, $–$$; *Bill Foster's Down East Lobster & Clambake,* Axholme Road off Route 1A, 363-3255, lobster pound and fish market, $$. Also see Portsmouth, page 243.

SIGHTSEEING *Old York:* Old York Historical Society, 140 Lindsay Road, PO Box 312, Dept. B, York, 363-4974. Buildings open mid-June to September, Tuesday to Saturday, 10 A.M. to 5 P.M. Tours from Jefferd's Tavern, off Route 1A facing the Old Burying Ground. Combined admission: Adults, $6; ages 6 to 16, $2.50; family rate, $16. Individual admissions available, $1 and $2.

INFORMATION The York Chamber of Commerce, Box 417, York, ME 03909, 363-4422.

Away from It All on Block Island

It's more than the 12-mile distance to the mainland that separates Block Island from the rest of the world. Block Island is a trip to yesterday.

Despite the ferry boats that bring more visitors every year, this exquisite island somehow manages to retain its wild beauty and the look and serenity of a time long gone by.

Around every bend, flower-splashed meadows and pond-dotted moors come into view, open and inviting, with little but criss-crossing stone fences and an occasional weathered clapboard home to show that anyone has been there before you.

The beaches bend for miles around the edges of the island: some of them easily accessible, some reached only by narrow sandy paths descending down bluffs as much as 200 feet above the ocean. The tallest of the cliffs, known as Mohegan Bluffs, is as spectacular a sight from below as from the top, where you can see forever out to sea.

Bicycles outnumber cars 100 to 1 here, adding to the tranquility. The islanders were so upset by the recent intrusion of mopeds that they threatened to secede from Rhode Island if a law was not passed banning the hated motorbikes from their quiet lanes. At present there is a compromise, with mopeds not allowed on dirt roads.

Though some of the old Victorian hotels have been spruced up in recent years, there's been no attempt to build resorts or amusements on Block Island, so the visitors who board the ferry boats from Rhode Island, Connecticut, and Long Island are precisely those who want to get away from all that. Even a weekend visit is enough to leave you refreshed, better able to cope with the pressures of the real world when you get back.

Most of the boats arrive at the pier in Old Harbor opposite a row of century-old, gingerbread-trimmed Victorian hotels now listed on the National Register of Historic Places. The most impressive is the spanking white National Hotel, meticulously restored to its original 1888 lines and resplendent with its dark green shutters, shiny black mansard roof, and elaborate cupola.

Lodgings on Block Island fall into two basic categories, the big wooden hotels that have been here for 100 years or more, and the newer, more intimate inns. Though some of the old hotels have refurbished their rooms, few Block Island lodgings are fancy places by mainland standards, and most island lovers like it just that way.

For faraway views, you'll want to climb the hill up Spring Street to the Spring House, or the neat and trim 1661 Inn, where a seat on the porch or the deck can keep you mesmerized for hours—gazing at that deep and unbelievably blue sea. The rooms here vary from tiny to enormous, with the bigger and costlier ones offering private decks. The Sea Breeze next door is also a prime little complex, cozy, recently redecorated, and with its own fine water views. The Atlantic Inn, not far away on High Street, is another old-time landmark offering ocean vistas.

Several attractive bed-and-breakfast inns have opened in recent years for those who prefer a bit of cozy country decor. Rose Farm Inn and the Old Town Inn are among the nicest. The Blue Dory in town has the most stylish furnishings.

To get your bearings on a first visit, you'll want to circle the island, not too difficult a task since it is only seven miles long and three miles wide. There are a dozen taxis that will gladly take you around if you've wisely left your car on shore, and bike shops all over the place will equip you to pedal your own path, poking down those tempting side roads as you ride to the beach. It's easy to get by on foot as well, especially with the beaches as tempting rest stops all along the way. Nature enthusiasts may want to join guided tours on summer weekends sponsored by the Rhode Island Department of Environmental Management, or the weekday tours led by the Block Island Conservancy. Check with the Chamber of Commerce for current schedules.

The island is shaped like a lamb chop, with Old Harbor situated just where the meatiest portion might begin. Heading north you'll come to Crescent Beach, which is really a whole string of beaches along the Atlantic Ocean, with the dunes growing steeper as you proceed farther north. Fred Benson Beach is the most crowded, since it has changing facilities and a lifeguard, but all it takes is a walk to find space to yourself.

The island is almost bisected at this point by the Great Salt Pond, with New Harbor sitting at the pond's most sheltered inland spot. Here's where the sailors and yachtsmen drop anchor at nearby marinas.

Continuing on the main (and only) roadway, Corn Neck Road, you'll come to Sandy Point with its historic 1867 granite lighthouse in the dunes and a Wildlife Sanctuary that is a favorite spring nesting ground for seagulls as well as one of the prime destinations for bird watchers on the East Coast. The North Light lighthouse has been restored and opened in 1993 as a museum.

Corn Neck Road was named for the crop grown there by the Narragansett Indians, Block Island's original inhabitants, who called their home "Isle of the Little God." They were spotted in 1524 by Giovanni da Verrazano, then in 1624 by Adrian Block, the Dutchman for whom the island was named. He was probably the first but by no means the last to sail over by yacht from Long Island.

Settler's Rock at Sandy Point marks the arrival of the English, who created the first real colony. Block Island abounds with legends of shipwrecks and tales of ghosts and eerie lights, passed on by generations of seafaring residents.

Sandy Point and its environs are flat. As you turn back toward the south past Old Harbor, the hills begin, and the dips and turns on Spring Street, Southeast Light Road, and the Mohegan Trail yield glorious views on all sides. It's at the southernmost end that you'll find the dramatic view from Mohegan Bluffs and the Southeast Light, a quaint brick building that has stood as a beacon to sailors for over 100 years. It had to be moved some 240 feet back recently to keep it safe from the eroding bluffs.

Stairs in the seagrass make it easy to descend to the rocky beaches below to gaze back at the bluffs and perhaps find a suitable perch on sand or rocks for basking on the beach.

The main road here cuts back inland past Rodman's Hollow, another of the island's five wildlife refuges, a great natural ravine left by a long-ago glacier. Once again, many paths wind through the meadows and marshes to the sea.

Once you've found your favorite spots, you'll likely want to spend most of your time occupying them and enjoying the beauty around you. If you want more activity, you can rent a sailboat at the Block Island Club or charter a fishing boat at Old Harbor dock.

Shopping is not a major occupation on Block Island, but there are some worthwhile stops in Old Harbor. They start right on Water Street, across from the docks. The Star Department Store is Block Island's general store, with everything from beach umbrellas to clothing. Around the corner on Dodge Street at the Sea Breeze Gallery are some appealing photos and drawings of Block Island, along with paintings and ceramics. Nearby on Dodge are several nice little stores, including Pottery by the Sea and Water Colors for fine arts and crafts. Spring Street Gallery is a special stop, a cooperative showing art, jewelry, stained glass, and quilts by local artists.

When the sun begins to set, one of the best views in town is off the deck at The Oar at Block Island Boat Basin on New Harbor. For dining, there is no shortage of places to enjoy Block Island swordfish, bluefish, and the other fresh seafood that is a specialty at this fisherman's paradise. If you want evening action, go to Ballard's, a boatman's hangout that is by far the noisiest and most popular place around. The music here is strictly '40s and '50s; younger action is at McGovern's Yellow Kittens, where there are live bands on weekends.

For an island souvenir, you might think of having Finn's Fish Market in Old Harbor pack up fresh fish or lobster for your trip home.

It may prove some small consolation for having to leave this extraordinary getaway at sea.

Area Code: 401

TRANSPORTATION Block Island is 45 minutes by ferryboat from Port Judith on the Rhode Island Shore, two hours from New London, Connecticut, and about two hours from Montauk on Long Island. There are also boats from Providence, stopping at Newport on the way, a four-hour ride. For schedules and rates, contact Nelesco Navigation, Box 482, New London, CT 06320, or Interstate Navigation Company, Galilee State Pier, Point Judith, RI 02882, both reached at (401) 783-4613. Bonanza buses from Providence connect to local bus service in Galilee. Amtrak trains stop at Westerly, Rhode Island, where there is air service via New England Airlines—a 12-minute flight, 596-2460 or (800) 243-2460. There are also flights from New London and the New York area on Action Airlines (203) 448-1646 or (800) 243-8623.

ACCOMMODATIONS Expect minimum-stay requirements in season; all Block Island addresses are zip code 02807. Unless indicated, all lodgings are in Old Harbor. **The hotel old-timers:** *Spring House,* Spring Street, 466-5844, refurbished rooms, $$$$–$$$$$ CP; *Atlantic Inn,* High Street, 466-2006, tennis and croquet courts, room 22 on top is prime; $$$–$$$$ CP; *National Hotel,* Water Street, 466-2901 or (800) 255-2449, $$$$ • **Inns and guest houses:** *1661 Inn,* Spring Street, 446-2421, huge buffet breakfast and cocktails served on deck overlooking the water, $$$$–$$$$$ CP; rooms with shared baths, $$–$$$; *Manisses House,* Spring Street, 466-2421, same owners as 1661 Inn, elegant small restored hotel, but no views, $$$$–$$$$$ CP; *Sea Breeze Inn,* Spring Street, 466-2275, small complex with a variety of rooms, some with smashing views, $$–$$$$ CP; *Rose Farm Inn,* off High Street, Box E, 466-2021, big rooms, pretty decor in a Victorian farmhouse or the new Captain Rose House, $$–$$$$ CP; *Blue Dory,* Dodge Street, 466-2254, tiny, elegant, antiques, water views, walking distance to town, $$$–$$$$ CP; *Old Town Inn,* Old Town Road, PO Box 351, 466-5958, spacious and gracious, midway between Old and New Harbor, long hike but easy bike, $$–$$$ CP; *Sheffield House,* High Street, 466-2494, pleasant modest guest house, $$–$$$$ CP; *Hardy Smith House,* PO Box 872, 466-2466, another welcoming guest house, $$–$$$ CP; *The Adrian,* Old Town Road, 466-2693, comfortable home, nice deck and lawn, $$–$$$$ CP; *Barrington Inn,* Beach and Ocean avenues, New Harbor, 466-5510, high on a knoll with wonderful views, $$–$$$ CP; *Gables Inn and Gables II,* Dodge Street, 466-2213, modest, old-fashioned guest houses near town, $$.

DINING   *Manisses House* (see above), attractive dining room with continental menu, $$–$$$ • *Dead Eye Dick's,* New Harbor, 466-2654, lively, waterfront deck, $$–$$$$ • *Winfield's,* Corn Neck Road, Old Harbor, 466-5856, intimate, special, $$–$$$ • *Atlantic Inn* (see above), excellent seafood, $$–$$$ • *Spring House* (see above), all-you-can-eat barbecue buffet lunch is a bargain, $, dinner, $$–$$$ • *Harborside Inn,* Water Street, Old Harbor, 466-5504, harbor view from the porch, $$–$$$ • *Mohegan Café,* Water Street, Old Harbor, 466-5911, nautical decor, popular for both lunch, $, and dinner, $$ • *Ballards,* Old Harbor, 466-2231, a madhouse, but the best lobster prices in town, $–$$$ • *Finn's Seafood,* on the piers near Ballards, Old Harbor, 466-2473, informal, attached to fish market, best bet on the island for simply prepared fish at reasonable prices, $–$$.

INFORMATION   Block Island Chamber of Commerce, Drawer D, Block Island, RI 02897, 466-2982.

High Notes Near Mt. Monadnock

They call it the "Quiet Corner" of the state, a world of apple orchards, covered bridges, mountain views, and tiny towns untouched by time.

But come summer each year, New Hampshire's southwestern Monadnock region comes alive with music. You can follow the melody from town to town—Schubert in Pine Hill tonight, Haydn at Jaffrey tomorrow, Mozart in Hancock the day after.

In all, more than 30 concerts are held in the hamlets and villages in this green and rolling region during the annual six-week festival known as Monadnock Music. The major concerts are on Fridays and Saturdays at the Pine Hill School's Waldorf Auditorium in Wilton, with recitals scheduled also on Sundays at the Old Meeting House in Jaffrey, and admission is charged. In addition, free concerts are held, moving from white-spired village church to meeting house in different small-town locales throughout the season, a perfect way to get acquainted with one of New England's least spoiled regions.

And these are just the beginning of the music. In 1992 the New England Marionette Opera debuted in their own specially constructed theater in Peterborough. Inspired by the famous Salzburg Marionettes, this delightful company presents classics from *Madame Butterfly* to *Porgy and Bess* performed to recorded music by lifelike, beautifully costumed 32-inch marionettes. There are special performances geared to children. The season extends into December, with special Christmas performances of operas such as *Amahl and the Night Visitors.*

There's something for every taste. The Apple Hill Chamber Players, artists-in-residence at Keene State College, perform in the Louise Shonk Keely barn in Nelson during the summer, and almost every town has a local band that struts its stuff with concerts on the greens. The Folkway in Peterborough is known as a center for folk music.

Besides this tuneful array, there is long-established summer theater in the area. The Peterborough Players have performed classics for over 50 years in a converted barn, and the American Stage Festival in Milford has been around since 1972. The Arts Center at Brickyard Pond at Keene State College also offers a variety of dance, music, and theater throughout the year.

The wonder is that the region remains relatively uncrowded, especially since Mt. Monadnock, the peak that Ralph Waldo Emerson called "the New Olympus," is, according to state authorities, the most-climbed mountain in the United States. A conservative estimate puts the number at 125,000 each year.

Part of the reason is that an ascent to the 3,165-foot summit is an accomplishment within reach of even novice hikers, who can then enjoy the soaring view of five states that is worthy of a far loftier peak. On a really clear day, the White Mountains to the north, the Green Mountains to the west, and the tops of Boston skyscrapers to the east are all in sight.

The view of the mountain from below can be equally impressive, for again it looms majestically out of all proportion to its size, visible from almost every town in the region. In the late nineteenth century, it attracted writers such as Emerson, Hawthorne, and Thoreau, who spent their summers here within sight of the inspiring peak. In the twentieth century many of America's most famous writers, artists, and composers also come here to be inspired at the MacDowell Colony, the famous retreat on a 450-acre estate in Peterborough.

With all the music and theater in the area, the only problem you'll have filling your evenings in the Monadnock region is choosing among the many offerings.

By day the options are equally tempting. If you're at all active, you'll want to head for Mt. Monadnock. Stop at the State Park Visitor Center in Jaffrey Center to pick up a trail map, and get some first-hand hiking pointers from the helpful staff members. There are 40 miles of trails and paths from one to ten miles long, for every ability level. A two-hour walk will take an average hiker to the top.

Don't miss the early-to-mid-July riot of color at Rhododendron State Park in Fitzwilliam. There are some 16 acres of the showy wild shrubs. The park offers a walking path around the entire glen, plus picnic grounds in shaded pine groves—and, of course, more of those ever-present views of Mt. Monadnock.

If you want to remain outdoors, there are many more parks to explore, and a number of local swimming holes. Among the highlights of the parks are the auto road to the summit of Pack Monadnock Mountain in Miller State Park in Peterborough, and the swimming area on Otter Lake in Greenfield State Park. A particularly lovely three-quarter-mile wilderness loop trail winds along a deep glacial stream in Chesterfield Gorge State Park in Chesterfield.

There are also lakes and rivers for canoeing or sailing, and with the necessary state fishing license, this is good country for anglers. Just stop at the Peterborough Information Center or ask—wherever you are staying—for directions to the nearest water. And this is excellent golfing territory, with four public 18-hole golf courses available in Francestown, Hillsboro, Jaffrey, and Keene. Those who want to be at the first tee bright and early can stay at Tory Pines Resort in Francestown, which is built around a golf course.

If indoor diversions such as antiques and art galleries are more to your taste, you'll still not lack for choices. The best plan is to make a tour of the pretty little towns to see what each has to offer.

Peterborough is a handsome hub that is attracting many as permanent residents. The Nubanusit River runs through the pic-turesque center. The enormous granite slabs used to build the structures on Grove and Main Street in 1847 have caused this to be dubbed the "Granite Block." Further on Grove, the Georgian red-brick buildings with photogenic white cupolas were built in this century, designed to complement the old. The Peterborough Library was the first free tax-supported public library in the country.

There are some intriguing small shops and galleries in town for browsing, and the North Gallery at Tewksbury, at the junction of Routes 101 and 123, has a nice selection of gifts and crafts. Another interesting stop is Vose Farm Road just off Route 202 north of town, where there are outlet stores for two companies headquartered in Peterborough: Brookstone, the catalog people with all those intriguing tools, and Eastern Mountain Sports, for outdoor wear.

Fitzwilliam is classic old New England, with a block-long green lined with fine white Colonial homes; it offers a trio of antique shops. In picture-postcard Hancock is The Barn, which is filled with furniture, crafts, and paintings by local artists.

Francestown, another front-runner in the local town beauty derby, has more antiques in its small town center, and flea market enthusiasts can treasure-hunt to their hearts' content at the event held regularly on weekends at the Cheshire Fairgrounds on Route 12 in Swanzey.

Keene does not qualify as quaint, but it does offer good shopping at the Colony Mill Marketplace, where Country Artisans Gallery showcases work by 300 craftsmakers and an antiques center includes over 100 dealers. You can see fine work from throughout New England at the Thorne-Sagendorph Art Gallery at Keene State College.

Back in the country, the Sharon Arts Center features top exhibits of art and crafts, as well as classes and a shop of fine crafts. Bacon's Sugar House in Jaffrey Center is one of several places to find locally produced maple syrup.

If you're still searching for more to do, just about every little town has its own sights or historic house museum. Dublin is notable as the home of *Yankee* magazine and of Friendly Farm, a place where youngsters can pet tame farm animals and see eggs being hatched. Some of the best views of the mountains are found on Route 101 through Dublin as the road curves around Dublin Lake and the mountain rises behind to the west.

Both Hancock and Milford boast Paul Revere bells in local steeples. The Hancock church is reputed to be the most photographed in New England.

Harrisville is one of the most perfectly preserved New England mill towns; the red-brick buildings around a group of ponds spilling into a waterfall attract both photographers and artists. A notable home for President watchers is the restored Franklin Pierce Homestead in Hillsboro. Or you can check out the local covered bridges. Swanzey is the covered bridge capital, with seven bridges within a five-mile area.

One final place you may want to see is Cathedral of the Pines in Rindge, an outdoor shrine with a panoramic view and an altar honoring American war dead.

Except for Keene, a small city, all the towns in the Monadnock region are small and little touched by time, and you'll hardly go wrong wherever you roam.

Nor are you likely to go wrong picking among the small country inns in the area. The Colonial John Hancock Inn is cozy and historic. The Amos A. Parker House is a charmer that does justice to its pretty hometown of Fitzwilliam, and the Hannah Davis House down the road is another beautifully restored village home. The Benjamin Prescott Inn is a historic house in the country, with antiques and lots of nooks and crannies for exploring, and the Apple Gate is a welcoming small 1832 Colonial in the countryside, convenient to both Peterborough and the Sharon Arts Center.

For vistas, the Inn at Crotched Mountain is the unquestioned winner, and you'll know why as soon as you drive up the long hill and see the 40-mile view. There is one hazard, however: Once you settle beside the pool with that scene before you, you may never be able to tear yourself away.

Area Code: 603

DRIVING DIRECTIONS The Monadnock region is in the southwestern corner of New Hampshire. It can be reached from the west via

I-91, taking the Route 119 exit to Hinsdale and on to Fitzwilliam, from the north off I-89 to Route 202; from the south via Route 2 to Route 202, which runs directly into Peterborough and Jaffrey. From the east, take Route 3 to Route 101 and go west to Route 202. The region is about 75 miles from Boston, 205 miles from New York, and 95 miles from Hartford.

PUBLIC TRANSPORTATION Vermont Transit bus service to Keene.

ACCOMMODATIONS First choices: *Amos A. Parker House,* Route 119, Fitzwilliam 03447, 585-6540, $$ CP • *Hannah Davis House,* Route 119, Fitzwilliam 03447, 585-3344, $–$$ CP • *John Hancock Inn,* Hancock 03449, 525-3318, $$–$$$ CP • *Benjamin Prescott Inn,* Route 124 East, Jaffrey 03452, 532-6637, $–$$ CP • *Inn at Crotched Mountain,* Mountain Road off Route 42, Francestown 03043, 588-6840, pool and tennis, $$$–$$$$ MAP • *Stepping Stones Bed and Breakfast,* RR1, Box 78, Wilton Center 03086, 876-3361, nineteenth-century home, artisan hostess, good value, $ CP • *Apple Gate Bed and Breakfast,* 199 Upland Farm Road (and Route 123 South), Peterborough 03458, 924-6543, $–$$ CP • **More options:** *Monadnock Inn,* Box B, Jaffrey Center 03452, 532-7001, old-timer, tired decor, but reasonable, $ • *Tory Pines Resort,* Route 47, Francestown 03043, 588-6352, recommended for golfers, $$–$$$ MAP • *Greenfield Inn,* Box 400, Greenfield 03047, 547-6327, gracious village home, $–$$ CP • *Inn at New Ipswich,* Porter Hill Road, PO Box 208, New Ipswich, 30371, 878-3711, comfortable 1790 farmhouse, away from the center of the region, but with reasonable rates, $ CP.

DINING *Latacarta,* 6 School Street, Peterborough, 924-6878, interesting menus, most say best in the area, $–$$ • *The Boilerhouse at Noone Falls,* Route 202 South, Peterborough, 924-9486, picturesque views, $$ • *The Folkway,* 85 Grove Street, Peterborough, 924-7484, informal, creative menus, folk music on weekends, $–$$ • *Fitzwilliam Inn,* on the green, Fitzwilliam, 532-8342, historic, cozy dining room, $–$$ • *John Hancock Inn* (see above), New England specialties, $$ • *Monadnock Inn* (see above), $$ • *Del Rossi's Trattoria,* Route 137, Dublin, 563-7195, Italian in a Colonial home, $–$$ • *Chesterfield Inn,* Route 9, Chesterfield, 256-3211, creative American cuisine in a 1700s farmhouse, $$–$$$ • *Birchwood Inn,* Route 45, Temple, 878-3285, home cooking, full dinners, $$. For lunch, try *Carolyn's Bistro & Deli,* 50 Depot Square, Peterborough, 924-2002, $, or the *Toadstool Bookshop Café* in Depot Square, 924-3543, $.

SIGHTSEEING *Monadnock Music,* PO Box 255, Peterborough 03458, 924-7610, six-week summer season. Write for schedule and prices • *Peterborough Players,* Middle Hancock Road, PO Box 1, Peterborough, 924-7585, changing repertory July and August, call for details • *New England Marionette Opera,* Main Street, Peterborough, 924-4333, June through mid-December. Prices vary, best to check • *American Stage Festival,* Route 13 North, Milford, 673-7515. Check for this year's plays and prices • *Sharon Arts Center,* Route 123, Sharon, 924-7256. Hours: Monday to Saturday, 10 A.M. to 5 P.M., Sunday from noon. Free • *The Friendly Farm,* Route 101, Dublin, 563-8444. Hours: May to Labor Day, daily, 10 A.M. to 5 P.M., weekends through mid-October. Adults, $3.50; children, $2.50 • *Cathedral of the Pines,* Route 110, Rindge, 899-3300. Hours: daily, May to October, 9 A.M. to 4 P.M. Free • *New Hampshire State Parks,* information for parks without a separate phone listing, 271-3556; unless noted, all parks have day's use fees, adults, $2.50; under 12, free; *Monadnock State Park,* Visitor Center off Dublin Road (Route 124), Jaffrey Center, 532-8862; *Rhododendron State Park,* Rhododendron Road, Fitzwilliam; *Miller State Park,* Route 101, Peterborough; *Greenfield State Park,* Route 136, Greenfield, 547-3497; *Chesterfield Gorge State Park,* Route 9, Chesterfield, 239-8153, free.

INFORMATION *Monadnock Travel Council,* 8 Central Square, Keene, NH 03431, 352-1303; Greater Peterborough Chamber of Commerce, PO Box 401, Peterborough, NH 03458, 924-7234; Information Center at the intersection of Routes 101 and 202, Peterborough.

Visiting Martha's Vineyard

If you're wealthy and/or a celebrity, chances are you have your own place on Martha's Vineyard, along with the likes of Carly Simon, Walter Cronkite, William Styron, and Beverly Sills.

The next best thing to owning is renting a place here, with time to get into the rhythm of the island and discover its private places and pleasures. More than most places, the Vineyard has two personalities, public and private, and though it's a perfectly lovely spot for a weekend, be forewarned that you'll only get a superficial look at the reasons why so many people fall totally in love with the island.

First of all, Martha's Vineyard is by far the biggest of the major vacation islands on the New England coast—108 square miles compared with roughly 30 for Block Island and 52 for Nantucket, its not-so-near neighbor off the Massachusetts shore. It takes a while to learn the ins and outs.

Martha's Vineyard is also quick to get to—just a 45-minute boat ride from Cape Cod. That attracts lots of summer vacationers, bringing the population from 10,000 people year-round to a summer glut of 70,000. Add hordes of daytrippers who want to see everything on a tour bus in a few short hours, and you can understand the problem.

But with all of that, the Vineyard still has magnificent beaches, seaside cliffs, woodlands, ponds, and wildlife preserves, and several diverse little towns to explore. What many like best about the island is its ambience, an unusual blend of green country retreat and beach resort, with great sailing waters thrown in as a bonus.

Among the towns, Edgartown, with its handsome sea captains' homes and ready supply of inns, is the first pick for lodgings for most weekend visitors since it has the greatest variety of inns and restaurants, most within walking distance of town. Since shuttle buses make regular rounds from the ferry docks at Vineyard Haven and Oak Bluffs to the Court House in Edgartown, this is an easy place to visit without a car.

There are attractive choices in the other towns as well, and some people prefer to be away from the crowds "up island" in West Tisbury or Menemsha. Wherever you stay, to really see the variety of the island's offerings, bring or rent a car, or rent a bicycle or moped when you get off the ferry. Like most islands, this is ideal biking country, though the hilly upcountry roads are not recommended for novices. There is a paved path for bicycles all the way from Oak Bluffs to Edgartown, and many miles of paths in the State Forest connecting Vineyard Haven, Oak Bluffs, Edgartown, and West Tisbury.

One of the first orders of business in understanding the makeup of Martha's Vineyard is a visit each of its disparate communities. The island was dubbed Martha's Vineyard by an early explorer, Bartholemew Gosnold, who landed there in 1602 and named it to honor one of his daughters as well as the wild grapes he found growing in profusion.

The first permanent white settlement on the island came 40 years later at Edgartown, known then as Great Harbor. With its rich farms and whaling expeditions from its harbors, the island prospered until the Revolutionary War. In 1778 the British fleet arrived to burn ships and raid more than 10,000 sheep and 300 head of cattle from local farmers.

In the 1820s the whaling industry revived and the fine homes in Edgartown were built by sea captains and merchants. Now a center for yachters instead of whalers, Edgartown still has the look of a nineteenth-century seaport. A walk around the little town, whose Water Street runs right beside the harbor, is a tour past spanking white Greek Revival homes that still display their dark shutters, fanlights, and "widow's walks," where worried wives watched for their husbands' safe return from the sea.

One of the houses on South Water Street belonged to Captain Valentine Pease, master of the ship on which Herman Melville made his only whaling voyage. Two other notable homes now serve as museums and another is the office of the *Vineyard Gazette*. The Federated Church, built in 1828, remains a landmark, along with the six-columned Old Whaling Church, which dominates Main Street and now serves as the local Performing Arts Center. Next door is the home of Dr. Daniel Fisher, the richest man on the island, a physician who was also the largest manufacturer of spermaceti candles and who held the contract to supply all the nation's lighthouses with whale oil.

Behind the Fisher House is the oldest remaining residence, the 1672 Vincent House. It has been preserved with the original brickwork, hardware, and woodwork to allow visitors to see how buildings were constructed 300 years ago.

The 1765 Thomas Cooke House is now The Vineyard Museum, headquarters of the Dukes County Historical Society. It is worth a stop to see the antique furniture, scrimshaw, ship models, costumes, and gear used by the earlier whalers and farmers on the island.

Drive to Oak Bluffs and you'll find a totally different kind of island history waiting. Just about the time the golden age of whaling was coming to an end, a new "industry" grew up: religion. It began in 1835, when the Edgartown Methodists held a camp meeting in an oak grove that later became known as Wesleyan Grove, on the bluffs at the northern end of town. The meeting, with worshipers and preachers living in tents and speakers standing on a driftwood platform, became a yearly affair of growing popularity. By 1859 the Martha's Vineyard Camp Meeting had become the largest in the world, with 12,000 people attending. Within 40 years, crowds of 30,000 gathered regularly for Illumination Night, which marked the end of the summer season with mammoth Japanese lanterns and fireworks displays. The event is still celebrated each year in August.

According to island history, many who attended the meetings found the seashore and lovely surroundings "as uplifting as the call to repent"—and thus began Martha's Vineyard's new era as a summer resort. The tents gave way to wooden cottages, with the owners often trying to outdo one another in colorful Victorian gingerbread. Wesleyan Grove turned first into Cottage City, then, as tourism grew, into Oak Bluffs, a town of 1,000 cottages plus boardinghouses and stores.

Religion remained a drawing card. In 1879 a new steel tabernacle replaced the old circus tent. The building and the remaining old cottages give a unique flavor to the present town of Oak Bluffs. The town also claims to own the oldest carousel in the country, The Flying Horses, which delights children today as it did in the 1870s.

Ironically, pious Oak Bluffs, along with Edgartown, is one of the few places on Martha's Vineyard that offers bar service with meals. Otherwise, it's BYOB in island restaurants.

Continuing along the coast to Vineyard Haven, the commercial center of the town of Tisbury, will bring you to seafaring territory again and the busy dock where most of the island ferries pull in. The Seaman's Bethel, once a refuge for sailors far from home, has been restored and is now a chapel and museum. The Jirah Luce House Museum in a 1796 house on Beach Road shows off the work of island artists. The Town Hall, once a Unitarian church, is one of the island's handsome architectural legacies from whaling days. Follow Main Street to the West Chop Lighthouse for a scenic drive past some of Vineyard Haven's finest homes.

Back in town, follow State Road through wooded West Tisbury to North Road and into Chilmark, an area of rolling green hills and exceptionally private coastline that is a choice location for summer homes. Watch for the turnoff to Menemsha, a tiny quintessential fishing village, and then follow Lighthouse Road to the brilliantly colored cliffs of Gay Head and its lighthouse. It is one of the first revolving lighthouses in the country, built in 1799.

You can vary your route back by taking South and West Tisbury roads into town. For a scenic detour off West Tisbury, take Deep Bottom for two miles and follow the sign to Long Point, a 580-acre preserve on the south shore with frontage on Tisbury Great Pond, as well as a couple of coves and a half mile of South Beach on the Atlantic.

Seeing the sights of Martha's Vineyard can fill a day, especially if you do it by bike. One highly recommended approach is to pack a picnic lunch and take time off for stops at a beach or walks through some of the nature preserves along the way.

Besides Long Point, there are Felix Neck, off the Vineyard Haven-Edgartown Road, and Cedar Tree Neck, on the north shore down Indian Hill Road off of State Road. These are places to see wildflowers, birds, and all manner of island pond life.

As for beaches, despite all those residents-only locations, there are many fine ones left from which to choose. One of the most beautiful of the public beaches is South Beach, also known as Katama Beach, on the south shore at Edgartown—three miles of powdery sand with surf on one side and protected salt pond on the other. East Beach on Chappaquiddick, a small island off Edgartown, is part of the Cape Pogue Wildlife Refuge, which includes most of the barrier beaches forming the northeastern tip of Martha's Vineyard. Much of Chappaquiddick is an untouched wilderness of dunes, cedar thickets, salt marsh, and scrubby upland, accessible only on foot or in a four-wheel-drive vehicle. No tour groups to contend with here.

You'll find every kind of outdoor recreation on the island—tennis courts in Vineyard Haven, Oak Bluffs, Edgartown, and West Tisbury; and an 18-hole golf course in Oak Bluffs and a nine-hole course in Vineyard Haven. Fishing boats go out of all the main island docks, sailboats are for rent in Vineyard Haven, and both sail and powerboats are available in Edgartown.

There are enough standard resort gift shops in island towns to keep die-hard shoppers occupied for a bit, and a dozen art galleries are spread around the island. Among the most interesting stops in Edgartown is the gallery on the main floor of the Charlotte Inn.

But shopping is the least of the reasons to come to Martha's Vineyard. Spend a weekend getting acquainted with the combination of country and seashore this lush island offers, its exceptional beaches and unspoiled natural beauty, and you may well find you're one of the many who come back for more.

Area Code: 508

TRANSPORTATION Passenger and car ferries to Martha's Vineyard run year-round from Woods Hole on Cape Cod (45 minutes), and ferries for passengers only in the warm months from the Cape Cod towns of Falmouth (40 minutes) and Hyannis (an hour and 45 minutes), and from New Bedford, Massachusetts (also an hour and 45 minutes). Bus service to Woods Hole from Boston and New York via Bonanza Bus Line (800) 556-3815. Woods Hole is 85 miles from Boston, 271 miles from New York, and 187 miles from Hartford. For ferry information: Steamship Authority, PO Box 284, Woods Hole, MA 02543, 477-8600. Air service is provided by Cape Air (800) 352-0714. For other ferry services and small airlines serving the island, contact the Martha's Vineyard Chamber of Commerce.

ACCOMMODATIONS *Charlotte Inn,* South Summer Street, Edgartown 02539, 627-4751, elegant, antique-furnished 1820 home with gallery and fine restaurant downstairs, $$$$–$$$$$ CP • *Daggett House,* 59 North Water Street, Box 1333, Edgartown 02539, 627-4600, snug historic sea captain's home with garden on the harbor, $$$–$$$$$ CP • *Point Way Inn,* Main Street and Pease's Point Way, Box 5255, Edgartown 02539, 627-8633 or (800) 942-9569, warm ambience, pleasant decor, croquet on the lawn, $$$–$$$$$ CP • *Shiverick Inn,* Pease's Point Way, Box 640, Edgartown 02539, 627-3797, formal, elegant, $$$$–$$$$$ CP • *Captain Dexter House,* 35 Pease's Point Way, PO Box 2798, Edgartown 02539, 627-7289, four-posters, pretty Laura Ashley decor, $$$–$$$$ CP • *Colonial Inn,* North Water Street, PO Box 68, Edgartown 02539, 627-4711, 42-room old-timer with hotel services, inn ambience, $$$–$$$$ CP • *Edgartown Inn,* 56 North Water Street, PO Box 1211, Edgartown 02359, 627-4794, comfortable, 1800 Colonial inn, $$–$$$$, with more modest annex, $$ • *The Arbor,* 222 Upper Main Street, PO Box 1228, Edgartown 02539, 627-8137, airy, attractive, good value, $$–$$$ CP • *Katama Shores Inn,* Katama Road, Edgartown 02539, 627-4747, beach lovers' choice, motel decor but facing lovely South Beach, tennis, pool, some kitchens, $$–$$$$ • *Beach Plum Inn,* North Road, Menemsha 02552, 645-9454, 1848 main house and a cottage complex, very private spot amid gardens overlooking the sound, $$$$–$$$$$ CP • *Menemsha Inn and Cottages,* Box 38B, Menemsha 02552, 645-2521, secluded contemporary inn with water views, special, $$$–$$$$$ CP • *Lambert's Cove Country Inn,* Lambert's Cove Road, West Tisbury (mailing address: Box 422, RR1, Vineyard Haven 02568), 693-2298, escapist's dream, charming farmhouse and cottages amid lawns, gardens, and an apple orchard, tennis, $$$–$$$$ CP • *The Oak House,* Seaview Avenue, Box 299, Oak Bluffs 02557, 693-4187, oak paneling, gingerbread and Victoriana, $$$–$$$$ CP • *Outermost Inn,* 1 Lighthouse Road, Gay Head, 645-3511, superb location on the cliffs, every room with ocean views, $$$$–$$$$$ CP • *Thorncroft Inn,* 278 Main Street, PO Box 1022, Vineyard Haven 02568, 693-3333, four handsomely restored and furnished homes, working fireplaces, Jacuzzi, $$$$–$$$$$ CP • *Captain Dexter House,* 100 Main Street, Vineyard Haven 02568, 693-6564, attractive furnishings, walking distance to the ferry, $$$–$$$$ CP.

LODGING RESERVATION SERVICE: Martha's Vineyard Reservations, PO Box 1322, Vineyard Haven, MA 02658, 693-7200.

DINING   *L'Etoille,* Charlotte Inn (see above), 627-8947, French, elegant and expensive, prix fixe, $$$$$ • *Warriners,* Post Office Square, Edgartown, 627-4488, can't be beat—gracious ambience, great food, wide choice, hamburgers to gourmet, $–$$$ • *Shiretown Inn,* North Water Street, Edgartown, 627-3353, highly regarded chef, $$–$$$ • *Savoir Fare,* Post Office Square, Edgartown, 627-9864, winning small café, creative menu, $$$–$$$$ • *Andrea's,* Upper Main Street, Edgartown, 627-5850, attractive airy setting, upscale Italian, $$–$$$ • *Square-Rigger,* Upper Main Street at West Tisbury Road, 627-9968, informal, tops for grilled seafood, good value, $$ • *David Ryans,* 11 North Water Street, Edgartown, 627-3030, popular, lively café, eclectic menu, $$ • *The Wharf,* Main Street, Edgartown, 627-9966, informal, "pub grub" and seafood in former blacksmith shop, $–$$ • *Seafood Shanty,* Dock Street, Edgartown, 627-8622, outdoor dining on the harbor, $–$$ • *Lambert's Cove Country Inn* (see above), gourmet fare, country setting, by reservation only, $$$; notable Sunday brunch, $$ • *Home Port,* Menemsha Road, Menemsha, 645-2679, nautical, informal, on picturesque harbor, $$–$$$ • *Beach Plum Inn* (see above), exceptional setting, reservations essential, $$$–$$$$ • *Louis' Tisbury Café,* 102 State Road, Vineyard Haven, 693-3255, tiny but highly regarded by island regulars, $$–$$$ • *Black Dog,* Beach Road, Vineyard Haven, 693-9223, informal, longtime waterfront favorite, $$ • *Le Grenier,* Upper Main Street, Vineyard Haven, 593-4906, excellent French café, $$$–$$$$ • *The Oyster Bar,* 162 Circuit Avenue, Oak Bluffs, 693-3300, Soho by the sea, big open bistro,

$$–$$$. For night life, try *Hot Tin Roof* at the airport, 693-1137, or the *Atlantic Connection,* Circuit Avenue, Oak Bluffs, 693-4516.

SIGHTSEEING *Vincent House and Old Whaling Church,* Main Street, Edgartown, 627-4440. Hours: late June to Labor Day, Monday to Friday, 10 A.M. to 2 P.M. Donation • *The Vineyard Museum and Dukes County Historical Society,* Cooke Street, Edgartown, 627-4441. Hours: July 4 to Labor Day, daily, 10 A.M. to 4:30 P.M. Adults, $5; students, $3; under 12, free. Columbus Day to Memorial Day, Wednesday to Friday, 1 P.M. to 4 P.M., Saturday, 10 A.M. to 4 P.M. Winter rates: Adults, $3; students, $2; under 12, free • *Seaman's Bethel,* Beach Street, Vineyard Haven, 693-9317. Hours: daily, 10 A.M. to 4 P.M. Donation.

INFORMATION Martha's Vineyard Chamber of Commerce, Beach Road, PO Box 1698, Vineyard Haven, MA 02568, 693-0085.

Moonlight and Mozart in Vermont

The sun was setting to the strains of Bach. As the concert played, lis-teners on the lawn were watching the big red ball dip behind the Adirondack Mountains across Lake Champlain, turning both sky and lake reflections into a progression of pink, rosy red, and smoky gray hues.

There are many summer music festivals in sylvan settings, and many larger and more famous than the Vermont Mozart Festival. But few can rival the beauty or the intimacy of this very special event. Since 1974, the three-week festival beginning in mid-July has been a movable musical feast in and around Burlington, switching locations from estates bordering Lake Champlain to college campuses and churches to the ferry boat on the lake. In recent years, concerts have moved as far afield as the Trapp Family Meadow in Stowe, the grounds of the Robert Frost Cabin in Ripon, and the Basin Harbor Club resort in Vergennes.

It is the lakeside lawn concerts, particularly those on the grounds of Shelburne Farms, that provide the most memorable moments. The music and the change in scene from sunset to intermission views of moonlight on the water provide a rare harmony of sights and sounds.

And the music is top-rate, featuring the Mozart Festival Orchestra as well as visiting chamber music groups and top soloists. The high caliber of the musicians is even more evident because the audiences are small enough so that no amplification is necessary to come between listeners and performers. The popular concerts have inspired a winter chamber music series as well.

For anyone who loves music, the Mozart Festival is the perfect reason for a trip to Vermont's largest city. As an encore, you can cruise on the lake and get acquainted with one of New England's most remarkable collections of folk art.

Not that Burlington (population 40,000) feels anything like a big city. With Lake Champlain as its western border, the Adirondacks across the water, the Green Mountains to the east, and the University of Vermont and several smaller college campuses adding green space to the center, Burlington has the feel of a cosmopolitan college town blessed with enviable surroundings.

There is scant evidence these days that this is a town dating back to 1773. The heart of the downtown business area has been trans-formed into a pleasant, modern, four-block pedestrian mall known as the Church Street Market Place, with colorful banners overhead and interesting shops, sidewalk carts, and open-air cafés along the way. This is one city whose downtown remains crowded and vibrant.

While there is a Radisson Hotel right off the Market Place, some of the most interesting lodgings are located a few minutes drive away from downtown. By far the most elegant is The Inn at Shelburne Farms, the exceptional manor house where the concerts are held, which is open to the public for lodging and dining. Reserve well in advance, and you'll find out how it feels to live like the lord of the manor.

On the outskirts of Burlington is the Inn at Essex, a new hotel complex in the Colonial country style, with an indoor pool, and a special lure—a branch of the New England Culinary Institute, whose students provide outstanding fare in the inn's restaurants.

Wherever you stay, you'll certainly want to take time for a look around the city. Burlington developed into a shipping center when the Champlain Canal, built in 1823, connected the lake to the Hudson River. Walk along the Battery and the King Street neighborhood near the waterfront to see the site of one of the earliest settlements, and then head for a stroll downtown and you'll see a time line of Burlington history. The discoveries along the way range from the 1798 Gideon King House at 35 King Street to Greek Revival homes of the 1860s on Maple Street, from the 1928 City Hall, designed by the famous architectural firm of McKim, Mead, and White, to Burlington Square Mall, a high-tech center done by Mies van der Rohe in the 1970s. Another pleasant uphill stroll or drive is to the Hill section, through the Champlain College and University of Vermont campuses and prosperous residential neighborhoods dating back to the city's heyday. The university, incidentally, was founded by Ira Allen, brother of Revolutionary War hero Ethan Allen.

The $7 million mall that transformed Church Street in 1982 houses dozens of merchants, from shops selling clothes, crafts, and books to Sweetwater's, a former bank converted into a restaurant. You'll have no trouble finding an outdoor café for lunch. Among the notable shops is a branch of the Vermont State Craft Center at Frog Hollow, with work by 200 Vermont artisans. Adjoining the Marketplace is Burlington Square Mall, with the Porteous department store and dozens of other specialty stores. Another interesting shop a block west of Church Street on College Street is Bennington Potters North, three floors stocked with pottery and all manner of attractive housewares.

If bargain shopping is your thing, Burlington has a growing number of outlet stores in shopping centers along Route 7 south of town. Tenney Brook Square includes Aileen, Van Heusen, and Timberland outlets. Stop at the nearby Vermont Teddy Bear Company and you can take a guided tour to see how the bears are crafted by hand. In the same shopping area is Chapter's, a combination bookstore and café.

Another outlet center is developing in Essex, including names such as Jones of New York, Mikasa, and London Fog. Champlain Mill in neighboring Winooski is another kind of shopping mecca, offering all kinds of shops and crafts in an atmospheric restored mill. The Waterworks Restaurant here is a top choice for Sunday brunch on the deck overlooking the Winooski River rapids.

However, on a fine afternoon, you may well prefer more summery diversions, such as town beaches or boat rides on Lake Champlain, unusually scenic cruises thanks to the billowy mountain views on the far side. A bike and jogging path along Lake Champlain also is accessible from the city's four lakeside parks.

Still another possibility is a tour of Shelburne Farms, principal site of the Mozart Festival Concerts, but well worth touring by day when you can really see the grounds. The 1,685-acre farm is a rolling landscape of open fields and woodlands laid out by Fredrick Law Olmsted, with striking views at every curve of the road through the property. It was the home of Dr. and Mrs. William Seward Webb, who had architect Robert Henderson Robertson design their magnificent mansion in shingle, slate, and limestone to blend with the landscape. Both the mansion, whose porch serves as main stage for the summer concerts, and the Coach Barn, where smaller concerts are held, are exceptional buildings. As mentioned, The Inn at Shelburne Farms also can be visited for dinner or an overnight stay.

The Webbs began their farm as an experimental agricultural showplace, and Webb descendants have continued it as a model of progressive cattle and dairy farming, as well as a demonstration bakery and cheese-making operation. Little or no fossil-fuel fertilizers, herbicides, or pesticides are used on the farm. The tour includes the manor house, the great barns and dairy building, exhibits of Vermont agriculture, and a small store featuring farm products, including some of the tastiest

Vermont cheese to be found. There are walking trails here, also, with stupendous water views. The latest addition is a Children's Farmyard, where youngsters can pet the animals.

You may well be back here on the lawn in the evening, since Saturday nights are usually reserved for concerts on the South Porch of Shelburne Farms.

When it comes to dinner, there are many excellent choices in Burlington. The names cited most frequently seem to be the lavish Inn at Shelburne Farms, Café Shelburne, and Pauline's. Déjà Vu Café gets the vote for decor, Ice House for its Lake Champlain views.

On Sunday, drive back to Shelburne to see another of the Webbs' legacies, the Shelburne Museum. There is no way to take in all of this amazing complex of Americana in a day, for this is the nation's foremost showcase of folk art. The museum's founder, Electra Havemeyer Webb, was a pioneer collector of Americana and American folk art and her interests were wide.

There are more than 40 buildings on the 45-acre site, which is probably best described as a "collection of collections." The beautifully landscaped grounds are set up like a New England village, and some of the buildings are simply homes furnished in period antiques. But within many of them are unmatched exhibits of quilts, decoys, cigar-store Indians and carousel figures, weather vanes, trade signs, accessories, primitive drawings and paintings, and painted furniture.

There seems to be no end to the variety of displays—dolls and dollhouses, Toby jugs and lustre pitchers, clocks, valentines, penny banks and puppets, embroidery, scrimshaw, and so on—all in prodigious numbers. Among the more unusual exhibits are a 525-foot hand-carved model of a circus parade and the big-as-life SS *Ticonderoga,* the last vertical-beam sidewheel passenger steamer intact in the United States. You can go on board to see the handsome paneling and elegant interiors.

Meanwhile, the pleasant little town of Shelburne has some interesting shops to bring you back to reality, everything from a delightful country store to Crafts in Common, a showcase of handcrafts. Or you can continue driving south for another half hour or so to Middlebury, stopping on the way to see the Vermont Wildflower Farm in Charlotte at its late July peak. Middlebury, a picture-book college town, is the original home of the Vermont State Craft Center at Frog Hollow, as well as the Vermont Folklife Center, where there are exhibits of traditional art from the state and the region. At 52 Seymour Street, you can also visit the bovine studio and shop of Woody Jackson, the man who made Vermont's black and white cows renowned.

Middlebury offers its own fine choices of dining. Swift House Inn, an 1815 estate, has traditional fare with a French influence; Woody's offers art deco decor, a creative menu, and a deck on the river; and the Dog Team Tavern, just off Route 7 about four miles north of Middlebury, is a traditional New England country inn with such regional specialties as sticky buns, country fried chicken, and baked ham with fritters. What nicer way to end a weekend in Vermont?

Area Code: 802

DRIVING DIRECTIONS   Burlington is in northwestern Vermont. I-89 goes directly into the city, as does Route 7. It is 225 miles from Boston, 300 miles from New York, and 200 miles from Hartford.

PUBLIC TRANSPORTATION   Burlington is served by several airlines, including Continental and US Air, as well as by Amtrak train service and Vermont Transit bus lines. Ferry service is available from New York State across Lake Champlain.

ACCOMMODATIONS   _The Inn at Shelburne Farms,_ Shelburne 05482, 985-8498, palatial, exceptional, open mid-May to mid-October, $$–$$$$$ (less expensive rooms share bath) • _Radisson Burlington,_ Burlington Square, Burlington 05401, 658-6500, downtown, $$–$$$ • _Sheraton Burlington Inn,_ 870 Williston Road, Burlington 05403, 862-6576, resort-motel near airport, tennis, indoor and outdoor pools, $$–$$$$ • _Econo Lodge,_ 1076 Williston Road, South Burlington 05403, 863-1125 or (800) 446-6900, budget option, $–$$ • **Outside town but a short drive:** _Inn at Essex,_ 70 Essex Way, Essex Junction 05452, 878-1100, outside Vermont (800) 288-7613, indoor and outdoor pools, $$–$$$ • _Marble Island Resort,_ Malletts Bay, 150 Marble Island Road, Colchester 05446, 864-6800, intimate resort, beautiful views, golf, tennis, boating, good value, $$$–$$$$ CP • **Within a half-hour drive:** _Charlotte's Web Bed and Breakfast,_ 1047 Greenbush Road, Charlotte 05445 (south of Shelburne), 425-3341, restored barn, $–$$ CP; _Swift House Inn,_ Stewart Lane and Route 7, Middlebury 05733, 388-9925, Federal-style estate, some fireplaces, whirlpools, $$–$$$$ CP; _North Hero House,_ PO Box 106, North Hero 05474, 372-8237, charming, away from it all in the Champlain Islands, beach, tennis, boating, $–$$.

DINING   _Déjà Vu Café,_ 185 Pearl Street, Burlington, 864-7917, striking decor, light and regular menu, crêpe specialties, $–$$$ • _Ice House,_ 171 Battery Street, Burlington, 864-1800, go for drinks on the deck, unbeatable lake view, $$–$$$ • _The Daily Planet,_ 15 Center Street, Burlington, 862-9647, ethnic, funky, fun, $–$$ • _Isabel's on the Waterfront,_ 112 Lake Street, 865-2522, inventive menus in a restored warehouse, excellent for lunch, $, or dinners on weekends, $–$$ • _Five Spice Café,_ 175 Church Street, Burlington, 864-4505, variety of Asian cuisines, $–$$ • _Pauline's,_ 1834 Shelburne Road (Route 7), South Burlington, 862-1081, creative menus, highly recommended, choice of café, $, and formal dining room, $$–$$$ • *Sweetwater's,* 120 Church Street, Burlington, 864-9800, on the Marketplace, snacks to meals, big Sunday brunch, $–$$ • *Leunig's Old World Café,* Church and College streets, 863-3759, another informal Marketplace choice for people watching, $ • *Shanty on the Shore,* 181 Battery Street, 864-0238, seafood, adjacent fish market, $–$$ • *Dockside,* 209 Battery Street, 864-5266, seafood near the waterfront, $–$$ • *Alfredo's,* 79 Mechanic's Lane, Italian on the Marketplace, $–$$ • *Vermont Pub & Brewery,* 144 College Street, 865-0500, pub fare and fresh-brew, brewery tours, $–$$ • *The Inn at Shelburne Farms* (see above), elegant, formal dining, $$–$$$ • *Café Shelburne,* Route 7, Shelburne, intimate, country French, tops, $$ • *Waterworks Restaurant,* Champlain Mill, Winooski, 655-2044, overlooking rapids, good for brunch, $–$$ • *Butler's,* Inn at Essex (see above), chefs from New England Culinary Institute, $$; NECI students also man the informal *Birch Tree Café* at the inn, $ • *Swift House Inn,* Middlebury (see above), $$–$$$ • *Woody's,* Bakery Lane, Middlebury, 388-4182, $–$$ • *The Dog Team Tavern,* off Route 7, Middlebury, 388-7651, $–$$. For lunch on the way to Shelburne, try *Chapter's Book Store and Café,* Teddy Bear Common, 2031 Shelburne Road, 985-1089, $.

SIGHTSEEING *Vermont Mozart Festival,* Box 512, Burlington 05402, 862-7352, three weeks, mid-July to August, write or phone for current schedule and concert prices • *Shelburne Museum,* Route 7, Shelburne, 985-3346. Hours: daily, mid-May to mid-October, 10 A.M. to 5 P.M.; rest of year, by guided tour only at 1 P.M.; hours may vary, so best to check. Adults, $15; ages 6 to 14, $6 • *Shelburne Farms,* Harbor and Bay roads, Shelburne, 985-8685. Hours: mid-May to mid-October, 9 A.M. to 5 P.M. Guided tours 9:30 A.M. to 3:30 P.M. Visitor center open year-round, 10 A.M. to 5 P.M. Adults, $6.50; ages 6 to 11, $3.50 • *Vermont Wildflower Farm,* Route 7, Charlotte, 425-3500. Hours: early April to late October, 10 A.M. to 5 P.M. Adults, $3; under 12, free • *Spirit of Ethan Allen Cruises,* Perkins Pier, Lake Champlain, 862-9685, summer day and dinner cruises aboard a paddle wheeler, $7.75 to $23.90, phone for schedules • *Lake Champlain Ferry,* King Street Dock, 864-9804, one-hour trips across Lake Champlain, mid-May to late October. Round trip for car and driver, $21; additional adults, $5.50; ages 6 to 12, $1.50; maximum fare, $28.

INFORMATION Lake Champlain Regional Chamber of Commerce, 60 Main Street, Suite 100, Burlington, VT 05401, 863-3489.

Scaling the Heights at Acadia

Mother Nature created many wonders along the coast of Maine, but when she got to Mount Desert Island she pulled out all the stops.

The heart of this ultimate down east destination, the easternmost point on the Atlantic coast, is Acadia National Park—32,000 spectacular acres that encompass everything from rugged rockbound coastlines to green hills, 26 lakes and ponds, and 18 mountains. One of the latter, Mt. Cadillac, is the highest point on the eastern seaboard.

Mount Desert (accent on the last syllable), a 16-by-13-mile retreat just across a causeway from the mainland, also includes Bar Harbor, once a mecca for the wealthy and now a thriving little waterside resort town of shops, restaurants, and lodgings, including lavish summer homes that have been transformed into attractive inns.

For boaters, or anyone who appreciates peerless water views, there is Somes Sound, which splits the far end of the island almost in half. This deep arm of the sea between mountainsides is the only fjord on the East Coast. The two sides provide ample coastline for scenic resorts in the peacefully removed fishing village of Southwest Harbor and in Northeast Harbor, a yachting town with just a bit more action. Northeast Harbor is closer to the park, but still far away from Bar Harbor's busy streets.

As if all that weren't enough of a lure, these are also absolutely prime lobstering waters, and almost all the restaurants on Mount Desert, as well as a couple of very reasonably priced "lobster pounds," offer the very best of Maine's most famous culinary treat.

The focal point for visitors is Acadia, one of the nation's most popular national parks. To make the most of your visit, start at the Visitors' Center, just off Route 3 at Hull's Cove, north of Bar Harbor, for a film on the park, information, park maps, and schedules of the many activities conducted by park rangers during the summer months. These include nature walks, mountain hikes, naturalist sea cruises, sunset photo walks, and evening activities, which sometimes include walks to look at the starry heavens.

Armed with maps, you're ready for the 26-mile Park Loop Road. Stopping points include Sieur de Monts Spring, featuring the Wild Gardens of Acadia with their profusion of native wildflowers, and many viewpoints along Ocean Drive, where the road becomes one-way, a plan no doubt wisely devised to make it easier to admire the views and pull over to the lookouts without causing traffic problems. Crescent-shaped Sand Beach is a favorite sunning spot off the drive, and there is always a crowd at Thunder Hole, named for the deafening thump of the surf as it roars into caverns carved in the cliffs.

When you get to Jordan Pond House, make a stop for a meal or the famous tea served with popovers on the lawn in midafternoon. The house is a contemporary edition of the landmark original that burned down a few years ago. It is a handsome structure with glass walls to take in the noted view of the pond and the two round peaks behind known as "The Bubbles." The melt-in-your-mouth popovers and legendary homemade ice cream can be had with lunch or dinner as well as with tea—and they're worth a wait in line.

Near the end of the Park Loop is the side road to the top of Cadillac Mountain and awesome views from every side of the 1,532-foot summit. As the first place where the sun reaches the nation each morning, the peak inspires some unique rituals, including the annual Fourth of July square dance at 12:01 A.M., followed by a sunrise breakfast.

Near the park exit on Route 3 you'll come to Seal Harbor, another popular beach and a village that gained some note as the summer home of Nelson Rockefeller. It was his father, John D. Rockefeller, Jr., along with Edsel Ford and some other early summer residents, who recognized the fragile beauty of the area and moved to preserve it for public use. They bought up nearly a third of the park's total acreage and turned it over to the federal government in 1919 as the basis for the first national park in the East.

Because cars were banned on Mount Desert for a time, the park contains some 50 miles of carriage roads—once the province of the horse-drawn carriages of the wealthy—which are ideal for hikers, bikers, horseback riders, and cross-country skiers in the winter.

Off Route 3 not far from the park entrance is my pick for the island's most delightful small lodging, the Inn at Canoe Point, a hideaway perched over the water at Hull's Cove, with stylish rooms and absolute privacy to enjoy the views.

Route 3 ends in Northeast Harbor, a yachtsman's haven and an elegant summer colony of large "cottages," special inns, and exclusive village shops. The big Asticou Inn, with an incomparable view of the harbor, is the most elegant of all Mount Desert hotels, though the atmosphere is a bit staid. Two exceptional smaller inns are found here also. The gracious, shingled Harbourside Inn, a welcoming place where the hostess takes particular pride in serving her guests homemade blueberry muffins for breakfast, offers big, comfortable, simply furnished rooms, many with working fireplaces. The Maison Suisse Inn, a nineteenth-century summer cottage right in the village, looks like a fairy-tale cottage set in a rustic garden. The rates include breakfast at the restaurant-bakery across the street.

To complete an island tour, follow Sargeant Drive, an enclave of secluded, lavish summer homes that parallels Somes Sound, and at the end take Route 198, which curves around the head of the sound into Somesville, a well-preserved village of Colonial homes that is the island's oldest settlement. The drive south from Somesville on Route 102 along Echo Lake will bring you to Southwest Harbor, a shipbuilding and fishing village that is also a popular summer community. The rooms at the 100-year-old Claremont aren't anything special, but the location on Somes Sound most definitely is. A bit farther on is the Moorings, a snug and cozy berth with nautical motifs and a popular restaurant looking out on the harbor. Every kind of boat, including a canoe, can be rented right next door.

While you're in Southwest Harbor, take time for two special attractions that are easy to overlook. The first is the tiny Wendell Gilley Museum, showing off the work of a local artist who became known for his extraordinary wooden bird carvings. The second is a branch of the Mount Desert Oceanarium, a great place for kids, with its "touch tanks" and other hands-on exhibits, including phones where you can listen to the "songs" of whales.

Appropriately, one of the best lobster pounds in the area is nearby on the docks. At Beal's Lobster Pier you can buy fresh lobster at very reasonable prices, wait for your choice to be cooked, and eat it on the spot at outside picnic tables beside the water.

Fisherman's Landing, a similar establishment on the pier in Bar Harbor, offers a rustic enclosed eating pavilion. Fisherman's Landing closes by 8:00 P.M. (Beal's even earlier), so if you want a relatively inexpensive lobster feast, plan an early dinner.

"Bah Hahba," as the natives call it, is filled with restaurants that offer fine dining as well as lobster specials. There are shops to keep you browsing for a while, though the offerings are very much on the touristy side. Though the towns are much smaller, the quality is higher in Northeast and Southeast Harbors.

Bar Harbor suffered a terrible fire in 1947 that destroyed a third of the fine old summer homes and ended its days as an elite resort. Many of the most gracious lodgings in town are in the remaining summer showplaces that line West Street and the shore path east of the Municipal Pier. Most exceptional are those with water views, such as The Tides, The Breakwater, and Balance Rock Inn, which has an extraordinary spot on Frenchman's Bay.

Bar Harbor can become clogged with tourists, but it is lively and offers visitors much to see and do within an easy stroll. There are a number of special events in the area during the summer. The Bar Harbor Festival and the Mount Desert Festival of Chamber Music featuring special musical events in late July and early August are worth noting. The local drama group is the Acadia Repertory Theater, which performs at the Masonic Hall in Somesville—a good evening out combined with an early lobster dinner at Beal's.

And should you want to get out on that deep blue water while you are here, you'll find a number of ways to do so. Besides the informative naturalist cruises sponsored by Acadia National Park, the Frenchman's Bay Company next to the Municipal Pier in Bar Harbor offers daily sightseeing cruises and deep-sea fishing boats. Sailing sloops go out from the Golden Anchor Pier, and the Bluenose Ferry offers a day-long "Sea Fun" outing to Yarmouth, Nova Scotia, with all the meals and trappings of a lavish ocean cruise. There are still more cruises to view lobstering, seals, and osprey, whale-watching cruises, fishing charters, and a variety of ferryboat and mailboat cruises to nearby islands out of Northeast Harbor plus the ferry to Swans Island at Bass Harbor. The Island Information Bureau on Route 3, just past the causeway leading to Mount Desert, and the Bar Harbor Chamber of Commerce Information Center at the Blue Nose Ferry Terminal on the harbor and on Main Street, will have all the current schedules.

If you find yourself facing a rainy day, don't despair. Take the opportunity to check out those museums in Southwest Harbor or to visit the other locations of the Oceanarium. At the Bar Harbor Oceanarium you'll find live harbor seals in a 50,000-gallon tank, as well as the Maine Lobster Museum, where a licensed lobsterman is on duty to fascinate you and your youngsters with a zillion little-known facts about how these tasty crustaceans live and how they are caught. He illustrates his narrative with live lobsters, sometimes including a mother carrying several dozen babies on her bottom. Having learned about these creatures of the deep, you can see them being born at the Lobster Hatchery on the Bar Harbor waterfront. The place is small, but you can see anywhere from 5,000 to 10,000 tiny newborn lobsters.

The College of the Atlantic's Natural History Museum is another place where visitors get involved with hands-on exhibits and live talks. The Bar Harbor Historical Museum in the basement of the Jesup Memorial Library displays photos and clippings of what it was like in the lavish old days of the grand hotels and steamers.

Sun is preferable, of course, to make the most of the natural beauty of the area, but whatever the weather, Mount Desert is an unbeatable destination. It's the place for unsurpassed down east scenery—and some of the best lobster dinners that Maine has to offer.

Area Code: 207

DRIVING DIRECTIONS   Take I-95 to Augusta, then Route 3 east to Mount Desert; or the Maine Turnpike to Bangor, follow Route 1A to Ellsworth and then Route 3 across the causeway. On Mount Desert, Route 3 leads to Bar Harbor, Route 102 to Southwest Harbor, and Route 198/3 to Northeast Harbor. Bar Harbor is 276 miles from Boston, 482 miles from New York, and 372 miles from Hartford.

PUBLIC TRANSPORTATION   Air transportation to Hancock County Airport, 12 miles, and Bangor Airport, 50 miles. There is Greyhound/Vermont Transit bus service from Boston to Bar Harbor.

ACCOMMODATIONS *Inn at Canoe Point,* Hull's Cove 04644, 288-9511, romantic hideaway, $$$–$$$$$ CP • *Harbourside Inn,* Northeast Harbor 04662, 276-3272, warm ambience, top choice in the price range, $$–$$$ CP • *Maison Suisse Inn,* Main Street, Northeast Harbor 04662, 276-5223, charming, $$$–$$$$ CP • *Asticou Inn,* Northeast Harbor 04662, 276-3344, formal old-time resort-hotel, $$$$–$$$$$ MAP • *The Claremont,* PO Box 137, Southwest Harbor 04679, 244-5036, landmark building and location, $$$–$$$$ MAP; cottages, $$$$ • **Mansion-inns:** *The Breakwater,* 45 Hancock Street, Bar Harbor 04609, 288-2313 or (800) 238-6309, 1904 showplace on the water, $$$$–$$$$$ CP; *Balance Rock Inn,* 21 Albert Meadow, Bar Harbor 04609, 288-9900, exceptional privacy and water views, $$$$–$$$$$ CP • *The Tides,* 119 West Street, Bar Harbor 04609, 288-4968, small, luxurious suites, on the water, $$$$–$$$$$ CP • *Ledgelawn,* 66 Mt. Desert Street, Bar Harbor 04609, 288-4596, grand manor and carriage house, pool, $$$–$$$$$ CP • *Manor House Inn,* 106 West Street, Bar Harbor 04609, 288-4759, turn-of-the-century ambience, big porch, $$–$$$$ CP; *Thornhedge Inn,* 47 Mt. Desert Street, Bar Harbor 04609, 288-5298, gracious shingled summer house, $$–$$$$ CP • *Nannau,* shingled shorefront estate, $$$–$$$$ CP • **More modest choices:** *Seacroft Inn,* 18 Albert Meadow, Bar Harbor 84609, 288-4669 or (800) 824-9694, rooms and efficiencies, quiet and convenient location, $$ • *Moorings,* Shore Road, Manset, Southwest Harbor 04679, 244-5523, main house and motel on the water, good value, $–$$ CP • **Four small Victorian bed-and-breakfast homes, all $$–$$$ CP:** *Graycote Inn,* 40 Holland Avenue, Bar Harbor 04609, 288-3044; *The Maples Inn,* 16 Roberts Avenue, Bar Harbor 04609, 288-3443, *Ridgeway Inn,* 11 High Street, Bar Harbor, 04609, *Black Friar Inn,* 10 Summer Street, Bar Harbor 04609, 288-5091 • *Golden Anchor Inn and Pier,* 55 West Street, Bar Harbor 04609, 288-5033, motel with balconies overlooking water, $$–$$$ • *Atlantic Eyrie Lodge,* Highbrook Road, Bar Harbor 04609, 288-9786, hilltop motel, water views, $$–$$$. For budget motels, call or write the Chamber of Commerce.

DINING *George's,* 7 Stevens Lane, Bar Harbor, 288-4505, long one of the best in town, $$ • *Porcupine Grill,* 123 Cottage Street, Bar Harbor, 288-3884, trendy menu, attractive decor, $$ • *The Fin Back,* 78 West Street, Bar Harbor, 288-4193, intimate café, excellent chef, $$. • *Jordan Pond House,* Park Loop Road, Acadia National Park, 276-3316, exceptional location, standard menu, best for lunch, $–$$; dinner, $$–$$$$ • *124 Cottage Street,* Bar Harbor, 288-4383, popular for giant salad bar, $–$$$ • *Maggie's Classic Scales,* 6 Summer Street, Bar Harbor, 288-9007, informal, seafood, $$ • *The Claremont* (see above), come for the view, $$ • *Brick Oven Restaurant,* 21 Cottage Street, Bar Harbor, 288-5861, informal, eclectic, $–$$ • *Clark Point Café,* Clark Point Road, Southwest Harbor, 244-6255, casual café with fine cuisine, $–$$ • **For lobster-by-the-pound:** *Abel's Lobster Pound,* Route 198, Northeast Harbor, 276-5817; *Beal's Lobster Pier,* Clark Point Road, Southwest Harbor, 244-3202; *Fisherman's Landing,* West Street on the Pier, Bar Harbor, 288-4632; *Oak Point Lobster Pound,* Route 230, Trenton, 667-8548, great views and great lobster; *Tidal Falls Lobster Pound,* Tidal Falls Road, Hancock, 422-6818, a drive but a remarkable location next to the falls. Prices vary by the season, but these are always the best values around.

SIGHTSEEING *Acadia National Park,* PO Box 177, Bar Harbor 04609, 288-3338. Hours: park open year-round; Visitors' Center, Route 3, Hull's Cove, open daily, July and August, 8 A.M. to 6 P.M.; May, June, September, October, 8 A.M. to 4:30 P.M. Park Head-quarters on Route 233 has information the rest of the year. Write for information, schedules. Admission to park: weekly pass, $5 per car • *Wendell Gilley Museum,* Southwest Harbor, 244-7555. Hours: April through December, peak summer season, Tuesday to Sunday, 10 A.M. to 5 P.M.; check off-season hours. Adults, $3; children, 5 to 12, $1 • *Mount Desert Oceanarium,* three locations, all open mid-May to late October, Monday to Saturday, 9 A.M. to 5 P.M., sometimes later in summer. *Oceanarium/Southwest Harbor,* Clark Point Road, 244-7330. Adults, $4.95; ages 4 to 12, $3.75. *Oceanarium/Bar Harbor,* Route 3, Bar Harbor, 288-5005. Adults, $4.95; ages 4 to 12, $3.75. *Oceanarium Lobster Hatchery,* 1 Harbor Place, Bar Harbor, 288-2334. Adults, $3; ages 4 to 12, $2.50 • *Natural History Museum at the College of the Atlantic,* Route 3, Bar Harbor, 288-5015. Hours: June to Labor Day, daily, 9 A.M. to 5 P.M. Adults, $2.50; children, $0.75 • *Bar Harbor Historical Society,* 34 Mt. Desert Street, Bar Harbor, 288-3838. Hours: mid-June to mid-October, Monday to Saturday, 1 P.M. to 4 P.M. Free.

INFORMATION Bar Harbor Chamber of Commerce, 93 Cottage Street, P.O. Box 158, Bar Harbor, ME 04609, 288-5103.

Supping with the Shakers in Hancock

Was it brown sugar? Honey? Maybe a touch of apple cider? No one at the long dinner table in the Believers Dining Room was sure of the secret ingredient in the old Shaker recipe. The guests knew only that cabbage, nobody's favorite vegetable, had been transformed into a treat that had everyone asking for more.

At the People's Dinners held at Shaker Village in Hancock, Massachusetts, you quickly discover that the industrious people who lived here a century ago definitely did not include good food among the worldly pleasures they disdained.

From their earliest years the Shakers paid careful attention to food and its preparation, and as the skill of the "Kitchen Sisters" became known, city excursionists began arriving to share the Shakers' Saturday and Sunday dinners. They still do. The "Evenings at Hancock Shaker Village" programs, featuring dinners made from original Shaker recipes, are the chance to sample menus that include traditional fare such as roast lamb with ginger and cider, turkey with sage dressing, Sister Clymena's chicken pie with mushroom sauce, Eldress Bertha's summer squash casserole, and Sister Mary's zesty carrots. The Shaker chocolate pound cake is a favorite, along with the rich lemon cake with raspberry sauce, but even "green and red cabbage" takes on added flavor from the seasoning and surroundings. The menus change each week, so if you've tasted one Shaker dinner, you definitely have not sampled them all.

Before dinner, guests are invited on a tour of the village with a guide in Shaker costume; afterward, they are offered beverages in the 1830 kitchen, where they can inspect the laborsaving devices used by the clever Kitchen Sisters.

The Shaker dinners are an added treat in the Berkshire region of western Massachusetts, which regularly serves up one of New England's most overflowing platters of summer pleasures. The Boston Symphony concerts at Tanglewood, the dance festival at Jacob's Pillow, top-notch summer theater at Stockbridge and Williamstown, and the Shaker Village are only the start of a true smorgasbord of weekend delights.

With all of this, it should come as no surprise that summer reservations are hard to come by, and when the Boston Symphony arrives for the weekend, prices almost double. Even for the motels on Route 7, several months in advance is none too soon to secure a room. Because weekend rooms are at such a premium, if you'll settle for student concerts at Tanglewood during the week, this is one area that is worth considering for a middle-of-the-week break.

The region known as "the Berkshires" actually runs the entire length of Massachusetts from its southern to northern borders on and around Route 7. Sheffield, the first of the towns, is an antiquer's haven. Next comes Great Barrington, a local commercial center that is gaining renown as a dining center, and Stockbridge, the quintessential New England village immortalized by its most famous resident, Norman Rockwell. To either side are South Egremont, New Marlborough, Lee, Becket, and West Stockbridge, the first four slightly removed from the crush of summer visitors, the latter a tiny boutique-strewn village often filled with strollers.

Lenox, the home of Tanglewood, was known as the inland Newport for its fine summer homes occupied by both the wealthy and by literary greats of the last century. It is the most gracious of the towns. Farther on are Pittsfield, another shopping center, and Williamstown, the handsome hometown of Williams College, also known for the fine Clark Art Institute, with its Impressionist paintings and other noted collections. The Williams College Museum of Art is also quite exceptional.

There are dozens of lodgings in these towns for every taste and pocketbook—historic inns, resorts, and two particularly lavish retreats: Wheatleigh, where you'll enjoy all the luxury of an Italian palazzo built by a contessa; and Blantyre, a summer mansion that is every bit as regal as the name implies. The wonderful old Red Lion on a downtown corner in Stockbridge, a classic Colonial inn, is the place where everyone seems to show up eventually for a drink on the porch or the patio. The Apple Tree Inn, a 22-acre retreat conveniently set at the gate of Tanglewood, shares with Wheatleigh the distinct advantage of allowing guests to walk to the concerts. It's a benefit you'll appreciate more when you see the lines of traffic.

The Roeder House in Stockbridge is a beautifully furnished smaller inn. It has a pool, as does the warm and welcoming Weathervane Inn, a converted farmhouse in South Egremont. Lenox offers lodgings in many former mansions transformed into inns.

As you might expect in such a popular area, dining is fine, with a price range from exorbitant to modest—something for everyone.

With the basics out of the way, you can begin the difficult task of choosing among the rich arts offerings throughout the area. Tanglewood, tops the list. It has been a major Northeast attraction since 1936, when it became the summer home of the Boston Symphony. The 6,000 seats in the open-air shed, which is noted for its acoustics, are frequently sold out; as many as 10,000 more people may congregate on the big lawn in back, enjoying elegant picnics along with a symphony concert under the stars. In 1994, the Seiji Ozawa Hall was inaugurated, a 1,200-seat theater that is an ideal home for chamber music and recitals. The full roster includes top pop music stars as well as the classics.

The grounds at Tanglewood can be seen best on Sunday afternoons, when visitors have a chance to stroll some of the 210 acres of William Aspinwall Tappan's former estate, past the formal gardens and the recreation of the red house where Nathaniel Hawthorne once worked.

Tanglewood is not the only mecca for music lovers in the Berkshires. There is chamber music at South Mountain in Pittsfield on the spacious grounds of the handsome summer home of Elizabeth Sprague Coolidge (bring a cushion for this one—the setting is lovely, but the benches are hard). Some 150 voices accompanied by the Springfield Symphony are the feature at the Berkshire Choral Festival in a shed on the campus of the Berkshire School in Sheffield, and Aston Magna presents early music on original instruments at the St. James Church in Great Barrington. The Berkshire Opera Festival has its home at the Cranwell Resort in Lenox.

For fans of the dance, Mark Morris, Merce Cunningham, and other major troupes from around the world can be seen at the Jacob's Pillow Dance Festival in Becket, the oldest event of its kind in the country. The theater also offers jazz concerts on Sunday. The Albany Berkshire Ballet also has a six-week summer season at the Arts Center of Berkshire Community College in Pittsfield.

Theater buffs have the happy choice of the long-established and excellent Berkshire Theater Festival in Stockbridge, with three arenas showing drama, musicals, and children's plays; or the highly acclaimed productions at the Williamstown Theater Festival. The Berkshire Public Theater presents repertory in Pittsfield year-round, and if the Bard's the thing, there is Shakespeare & Company, performing in a natural amphitheater on the grounds of The Mount, Edith Wharton's former estate high above Laurel Lake. Wharton stories are dramatized in the intimate theater in the main house.

In addition to the arts, there are enough sightseeing attractions in the mountains and woodlands and lovely towns of the Berkshires to keep you busy even if you had nothing else to do. Priority goes to two special places. The first is the Norman Rockwell Museum, featuring the well-known illustrations of the artist in the town where he spent his last 25 years. The world's largest collection of his work can be seen in this stunning museum, which opened in 1993 on a 36-acre former estate just outside Stockbridge. The museum inspires new appreciation for Rockwell's talents at mirroring changing American society. His studio has also been moved to the site. Not the least of the museum's pleasures are the grounds, which offer expansive views of the Housatonic River Valley and the Berkshire countryside.

The second is Hancock Shaker Village, the most elaborate of all the Shaker museums, where 20 buildings have been restored of the original 100 structures in a settlement that was established in 1790 and reached its height in the 1830s.

You'll learn a lot about the ingenious Shaker people, whose faith was founded on four fundamental principles: separation from the world, common property, confession of sin, and celibacy, meaning separation in living quarters but equality in privileges for the sexes. The name "Shaker" came from the lively dance that worshipers practiced to drive evil away.

The Shakers had a genius for finding the most functional way of doing things, exemplified by their classically simple tables and chairs and pegs, precursors of modern design. Their legacy to us includes the first packaged garden seeds and herbal remedies, and such practical inventions as the circular saw, the flat broom, and the clothespin.

The trilevel round stone barn in Hancock is the most striking reminder of Shaker ingenuity, with a shape as practical as it is beautiful, a design that enabled as many as 54 head of cattle to be fed by a single farmhand from a central core. Among the other buildings to be toured are the Brethren's and Sisters' shops, where you'll see the chair, broom, and oval box-making industries that were run by the men, and the dairy, medical department, and weaving facilities that were the province of the women. Craftspeople, on hand to demonstrate these various occupations, reproduce Shaker small goods, wooden objects, and furniture for sale to visitors.

One of the most important buildings is the Brick Dwelling, which housed 100 and contained the communal dining room and meeting room used for weekday worship. Here is where the dinners are now held on Saturday nights, and where you will often find demonstrations going on in the 1830 kitchen in the basement. Homemade bread, preserves, and other foods made from Shaker recipes are for sale here in the appropriately named Good Room.

On the grounds, this remains a working farm, where you can see historic breeds of sheep, cows, horses, and chickens, as well as tour an heirloom garden where nineteenth-century varieties of vegetables and herbs are grown using Shaker planting and cultivation methods.

If you want to check out the best of the area shops, try the main streets of Stockbridge, Lenox, and West Stockbridge. The Curtis House shops in Lenox are worthy of note, as is the G/M Gallery in West Stockbridge, worth a stop for its interesting combination of new and antique jewelry and ethnic arts. For bargain hunters, an outlet mall is located north of Lenox on Route 7.

On a beautiful summer day, you might prefer to forget about sights or shops and enjoy a swim. Try York Lake in New Marlborough, Benedict Pond in Beartown State Forest near Great Barrington, or Pontoosuc Lake on Route 7 south of Pittsfield, which offers boat rentals as well as a little beach.

For hikers there are several choices, including Monument Mountain between Great Barrington and Stockbridge, 39 miles of the Appalachian Trail, and Mount Greylock, the highest in the state. Serious hikers or anyone who is on a budget and is willing to put up with spartan furnishings and shared rooms can stay on top of Mount Greylock in the Bascom Lodge, run by the Appalachian Mountain Club. The club sponsors many guided walks and programs. You can pick up a schedule at the visitors' center, just off Route 7 in Lanesboro, north of Pittsfield. The road is plainly marked.

Should you have the time, there are more places of interest to be visited, two of them monuments to famous sculptors. Chesterwood, an estate set beside the Housatonic River overlooking the mountains, was aptly described as "heaven" by its former owner, Daniel Chester French, the sculptor of the seated Lincoln figure at the Lincoln Memorial in Washington. Tyringham Art Galleries is a curiosity. The studio of Sir Henry Kitson, best known for his Minuteman statue at Lexington, it is a Hansel-and-Gretel affair appropriately called the Gingerbread House, with a "thatched roof" that is itself a sculpture, weighing 80 tons.

Naumkeag, a Stockbridge mansion designed by Stanford White, is one of the grander homes in the area, and Arrowhead in Pittsfield is of interest as the home where Herman Melville wrote *Moby-Dick.* Flower lovers will also enjoy Bartholomew's Cobble, a 200-acre world of meadows and woods and wildflowers in Ashley Falls; and the Berkshire Botanical Garden, a 15-acre show garden in Stockbridge.

All these attractions simply can't be seen in one weekend, which is probably a very good thing. The Berkshire mountainsides are beautiful in autumn, offer skiing in the winter, and take on a special glow in the bloom of spring—which gives you lots of excuses to come back and see what you've missed.

Area Code: 413

DRIVING DIRECTIONS   Lenox, the heart of Tanglewood Country, is on Route 7, about 150 miles from both Boston and New York, and 53 miles from Hartford. Hancock Shaker Village is about 15 minutes away in Pittsfield; make a left turn off Route 7 in Pittsfield to Route 20, which takes you directly to the village.

PUBLIC TRANSPORTATION   Bonanza Lines provides bus service to the area. Amtrak serves Pittsfield from Boston. Closest major airports are Springfield, Massachusetts, 70 miles away, or Albany, New York, 37 miles. If you stay near Tanglewood, you can manage without a car, but you'll miss a lot of the sights.

ACCOMMODATIONS   Rates given are for weekends in July and August concert season and foliage season; all are less on weekdays and in September—and much less after October. All inns have minimum-stay requirements in season. *Apple Tree Inn,* 224 West Street, Lenox 01240, 637-1477, lovely hilltop location, $$–$$$$ CP (less expensive rooms are in a modern motel-lodge on the grounds) • *Williamsville Inn,* Route 41, West Stockbridge 01266, 274-6118, charm, pool, tennis court, excellent dining room, $$$–$$$$ CP • *The Roeder House,* Route 183, Stockbridge 01262, 298-4015, fine furnishings and good taste, pool, $$$–$$$$ CP • *Weathervane Inn,* Route 23, South Egremont 01258, attractive converted farmhouse, pool, 528-9580, $$$$$ MAP • *Brook Farm Inn,* 15 Hawthorne Street, Lenox 01240, 637-3013, Colonial charm, poetry readings and concerts, pool, $$–$$$$ CP • *Walker House,* 24 Walker Street, Lenox 01240, 637-1271, art-filled, offbeat, and interesting, $$–$$$$ CP • *Garden Gables Inn,* 141 Main Street, Lenox 01240, 637-0193, cozy, Colonial decor, big pool, $$–$$$$ CP • *Merrell Tavern,* Route 102, South Lee 01260, 243-1794, authentically restored 1800 stagecoach inn, $$–$$$$ CP •

Chambery Inn, Main and Elm streets, Route 20, Lee 01238, 243-2221, restored schoolhouse in the village, big rooms, $$–$$$$ CP • *Applegate Bed and Breakfast,* 279 West Park Street, Lee 01238, 243-4451, Southern mansion transplanted to New England, pool, $$$–$$$$ CP • *The Red Lion Inn,* Main Street, Stockbridge 10262, 298-5545, $$$–$$$$ • *Staveleigh House,* Route 7, Sheffield, 229-2129, ideal for antiquers, good value for all, $$ CP. **Some of the mansions-turned-inns in Lenox:** *Birchwood Inn,* 7 Hubbard Street, Lenox 01240 (800) 524-1646, spacious historic house with canopy beds, handsome garden, $$–$$$$ CP • *Cliffwood Inn,* 25 Cliffwood Street, Lenox 01240, 637-3330, Belle Epoque showplace, breakfast on the veranda overlooking the grounds, $$$–$$$$ CP • *Underledge,* 76 Cliffwood Street, Lenox 01240, 637-0236, manor house on four acres, $$$–$$$$$ CP • **The top of the line:** *Blantyre,* Route 20, Lenox 01240, 298-3806, $$$$$ • *Wheatleigh,* West Hawthorne Road, Lenox 01240, 637-0610, $$$$$ CP. Also see Williamstown, page 197.

DINING *Wheatleigh* (see above), continental, prix fixe, $$$$$ • *Blantyre* (see above), prix fixe, $$$$$ • *The Old Mill,* Route 23, South Egremont, restored gristmill, long a local favorite, $$–$$$ • *Williamsville Inn* (see above), continental, $$–$$$ • *Federal House,* Route 102, South Lee, 243-1824, continental, $$–$$$ • *Gateways Inn,* 71 Walker Street, Lenox, 637-2532, continental, $$$–$$$$ • *Church Street Café,* 69 Church Street, Lenox, 637-2745, excellent bistro, $$ • *Café Lucia,* 90 Church Street, Lenox, 637-2640, Italian, $$–$$$ • *The Dakota,* Route 7, Lenox/Pittsfield line, 499-7900, informal, fun, popular, $–$$ • *Apple Tree Inn* (see above), continental with an Italian accent, $$–$$$ • *Lenox 218,* 218 Main Street (Route 7A), Lenox, 637-4218, continental, $$–$$$ • *La Bruschetta,* 1 Harris Street, West Stockbridge, 232-7141, Italian, $$–$$$ • *The Old Inn on the Green,* Route 57, New Marlborough, worth the drive for five-course dinners in an eighteenth-century dining room, by reservation only, prix fixe, $$$$$ • *The Red Lion Inn* (see above), New England fare, good for people watching, $$–$$$ • *The Painted Lady,* 285 South Main Street, Great Barrington, 528-1662, northern Italian, $$–$$$ • *Castle Street Café,* 10 Castle Street, Great Barrington, 528-5244, bistro menu, well-regarded chef, $$–$$$ • *The Orient Express,* off Main Street, West Stockbridge, 232-7110, Vietnamese, very popular, $. For lunch, in Stockbridge try *The Café* in the Mews around the corner from the Red Lion; and in West Stockbridge, *Shaker Mill Tavern,* which also has light supper fare and entertainment. For Tanglewood picnics, call *Cheesecake Charlie's,* 637-3411. Also see Williamstown listings, pages 197–198.

SIGHTSEEING *Hancock Shaker Village,* Route 20 at 41, Pittsfield, 443-0188. Hours: May 1 to October 31, daily, 9:30 A.M. to 5 P.M.; April and November, daily, 10 A.M. to 3 P.M. Adults, $10; children, 6 to 17, $5; family rate, $25; *An Evening at Hancock Shaker Village,* tour, candlelight dinner, and entertainment, most Saturday nights mid-June to mid-October; reservations required. $35 • *Norman Rockwell Museum,* Route 183, Stockbridge, 298-4137. Hours: May to October, daily, 10 A.M. to 5 P.M.; November to April, weekdays, 11 A.M. to 4 P.M., weekends, 10 A.M. to 5 P.M. Adults, $8 ($7.50 in winter); children, $2 • *Chesterwood,* Route 183, two miles west of Stockbridge, 298-3579. Hours: May to October, daily, 10 A.M. to 5 P.M. Adults, $6; students, $3; children 6 to 12, $1 • *Naumkeag Museum and Gardens,* Prospect Hill, Stockbridge, 298-3239. Hours: Memorial Day to Labor Day, Tuesday to Sunday and Monday holidays, 10 A.M. to 4:15 P.M. Labor Day to Columbus Day, weekends and holidays only. House and garden, adults, $6, children 6 to 12, $4; garden only, adults, $4, children, $1.50 • *The Mount, Edith Wharton Restoration,* Plunkett Street, Lenox, 637-1899. Hours: Memorial Day through Labor Day, Tuesday to Sunday, 10 A.M. to 5 P.M.; September and October, Thursday to Sunday, 10 A.M. to 5 P.M. Adults, $4.50; students, $3 • *Tyringham Art Galleries,* at Routes 102 and 20, Tyringham, 243-3260. Hours: Memorial Day to Columbus Day, 10 A.M. to 5 P.M. Adults, $1; children, free • *Arrowhead,* 780 Holmes Road, Pittsfield, 442-1793. Hours: Memorial Day to Labor Day, Monday to Saturday, 10 A.M. to 5:00 P.M.; closed Tuesday and Wednesday after Labor Day; by appointment in winter. Adults, $4.50; ages 6 to 16, $3 • *Bartholomew's Cobble,* off Route 7A, Ashley Falls, 229-8600. Hours: museum, April 15 to October 15, Wednesday to Sunday, 9 A.M. to 5 P.M.; grounds open year-round. Adults, $3.50; under 12, $1 • *Berkshire Botanical Garden,* Routes 102 and 183, Stockbridge, 298-3926. Hours: mid-May to October, daily, 9:30 A.M. to 5 P.M. Adults, $5; under 12, free • *Berkshire Scenic Railway Museum,* PO Box 298, Lee, 637-2210. Trains leave from the Lenox station on Willow Creek Road; phone for schedules. Also see Williamstown attractions, page 198.

PERFORMING ARTS   For all the following listings, it is best to write or call for current schedules and prices, as they change from season to season: *Tanglewood,* West Street (Route 183), Lenox, 637-1940; before June (617) 266-1942. Tickets also available from Ticketmaster (212) 307-7171; concerts July through Labor Day • *Jacob's Pillow Dance Festival,* off Route 20 on George Carter Road, Becket, 243-0745, late June through August • *Shakespeare & Company,* The Mount, Route 7, Lenox, 637-3353, late May through October • *Berkshire Choral Festival,* Berkshire School, Sheffield, 229-3522, July and August • *Berkshire Theater Festival,* Main Street, Stockbridge, 298-5576, late June to early September • *Williamstown Theater Festival,* Park and Main (intersection of Routes 7 and 2), Williamstown, 597-3399, July and August • *Aston Magna Foundation,* PO Box

1035, Great Barrington, 528-3595, July to early August • *Berkshire Opera Company,* 17 Main Street, Lee, 243-1343 • *Berkshire Public Theater,* 30 Union Street, Pittsfield, 445-4634, performances year-round • *Albany Berkshire Ballet,* 51 North Street, Pittsfield, 442-1307 • *South Mountain Concerts,* Route 7, one mile south of Pittsfield, 442-2106, September to early October.

INFORMATION   Berkshire Visitors' Bureau, Berkshire Common, Pittsfield, MA 01201 (800) BERKSHR or 443-9186 • Lenox Chamber of Commerce, 75 Main Street, Lenox, MA 01240, 637-3646, for local information and lodging referral service.

Show-and-Tell at Lake Sunapee

I almost hate to tell about New London, New Hampshire. After all, if too many people find out about this classy little college town at the top of Lake Sunapee, the congenial and reasonably priced inns in town may be booked solid when I want to go back.

There's no problem, however, talking about the annual summer show of the League of New Hampshire Craftsmen Foundation at Mount Sunapee State Park, because it is already one of the region's most eagerly awaited annual events, so popular that it has grown from a weekend affair to a full nine days.

Fine crafts seem to flourish best in the country, where artisans still take time and pains with handwork, and in New Hampshire, a state that remains largely rural, with lots of country to go around, the crafts tradition is strong and still growing. Much of the impetus is due to the efforts of the league, which began holding the nation's first crafts fair more than 60 years ago.

The dozen big, brightly striped tents set up in front of the grassy ski slopes host a range of artisans—from potters and silversmiths to basket makers and bird carvers. One of the most popular features of the fair is the "Living with Crafts" exhibit, a display showing off handicrafts in model-room settings, giving new ideas and inspiration to take back home. The handmade furniture pieces, which include modern versions of the old cabinet-maker's work of art, the highboy, are the priceless antiques of the future. In the same building is an exhibit of handcrafted clothing and accessories called "Craftwear."

But this lively affair is more than displays. There are demonstrations by talented men and women from various guilds around the state—

perhaps a blacksmith laboring at the forge, a basket maker, or a seamstress turning flax into yarn at a spinning wheel—much to the delight of an audience of fascinated children. Both children and adults are welcome to take craft workshops as well as watch others at work.

The kids have their own Children's Tent for supervised creative play, art activities, and special entertainment—and many of them manage to coax their parents into a ride on the Mount Sunapee ski gondola, allowing everyone a bird's-eye view of the mountains and lakes of the area.

The big lake is Sunapee, and there's a public beach right in the state park to make the most of it. It is pleasant, albeit crowded.

Boating is another favorite pastime. You can either rent your own small craft or go out for a two-hour cruise on the big *MV Mt. Sunapee II.* Dinner cruises are also offered on the *MV Kearsarge,* featuring buffet suppers and beautiful sunsets.

The Sunapee area has a variety of lodgings away from the crowds. Dexter's Inn and Tennis Club is a delightful hideaway, tucked high up on a hill with a choice of views—lake on one side, mountain on the other. There's a lot of emphasis on tennis here, with clinics and round-robins scheduled.

The Inn at Sunapee is a homey farmhouse on a spectacular site with views of lakes and mountains, and it also offers a pool and tennis court. Other options not far away are the Follansbee Inn, an 1840 farmhouse with private frontage on Kezar Lake in North Sutton, and the Inn at Coit Mountain in Newport, a handsome 1790 Georgian home.

But there's no getting away from it—you can't talk about the Sunapee area without mentioning New London, though many genera-tions of Dartmouth students who made their way here to date the women at Colby-Sawyer College will need no introduction to the town.

Don't expect anything big or flashy. The New London Barn Players have been resident summer performers here since 1933, and there are summer concerts on the Colby Campus as well. Even so, New London is light-years away from being a tourist town—and that's part of its charm. The real pleasure of New London is simply strolling the pretty and unspoiled streets and savoring the relaxed small-town ambience that can make workaday pressures seem a faraway illusion.

The traditional red-brick buildings of the Colby campus are right in the center of things on Main Street, and they lead on to a row of handsome white Colonial homes and the requisite white-spired New England church. There are a few crafts and antiques shops for browsing—nothing fancy, but enough to pass the time. Baynham's has a potpourri of gifts, a 1950s soda fountain, and a pleasant café.

Eventually you'll find your way to the New London Inn, either for a meal or for lodgings at night.

The inns in town are not sophisticated resorts, but homey and simple lodgings with down-to-earth rates. The New London Inn is the most historic: The "new wing" was built in 1806; the rest of the building dates back to 1792. It's a warm and unpretentious place with a fine dining room. Guests at the inn are given passes to the residents-only beach at Little Sunapee, about a mile and a half away and much less crowded than the big beach at the big lake.

More of a hideaway is the Pleasant Lake Inn outside town, an eighteenth-century farmhouse with views of Pleasant Lake on one side and Mt. Kearsarge on the other. Once again, it's not elaborate, but reasonable, attractive, and comfortable, and it has a dining room overlooking the lake and guest privileges at the private beach club just across the way. The Hide-Away Inn is just that, a cozy, rustic retreat up the hill from Little Lake Sunapee.

Colonial Farm Inn has a highly praised dining room, attractively decorated rooms, and an antiques shop on the premises, but the disadvantage of a setting on the main highway. Golfers may want to check out the Fairway Motel at the Lake Sunapee Country Club, which lets you stay within a putt of the starting green and offers tennis and a pool as well. Golfers may also want to check the Country Club of New Hampshire in North Sutton, rated as one of New England's best public courses.

The crafts fair, the boating and swimming, a game of golf or tennis, some back-roads exploring plus a stroll or two down New London's Main Street, should easily fill a pair of peaceful country-style days. For more shopping, check nearby towns such as Georges Mill, where Prospect Hill has a big display of antiques, or Andover, where Potter Place Gallery exhibits work by New England artisans.

If you have time for an extra drive one day, head north on I-89 to exit 17, Enfield, and follow signs to Route 4A and the Lower Shaker Village, a restoration of a Shaker community. Founded in 1793, the village numbered 330 residents at the community's peak in the 1850s, but had dwindled to just eight when the last members moved to Canterbury in 1923. The La Salette Brothers took over four years later, and used the spot to build a shrine and establish a school for boys. In 1985 the property was sold and is now being restored. There are nine original Shaker buildings on the site.

This is not a slick restoration, but it holds interest for its authenticity. Among the sights are a small museum in the Laundry/Dairy building, which dates to 1813, the East and West Brethren's Shops (circa 1819 and 1820), the cow barn, the old cemetery, and lovely herb gardens. The impressive church was added by the La Salette Brothers in 1930.

To keep things lively, the museum schedules many special performances, demonstrations, workshops, and festivals all summer, and the 1,300-acre grounds offer many walking trails besides.

Reproductions of Shaker crafts are sold in the shop and you may well be inspired to buy some of the fine reproduction furniture at the showroom of Dana Robes just opposite the village.

When you're ready for a meal, the big, gray stone Shaker Inn will be ready for you. Known as the Great Stone Dwelling, it is one of the most impressive examples of Shaker architecture, and was the tallest building north of Boston when it was completed in 1841. It has been nicely restored as a restaurant and inn, and filled with Shaker furnishings. The dinner menu is continental, but traditional candlelight Shaker dinners are offered on Sunday evenings from June to mid-October. A documentary on the Shakers, "Hands to Work, Hearts to God," is shown preceding the meal.

While the rooms upstairs are on the spare side, those in the Victorian Mary Keane House on the grounds overlooking Lake Mascoma may tempt you to come back for a longer stay.

Evenings in the Sunapee area hold a choice of the New London Players or the Dartmouth Players Repertory Company in Hanover, just half an hour away, as well as the Music at King Ridge summer concerts at the King Ridge ski area and free old-fashioned band concerts on the New London common.

A highly recommended end to the weekend is a detour north on Route 12A to Cornish and the late-afternoon Sunday concerts at Saint-Gaudens National Historic Site. This is the magnificent home, gardens, and studio of Augustus Saint-Gaudens, one of America's greatest sculptors, whose famous "Standing Lincoln" and many other works led the way toward realism in sculpture. The mansion is a showplace, the many-acred grounds are even more spectacular, with a soaring view of hills and mountains beyond. The chamber music series is held in the sky-lighted studio, but many people prefer staying out on the lawn to listen while they contemplate the beauty around them.

Saint-Gaudens is another little-heralded treat in an area filled with unexpected pleasures, not the least of them the no-longer-hidden charms of New London.

Area Code: 603

DRIVING DIRECTIONS   To reach the Lake Sunapee area from the east, take I-93 to I-89 west to New London, south on Route 11 to Mount Sunapee State Park. From the west, take I-91 to Exit 8, go about 13 miles east on Route 103 to the park, then north on Route 11 to New London. New London is 110 miles from Boston, 260 miles from New York, and 150 miles from Hartford. Mt. Sunapee Park is about 10 miles away.

PUBLIC TRANSPORTATION   Vermont Transit bus service from Boston to New London.

ACCOMMODATIONS   *New London Inn,* Main Street, New London 03257, 526-2791 or (800) 526-2791 out of state, $–$$ CP •

Pleasant Lake Inn, Box 1030, Pleasant Street, New London 03257, 526-6271 or (800) 626-4907, $$ CP • *Hide-Away Inn,* Twin Lake Villa Road, New London 03257, 526-4861 or (800) 457-0589, $$ CP • *Colonial Farm Inn,* Route 11, New London 03257, 526-6121 or (800) 805-8504, $–$$ CP • *Fairway Motel,* Lake Sunapee Country Club and Inn, Route 11 East, New London 03257, 526-6040, ask about golf packages, $–$$ • *Dexter's Inn and Tennis Club,* Stagecoach Road, Sunapee 03782, 763-5571, $$$–$$$$ MAP, tennis packages available • *The Inn at Sunapee,* Box 336, Sunapee 03782, 763-4444, $$ CP • *Seven Hearths,* Old Route 11, Sunapee 03782, 763-5657 or (800) 237-2464, new owners at press time, $$$–$$$$ CP • *The Inn at Coit Mountain,* Route 10, HCR 63, PO Box 3, Newport 03773, 863-3583 or (800) 367-2364, $$–$$$$ CP • *Follansbee Inn,* Route 114, PO Box 92, North Sutton 03260, 927-4221, $$ CP • *The Chase House,* Route 12A, Cornish 03745, 675-5391, $$–$$$ CP • *The Shaker Inn,* Lower Shaker Village, Route 4A, Enfield 03748, 632-7800, inn rooms or Keane House suites, $$–$$$ • *Blue Goose Inn,* Route 103B, Mount Sunapee 03772, 763-5519, modest roadside farmhouse, closest lodging to the craft fair, $ CP.

DINING   *New London Inn* (see above), tops in town, $$ • *Colonial Farm Inn* (see above), highly regarded locally, $$ • *La Meridiana,* Route 11, Wilmot (just east of New London), 526-2033, northern Italian, well recommended, $–$$ • *The Millstone,* Newport Road, New London, 526-4201, continental menu, good Sunday brunch, $$ • *Peter Christian's Tavern,* Main Street, New London, 526-4042, branch of the Hanover standby, informal, reliable, $–$$ • *Four Corners Grille,* Route 11 at Route 114, New London, 526-6899, burgers to full meals, great views of Mt. Kearsarge, $–$$ • *Pleasant Lake Inn* (see above), full meal, $$–$$$ • *The Inn at Sunapee* (see above), $$ • *Dexter's Inn* (see above), very popular, $$ • *Woodbine Cottage,* River Road, Sunapee Harbor, 763-2222, cozy, New England fare, $$ • *Tommy's Anchorage,* Sunapee Harbor, 763-4777, light fare, deck on the harbor, $ • *Murphy's Grille,* Route 103, Sunapee, 763-3113, casual dining, $–$$ • *MV Kearsarge* dinner boat, Lake Avenue, Sunapee, phone 763-5477 for current rates • *The Shaker Inn* (see above), 632-5466, $$, phone for dates of traditional Shaker dinners.

SIGHTSEEING   *League of New Hampshire Craftsmen Fair,* Mount Sunapee State Park, Route 103, Newbury, NH, held annually in early August. Adults, $7; under 12, free. For dates, contact the League at 205 North Main Street, Concord, NH 03301, 224-1471 • *Mount Sunapee State Park Beach,* 763-2356, June 16 to Labor Day. Adults, $2.50; under 12, free with adult • *MV Mt. Sunapee II* sails from Sunapee Harbor, call 763-4030 for current schedules and rates • *Saint-Gaudens National Historic Site,* Route 12A, Cornish, 675-2175.

Hours: late May through October, buildings 8:30 A.M. to 4:30 P.M., grounds until dark. Adults, $2; under 17, free. Write for current concert schedule • *The Museum at Lower Shaker Village,* Route 4A, Enfield, 632-4346. Hours: June to mid-October, Monday to Saturday, 10 A.M. to 5 P.M., Sunday from noon; rest of year to 4 P.M. Adults, $3.50; children, $1.50. Winter admission: adults, $2; children, $0.75.

INFORMATION New London Area Chamber of Commerce, PO Box 532, New London, NH 03257, 526-6575; Lake Sunapee Business Association, PO Box 400, Sunapee, NH 03782, 763-2495, out of state (800) 258-3530.

Smooth Sailing in Boothbay Harbor

Picture-postcard photographs of Boothbay Harbor, Maine, resemble paintings of a perfect seacoast village. Views from the land show shimmering light on the water, a montage of masts and deep blue sea studded with pine-rimmed islands. From the sea you can see the harbor backed by a row of wharves and tiny shops, with trim New England homes, church steeples, and green hills in the distance.

The pictures don't lie. This is as idyllic a spot as you'll find on the Maine coast—or any coast. It is also a lively community, full of crowds in summer, a town that can rightfully boast of being "The Boating Capital of New England." Boothbay becomes even more picturesque in late June during Windjammer Days, when a whole fleet of many-rigged tall ships makes a stately procession into the harbor. Parades, band concerts, and fireworks also mark the occasion.

But this is one place that needs no special occasion to make your visit an event. You need only board one of the many crafts waiting in the harbor to appreciate just why this area is a perennial favorite for sailors and yachtsmen. The trip from Boothbay to Monhegan Island in particular is a not-to-be-missed experience for anyone who appreciates untouched natural beauty.

But first you'll want to settle on land, and that can be a pleasantly difficult decision. There are four parts to Boothbay, the village and three fingerlike peninsulas jutting out to sea. Each has its own attractions.

If you want to be within walking distance of the village piers, shops, and restaurants but a bit removed from the bustle, two choices are just up the steep hill on McKown Street, where simple lodgings come with an unbeatable water view. Topside offers both home and motel units with balconies; Welch House gives you the same view in a nineteenth-century sea captain's home or a more modern motel section, known as the Sail Loft.

Spruce Point, a scenic rocky peninsula about five minutes' drive from the village, offers the area's most elegant resort, Spruce Point Inn (coat and tie for dinner).

Ocean Point is a bit farther out and a bit more rugged, with a classic rocky shoreline to explore. Ocean Point Inn is off by itself at the entrance to Linekin Bay, a complex of inn and lodge, motel and cottages, with its own dining room, boat excursions, and again, that handy heated pool.

But if you really want the sense of being away from it all, head across the bridge from Boothbay to Southport Island. Two rustic inns here have water views to stop you in your tracks. Don't expect fancy decor at Newagen Inn, but do expect an extraordinary site in the middle of a nature preserve jutting directly into the Gulf of Maine. Albonegon Inn (accent on the *nee*), a cozily cluttered little place, has an equally smashing site on its own tiny island off the mainland with a view of harbor islands, forested peninsulas, and the fisherman's passage that is the gateway to the Atlantic. These are places where you could easily settle in not just for a relaxing weekend but for a quiet, rejuvenating week or two, happily contemplating the view.

For fans of smaller bed-and-breakfast inns, there are an increasing number in and around town. Those listed below give the bonus of water views.

One thing to be done as soon as you get to Boothbay Harbor is to head straight for the wharf to make your reservation for an outing on the water. There is a wide choice of boats—more than 50 kinds of trips—from an hour's sail to a 41-mile cruise up the Kennebec River to see the ships being built at the Bath Iron Works.

Whichever you choose, you'll be gloriously out to sea among picturesque pine-covered islands and lighthouses, where ospreys soar and herons skim, dolphins and seals play, and (with a little luck), whales can be sighted in the distance.

For the most extraordinary trip of all, board the *Balmy Days* for Monhegan Island. Jamie Wyeth, one of the many artists who summer on Monhegan, described the island to a reporter as "like living on a ship, out of sight of land."

The living here is primitive—few telephones, little electricity—and that's just the way those who love the place want to keep it. Part of Monhegan's beauty is its wildness and the amazing variety of terrain—200-foot cliffs jutting into the sea, virgin forests, ponds and coves, and sighting places along the way for bird and seal watchers with binoculars in hand. The harbor seals are seen best at half tide on Seal Ledge, and sometimes they can be spied at Lobster Cove and off Fish Beach as well.

You'll be given a map as you come onto the island to guide your way. There are a few sights to visit—a museum, a lighthouse, and many artists' studios—but the island's most fabulous sight is itself. Walking trails are clearly marked on the map as to distance and difficulty. The Cathedral Woods are pleasant, cool, and shady, and strewn with wild-flowers, ferns, and "fairy houses" of sticks and bark, built (according to the guide) to entice woodland fairies to set up housekeeping. The most spectacular walks go straight across the top of the cliffs, offering overviews of waves crashing on rocky headlands, which may well remain your favorite memories of Maine.

Monhegan takes up an entire day. The *Balmy Days* ships out at 9:15, arrives at 10:50, and allows you four hours on shore before heading back for a 4:30 arrival in Boothbay Harbor. Lunch is available at both the island's laid-back hotels, the Island Inn and the Trailing Yew, and if you are so taken that you want to come back to stay a while, you can make your reservation now for the next season—the hotels are often booked a full year ahead.

You'll be back on the mainland in plenty of time to try some of the many restaurants for dinner, and to make the rounds of the shops, most of which are conveniently open in the evening. If you wander the wind-ing, narrow streets of town, you'll find some worthwhile stops tucked among the souvenir emporiums. The Custom House on Wharf Street is headquarters for crafts by natives of the state, including original blue-berry pottery. Working metalsmiths are on hand at Silver Lining, and you can watch glassblowers at their craft at Maine Blown Glass.

There are many art galleries for pleasant browsing, including the community-supported Boothbay Region Art Foundation Gallery on Townsend Avenue, which displays some of the better work of area artists in changing shows each season. The Gleason Gallery is housed in The Old Brick House, circa 1807, built by a well-known early builder, John Leisman, Jr., who had the bricks imported from England.

The other attractions in town are recommended only for a rainy day, though kids may enjoy the steam train ride at the Boothbay Railroad Museum.

The town of Boothbay Harbor extends across the river via a foot-bridge. The main incentive to cross over to the east side is dining. Choices include the deck of the Rocktide with its postcard view of the harbor across the water, Brown's Wharf, or the Lobsterman's Co-op. The Sea Pier aquarium on Atlantic Avenue near the Lobster-man's Co-op is stocked by local fishermen.

Evening entertainment is informal, mostly just live music in places such as Fisherman's Wharf. The Carousel Music Theater provides Broadway revues, but remember that you're very far off-Broadway. And there's always the Dolphin Mini-Golf Course on Route 27 in Boothbay, which includes its own New England lighthouse and covered bridge.

If you spend your Saturday at sea, you might relax on Sunday and enjoy the scenery, try another kind of boat excursion, check out the art, or perhaps make the half-hour drive to Pemaquid Point, another of those convoluted peninsulas that mark this part of the coast. This one is reached through the neighboring town of Damariscotta, back on U.S. Route 1.

One of the lesser-known gems of Maine's shoreline, Pemaquid Point is a prime example of that much vaunted "rockbound coast," with a photogenic old lighthouse, a little fishermen's museum and art gallery, and shelves of granite descending into the sea that are especially fun for rock clamberers. The area around the lighthouse has been turned into a park, and the crescent-shaped beach around the bend is open to the public for a fee. The 1827 lighthouse offers one of the best perspectives on the pounding surf.

Not only is Pemaquid as dramatic a viewpoint as any you'll encounter on the coast, it offers a bonus for history and archaeology buffs at Fort William Henry in the state park that has been developed near the beach. This is where England held off the French in four successive forts built between 1605 and 1729. The Old Fort House, built for the last battles, has been restored and shouldn't be missed, even if all you want to do is take a scenic snapshot.

North of the fort are the remains of a once-thriving settlement that existed as early as 1620. Archaeologists have unearthed many of the old cellars, including that of the Customs House, where clearance was required of all ships. Some 40,000 artifacts have been recovered, and a small museum known as Colonial Pemaquid, holds the results of the digs—tools and pottery shards and all manner of possessions reflecting the lives of those who settled here over 350 years ago.

Also in Damariscotta is the restored St. Patrick's Church, the oldest surviving Catholic Church in New England, complete with Paul Revere bell in the tower and an adjacent old cemetery.

If you want to have a meal on Pemaquid Point, there's the New Harbor Co-op for lobster served indoors or on the deck, or the Bradley Inn, a Colonial-style inn on Route 320. The inn is attractive, something to keep in mind if you decide to come back to Pemaquid. Like Monhegan and Southport Island and the rest of the beautiful midcoast around Boothbay Harbor, it seems to beg for a longer visit.

Area Code: 207

DRIVING DIRECTIONS   Boothbay Harbor is 12 miles off U.S. Route 1 on midcoastal Maine, 55 miles east of Portland. Turn south off Route 1 onto Route 27 about a mile north of Wiscasset and follow it into town. It is 164 miles from Boston, 374 miles from New York, and 264 miles from Hartford.

PUBLIC TRANSPORTATION   Air service to Portland; taxi service is available from the airport into Boothbay. You can manage without a car if you stay right in town.

ACCOMMODATIONS   *Topside,* McKown Hill, Boothbay Harbor 04538, 633-5405, $$ • *Welch House,* McKown Hill, Boothbay Harbor 04538, 633-3431, $–$$ • *Spruce Point Inn,* Boothbay Harbor 04538, 633-4152, $$$$$ MAP • *Ocean Point Inn,* PO Box 409, Shore Road, East Boothbay 04544, 633-4200, $$–$$$ • *Albonegon Inn,* Capitol Island 04538, 633-2521, $ CP • *Newagen Inn,* Southport Island, Cape Newagen 04552, 633-5558 or (800) 654-5242, $$–$$$ CP • *Five Gables Inn,* Murray Hill Road, East Boothbay 04544, 233-4551 or (800) 451-5048, century-old summer house, attractive, $$–$$$ CP • *The Lion's Den,* 106 Townsend Avenue, Boothbay Harbor 04538, 633-7367 or (800) 887-7367, good budget choice, $–$$ CP • **Bed-and-breakfast inns with water views:** *Water's Edge,* 8 Eames Road, Boothbay Harbor 04538, 633-4251, quiet location, $–$$ CP; *Harbour Towne Inn,* 71-A Townsend Avenue, Boothbay Harbor 04538, $–$$, spacious penthouse, $$$, all CP; *Anchor Watch,* 3 Eames Road, Boothbay Harbor 04538, 633-7565, $$ CP; *Atlantic Ark,* 64 Atlantic Avenue, Boothbay Harbor 04538, 633-5690, $–$$ CP; *Captain Sawyer's Place,* 87 Commercial Street, Boothbay Harbor 04538, 633-2290, $–$$ CP • **Among the nicest of the motels:** *Ocean Gate,* Southport 04576, 633-3321, $$$–$$$$; *Lawnmeer Inn,* Southport 04575, 633-2544, $; and *Rocktide,* in East Boothbay 04538, 633-4455, $$–$$$; *Island Inn,* Monhegan 04852, 596-0371, $$$ MAP; *Trailing Yew,* Monhegan 04852, 596-0440, $$ MAP.

DINING   **First things first: Lobster!** (Prices vary with the year, but always are less at these informal outdoor eateries.) *Boothbay Region Lobstermen's Co-op,* Atlantic Avenue, East Boothbay, 633-4900, no-frills lobster at waterside picnic tables; *Robinson's Wharf,* Route 27 at the bridge, Southport, 633-3830, full menu as well as lobster, $$; *Cabbage Island Clambake,* 633-5490, includes cruise to Cabbage Island • **Other recommended restaurants:** *Rocktide,* 45 Atlantic Avenue, 633-4455, seafood, buffets, great view, $–$$$; a free trolley runs to and from the village (jackets required in the Dock Room, but not in the Chart Room), $–$$ • *Lawnmeer Inn* (see above), inlet view, $–$$ • *Tugboat Inn,* overlooking the harbor, 633-4434, seafood, $$–$$$; *Black Orchid,* on the By-Way, 633-6659, Italian and seafood specialties, $–$$$ • *Maxfield's,* 33 Oak Street, 633-3444, pleasant ambience, $$ • *Brown's Wharf,* 633-5440, old standby, $$ • *Chowder House,* at the Footbridge, Boothbay Harbor, 633-5761, outdoor deck on the water, also good for breakfast and lunch, $–$$; *Bradley Inn,* Pemaquid Point Road, New Harbor, 677-2105, $$; *New Harbor Co-op,* New Harbor, 677-2791, prices vary with season's catch.

SIGHTSEEING   Boat trips: *Argo,* Pier 6, 633-7200, sightseeing cruises daily in season; *Balmy Days* to Monhegan, Pier 8, 9:30 A.M. daily, 633-2284; *Cap'n Fish's Sightseeing Boat Trips,* daily excursions from Pier 1, also sunset cruises, lobster fishing, and nature cruises, 633-3244; *Maranbo II,* Pier 8, 633-2284, daily cruises; *Miss Boothbay,* 5 Williams Street, 633-6445, lobster boat cruises • **Sailboat cruises:** *Bay Lady,* Fisherman's Wharf, 633-6990; *Eastward,* 633-4780; *Appledore V,* Pier 6, 633-6598, 60-foot windjammer • For any new additions and fishing boat schedules, contact the Chamber of Commerce • *Boothbay Railway Village,* Route 27 outside Boothbay, 633-4727. Hours: mid-June to mid-October, daily, 9 A.M. to 5:30 P.M. Adults, $5; children, $2 • *Boothbay Region Art Foundation Gallery,* 7 Townsend Avenue, Boothbay Harbor, 633-2703. Hours: Monday to Saturday, 11 A.M. to 5 P.M., Sunday, 2 P.M. to 5 P.M. Free • *Sea Pier Aquarium,* Atlantic Avenue, East Boothbay, 633-4900. Hours: Memorial Day to Columbus Day, 10 A.M. to 5 P.M. Small admission fee.

INFORMATION   Boothbay Harbor Region Chamber of Commerce, Route 27, Boothbay Harbor, ME 04538, 633-2353.

Discovering the Other Nantucket

The day-trippers hardly know it exists. For most of the passengers pouring off the ferry, Nantucket Island means the quaint cobblestoned village with its whaling captains' mansions, rose-covered cottages, shops, beaches—and crowds.

But just a few miles away there's another Nantucket, Siasconset and Wauwinet, two tiny settlements that still miraculously match one eighteenth-century visitor's description: "Perfectly unconnected with the real world and far removed from its perturbations." That visitor might be surprised to find that on an island known for its fine dining, the two most lauded restaurants are in these outposts.

The better known of the two, universally called 'Sconset, is a beguiling village set between the cranberry bogs and the rose-grown bluffs overlooking the Atlantic. The miniature cottages winding along 'Sconset's lanes suggest its seventeenth- and eighteenth-century origins as a whaling outpost. They are fishermen's shanties that have been altered and added to over the centuries. Many are unique, built with used wood brought from town or retrieved from shipwrecks, giving rise to the town's nickname of "Patchwork Village."

'Sconset's special flavor began to attract visitors as early as the

1800s. By the end of the century, when the Nantucket Central Railroad extended its narrow-gauge tracks to provide a fast, 35-minute ride from town to the village, the passengers included a "who's who" of the American stage. Stars such as Lillian Russell and Joseph Jefferson came to vacation in what had become a summer haven for Broadway luminaries.

With the rise of Hollywood, the actors' colony moved westward, leaving 'Sconset's glorious beaches in peace. With the exception of one pleasant little café and a spot offering gourmet box lunches, the village square offers little more than basics—food, papers and magazines, liquor, and gasoline. It is marked by the antique water pump that once served the entire community.

Tucked behind hedges and a garden down the lane, however, is The Chanticleer, where chef Jean-Charles Berruet has held sway for more than two decades as the island's most lauded chef, creating delicacies such as scallops poached in Madeira sauce with truffles or gratin de homard in a lobster sauce with cognac. For lunch, tables are set in a vine-covered arbor outside.

Though many people rent houses here during the summer, there are few lodgings in 'Sconset for transient visitors, which is one reason the village retains its peaceful air. The Summer House, on a bluff at the southeastern edge of the island, is the best of the choices, offering cottage accommodations with access to the beach, plus its own pool and cheerful dining spaces. The other possibility is Wade Cottages, a former estate perched on a magnificent seaside bluff. You can rent an entire cottage or a single room here.

Wauwinet, Nantucket's other faraway retreat, is even less developed. It consists of miles of ocean and bayfront beach to tempt strollers, sun worshipers, and fishermen. There are a few houses, one hotel, and not another commercial establishment in sight.

Fishermen were originally attracted to Wauwinet because of the strand of land they dubbed "the haulaway," a strip separating the calm inner harbor from the open Atlantic where they could literally haul their dories across from one to the other. As in 'Sconset, the fishermen built huts that were expanded over the years, but this community soon centered on Wauwinet House, a rambling gray shingled beach house opened by James Backus in 1897 to serve meals for fishermen on its big screened porch.

People began asking to stay overnight, and Wauwinet was soon a thriving summer hotel. It remained so over many years, turning into a no-frills haven for nature lovers and escapists.

Then new owners came in, renovated to the reported tune of $8 million, and the hotel was reborn as Nantucket's poshest retreat, now called simply "The Wauwinet." For those who can afford the tab, there's no better place to escape the crowds and still enjoy all the luxuries of civilization. The shingled facade is almost unchanged, but the interior of the hotel is now a stylish world of chintz and antique pine, stenciling, folk art, and faux ceiling clouds—all the accoutrements of country chic. Amenities include free shuttle service into town.

The cool restaurant, named Topper's after the owner's dog, quickly rivaled The Chanticleer for the title of "best on the island" for its "New American" cuisine. Even the sumptuous breakfasts served to guests are extraordinary. Leave the calorie counter at home.

Those who stay in town and want to come to Wauwinet for lunch or dinner can do so via a free cruise on the *Lady Wauwinet,* a wonderful outing. The terrace is an unbeatable place for watching glorious island sunsets.

One thing that has not changed at Wauwinet is unending vistas of blue sea. You can play tennis or rent a boat, but this is really a place to do absolutely nothing—just appreciate the rare tranquility ensured for years to come by the Backus's gift of more than 500 acres of surrounding land to the Massachusetts Trustees of Preservation.

Almost everyone eventually takes off along the four-mile curved beach to Great Point and its lighthouse, rebuilt after a storm and now solar-powered. The hotel offers guided walks for guests.

If you want more action, take the hotel shuttle, drive, or bike the eight miles or so and join the tourists on the cobbled lanes in Nantucket Village, where there are scores of restaurants, two movie theaters, nightlife, and plenty of shops to keep you occupied. The Whaling Museum is just the thing for a cloudy day, as are the elegant homes of the old whale-oil merchants. See page 25 for more about Nantucket sights, and visit the Chamber of Commerce for information on guided walking tours of the beautiful village.

When you've had your fill of sights, you can come back to 'Sconset or Wauwinet, leaving crowds and cares behind for the company of the gulls and the sea.

Area Code: 508

TRANSPORTATION   See page 23.

ACCOMMODATIONS   *Summer House,* Box 313, Shore Road, Siasconset, Nantucket 02564, 257-9976, late April to early October, $$$$$ CP • *Wade Cottages,* Box 211, Siasconset, Nantucket 02564, 257-6308, late May to mid-October, $$$–$$$$ CP • *The Wauwinet,* Wauwinet, Nantucket 02584, 228-0145 or (800) 426-8718, April to October, $$$$$ CP • A three-day minimum may be required in season; all accommodations are less in spring and fall.

DINING   *The Chanticleer,* Siasconset, 257-6231, reservations essential, open late May to mid-October, lunch served June through September, $$$–$$$$; dinner, prix fixe, $$$$$ • *Topper's,* The Wauwinet (see above), lunch, $$; dinner, $$$$ • *Summer House* (see above), $$$–$$$$ • *'Sconset Café,* on the square, Siasconset, 257-4008, $–$$ • *Claudette's Box Lunches,* on the square, Siasconset, 257-6622 • For additional Nantucket suggestions, see pages 24–25.

SIGHTSEEING   See page 25.

INFORMATION   Nantucket Island Chamber of Commerce, 48 Main Street, Nantucket, MA 02554, 228-1700.

Fall

Overleaf: *Autumn in Woodbury, Vermont. Photograph Courtesy of Vermont Travel Division.*

Indian Summer in Kennebunkport

Kennebunkport, Maine, is picturesque . . . posh . . . and packed with people and cars in midsummer. After part-time resident George Bush became President, the numbers grew even larger, and though he is out of office, gawkers still come trying to get a glimpse of the Bush family compound on the water.

Celebrity watcher or not, there's good reason to head for this delightful seafaring town, but since its special pleasures are not limited to July and August, there's no reason to put up with the crowds.

Instead, mark Kennebunkport down for a warm Indian Summer weekend after Labor Day. You can still live in a sea captain's mansion, see the lovely shuttered Colonial homes and enormous summer "cottages," walk the cliffs and the wide beaches, watch the foam spout at "Blowing Cave" and the sun set at Porpoise Point, and eat all the lobster you can hold—without having to fight for space to do it all.

Kennebunkport has always been a desirable place to be. Even Maine's Indians chose to set up their campgrounds along the beautiful beaches here, and countless artists and writers have been inspired by the views. Kenneth Roberts, a native, immortalized the town in his novel *Arundel* (the name of the village until 1821), and Booth Tarkington wrote his novels aboard his schooner *Regina,* which was moored on the Kennebunk River for years.

The village became a favorite summer resort for the wealthy in the late 1880s, and has boasted prominent summer residents ever since.

In the 1700s, Kennebunkport grew into a port and shipbuilding center second only to Portland on the Maine coast. Eight hundred vessels were launched from here in less than 80 years. The unusual profusion of fine Colonial residences in the central Historic District are testament to the fortunes that were made in the shipbuilding trade.

Though there are excellent lodgings of every kind to be found, one of the particular pleasures of Kennebunkport is to stay in one of the old mansions that now serve as elegant inns. The best known (and for good reason) is the Captain Lord Mansion, built by a wealthy shipbuilder who kept his carpenters occupied during the British blockade of the harbor in 1812 by putting them to work constructing the town's most imposing residence. And grand it remains, a three-story, creamy yellow clapboard, Federal-style structure with rows upon rows of tall shuttered windows and an octagonal cupola on top. The three-story stairway, many fireplaces, and ornate Victorian furnishings in the inn's 16 rooms are exceptional.

Needless to say, your odds of getting a reservation are better off-season, but do write well ahead anyway.

If the Captain Lord is full, all is far from lost, for the Captain Jefferds Inn, circa 1804, is another beauty built by an affluent merchant captain, and its antique-filled interior is also exceptional. It was once featured in *House Beautiful*.

The Captain Fairfield Inn, built in 1813, has also been beautifully restored, and is a bit cozier in feel. The Inn on South Street and Kylemere House are gracious smaller homes turned inns.

The Lower Village, the heart of Kennebunkport, is a short stroll from any of these inns. It is a compact area that is best appreciated on foot. The 1824 South Congregational Church, across the way from the shopping area, with its 100-foot white steeple and weather-vane-topped Christopher Wren cupola and belfry, is a quintessential New England sight and the subject of many photographs.

Across the way, in the Temple Street Post Office, you can see a Gordon Grant mural depicting the harbor as it was in the old days, when the air was filled with the clang of shipbuilders' hammers and the cries of crews unloading cargo from around the world. Dock Square, where square-riggers were once moored, is no less busy today as a complex of weathered buildings housing all manner of shops and restaurants. The Dock Square Market building, moved here in 1849, once housed a Baptist church and a school. The Bookport Building started life as a rum warehouse for Perkins' West India Goods. You'll find almost every kind of clothing and craft for sale here, though the emphasis is on fashions that are on the preppy side.

From Dock Square, walk down Ocean Avenue past more shops and turn left on Pearl Street, then right on Pleasant to view some of the finest of the sea captains' homes. Green and Maine streets offer more architectural delights.

You'll find art galleries almost everywhere you go, since Kennebunkport remains a magnet for artists. The Art Guild brochure, available in most inns and shops, lists almost two dozen galleries.

Return to Ocean Avenue and take a very long walk or a drive around rocky Cape Arundel and you'll begin to see what inspires the artists. The rugged coastline here is superb, and there's a bonus if you clamber down the rocks to Spouting Rock and Blowing Cave, where the waves perform a foaming leaping dance in rhythm with the tide. Keep going and you'll see St. Ann's Episcopal Church, built of sea-washed stone just beyond reach of the waves, with the ocean in sight beyond the altar of an outdoor chapel. When you spy the Secret Service men on guard, you'll know you've reached the Bush family residence at Walker Point.

There is a beach off Ocean Avenue in town, but the better bet is Goose Rocks Beach, about a ten-minute drive along King's Highway off Route 9. The beach is near Cape Porpoise, whose pier is a center for lobstering and much of the commercial fishing activity of Kenne-bunkport. It is a scenic spot for taking photos, especially near sunset.

One of the most delightful of Kennebunkport's small inns is The Inn at Harbor Head, hidden away high on a hill overlooking Cape Porpoise Harbor and the ocean beyond. Canopy beds, antique pine, and artistic taste make each of the four bedrooms special.

Some of the best eating in town is also found at Cape Porpoise. For lobster sans frills, there's Nunan's Lobster Hut, for more formal dining, Seascapes offers both harbor views and gourmet menus.

Another local eating experience that shouldn't be missed is breakfast at the Green Heron, a many-course delight with wonderful fresh fruits and baked goodies that has become a local institution—as the long waiting lines outside the inn on weekend mornings suggest.

If the shops and galleries pall and the weather isn't conducive to beach walks, visit the Seashore Trolley Museum, one of the largest collections of electric and railway cars in the country, for a bit of nostalgia and an old-fashioned trolley ride. If bargains are of more interest than trolleys, head for Wells and its array of discount stores.

Another possibility is the short drive to Kennebunk to see another magnificent early New England church, the First Parish Unitarian Church, built in 1772. The Christopher Wren steeple was added when the church was enlarged in 1803–1804, and a Paul Revere bell was hung at the same time. Kennebunk's tiny Brick Store Museum on the main street offers interesting exhibits from the town's early days, including furniture, paintings, and ship models. Kennebunk lacks its seaside sister's charm, but it does have some interesting historic homes and some fine beaches of its own.

If the sun is shining, there are boats waiting to take you out to sea for a scenic cruise, a fishing excursion, or whale watching in season.

In truth, though, it's hardly likely you'll stray far from Kennebunkport. Ensconced in your own sea captain's quarters with magnificent seascapes, historic homes, and half a hundred shops and galleries just around the corner, why on earth would you want to leave?

Area Code: 207

DRIVING DIRECTIONS   Kennebunkport is on the southern coast of Maine, about 25 miles below Portland. From I-95 or U.S. Route 1, follow Route 35 east into town. Route 9, closer to the shore, also leads to Kennebunkport. It is 88 miles from Boston, 298 miles from New York, and 188 miles from Hartford.

PUBLIC TRANSPORTATION   Greyhound bus service to Biddeford, 7 miles; nearest air service is Portland.

ACCOMMODATIONS *Captain Lord Mansion,* Box 800, Pleasant and Green streets, Kennebunkport 04046, 967-3141, $$$$–$$$$$ CP (less from January 1 to April 30, and the rooms have fireplaces!) • *Captain Jefferds Inn,* Pearl and Pleasant streets, Box 691, Kennebunkport 04046, 967-2311, $$–$$$ CP • *Captain Fairfield Inn,* Pleasant and Green streets, Kennebunkport 04046, 967-4454, $$$–$$$$ CP • *The Inn at Harbor Head,* Pier Road, Box 1180, Cape Porpoise, Kennebunkport 04046, 967-5564, exceptional location and decor, $$$–$$$$$ CP • *Old Fort Inn,* Old Fort Avenue, Kennebunkport 04046, 967-5353, secluded and rustic, with pool and tennis court, $$$–$$$$$ CP • *White Barn Inn,* Beach Street, Kennebunkport 04046, 967-2321, inn and luxurious restored carriage houses, member Relais & Châteaux, $$$–$$$$ CP • *The Inn on South Street,* Box 478A, Kennebunkport 04046, 967-5151, attractive nineteenth-century Greek Revival home, $$–$$$ CP • *Kylemere House,* South Street, Box 1333, Kennebunkport 04046, 967-2780, another attractive 1818 home, $$ CP • *1802 House,* Box 646A, 15 Locke Street, Kennebunkport 04046, 967-5632, cozy, quiet, $–$$$ CP • *Bufflehead Cove,* off Route 35, PO Box 499, Kennebunkport 04046, 967-3879, rural location only a mile from town, serene water views, simple charm, $$ CP • *Inn at Goose Rocks,* Dyke Road, Goose Rocks, Kennebunkport 04046, 967-5425 or (800) 457-7688, wooded setting on marshes, near the beach, pool, $$–$$$ CP • *The Colony,* Ocean Avenue and King's Highway, Kennebunkport 04046, 967-3331, big, staid classic old hotel in town, $$$$–$$$$$ AP.

DINING *White Barn Inn* (see above), charmingly restored barn, excellent fare, $$$ • *Kennebunkport Inn,* Dock Square, 967-2621, gracious, $$$ • *The Olde Grist Mill,* Mill Lane off Route 9, 967-4781, New England menu in a real old mill, $$–$$$ • *Windows on the Water,* Chase Hill Road, Kennebunkport, 967-3313, no views despite the name, but highly regarded, $$–$$$ • *Cape Arundel Inn,* Ocean Avenue, 967-2125, views and fine dining, $$–$$$ • *Breakwater Inn,* Ocean Avenue, Kennebunkport, 967-3118, harbor views, $–$$ • *Tides Inn by the Sea,* 737 Goose Rocks Beach, Kennebunkport, 967-3757, rustic setting overlooking the beach, interesting menu, $$, also tavern fare, $ • *Seascapes,* Cape Porpoise Harbor, 967-8500, elegant dining, views, $$–$$$ • *Nunan's Lobster Hut,* Route 9, Cape Porpoise, 967-4435, informal lobster spot, $–$$ • *Cape Porpoise Lobster Co., Inc.,* 15 Pier Road, Cape Porpoise, 967-4268, lobster rolls, chowder, etc., $$ • *Kellett's Lobster Pot,* Route 9, Cape Porpoise, 967-4607, family restaurant, $–$$ • For breakfast, *The Green Heron,* Ocean Avenue, 967-5353; for a take-out lobster-roll lunch, *Port Lobster Company,* Ocean Avenue, 967-2081, $.

SIGHTSEEING *Seashore Trolley Museum,* Log Cabin Road, Box 220, Kennebunkport, 967-2800. Hours: Memorial Day to Labor Day, daily, 10 A.M. to 5:30 P.M., early May and Labor Day through October, weekends only, 10 A.M. to 4 P.M.—may be open weekends to mid-November, best to check. Adults, $6; ages 6 to 17, $4; family rate, $20 • *Brick Store Museum,* 117 Main Street, Kennebunk, 985-4802. Hours: museum, Tuesday to Saturday, 10 A.M. to 4:30 P.M., closed Saturday January to April; house, June to September, Tuesday to Friday, 1 P.M. to 4 P.M. Adults, $3; children, $1; house admission, adults, $2; children, $1; combination ticket, $4. • *Kennebunkport Maritime Museum and Gallery,* Ocean Avenue, Kennebunkport, 967-4195. Hours: mid-May through November, Monday to Saturday, 10 A.M. to 5 P.M., Sunday 11 A.M. to 4 P.M. Admission, $2; under 6, free • *Cape Arundel Cruises,* Arundel Shipyard, Route 9 by the bridge, PO Box 840, Kennebunkport 967-5595, phone for rates and schedules.

INFORMATION Kennebunk-Kennebunkport Chamber of Commerce, PO Box 740, Kennebunk, ME 04043, 967-0857.

Inns and Arts of Vermont

Inn fever is an epidemic that strikes thousands in New England, and it is highly contagious. You'll find victims in small towns and on back roads everywhere, ready to travel any lengths to track down a new and choice country inn.

If you share this delightfully incurable affliction, you'll find the southwestern corner of Vermont happy inn-hunting grounds. There are dozens of inns within a wiggly scenic rectangle roughly 30 by 21 miles, with Dorset, Bennington, Wilmington, and Jamaica as the corners. Many can rightfully be called exceptional, each in its own way.

And to make the quest even more rewarding, this is a route rich in art, where you will find prize galleries as well as one of Vermont's major annual exhibitions, the month-long fall Stratton Arts Festival, plus other fall art and crafts events. Add the scenery of an area with four ski mountains, lots of opportunity for hiking and canoeing, and more shops than can fit into a month of weekends, and you have a year-round destination that becomes unbeatable in foliage season.

The major commercial center is Manchester, a town that likes to call itself Manchester and the Mountains, to underscore its role as the heart of this cluster of villages. Since it is within easy reach no matter where you choose to stay, Manchester makes an ideal starting point for an inns-and-arts tour.

There's plenty to see and do right here, and you'll find lots of information at the Visitors' Center in Manchester Center. You'll also find cars—long lines of them— clogging the intersections of Route 30, 11, and 7. The lure is Manchester Commons, a shopping complex that includes outlets for Polo/Ralph Lauren, Coach leather, Cole Hahn shoes, and many other upscale labels. Right across the street is Battenkill Plaza, where Anne Klein, Donna Karan, Ellen Tracy, and Van Heusen stores beckon. And the shops continue to march eastward farther and farther along Route 30, including a major new mall that includes Brooks Brothers, Armani, Esprit, and other fashionable names. Across the road is an outlet for Orvis, the outdoor outfitters whose headquarters are on Route 7A farther south.

If shopping is not your sport, outdoor enthusiasts should note that there are three golf courses as well as public tennis courts in town, and more facilities not far away at Stratton Mountain. For more outdoor activity, bikes are for rent at Battenkill Sports at the intersection of Routes 7/11/30 in Manchester Center, and there's plenty of hiking in the area, with both the Long Trail and the Appalachian Trail nearby. Stop at the U.S. Forest Service headquarters on the way to Bromley Mountain, north of Manchester on Routes 11/30, for maps and guidance.

Though many pleasant inns line Route 7A, the traffic has taken away the feeling of a country getaway. The best bet in Manchester Center is Birch Hill Inn, set an 240 acres away from the bustle and offering mountain views from every room.

Or head for Dorset, the northern tip of your driving tour, for a tranquil Colonial oasis. Barrows House is a world of its own, a collection of houses centered on a 1784 mansion, all set amid towering trees and well-groomed gardens. Guests here enjoy tennis courts, a pool, a croquet court, and a gazebo for enjoying the setting. The restaurant is excellent, and new owners have refurbished the rooms, added a few more fireplaces, and a playroom for families.

The Dorset Inn is another very attractive possibility, on the green right on the pretty little Main Street of town. It offers lots of Colonial atmosphere and a highly regarded dining room. Just across the road is the Dovetail Inn, a relaxed, reasonably priced Colonial-style bed-and-breakfast inn in a pair of the town's appealing old homes, highly recommended for those on a budget. You'll look hard to find a more charming stop than the Cornucopia of Dorset, located just down the block in a nineteenth-century home. The decor is tasteful, the breakfasts are sumptious, and the rates include afternoon tea.

The fighting-mad Green Mountain Boys signed their personal declaration of independence in Dorset, an event remembered by a marker in the center of town. In the peaceful, moneyed Dorset of today, a more significant claim to fame may be what is reputedly the oldest nine-hole golf course in the country at the Dorset Field Club. The Dorset Playhouse is one of the few summer theaters that remains open into the foliage season, and the town has several stops for antiquers.

Though you'll spy plenty of antiques shops all along your drive, avid antiquers may want to detour a couple of miles north on Route 7 to the

1812 House Antiques Center, a collective of 30 dealers. A detour for apples instead will take you to Mad Tom's Orchard in East Dorset, where you can pick your own apples to go with the Vermont cheese and maple syrup you'll probably acquire at a country store en route.

Returning to Manchester and heading south, take historic Route 7A to Manchester Village and the two main sightseeing stops in the region, both offering expansive hilltop views as well as a chance to get out and walk. The Southern Vermont Art Center, a gracious mansion on 407 sylvan acres, has changing exhibits of art, sculpture, and photography and also offers nature walks, including a Botany Trail with 67 varieties of wildflowers. Concerts are held throughout the year, for every taste from classical to jazz. The Garden Café here is a highly recommended stop for lunch or brunch with a view.

Hildene is the Georgian mansion built by Robert Todd Lincoln, Abraham's son, and occupied by descendants of the Lincoln family until 1975. It is one of the most fascinating historic houses to visit. Guided tours include a demonstration of the mansion's 1,000-pipe Aeolian organ. Hildene sits on 412 acres with formal gardens and walking trails, and you can picnic here with the valley below spread before you in its best autumn colors. The first weekend in October brings an annual Harvest and Craft Festival to the grounds. If you come back in winter, there's excellent cross-country skiing on the grounds.

The American Museum of Fly Fishing is another local institution, of interest not only to the many who come to try their luck in the nearby Battenkill River, a noted trout stream. Masterworks of America's best fly-tiers are displayed, along with the tackles of such notable fishermen as Daniel Webster, Dwight Eisenhower, Andrew Carnegie, and Ernest Hemingway. Should you be inspired to improve or take up the sport, the Orvis store nearby is fly-fishing headquarters, and holds teaching clinics regularly.

Manchester Village was a posh resort during the pre–Civil War days when its Equinox House was a well-known summer retreat, and it still boasts the marble-slab sidewalks and handsome homes from those glory days. The village is looking very spiffy once again since restoration of the grand old hotel was completed, and there are now many upscale shops to tempt the upscale visitors. The hotel offers golf, tennis, and a well-equipped spa.

Another old-timer is the Wilburton Inn, a Tudor-style summer mansion built in the early 1900s on a high knoll with soaring mountain views. The rooms are huge, amenities include tennis courts and a pool, and the food lives up to the setting.

Two choice small inns are just a stone's throw from the Equinox. The Reluctant Panther Inn, a 150-year-old house easy to spot for its lavender paint, is country elegant and is an excellent dining choice. The 1811 House, which was actually built in the 1770s, is a showcase for period antiques and is surrounded by a nice lawn and gardens.

One of those ubiquitous country stores awaits on Route 7A in Arlington, as well as a shop and museum featuring the works of Norman Rockwell, a onetime village resident. Follow the road to East Arlington for Candle Mill Village, eight shops in a former gristmill beside a waterfall. The specialty here is candles—some 50,000 of them—and if none of them please, you can dip your own. There are also shops that offer 1,000 kinds of cookbooks and more than 600 kinds of music boxes. And the East Arlington Antique Center offers wares from 45 dealers under one roof.

Take the road just opposite the columned Arlington Inn (a good bet for dinner) to the West Mountain Inn, a wonderful hideaway near the Battenkill River, with warm country ambience and an unbeatable mountain view. Children will like the resident llamas and goat; trout fishermen and canoers will enjoy the river. On the way, you will pass The Keelan House, an antique-filled 1820 Federal home on the river, a perfect B & B choice when you are looking for moderate rates.

Continue on scenic River Road to West Arlington and you'll come to an inn with a special history. The Inn on Covered Bridge Green, a 200-year-old Colonial home, was Norman Rockwell's home for part of his stay in Arlington; his former studio can be rented as a two-bedroom cottage. When you see the New England views from the master bedroom of the little white Church on the Green and the Covered Bridge, you'll understand why this location would have appealed to the artist.

When you come into Bennington, turn right on Route 7 to historic Old Bennington, a stately beauty of a village with a host of magnificent eighteenth- and nineteenth-century homes. On the way you'll pass the columned Bennington Museum, which offers free walking-tour pamphlets of the old part of town and a delightful gallery devoted to one of the region's better-known painters, former resident Grandma Moses, who captured the surrounding Vermont landscapes with so much naive charm. There are 32 of her works on display, and if perchance you've never seen an original Grandma Moses, you have a treat in store.

Outside is the Grandma Moses Schoolhouse, the 1834 one-room school that she attended as a child with a photo story of her life. The museum also offers a military gallery; a comprehensive collection of American pressed glass, including pieces by Louis Comfort Tiffany; and the largest collection of the well-known brown-glazed early Bennington pottery.

Continuing west on Route 9, turn right on the main street of Old Bennington and drive up the hill to the impressive 360-foot stone obelisk commemorating the famous Battle of Bennington, a major turning point in the Revolutionary War. It was here that General John Stark turned back the British, saying, "There are the Redcoats and they are ours, or this night Molly Stark sleeps a widow." The tall monument on the hill can be seen for miles around, and the elevator ride to the top affords an unforgettable view of the countryside. There is also a diorama in the monument depicting the battle, created by Vermont artist Paul Winters.

Take a walk down the hill from the Monument to really appreciate the details of the gracious houses on both sides of the road, with the walking tour as a guide to each home's history. At the bottom on the green is the Walloomsac Inn, said to be the oldest continuously operating inn in Vermont. It's doubtful you'll want to stay in this inn, which is looking rather the worse for its 220-plus years of wear, but it is definitely worth a look.

You probably *will* want to stay or at least dine at the Four Chimneys, an Old Bennington mansion converted to a luxury inn and restaurant by Alex Koks, a highly regarded Vermont chef.

Another place to visit in town is the Potter's Yard. Follow Route 7 two lights north of Route 9, then turn on County Street to the place where Bennington Pottery was founded more than three decades ago on the site of a former gristmill. Though the pottery is still very much in operation, most of the pieces now are modern rather than copies of the originals. There is a tremendous collection of pottery for sale in an attractive shop that also sells woven goods and baskets from around the world. Nearby shops have more attractive accessories for the home. Time your visit for lunch to sample the gourmet fare at The Brasserie, an outstanding restaurant adjoining the shops.

Antiquers may want to make time for the Camelot Village Antique Center on Route 9, a barnlike building with two floors filled with antiques and gifts.

From Bennington, proceed west on Molly Stark's Route 9, a heavily wooded, very scenic road along a river that will bring you to Wilmington. Once a sleepy village, Wilmington has had an infusion of energy from all the skiers who come to town for Haystack Mountain or nearby Mount Snow, and is now pleasantly alive with restaurants, inns, and shops that make for pleasant browsing. Check out Quaigh Design Center for Vermont crafts. There's another shot at a country store here, too.

Turn left onto Route 100 north and then make another left at Coldbrook, the road to Haystack Mountain, for The Hermitage, a gracious old inn above the mountain, set on 24 acres of woods and fields that make for prime ski touring in winter and provide a view that goes on forever. Prize game and fowl, raised by the owner, are a specialty of the inn's dining room, along with trout from a pond on the property. The rooms here are big and handsome, each with a fireplace.

Come back to Route 100, continue north a few miles to West Dover, and cross the bridge to The Inn at Sawmill Farm. This onetime barn and stable is now an antique-filled inn that makes the best possible use of the soaring heights and beams of the old barn. The rustic setting is softened with warm brick and fieldstone, and comfortable upholstered pieces. It's elegant yet country in feel, the rooms are posh and enormous (ten of them have fireplaces), and the fare in the dining room does justice to its surroundings. The tab is hefty, but the inn is special.

If you've timed your visit right, while you are in the area, you can take in the annual Mount Snow Craft Show, usually held in the base lodge over the Columbus Day weekend. To end your tour with the arts, turn west on Route 30 to the mammoth show at Stratton Mountain. The Stratton Arts Festival, a nonprofit event that began in 1963 as a Columbus Day art show with 30 participants, has grown into one of the largest displays of Vermont talent. The highly selective, juried show feature more than 200 exhibitors showing oils and watercolors, metal and stone sculpture, prints and photographs, and handcrafted clay, metal, ceramic, and fiber pieces. All of the work is for sale.

Exhibitors are present on weekends to demonstrate their work and talk about their craft, and each Saturday afternoon features free musical performances, from jazz to rock to classical.

It might be possible to take in all of this in a day, but it's not probable—or advisable. You'd do better to head back to your inn when your energy flags and save half the route for a second day, allowing plenty of time to enjoy the views, the outdoors, and your own discoveries along the way.

In fact, you could spend many happy weekends exploring the varied pleasures of this rich section of southern Vermont. When you've returned home, stored the apples and cheese and maple syrup, settled on spots for your newly purchased finds, and taken the film to be developed, you can begin figuring out which of those wonderful inns to try when you come back for a repeat performance.

Area Code: 802

DRIVING DIRECTIONS   Manchester Center is on Route 7A at the intersection of Routes 11 and 30. It is 160 miles from Boston, 248 miles from New York, and 138 miles from Hartford.

PUBLIC TRANSPORTATION   Vermont Transit provides bus service to Manchester and Bennington. Closest air service is Albany, New York, 90 minutes away.

ACCOMMODATIONS   **First choices, in alphabetical order:** *The Barrows House,* Dorset 05251, 867-4455, $$$$–$$$$$ MAP • *Birch Hill Inn,* West Road, Manchester 05254, 362-2761 or (800) 372-2761, $$$ CP • *Cornucopia of Dorset,* PO Box 307, Route 30, Dorset 05251, 867-5751, $$$ CP • *The Dorset Inn,* Church and Main streets, Dorset 05251 $$$–$$$$ MAP • *Dovetail Inn,* Route 30, Dorset 05251, 867-5747, $$ CP • *1811 House,* Route 7A, Manchester Village

05254, 362-1811, $$$$ CP • *Equinox Hotel,* Route 7A, Manchester Village 05254, 362-4700 or (800) 362-4747, many special packages, $$$$–$$$$$ • *The Hermitage,* Coldbrook Road (off Route 100), Wilmington 05363, 464-3711, $$$$$ MAP • *West Mountain Inn,* Route 313, Arlington 05250, 375-6516, relaxed country charm, $$$–$$$$ MAP • *Inn on Covered Bridge Green,* River Road, Arlington 05250, 375-9489 or (800) 726-9480, $$$–$$$$ CP • *The Inn at Sawmill Farm,* Box 367, Mt. Snow Valley, West Dover 05356, 464-8131, $$$$$ MAP • *The Keelan House,* Route 313, Arlington 05250, 375-9029, $ CP • *Reluctant Panther Inn,* West Road (off Route 7A), Manchester Village 05254, 362-2568, $$$$–$$$$$ CP • *Wilburton Inn,* River Road, Manchester Village 05254, 362-2500 or (800) 648-4944, $$–$$$ CP • **More good options:** *Arlington Inn,* Arlington 05250, 375-6532, $$–$$$ CP; *Four Chimneys Inn,* 21 West Road, Old Bennington, 447-3500, $$$ CP • *Inn at West View Farm,* Route 30, Dorset 05251, 867-5715, $$–$$$ CP; *The Inn at Manchester,* Box 41, Route 7A, Manchester 05254, 362-1793 or (800) 273-1793, a charming inn, but on very busy road, $$–$$$ CP; *Manchester Highlands Inn,* Highland Avenue, Manchester 05255, 362-4565 or (800) 743-4565, Victorian house, quiet spot, reasonable, $$–$$$ CP; *South Shire Inn,* 124 Elm Street, Bennington 05201, Queen Anne mansion in a residential neighborhood, $$–$$$$ CP • For motels and ski lodges, try the Manchester Chamber of Commerce Lodging Service, 824-6915, or Stratton Mountain Reservation Service (800) 843-6867.

DINING *Reluctant Panther Inn* (see above), $$$ • *Wilburton Inn* (see above), $$–$$$ • *Mistral's,* Toll Gate Road, Manchester Center, 362-1779, classic French menu, country decor, $$–$$$ • *The Black Swan,* Route 7A, Manchester, 362-3807, continental fare in an old farmhouse, $$–$$$ • *Bistro Henry,* Route 30, Manchester, 362-4982, French accent, $–$$ • *Chanticleer,* Route 7, East Dorset, 362-1616, Swiss and Provençal specialties, $$–$$$ • *The Dorset Inn* (see above), $–$$ • *The Barrows House* (see above), $$–$$$; lighter menu, $ • *Arlington Inn* (see above), $$–$$$ • *The Hermitage* (see above), $$–$$$ • *West Mountain Inn* (see above), prix fixe, $$$$ • *The Inn at Sawmill Farm* (see above), $$$$ • *Four Chimneys Inn* (see above), $$–$$$ • *Alldays & Onions,* 519 Main Street, Bennington, 447-0032, American, light to formal, $–$$$ • **Informal dining:** *Laney's,* Route 11/30, Manchester Center, 362-4456, lively, open kitchen, ribs, chicken, brick-oven pizza, $–$$; *The Brasserie,* 324 County Street, Bennington, 447-7922, lunch and light dinners until 8 P.M., $; *Main Street Café,* 1 Prospect Street, North Bennington, 442-3210, Italian, $–$$; *Garlic John's,* Routes 11/30, Manchester Center, 362-9843, cheerful spot for pasta and spaghetti, $–$$; *River Café,* Route 30, Bondville, 297-1010, sandwiches, salads, pasta, deck with river view, $–$$; *The Garden Café,* Southern Vermont Art Center, Manchester,

362-4220, wonderful spot for lunch, $ • For breakfast, the place is *Up for Breakfast,* 710 Main Street, Manchester Center, 362-4204, great muffins, scones, etc., $.

SIGHTSEEING   *Stratton Mountain Arts Festival,* Stratton Mountain Base Lodge, Route 30, Bondville, 297-2200. Hours: mid-September to mid-October, daily, 9:30 A.M. to 5:00 P.M. contact for current dates and admission • *Historic Hildene,* Route 7A, Manchester Village, 362-1788. Hours: mid-May through October, daily, tours 9:30 A.M. to 4 P.M. Adults, $6; children, $2 • *Southern Vermont Art Center,* West Road off Route 7A, Manchester, 362-1405. Hours: late May to October, Tuesday to Saturday and Monday holidays, 10 A.M. to 5 P.M., Sunday from noon. December to April, Monday to Saturday, 10 A.M. to 4 P.M. Adults, $3; students, $0.50; under 13, free; free to all on Sunday • *American Museum of Fly Fishing,* Route 7A, Manchester Village, 362-3300. Hours: April 1 to November 1, daily, 10 A.M. to 4 P.M.; rest of year closed weekends. Admission, $2 • *Norman Rockwell Exhibition,* Route 7A, Arlington, 375-6423. Hours: daily, May to October, 9 A.M. to 5 P.M., November to April, 10 A.M. to 4 P.M. Admission, $1 • *Bennington Museum,* West Main Street, 447-1571. Hours: daily, 9 A.M. to 5 P.M. Adults, $5; under 12, free.

INFORMATION   Manchester and the Mountains Chamber of Commerce, Box 928, Manchester Center, VT 05255, 362-2100; Bennington Chamber of Commerce, Veterans Memorial Drive, Bennington, VT 05201, 447-3311; Stratton Mountain, Stratton Mountain, VT 05155, 297-2200 or (800) 843-6867.

Back to Nature on Cape Cod

For true beach and nature lovers, the real Cape Cod begins at the "elbow," the bend that marks the break from the calm waters of Nantucket Sound to the rough surf of the Atlantic.

The wide, dune-backed ocean shores of the Outer Cape, stretching for 40 unbroken miles from Chatham and Orleans to the tip of Provincetown, are as fine as any beach area in the country. Thanks to the National Park Service, which took over when most of the area was declared a National Seashore in 1961, not only the beach but 27,000 acres of marshes, meadows, and ponds around it have been protected to provide recreation and beauty for swimmers, surfers, hikers, bikers, horseback riders—or anyone who just wants to sit on an uncrowded beach and contemplate the hypnotic rhythms of the sea.

This extraordinary seashore is at its most glorious in autumn, just when most of the tourists leave. The days are generally bright and sunny, but not too hot for outdoor activity; the evenings are cool and breezy, the better to enjoy the indoor pleasures of dining in good restaurants now relieved of their summer crowds. To add to the pleasure, some inns lower their rates starting in mid-September.

You'll find the pick of the inns in and around Orleans, at the start of the Outer Cape. A personal favorite is the Nauset House Inn, an antique-filled renovated farmhouse with a big inviting living room where guests congregate, and a wicker and plant-filled conservatory that is cheerful on even the gloomiest day. The warmth of the owners makes everyone feel at home here.

Nauset House Inn is within walking distance of Nauset Beach, a glorious unending stretch of sand, but even closer is the Ship's Knees Inn, a snug nautical haven with a pool and tennis court. Hillbourne House, set on spacious lawns facing Pleasant Bay, is another choice stop, with rooms in a cozy pine-paneled 1798 home as well as a small adjacent motel and cottage units. And there's peace and privacy at the Whalewalk Inn, just across the Orleans town line in Eastham. This 1830 whaling master's home is furnished with a mix of antiques and comfortable contemporary, and offers lodgings in the main house, in the barn, or in cottages on the grounds.

As the shopping center for the Lower Cape, Orleans has been invaded by discount stores and fast-food outlets, but outside the commercial center it remains a placid and attractive town with some of the best restaurants in the area. The sections toward Rock Harbor and Cape Cod Bay, where early packet boats landed from Boston, is filled with gray-shingled cottages and white picket fences. Fishing boats are still a presence in the pretty harbor. The lanes of East Orleans, near the ocean, are equally old New England in feel.

Orleans also provides necessary shops and diversions in the unhappy event of rain. The Artful Hand, Trees, and Peacock Alley are the pick of the galleries. And there are such worldly pleasures as gourmet ice cream in a branch of Boston's Emack and Bolio's or in the local outlet known as the Sundae School in East Orleans.

Farther down the coast are more lodging choices in Wellfleet and Provincetown. This is prime country for using the area bed-and-breakfast services, since private-home accommodations allow you to stay in wooded settings in towns such as Truro, which offer few inns. Staying in these towns will give you access to their beautiful private beaches.

Once you've settled in, begin your exploration with a stop at the Salt Pond Visitors' Center at Eastham or the Province Lands center near Provincetown, each right off the main highway (Route 6) and clearly marked. Both lead to excellent hiking, biking, and riding trails and beaches, and both have schedules of many ranger-guided walks and talks at the National Seashore.

The trails of the National Seashore are designed to show the variety of the terrain as well as the ever-changing effects of wind and water on this fragile land. The power of erosion is clearly seen at the Marconi Wireless Station at Wellfleet, where the Cape is only a mile wide. Much of the cliff has disappeared, along with the towers that Guglielmo Marconi built here to transmit the first wireless communication from America to Europe in 1903—victims of the relentless tides that take away an average of three feet of coastline each year.

The Marconi site leads into the Atlantic White Cedar Swamp Trail, where lush green vegetation surrounds walkers as they thread their way through the swamp on an elevated boardwalk. There are many other trails for taking in the salt ponds, forests, and dunes. On any of the paths, you are also liable to find yourself suddenly in a clearing with pond or ocean views, a scenic bonus.

There are still more nature trails to be found at the Massachusetts Audubon Society headquarters in Wellfleet, which sponsors many guided activities. And when you've had enough nature for one day, there are two more worldly visitors' paths away from the seashore for a pleasant change of pace. One afternoon will do nicely for the galleries in Wellfleet and the historic narrow streets of Provincetown, and either is a good choice for dinner.

Wellfleet, a small, no-longer-sleepy town of church spires and Colonial homes, has developed into an art center. The local guide, available in any of the shops, lists a dozen galleries and shops offering paintings, crafts, and sculpture. The shops are easy to find, since most are right on Main Street or around the bend on Commercial Street. The Blue Heron, representing more than 30 artists, and Kendall Art Gallery, with a sculpture garden in back, are special stops.

Another ten-minute drive to the tip of the Cape will bring you to Provincetown. With its spectacular dunes and open beach, this is the most beautiful area of the seashore, and the view from the deck of the Visitors' Center should not be missed.

It was at Provincetown, not Plymouth, that the Pilgrims first landed in 1620. The Mayflower Compact, drawn up during their five-week stay before heading for more sheltered waters, is considered the root of democratic government in America. A bronze plaque set into a boulder at the west end of Commercial Street on the present-day harbor marks their landing place. The tallest granite structure in the United States, the 255-foot Pilgrim Monument was added in 1910 as a memorial and landmark for fishermen, sailors, and tourists alike. Climb to the top for a view of the entire Cape and across the bay to Plymouth. On a clear day you can even see Boston.

Provincetown itself is a town with several distinct personalities. The Provincetown Heritage Museum, a national landmark, houses both reminders of the nineteenth-century whaling and fishing village and works that reflect the town's later emergence as an art colony. Local luminaries include Hans Hofmann and Edward Hopper.

The Provincetown Art Association and Museum, established in 1914, has an outstanding permanent collection of 500 works, and features emerging artists as well. Its membership is a "who's who" of the American art world.

Writers and poets have also been inspired by the beauty of Provincetown. The list is an eminent one, boasting Eugene O'Neill, John Dos Passos, Tennessee Williams, and Sinclair Lewis. Many famous actors also appeared at the Provincetown Playhouse early in their careers.

Present-day Provincetown retains some of the flavor of the past. Artists and writers are still present, and fishermen can still be seen at work at MacMillan Wharf, their presence adding the bonus of good Portuguese food in town. And the waterfront along Commercial Street remains as beautiful as ever, despite the crowds that clog the sidewalks. Walk all the way east to find quiet lanes, some of the best of the galleries, and some very nice lodgings, many with harbor views.

The Dolphin Fleet at the wharf is the best known of the groups offering a taste of the past on whale-watching cruises, a popular Provincetown diversion.

The center of Commercial Street has become a kind of outdoor theater for the arty and the showy, and for strolling couples of the same sex and opposite sex. Some find it fascinating; others consider it a turn-off. Whatever your reaction, you'll find things considerably calmer off-season—and if you have dinner at one of the town's host of fine restaurants on the waterfront, rest assured that you'll have no quibble about the view.

Area Code: 508

DRIVING DIRECTIONS   Cape Cod is reached via Route 3 south from Boston, or via I-95 or I-495 from the west. The Mid-Cape Highway, Route 6, goes directly to Orleans and is the only main road that continues from there to the tip at Provincetown. Orleans is 86 miles from Boston, 296 miles from New York, and 186 miles from Hartford.

PUBLIC TRANSPORTATION   Several airlines and Amtrak service Hyannis. Bus service to Cape Cod is available via Peter Pan, Bonanza, and Plymouth and Brockton (508) 746-0370; several buses connect with Boston's Logan Airport. Finally, there is service from Boston to Provincetown via Bay State Cruise Company (617) 723-7800. Carriers change, so it's best to contact the Cape Cod Chamber of Commerce for current information.

ACCOMMODATIONS *Nauset House Inn,* Beach Road, PO Box 774, East Orleans 02643, 255-2195, $–$$$ • *Ship's Knees Inn,* Beach Road, PO Box 756, East Orleans 02643, 255-1312, tennis, pool, $–$$$ CP (Don't stay at their Cove House Annex—it's all the way in town.) • *Hillbourne House,* Route 28, PO Box 190, South Orleans 02662, 255-0780, $–$$ CP • *Whalewalk Inn,* 220 Bridge Road, Eastham 02642, 255-0617, $$–$$$$ CP • *The Inn at Duck Creeke,* East Main Street, Wellfleet 02667, 349-9333, modest, comfortable, $–$$ CP • *Bradford Gardens,* 178 Bradford Street, Provincetown 02657, 487-1616, antiques and fireplaces, $$–$$$$ CP • *Watermark Inn,* 603 Commercial Street, Provincetown 02657, 487-0165, attractive modern suites with kitchens, on the water, $$$–$$$$$ • *Hargood House,* 493 Commercial Street, Provincetown 02657, spacious waterfront studios and apartments, usually by the week but available for weekends out of season, $$–$$$ • A motel worth noting is *Nauset Knoll Motor Lodge,* PO Box 642, East Orleans 02643, 255-2364, $$$, directly across from Nauset Beach. • There are dozens of additional motels all along busy Route 6, and one pleasant Victorian inn, *The Over Look Inn,* Route 6, PO Box 771, Eastham 02642, 255-1886, $$–$$$ CP.

DINING *Captain Linnell House,* Skaket Road, Orleans, 255-3400, 1840s mansion, formal dining, continental, $$–$$$ • *The Arbor,* Route 28, Orleans, 255-4847, continental menu, good value, $$–$$$ • *Binnacle Tavern,* part of The Arbor, terrific gourmet pizza, outdoor seating, $ • *Nauset Beach Club,* 222 East Main Street, East Orleans, 255-8547, gourmet seafood and Italian specialties, excellent, $$$–$$$$ • *Off the Bay Café,* 28 Main Street, Orleans, 255-5505, chic decor, good seafood, and excellent Sunday brunch, some say overpriced, $$–$$$ • *Christian's* and *Upstairs at Christians,* 443 Main Street, Chatham, 945-3362, excellent formal dining downstairs, $$–$$$; lively atmosphere, light menu upstairs, $–$$ • *Aesop's Table,* 508 Main Street, Wellfleet, 349-6450, creative cooking in an 1805 home, $$–$$$; jazz and desserts in the upstairs bar • *Sweet Seasons,* The Inn at Duck Creeke (see above), "new American menu," $$ • *Flying Fish Café,* Briar Lane, Wellfleet, 349-3100, quiet, no-frills, well-recommended café, $$ • *Adrian's,* in the Outer Reach Motel, Route 6, North Truro, 487-4360, creative pasta and pizza, great breakfasts, $–$$ • *The Blacksmith Shop,* Truro Center, 349-6554, try the cioppino, a delicious Portuguese seafood stew, $–$$ • *Napi's,* 7 Freeman Street, Provincetown, 487-1145, delightful eclectic menu, $–$$ • *The Mews,* 429 Commercial Street, Provincetown, 487-1500, charm and water views, $$$; *Café Mews,* lighter fare, $ • *Front Street,* 230 Commercial Street, 487-9715, reliably one of the best in town, $$–$$$ • *Sal's Place,* 99 Commercial Street, 487-1279, pasta and seafood by the sea, $–$$ • *The Moors,* Beach Road and Bradford Street, Provincetown, 487-0840, the place to sample Portuguese cooking, $$ • **For lobster and informal seafood, all $–$$:** *The Lobster*

Claw, Route 6A, Orleans, 255-1800; *Kadee's Lobster and Clam Bar,* Main Street, East Orleans, 255-9706; *The Eastham Lobster Pool,* Route 6, Eastham, 487-0842; *The Lobster Pot,* 321 Commercial Street, Provincetown, 487-0842; and the *Bayside Lobster Hutt,* Commercial Street, Wellfleet, 349-6333, where you order at the window, eat family-style, and get good food at good prices • **Other places of note in Orleans:** *Cap'n Cass* on Rock Harbor, no phone, a tiny place with the best lobster roll to be found; *Land Ho,* Route 6A and Cove Road, 255-5165, for pub fare and fun; *Philbrick's Fish & Chowder House,* 54 Main Street, Orleans, 240-1144, new address for the beach stand long famous for its fried onions and clams, $–$$; and the *Brown Bag,* Old Colony Way, 255-4431, for terrific breakfasts.

SIGHTSEEING *Cape Cod National Seashore,* five public beaches, ten guided nature trails, three bicycle trails, riding trails, ranger lectures and walks • *Salt Pond Visitor Center,* Route 6, Eastham, 255-3421. Hours: 9 A.M. to 6:30 P.M. in fall, extended hours in summer. Ten-minute orientation film, much free literature • *Province Lands Visitor Center,* off Race Point Road, Provincetown, 487-1256. Hours: July and August, daily, 9 A.M. to 6 P.M.; rest of year to 4:30 P.M. Twenty-minute orientation film, free literature, great view from the deck • *Provincetown Heritage Museum,* Commercial and Center streets, 487-7098. Hours: June to mid-October, daily, 10 A.M. to 6 P.M. Adults, $2; under 12, free • *Provincetown Art Association and Museum,* 460 Commercial Street, 487-1750. Hours: Memorial Day to Labor Day, daily, noon to 5 P.M. and 7 P.M. to 9 P.M.; in October, closed at 5 P.M. weekdays, open Friday and Saturday evenings; rest of year, Tuesday to Saturday, noon to 4 P.M. Adults, $2; children, $1 • *Pilgrim Monument,* High Pole Hill off Route 6, 487-1310. Hours: July and August, daily, 9 A.M. to 7 P.M., April to June and September to October, to 5 P.M.; rest of year varies, best to call. Adults, $5; children, $3 • **Whale watching:** Cruises are available mid-April through October; phone for schedules and current rates. *Dolphin Fleet,* MacMillan Wharf, Provincetown (800) 826-9300; *Provincetown Whale Watch Inc.,* MacMillan Wharf, Provincetown, 487-3322 or (800) 992- 9333, naturalists on board; *Portuguese Princess Whale Watch,* 487-2651 or (800) 442-3188 • The best beaches open to the public (all have parking fees in season; town beach fees are often steep). **Town beaches:** *Nauset Beach,* Orleans; *Cahoon Hollow,* Wellfleet; *Ballston,* Truro. **National Park Service beaches:** *Head of the Meadow,* Truro; *Race Point,* Provincetown (the last is the best for watching sunsets).

INFORMATION Orleans Chamber of Commerce, PO Box 153, Orleans, MA 02653, 255-1386; Wellfleet Chamber of Commerce, PO Box 571, Wellfleet, MA 02687, 349-2510; Provincetown Chamber of Commerce, 307 Commercial Street at MacMillan Wharf,

PO Box 1017, Provincetown, MA 02657, 487-3424; Cape Cod
Chamber of Commerce, Routes 6 and 132, PO Box 16, Hyannis, MA
02601, 362-3225.

Fair Weather at Fryeburg

When's the last time you saw an oxen-pull competition? How about a
pig scramble, or a sheep judging show, or an old-time fiddlers' contest?
For that matter, when did you last watch someone milking a cow?

From July to October country fairs are in high gear all over the New
England states, a harvest ritual that gives farmers a showcase for their
crops and livestock, homemakers a place to exhibit their prize baking
and canning, and city folks the opportunity to enjoy some old-
fashioned down-on-the-farm fun.

Maine saves her best for last, early October in Fryeburg, a town in
the western part of the state near New Hampshire's White Mountains.
This affair celebrated its 140th year in 1990. It's the biggest fair in
Maine, in what just might be the prettiest fairground setting in New
England, with a mountain peak as a backdrop.

And to make it even better, Fryeburg is an easy drive from the heart
of lake country as well as from Maine's share of the White Mountain
National Forest, so you can have your pick of scenery at the height of
foliage season.

At Fryeburg you'll see the traditional "pull" competitions—oxen,
horses, ponies, and tractors all hauling heavy loads that make moving,
much less racing, almost impossible. There's a woodman's field day
when axe-chopping contests make chips fly, a milking parlor, and all
the livestock and agricultural judging you'd expect at a major event of
this kind.

Some things you might not expect have included a wreath maker's
demonstration, a flower show, and a shuffleboard tournament. The
exact schedule of events may change, but fun is always assured. Of
course, there is a midway with plenty of rides and games for kids big
and small, plus country music shows, and harness racing to keep things
lively at night. Friday night's fun is usually capped with fireworks.

Assuming you are working your way west to Fryeburg from Portland
on Route 302, you'll pass through Naples, the place to board for boat
rides on the lakes, and Bridgton, a shopping center of the lakes area.

From the top of Pleasant Mountain in Bridgton, you can get the lay
of the land, or rather the lakes, for some 50 bodies of water can be seen
here. The Sebago-Long Lake chain, made up of Sebago, the state's
second largest lake, plus Little Sebago, the Songo River, Long Lake,

and numerous lesser lakes and streams, covers hundreds of square miles. The 1,300-acre Sebago Lake State Park makes a fine place for a picnic with a water view.

Deciding where to stay is something of a dilemma. Once the peak vacation period ends, weekend reservations become available at one of the loveliest of the lakeside resorts, Migis Lodge on Sebago, where a week's stay is usually required in summer. Migis is an escapist's dream, with cottages in the pines on 90 acres bordering the deep blue lake. Though autumn nights can be cool in lake country, you won't mind them here with your own fireplace in your own cozy cottage. And since late September days are often warm and sunny, the location is ideal for hiking the many woodland trails on the grounds or enjoying the lodge's fleets of boats.

Through September you can also enjoy a ride on the *Songo River Queen II,* a 90-foot paddle wheeler out of Naples that offers one-hour cruises on Long Lake and longer trips through the narrow Songo River Lock into the expanse of Sebago Lake. The pier is headquarters as well for pleasure boats, windsurfers, and parasailers. Conveniently situated just up the hill is the Inn at Long Lake, a small hotel furnished with taste and country charm.

For those who prefer to paddle their own canoe, the Saco River is a popular waterway, especially the broad, flat portion from the New Hampshire state line to Hiram. There are many places to rent canoes, including Saco River Canoe & Kayak on Route 5 north of Fryeburg, and Saco Bound in Conway, just across the New Hampshire line.

Water lovers will also enjoy Westways on Kezar Lake in Center Lovell, another attractive lakefront cottage resort. And The Noble House, a pleasant and welcoming bed-and-breakfast inn in Bridgton, offers swimming privileges and boating on Highland Lake. The knowledgeable owners help guests make the most of the area.

Golfers should note that the Bridgton Highlands Country Club is expanding their golf course from 9 to 18 holes and will be a first class layout in a very picturesque setting. The expected completion date is 1995.

North of Bridgton there are two other possibilities for lodging, both quaint, picture-perfect New England villages, which are lovelier than ever when their white clapboard homes and church steeples stand out against the bright autumn foliage.

In Bethel, the gracious Bethel Inn & Country Club faces an entire village common that has been declared a National Historic District. Golfers will enjoy the course here with its splendid views. There are many bed-and-breakfast inns in town as well. Rockhounds, too, may enjoy being in Bethel, an area rich in minerals. Stop at the Mt. Mann shop in Bethel or Perham's in West Paris to see some of the local finds. The shops can tell you where to go for your own finds.

The second town, Waterford, is best described by its most celebrated resident, Charles Farrar Browne, better known as Artemus

Ward, one of America's most famous early humorists. Ward said: "The village . . . is small. It does not contain over 40 houses, all told; but they are milk white with the greenest of blinds and for the most part are shaded with beautiful elms and willows. To the right of us is a mountain—to the left a lake. The village nestles between." There are three inns in this gem of a village, all recommended. If you stay in Waterford, you'll find Mt. Tir'em a relatively easy climb that is rewarded with a view of five lakes.

Finally, there are two excellent choices right in Fryeburg. The Oxford House Inn has Victorian charm and a highly regarded dining room, and the Admiral Peary House is a tastefully furnished bed and breakfast with spacious rooms, a big back lawn, and a clay tennis court. If you've forgotten your racket, the owners will provide a "loaner."

Wherever you stay, a loop taking in these towns will provide peak foliage vistas. From Fryeburg, take Route 302 east to Bridgton, Routes 37 and 35 north to Waterford, then Route 118 west to Route 5 south through Lovell and back to Fryeburg. While you are in Fryeburg, take a short drive to see one of Maine's picturesque covered bridges, the 1857 Hemlock Bridge, located off Route 302 three miles northwest of East Fryeburg, spanning an old channel of the Saco River.

What with time at the inn, the Fryeburg Fair, the lakes, some scenic drives, and a few country walks, you've almost filled a weekend. But be sure to block out some time for the nearby White Mountain foothills—spectacular scenery that shouldn't be missed, especially during foliage season. For a rewarding day, pack a picnic, lace up the walking shoes, and head north from Fryeburg on Route 113 to the White Mountain National Forest and Evans Notch. This scenic pass through the peaks offers any number of memorable views, including The Roost, a suspension bridge high above the Wild River that is a favorite of photographers. An easy half-mile trek will get you to the top of The Roost. There's good hiking territory for all capabilities, with some difficult and rewarding climbs to rocky ledges overlooking the river valley. Stop in Bethel at the Evans Notch Ranger District on Bridge Street for advice and maps.

Save the picnic, however, until the views get even better farther north. Take Route 2 west to Bethel, then north on Route 26 to Grafton Notch State Park. Screw Auger Falls, the best-known spot in the park, fits its name; it cascades down the mountain in a series of spirals through the rocks. If you're up for a steep hike from the falls, you can reach the scenic overlook at Table Rock.

When you can't wait another minute for lunch, head for Cascade Falls and its prize picnic area nearby. Other sights to see are Mother Walker Falls and Moose Cave, a fascinating cavern in the rocks that is just a quarter of a mile from the main road. The trails are clearly marked off the road as you drive through. For serious hikers, there are trailheads for the Appalachian Trail and a loop trail up Old Speck, the third highest mountain in the state.

If luck is against you and it rains, you can still while away a pleasant afternoon in area shops. Bridgton, Naples, and Harrison hold many temptations for antiquers.

The Jones Museum of Glass and Ceramics off Route 107 in Sebago is a rarity, displaying over 6,000 pieces of exquisite glass and ceramics, from ancient Egypt to the present day; an adjacent shop sells ceramics and glassware. In Bethel, Bonnema Pottery is an interesting shop where craftspeople can be seen at work.

Bridgton has several shops showcasing crafts. Emphasis on Maine shows handcrafts by state artisans as well as artists from all over New England, and over 40 artisans display work of all kinds at Craftsworks. Stone Soup Artisans is a cooperative sponsored by the Society of Southern Maine Craftsmen, stocked and staffed by members of the society. Cry of the Loon in South Casco is another fine gallery for art and crafts.

For sightseeing, the Bridgton Historical Society is restoring the 1797 Narramissic Farm in South Bridgton, recapturing rural farm life on the eve of the Civil War. The Fryeburg Library has its own attraction, a room devoted to Clarence Mulford, creator of Hopalong Cassidy. A drive to Newfield, off Route 11, will bring you to Willowbrook, a restored nineteenth-century village. Another worthwhile drive of about half an hour will bring you to the Sabbathday Lake Shaker Community, and a fascinating tour of the last settlement where Shakers are still living and working. The village includes a library, a museum, an herb distributor, and a sheep farm. A wealth of Shaker furniture, tin and woodenware, folk and decorative arts, textiles and early tools and farm implements, are displayed in the Meeting House, Ministry's Shop, Sisters' Shop, and Boys' Shop.

You can pick up pumpkins, apples, and other produce of the season at roadside stands beside the farms on almost any back road; just watch for signs on village main streets pointing the way.

In an area where unspoiled villages, lakes, mountains, and forest wilderness come together within one superb back-country area, fall in western Maine forecasts a fair weekend indeed.

Area Code: 207

DRIVING DIRECTIONS Fryeburg is on the western border of Maine, about 60 miles from Portland and about 6 miles from Conway and the White Mountains of New Hampshire. Take Route 302 west from Portland or Route 113 to 302 east from Conway, New Hampshire. Fryeburg is 180 miles from Boston, 380 miles from New York, and 270 miles from Hartford.

PUBLIC TRANSPORTATION   Air service to Portland. Fryeburg is an easy drive by rental car from the Portland airport. Vermont Transit and Concord/Trailways offer bus service to nearby North Conway, New Hampshire.

ACCOMMODATIONS   *Oxford House Inn,* Route 302, Fryeburg 04037, 935-3442, $$ CP • *Admiral Peary House,* 9 Elm Street, Fryeburg 04037, 935-3365, $$ CP • *The Noble House,* on Highland Lake, Box 180, Bridgton 04009, upstairs suites perfect for families, $$ CP • *Inn at Long Lake,* Lake House Road, Naples 04055, 693-6226 or (800) 437-0328, $$–$$$ • *Lake House,* Routes 35 and 37, Waterford 04088, 583-6078, simple country charmer, $$ CP, $$$ MAP • *Kedarburn Inn,* Route 35, Box A-1, Waterford 04088, 583-6182, 1858 house on a brook, $–$$ CP • *Waterford Inn,* PO Box 49, off Route 37, East Waterford 04088, 583-4037, serene location with a gorgeous view, $–$$ • **Resorts:** *Westways,* on Kezar Lake, Center Lovell 04016, 928-2663, $$$–$$$$$ or $$$$–$$$$$ MAP; *Migis Lodge,* off Route 302, South Casco 04077, 655-4524, $$$$$ AP; *Bethel Inn & Country Club,* on the common, Bethel 04217, 824-2175, $$$$–$$$$$ MAP; ask about weekend packages • For other Bethel lodgings, see pages 266–267.

DINING   *Oxford House* (see above), excellent, $$–$$$ • *Epicurean Inn,* Routes 302 and 35, Naples, 693-3839, for fine dining, $$–$$$ • *Black Horse Tavern,* Route 302, Bridgton, 647-5300, informal, Cajun touch, $–$$ • *Lobster Pound,* Route 302, Naples, 693-6580, no frills, $–$$ • *Westways* (see above), lovely view, $$ • *Lake House* (see above), top reviews, $$–$$$ • *Kedarburn Inn* (see above), American and continental, $$ • *Waterford Inn* (see above), advance reservations essential, prix fixe, $$$ • Lake House and Kedarburn Inn are also good choices for Sunday brunch. • Also see Bethel dining, page 267.

SIGHTSEEING   *Fryeburg Fair,* Route 5, Fryeburg, runs for one week beginning the first Sunday in October; admission and parking charge. For current dates and fees write or call H. Ted Raymond, Box 36, Fryeburg 04037, 935-2155 • *Songo River Queen II,* Route 302, Naples, 693-6861. Hours: daily, July to Labor Day; weekends in June and September. Two-hour Songo River cruise. Adults, $9; children, $6 • *Willowbrook,* Box 80 Newfield, 793-2784. Hours: daily, May 15 to September 30, 10 A.M. to 5 P.M. Adults, $6.50; ages 6 to 18, $3.25 • *Jones Museum of Glass & Ceramics,* Douglas Hill off Route 107, Sebago, 787-3370. Hours: May to mid-November, Monday to Saturday, 10 A.M. to 5 P.M., Sunday, 1 P.M. to 5 P.M. Adults, $3.50; children, $0.75 • *The Shaker Museum,* Sabbathday Lake, Route 26, New Gloucester, 926-4597. Hours: Memorial Day to Columbus Day, Monday to Saturday, 10 A.M. to 4:30 P.M. Introductory tour, adults, $4, children, $2; extended tour, adults $5.50, children, $2.75.

INFORMATION Bridgton-Lakes Region Information Center, Route 302, PO Box 236, Bridgton, ME 04009, 647-3472.

Leafing Through the Northeast Kingdom

Anyone who despairs of making a fortune in this world can take heart from the story of Thaddeus Fairbanks.

Thaddeus is the man who invented the platform scale, which registers weight at eye level when an object or person is on the platform. Not such a remarkable notion, you say? Well, that simple invention made the Fairbanks family one of the ten wealthiest in the world back in the 1800s. And since members of the Fairbanks clan were generous with their fortune, their hometown of St. Johnsbury, Vermont, was transformed.

Thanks to the Fairbanks family, when you visit St. Johnsbury today you discover not just a center of the state's maple sugar industry, but a town boasting one of the handsomest small-town public libraries and art galleries to be found, not to mention one of the most elaborate small museums. It's a surprise, way up here in rural northern Vermont—and only the first of the happy surprises waiting in this beautiful and relatively unexplored area known as the Northeast Kingdom.

Not the least of the reason to plan your trip here during foliage season is the very fact that not too many people have discovered the mountains and lakes and exceptional inns in this quiet corner of the state. So while the roads are clogged farther south, you can drive the scenic routes and walk the wooded trails here without ever feeling jostled by the rest of the foliage watchers of the world.

A Northeast Kingdom weekend itinerary ideally includes half a day in St. Johnsbury, with the rest of the time allotted to the scenic backroads, country walks, oohs and ahs, and photos.

Don't expect traditional rural motifs when you step inside the Fairbanks Museum and Planetarium in St. Johnsbury. Franklin Fairbanks, a nephew of Thaddeus, founded the museum in 1891, donating his own "Cabinet of Curiosities," a natural science collection that had outgrown his home. Franklin wanted nothing but the best and hired Lambert Packard, one of the great Victorian architects, to design the building. Packard did them proud, with soaring 30-foot barrel-vaulted ceilings, stained-glass windows (some by Tiffany), and lavish use of wood.

The exhibits are a mélange of history, archaeology, and science, with collections of dolls and Japanese Netsuke carvings, "tapestries" of George Washington made of moths, beetles, bugs, and tools of nineteenth-century life in northeastern Vermont, and enough stuffed animals and birds to gladden a taxidermist's heart. The building also features northern Vermont's official weather station and its only public planetarium. The wacky variety adds to the fun of a visit. And downstairs you can see some of the scales that made the Fairbanks fortune—and the museum—possible.

Visiting the St. Johnsbury Athenaeum means reentering the gracious world of the nineteenth century. It was built as a public library and presented to the town in 1871 by Horace Fairbanks, a nephew of the inventor, who became president of the scale-manufacturing company and eventually governor of the state of Vermont. The cathedral ceilings, tall windows, spiral staircases, and elaborate woodwork and floors with alternating strips of oak and walnut make for a truly elegant structure.

In 1873 an art gallery was added to the main building to hold some of Horace Fairbanks's growing art collection. It is now the oldest unaltered art gallery in the country. The unusual design of the gallery was determined by the need to house Fairbanks's prize canvas, *The Domes of Yosemite,* an enormous 10-by-15-foot painting by Albert Bierstadt. The exceptional landscape, placed opposite the entrance to the gallery, benefits from natural light provided by an arched skyway, which enhances the feeling of looking down into the valley.

St. Johnsbury's additional claim to fame has nothing to do with its illustrious benefactors. This is the heart of Vermont maple sugar country, which in a typical year produces about two-thirds of the nation's supply. Maple Grove, the world's largest maple candy factory, has been operating since 1915 and creates more than 200 kinds of delectable maple sweets. On weekdays you are invited to tour the Maple Grove factory for a close-up view of the vats of boiling sap being poured into different kinds of candy molds, to emerge in familiar Vermont shapes from maple leaves to pine trees.

Visitors are welcome anytime to visit the Maple Cabin here to see a 15-minute film on the maple sugar process. Actual kettles of sap are boiling year-round in the adjacent small Maple Museum, which features exhibitions of sugar-making equipment, both ancient and modern. After the tour you can taste free samples of the final result and stock up for the future at the gift shop.

Before you leave St. Johnsbury, have a look at the fine houses to be seen along Main Street. Then, leave "city" business behind and strike out for the country roads waiting to show off their autumn colors. One prime route for scenery is to drive north from St. Johnsbury on Routes 5 and 114 to East Burke and Burke Mountain. On the way you'll pass through Lyndonville, whose claims to fame are the five covered bridges nearby, antiques at Lyndonville's Collectibles Plus and the East Burke Antiques Center, both multidealer emporiums, and the delightful Bailey's Country Store in East Burke. Near Bailey's, detour at the sign to West Burke and go up to the top of Darling Hill for a fantastic view of Burke Mountain. Then take the auto road to Burke's 3,267-foot summit for even more sweeping views of the countryside.

From here, head for Vermont lake country by connecting again with Route 5, then turning onto Route 5A north to Lake Willoughby. Two cliffs, Mt. Pisgah and Mt. Hor, rise from opposite sides of this lake, making a majestic vista. To get an even more spectacular view, take of the well-maintained hiking trails in the 7,000-acre state forest surrounding the lake. The view from the cliffs is worth the climb.

There are some 15 lakes in this general area, providing recreation for boaters and fishermen and scenery for all. Almost all the lakes are surrounded by hills, and Crystal Lake, back on Route 5, is another beauty set against a dramatic cliff. If you detour off Route 5 a few miles north to Brownington Center, you'll come to The Old Stone House, run by the Orleans County Historical Society. This handsome granite-block building was designed and built as a school dormitory in the 1830s by the Reverend Alexander Twilight, the man believed to be America's first black college graduate and first black legislator. Twilight taught the region's children here for two decades. The 30-room building now serves as a showcase for furnishings, tools, needlework, art, and crafts of the region's past.

Turn south again and follow Route 14 to Craftsbury, another charmer. It is actually made up of a string of villages so minute you can easily pass through before you know you have arrived—until you reach Craftsbury Common, with its picture-book green surrounded by dazzling white clapboard buildings and a church. It is an appropriate setting for The Inn on the Common, an uncommon inn where guests play croquet on the lawn and men don jackets for a multicourse dinner served on Tiffany china with heirloom silverware. The inn is frequently filled with sophisticated travelers who want to get away from it all. It offers many special weekends, some including walking and biking. If the tab is too high, the Craftsbury Inn, a handsomely furnished 1850 country home, is also appealing.

The Craftsbury Center is another asset in this area, offering biking, sculling, running, and horseback riding, and walking tours plus cross-country skiing in winter. The center has its own dorm and apartment lodgings, as well as packages in cooperation with local inns.

Craftsbury is one of four choice areas that can serve as an excellent home base for Northeast Kingdom exploring. Another prime candidate is Lower Waterford, about ten miles east of St. Johnsbury, a picture-book hamlet with wonderful views across the Connecticut River to the New Hampshire mountains. Rabbit Hill Inn, a lovely, columned, antique-filled inn in town, is known for its fine cuisine.

Farther north, heading toward Burke Mountain, is The Wildflower Inn, a country charmer set on a ridge with views that go on forever and with lots of windows to make the most of them. The inn has a tennis court, and welcomes young guests with their own game room, a summer activity program, and a children's menu. If you don't stay here, pay a visit to the Tiffin Gallery, in a barn, featuring North Country artists, crafts, and gifts. Dinner here is also highly recommended.

The rustic little Old Cutter Inn on the Burke Mountain Access Road also is well known locally for its Swiss fare.

Finally, for lake views, there is the attractive Willoughvale Inn. Especially appealing are the inn's fresh, pretty housekeeping cottages right on the shore of Lake Willoughby, with sunrooms, screened porches, and decks. Across the lake is Fox Hall, a modest, homey, bed-and-breakfast inn that offers guests a private waterfront with boats, canoes, and windsurfers, and cross-country ski trails in winter.

As you drive around, watch for special places such as Laplant's Sugarhouse in Sutton, where horse-drawn hayrides into the country-side are offered in summer and fall, sleigh rides in winter, and maple sugaring in the spring.

In late September each year, several of the tiny towns in the area join in the Northeast Kingdom's Foliage Festival, taking turns holding church lunches and suppers, crafts shows, and special events. These are small affairs, nothing to write home or drive miles out of the way for, but if you plan your driving itinerary to pass through any of the towns on the day of the festivities, it may add a down-home touch and a home-cooked meal to your memories.

If you head for Cabot, you can add a visit to the Cabot Farmers' Cooperative, watch the making of Vermont's best known cheddar cheese, and enjoy tasting at the sample table. Most of the activity takes place before 1:00 P.M. In pretty Peacham, the town founded in 1776 that boasts it is the most photographed in the state, don't miss a stop at the Peacham Store, where the hostess turns out delicious hot gourmet lunches to go. Other towns on the tour are Plainfield, Barnet, Groton, Marshfield, and Walden. An advance schedule of events is available from the Chamber of Commerce.

It was former U.S. Senator George Aiken who dubbed this area the Northeast Kingdom when he saw its untouched beauty during one bril-liant fall foliage season some years ago. When you view the peaceful mosaic of the mountains and lakes, unspoiled villages, and placid farms, you may well agree that this corner of Vermont is, indeed, a kingdom of its own.

Area Code: 802

DRIVING DIRECTIONS   St. Johnsbury is off I-91 at Exit 20. It is 150 miles from Boston, 300 miles from New York City, and 190 miles from Hartford.

PUBLIC TRANSPORTATION Vermont Transit has bus service to St. Johnsbury; Amtrak services to Montpelier. Closest air service is Burlington, Vermont, or Lebanon, New Hampshire.

ACCOMMODATIONS *Rabbit Hill Inn,* Route 18, Lower Waterford 05848, 748-5168 or (800) 76-BUNNY, $$$$–$$$$$ MAP • *The Wildflower Inn,* Star Route, Lyndonville 05851, 626-8310 or (800) 627-8310, $$–$$$ CP • *The Old Cutter Inn,* Burke Mountain Access Road, East Burke 05832, $ or $$–$$$ MAP • *The Inn on the Common,* Craftsbury Common 05827, 586-9619 or (800) 521-2233, $$$$–$$$$$ MAP • *Craftsbury Inn,* Craftsbury 05826, 586-2848 or (800) 336-2848, $–$$$ CP or $$$–$$$$ MAP • *Craftsbury Center,* Box 31 Craftsbury Center 05827, 586-7767, dormitory bunks to apartments, $–$$$ MAP • *Willoughvale Inn,* Route 5A, Westmore 05860, 525-4123 or (800) 541-0588, $$ CP, cottages, $$$ • *Fox Hall Inn,* Willoughby Lake, Barton 05822, 525-6930, $–$$ CP • For more small inns, write to Chamber of Commerce for Vermont's Bed & Breakfasts of the Northeast Kingdom brochure.

DINING *Rabbit Hill* (see above), prix fixe, $$$$ • *Wildflower Inn* (see above), $$; also children's menu, $ • *The Old Cutter Inn* (see above), $–$$ • *The Pub Outback,* Route 114, East Burke, 626-5187, casual, lively, $–$$ • *The River Garden Café,* Route 114, East Burke, 626-3514, light fare to full dinners, $–$$ • *Willoughvale Inn* (see above), $$ • *The Creamery,* Hill Street, Danville (near St. Johnsbury), 684-3616, seafood and home-baked pies in a converted creamery, $$ • *Aime's Restaurant,* Route 2 at Route 18, St. Johnsbury, 748-3553, old-timer, game specialties, simple pine-paneled decor, $–$$ • *Tucci's Bistro,* 43 Eastern Avenue, St. Johnsbury, 748-4778, Italian, $$. • For a light lunch and/or dessert, *Rainbow Sweets,* Route 2, Marshfield, 426-3531, bakery-café, $; *Northern Lights Bookshop & Café,* 79 Railroad Avenue, St. Johnsbury, 748-4463 • And for good, plain country cooking, and lots of it, join the locals at the *Miss Vermont Diner,* Route 5, St. Johnsbury, 748-9751, or its sister, the *Miss Lyndonville Diner,* Route 5, Lyndonville, 626-9890, both $.

SIGHTSEEING *Fairbanks Museum and Planetarium,* Main and Prospect streets, St. Johnsbury, 748-2372. Hours: Monday to Saturday, 10 A.M. to 4 P.M., to 6 P.M. July and August, Sunday, 1 P.M. to 5 P.M. Adults, $4; children, $2.50; families, $9 • *St. Johnsbury Athenaeum,* 30 Main Street, 748-8291, library and art gallery. Hours: Monday and Wednesday, 10 A.M. to 8 P.M., Tuesday, Thursday, Friday, 10 A.M. to 5:30 P.M.; Saturday 9:30 A.M. to 4 P.M. Donation • *Maple Grove Museum,* Route 2 on eastern edge of St. Johnsbury, 748-5141. Hours: Memorial Day to late October, daily 8 A.M. to 4:45 P.M., factory tours weekdays. Admission $0.75 • *The Old Stone House,* Brownington Center, 754-2022. Hours: July and August, daily, 11 A.M. to 5 P.M.;

May 15 to June 30 and September to October 15, Friday to Tuesday only, 11 A.M. to 5 P.M. Adults, $3; children, $1 • *Cabot Farmers' Cooperative Creamery,* Main Street, Cabot, 563-2231. Hours: June 15 to October 15, Monday to Saturday, 9 A.M. to 5 P.M.; Sunday 11 A.M. to 4 P.M.; rest of year, Monday to Saturday, 9 A.M. to 4 P.M., closed Sunday. Adults, $1; under 12, free • *Laplant's Sugarhouse,* Route 5, Sutton (three miles north of West Burke), 467-3900, phone for information and reservations for hayrides • *Northeast Kingdom Fall Foliage Festival,* PO Box 38, West Danville, VT 05873, write for current year's schedule of events. Outdoor recreation: *Craftsbury Center,* Craftsbury Common, 586-7767, hiking, biking, cross-country skiing, horseback riding • *Burke Mountain,* East Burke, 626-3305 or (800) 541-5480, downhill and cross-country skiing.

INFORMATION Northeast Kingdom Chamber of Commerce, 30 Western Avenue, St. Johnsbury, VT 05819, 748-3678.

Making a Pilgrimage to Plymouth

When the cranberries ripen to ruby red, that's the time to plan your pilgrimage to Plymouth, Massachusetts.

In case you didn't know, cranberries became part of our traditional Thanksgiving feast because the Mayflower Pilgrims happened to come to rest in the heart of America's cranberry-growing center.

The Pilgrims used this wild native fruit as a dye, to make poultices, and in a dried cake called pemmican, a mixture of berries, venison, and grains learned from Native Americans who called the berry "sassamanash." There are more than 13,000 acres of cranberry bogs in southeastern Massachusetts today, continuing a tradition of formal cultivation begun in 1816.

Come late September, when the berries are ready for harvest, the countryside around Plymouth is transformed into a remarkable landscape of glowing red. Federal Furnace Road between Plymouth and South Carver is lined with bogs. Columbus Day weekend marks the annual Massachusetts Cranberry Harvest Festival in South Carver. It's an extra splash of color for a trip that ought to be made anyway by anyone who is interested in how our country began.

Don't expect a dull history lesson. Plymouth Rock and a reproduction of the *Mayflower* are here, of course, but the real story of the Pilgrims who landed at Plymouth is told best at Plimoth Plantation, an amazingly realistic re-creation of New England's first settlement. This authentic replica of the 1627 Pilgrim village is peopled with "residents" who have been intensely trained to re-create the atmosphere of the first surviving colony in New England.

You'll be entering a farming community where everyone is at work at typical seasonal tasks, and you can see firsthand what it was like to settle in a new land where almost everything had to be grown or made on the spot. The crafts that helped the settlers to be self-sufficient are demonstrated at the Carriage House Crafts Center. The Pilgrim residents are so authentic they even have differing dialects to match the regions they left in England.

You may meet Miles Standish or John Alden and lots of other people who may tell you in the most believable way how it felt to make a home in the wilderness. They'll describe life in the old country as well as the new, talk about the *Mayflower* voyage—in fact, they'll answer any question you ask as long as it doesn't involve knowledge of anything past the year 1627.

The village is so well done that you'll almost forget it isn't real, just like the visiting kids eagerly approaching one after another of the residents to find out who is married to whom and which child belongs to which parent. Make Plimoth Plantation your first stop while you're fresh on Saturday morning, and at least three hours to really make the most of this experience.

Check also for special activities at the village. These include gallery talks, bread baking and hearth cooking workshops (the cooking workshops include dinner in the village), lessons in herbal wreath making and seventeenth-century coat making, basket making, and many children's activities, from storytelling to Pilgrim games to talks on Pilgrim life.

Back in Plymouth, you can get some notion of how it felt for 102 passengers to cross the ocean on a 106-foot boat by boarding the reproduction of the *Mayflower,* the second part of the Plantation's "living museum." Once again the sailors and passengers aboard represent the real ones.

Mayflower II is docked at the harbor in town, next to what is probably the best-known boulder in the country, Plymouth Rock. An elaborate columned monument has been built over the rock to protect it and provide a viewing platform, and the waterfront area around it has been turned into a grassy promenade that is now a state park.

Across the street is Coles Hill, where you can get a panoramic view of Plymouth harbor. The Pilgrims buried their dead in unmarked graves here during their first terrible winter. Also on Coles Hill is the statue of Massasoit, chief of the Wampanoag Indians, who befriended the newcomers and helped them to survive that winter. The 81-foot Pilgrim Monument on Allerton Street was built between 1859 and 1899, at the then-enormous cost of $155,000, to commemorate the bravery of these early settlers. Don't overlook the statue dedicated to the Pilgrim women; 25 made the crossing, but only four survived.

Follow the signs inland a block or two for a visit to America's oldest public museum, Pilgrim Hall, which has preserved the possessions the Pilgrims used over 350 years ago. You'll see John Alden's Bible, William Bradford's chair, William Brewster's books, Myles Standish's sword, and many other possessions and furniture of the early settlers, as well as paintings by Gilbert Stuart and the only painting of a Mayflower Pilgrim, Edward Winslow.

There are several historic houses to be seen in Plymouth, the most impressive being the Mayflower Society House, headquarters of the General Society of Mayflower Descendants. The oldest house of all, the 1640 Richard Sparrow House, is now a pottery-making center and shop. The Harlow Old Fort House offers hands-on experience with such Colonial arts as spinning, weaving, and candle dipping. The house was built with timbers from the original fort.

A particularly pleasant walk will take you through Brewster Gardens with its placid duck pond to see Jenney Grist Mill, a working twentieth-century reconstruction of a seventeenth-century mill. The meal at the mill is for sale, and there are several other shops around.

All these shops are a sign that the waterfront in Plymouth is packed with tourists in season. The town has gone slightly commercial to take advantage of that fact, but so far things are not out of hand. The most extensive town shopping is in a complex called Village Landing, a group of clapboard and shingle shops built to re-semble a nineteenth-century village. These shops are pleasant enough, offering everything from jewelry to hand-stenciled plaques to quality brassware and antiques. There's also a shop with homemade ice cream and a candy store.

Serious shoppers will want to drive another mile and a half west on Main Street to Cordage Park, a cluster of outlet stores and shops in a former rope factory.

The two favorite restaurants recommended by Plymouth residents are the Inn for All Seasons, housed in an attractive restored mansion high on a hill, and Mamma Mia, an Italian restaurant across from the harbor. Visitors, however, may prefer to join the crowds concentrating on the informal restaurants around the waterfront offering traditional New England seafood, such as lobster, fried clams, and chowder. Modestly priced take-out stands where you can have your seafood at picnic tables with a water view are a real boon for families.

Save time for a walk along the long rock jetty into the harbor for a close-up look at the many sailboats and yachts that fill Plymouth Harbor today. If you want to get out on the water, several boat outings are available through the early fall, both harbor cruises and whale-watching excursions.

A pleasant way to see Plymouth's historic district and hear some fascinating tales of early life is on the guided Colonial Lantern Tours offered in the evening.

If you spend Saturday seeing the sights, you can devote Sunday to those cranberries. Visit the Ocean Spray Cranberry World Visitor Center on Water Street for a tour that traces how the berries have been grown and harvested throughout history. You'll learn how the quality of a berry is judged by its bounce, see a scale model cranberry farm, and be able to inspect the tools for both dry and wet harvesting. At the demonstration kitchen downstairs, you can watch cranberry dishes being prepared and taste some of the goodies. There is the chance to sample a variety of cranberry juice products as well.

Free samples are also offered at the Plymouth Colony Winery just outside town, where cranberry wine is made. Here, you can take a stroll around the cranberry bogs.

But a more spectacular show is found if you drive west on Route 44 toward Carver, where the roadside is lined with bogs and you can watch harvesting in action. Many growers flood their bogs, then gently stir the water to bring the berries to the surface, where they are corralled and loaded on trucks via conveyers. Some growers have taken to using helicopters to hoist the bins away, a colorful sight.

On Columbus Day weekend, the Massachusetts Cranberry Harvest Festival takes place on Rochester Road, off Route 58, in South Carver, near one of the oldest of the bogs. Activities include guided tours of the bogs, cooking demonstrations and contests, art, photography and crafts displays, a farmers' market, live music, and lots of food.

October also brings celebrations of seventeenth-century foods and lifestyles at Plimoth Plantation, and Harvest Feasts, a re-creation of the feasts and games that marked the end of the colony's successful growing season. Feasts continue into November, culminating with a New England Thanksgiving Buffet.

Come back in November, if you can, but early October is the ideal time to visit Plymouth. You'll leave with a lot more knowledge about your country and with a rosy cranberry glow as well.

Area Code: 508

DRIVING DIRECTIONS   Plymouth is off Route 3 on Route 3A, 40 miles south of Boston, 245 miles from New York, and 135 miles from Hartford.

PUBLIC TRANSPORTATION   Plymouth and Brockton bus lines run from Boston and Hyannis, 746-0378, or, in MA (800) 328-9997. Nearest air service is Boston.

ACCOMMODATIONS   All Plymouth area codes 02360. *Sheraton Inn,* 180 Water Street at Village Landing, 747-4900, best in town, $$$
• *John Carver Motor Inn,* 25 Summer Street, 746-7100, walking

distance to town, $$–$$$ • *Governor Bradford Motor Inn,* Water Street, 746-6200, across from the water in the middle of town, $$–$$$ • *Pilgrim Sands,* 150 Warren Avenue, 747-0900, waterfront location, three miles south of town near Plimoth Plantation, $$–$$$ • *Jackson-Russell-Whitfield House,* 26 North Street, 746-5289, charmingly restored 1782 home just steps from the waterfront, antiques, no children under 12, $$ CP • *Foxglove Cottage,* 101 Sandwich Road, 747-6576, restored 1820 Cape in a country setting five minutes from town, Victorian decor, floral prints, no children under 12, $$ CP.

DINING *Inn for all Seasons,* 97 Warren, 746-8823, dancing on weekends, $$ • *Mama Mia,* 122 Water Street, casual Italian dining across from the waterfront, $ •*Café Nanina,* 14 Union Street, 747-4503, on the waterfront but away from the crowd, formal dining, $$, and lighter menu, $ • *McGrath's,* 746-9751; *Lobster Hut,* 746-2270; and *Wood's,* 746-0261, on the Town Pier, Water Street, are busy waterfront spots for sit-down and take-out seafood and water views, $–$$ • *1620 House,* Water Street, 746-9565, seafood, across the street from the harbor, not quite so frantic, $$ • *Iguana's,* 170 Water Street, Village Landing, 747-4000, change of pace Mexican fare, $ • *Harbor Grille,* Sheraton Inn (see above), pleasant setting for more formal dining, reasonable, $–$$ • *Ernie's,* 330 Court Street, 746-3444, informal old-timer, seafood and Italian dishes, pizza, good for families, $–$$ • *Crane Brook Restaurant,* Tremont Street, South Carver, 866-3235, excellent innovative American fare, $$–$$$.

SIGHTSEEING *Massachusetts Cranberry Harvest Festival,* Edaville Cranberry Bog, Rochester Road (off Route 58), South Carver. Held for three days on Columbus Day weekend, 10 A.M. to 4 P.M. Free. For information, phone Cranberry World, 747-2350 • *Plimoth Plantation,* Route 3A, three miles south of Plymouth, 746-1622. Hours: April through November, daily, 9 A.M. to 5 P.M. Combination tickets for Pilgrim Village and Mayflower II: adults, $18.50; ages 5 to 12, $11. Admission good for two days. Village alone, adults, $15, children, $9; Mayflower II alone, adults, $5.75, children, $3.75. Write for schedule of special events and children's activities. • *Cranberry World Visitors' Center,* Water Street, Plymouth, 747-2350. Hours: May to November, daily, 9:30 A.M. to 5 P.M. Free • *Pilgrim Hall Museum,* 75 Court Street (Route 3A), 746-1620. Hours: daily, 9:30 A.M. to 4:30 P.M. Adults, $5; ages 6 to 12, $2.50 • *Harlow Old Fort House Museum,* 119 Sandwich Street, 746-3017. Hours: July 1 to Labor Day, Tuesday to Sunday, noon to 5 P.M.; June and Labor Day to Columbus Day, Wednesday to Saturday, noon to 5 P.M. Adults, $2.50; children, $0.50 • *Spooner House Museum,* 27 North Street, 746-0012. Hours: same as Harlow Museum above. Adults, $2.50; children, $0.50 • *Mayflower Society Museum,* 4 Winslow Street, 746-2590. Hours: July and August, daily,

10 A.M. to 5 P.M.; June, September to mid-October, weekends only, 10 A.M. to 5 P.M. Adults, $2.50; ages 6 to 12, $0.50 • *Richard Sparrow House,* 42 Summer Street, 747-1240. Hours: daily except Wednesday, 10 A.M. to 5 P.M. Donation • **Cruises:** *Capt. John Boats,* Town Wharf, 746-2643; *Cape Cod Cruises,* Mayflower II Pier, 747-2400 • *Lantern Light Walking Tours,* PO Box 3541, 747-4161. Hours: June to October, nightly, 7:30 P.M. 90-minute tours from the lobby of the John Carver Inn. April, May, November, weekends only. Adults, $7; children, $5

INFORMATION   Destination Plymouth, 225 Water Street, Suite 202, Plymouth, MA 02360 (800) USA-1620 or 747-7525. Ask about weekend packages and sightseeing pass for all attractions.

Fall Foliage in Franconia

Men hang out signs indicative of their respective trades; shoemakers hang out a giant shoe; jewelers a monster watch; and a dentist hangs out a gold tooth; but up in the mountains of New Hampshire God Almighty has hung out a sign to show that there He makes men.

It was Daniel Webster who wrote these words upon viewing the Old Man of the Mountain, an unmistakable craggy profile in stone carved on a mountainside by some celestial sculptor.

The rugged visage of the Old Man, now the official symbol of New Hampshire, the Granite State, can be seen clearly, high on a rock cliff at the end of the eight-mile mountain pass called Franconia Notch, where he presides over a panorama of peaks and valleys, awesome gorges, tumbling waterfalls, and ice-blue mountain lakes, a vista that has few peers in New England.

Add the region's most scenic highway, aflame in fall foliage, and a chance to view it all from a cable car that travels 4,200 feet into the sky and you have all makings of an unforgettable fall outing.

Since this is a deservedly popular destination in the fall and inns are small, it's well to begin by reserving a place early. The pick of the crop is just above Franconia in the little town of Sugar Hill. The local guide aptly describes this region as an area of small villages and big mountains, and Sugar Hill is the quaintest of the villages. The one main road, Route 117, climbs up, up the hill with views all the way. Along the way is the Sugar Hill Inn, a tasteful 1748 Colonial with charming rooms done in traditional Laura Ashley. Farther up the hill is the Hilltop Inn, a cozy Victorian guest house. Both inns serve dinners to the public as well as their guests. A newer entry on the same road is Foxglove, a designer-decorated turn-of-the-century home.

The Franconia Inn, off on quiet Route 116 south of Franconia in the Easton Valley, is a longtime mainstay, set on 107 acres. It was rebuilt after a 1934 fire to resemble the original Colonial inn of the 1860s, and has been refurbished once again to provide modern baths and a few Jacuzzi tubs. Here you have your pick of views, meadow, or mountain, and there are horses for riding, tennis courts, a pool, a fishing stream, and a hot tub for guests. In winter, the inn offers ice skating and its own cross-country skiing center.

Continue farther on Route 116 for the Bungay Jar, a delightful eighteenth-century barn turned bed and breakfast. There are heavenly views from the inn's many decks, a sauna for relaxing, and room to wander wooded paths to a hidden river out back.

Another possibility north of Franconia is the Adair-A Country Inn, a country estate on 200 acres, with a pool and tennis courts.

Near the start of the Kancamagus Highway to the south in Lincoln, the Mill House Inn is another kind of option, a pleasant modern hotel that is part of a restored mill complex, offering tennis, indoor and outdoor pools, exercise equipment, and shopping.

Once you've made your choice and settled in, you're in for two days of spectacular sights. If you want to enjoy the area to the fullest, you can easily spend an entire day driving, walking, and picnicking in the fantastic beauty of Franconia State Park. Route 93, a limited-access parkway, takes you directly through, with exits at major points. A nine-mile bike path separate from the road is a treat for pedalers.

You might as well drive right to that famous profile at Franconia Notch. Profile Lake has been dubbed the "Old Man's Washbowl" for its location 1,200 feet below the outline of the Old Man himself. A parking area along the lake gives a magnificent view of mountains reflected in the deep blue water and is also the best vantage point for seeing the distinct face above, which is actually composed of five separate granite ledges. The forehead alone is made of a 20-foot-long granite block weighing about 30 tons. The profile is 25 feet wide and measures about 40 feet from chin to forehead.

Continuing on the main road, you'll come to a waterfall cascading into a granite pool called The Basin. It is believed that the granite was eroded by a melting glacier 25,000 years ago. Below is a water-eroded rock formation, then comes the rushing water of the Baby Flume, a forerunner of what lies ahead.

The Flume is a natural gorge whose 70- to 90-foot granite walls extend for 800 feet along the southern flank of Mount Liberty. A bus takes you to within 500 yards of the gorge, then it's an easy two-mile round-trip hike along the paths and wooden walkways crisscrossing the stream to reach the actual Flume and the crescendo of sound that announces Avalanche Falls, a torrent of water crashing 23 feet down the canyon into a pool. A short trail leads you to the Cascades, another rush of mountain streams tumbling into a narrow valley known as Liberty

Gorge. On the way back you'll pass a deep basin called simply The Pool, fed by a cascading river. In 1938 a giant pine uprooted by a hurricane fell across the river and now forms a base for the Sentinel Pine Bridge, which offers the best viewing point for The Pool.

By now you've surely worked up an appetite for lunch. There is a cafeteria at the Flume Visitor Center, but with all that scenery around, it's better to bring a picnic. The closest picnic grounds are right across from the Flume; the most scenic are back in the other direction at Echo Lake, a pool of blue in a setting of granite cliffs.

There's boating and fishing at Echo Lake, and a sandy beach near the picnic area. If you're up for a 1½-mile walk, Artist's Bluff up above is a rocky palisade with fine views of the Franconia and Kinsman ranges. The name comes from yet another profile carved in the mountain, this one known as "The Artist."

Now it's time for the view that beats them all, the thrilling cable car ascent via the Cannon Mountain Aerial Tramway to the 4,200-foot peak of Cannon Mountain. This was the first such lift in America, and it is still one of the most spectacular. The present tram, completed in 1980, goes a mile straight up, a five-minute ride that affords amazing views of all the White Mountain ranges in their best fall dress. There are trails at the summit up to an observation tower for a longer view.

At the base of the tramway is the New England Ski Museum, which claims the most extensive collection of historical ski equipment, clothing, art, and photography in the Northeast.

If you still have energy, another area attraction worth a visit is Frost Place, the simple frame house where poet Robert Frost lived and worked. You can stand at his desk or on the front porch, sharing the mountain views that inspired him.

After a hearty breakfast at the inn, start Sunday by exploring one of the less heralded but no less intriguing natural attractions of the area, the strange formations known as Lost River. The river here flows through a narrow, steep-walled glacial gorge and disappears beneath immense blocks of granite that tumbled into the gorge eons ago. You can follow its course on a wooden walkway as it moves through the gorge and canyons and down Paradise Falls. There are bridges and ladders all along the way that let you wander into caves and through hidden passages in the boulders. Kids absolutely love it—but then, so do the grown-ups. The walk takes about an hour.

In Lincoln you can get another bird's-eye view of the colorful mountains from the Loon Mountain Gondola, which bills itself as the state's longest aerial ride. At the top, the Summit Cave Walk explores the area's unique glacial caves, or you can climb the four-story Sky Tower for an even loftier view.

But the major attraction for this day is down to earth, a drive that gets my vote as the most beautiful in New England. The Kancamagus Highway (Route 112) runs for 32 miles between the villages of Lincoln and Conway through the heart of the White Mountain National Forest. It was designed by the U.S. Forest Service to make the most of the views and to give access to the magnificent wilderness on either side with picnic areas and hiking trails. The road was designated a National Scenic Byway in 1989.

The drive alone is extraordinary, especially with the added glow of autumn color, but to make the most of the highway you really should get out and investigate the scenic areas on the way. A special one is the Rocky Gorge area, where the Swift River has worn a cleft in the rock now known as Rocky Gorge. Within this area is Falls Pond, a five-minute walk over the gorge via a rustic footbridge.

Some other easy walks are to Boulder Loop, which gives a spectacular view of Mt. Chocorua and the Swift River Valley from the ledges, and Sabbaday Falls, a picturesque series of cascades in a narrow flume. You can spend an hour here—or a day.

At the end of the road in Conway, you're very much back in civilization, with many shops to choose from, and lots of good restaurants as well. But somehow it seems a shame to lose the glow of all that pristine beauty. A better move may be to take the return trip on the Kancamagus, seeing it all from a different perspective this time, and heading home with the glorious New Hampshire autumn recorded in your mind's eye to sustain you through the winter ahead.

Area Code: 603

DRIVING DIRECTIONS Franconia is on the west side of the White Mountains in upper New Hampshire and can be reached via I-93. It is 115 miles from Boston, 325 miles from New York, and 215 miles from Hartford.

PUBLIC TRANSPORTATION Air service to Manchester or Lebanon, New Hampshire; closest bus service is Vermont Transit to St. Johnsbury, Vermont, or Concord Trailways to Conway, New Hampshire.

ACCOMMODATIONS *Sugar Hill Inn,* Route 117, Sugar Hill 03580, 823-5621, $$$$ MAP, • *Foxglove,* Route 117, Sugar Hill 03585, $–$$ CP • *Hilltop Inn,* Main Street, Route 117, Sugar Hill 03585, 823-5695, $$–$$$ CP • *Franconia Inn,* Easton Road (Route 116), Franconia 03580, 823-5542, $$–$$$ CP, $$$$–$$$$$ MAP • *Bungay Jar,* PO Box 15, Easton Valley Road (Route 116) Franconia 03580, 823-7775, $–$$$ CP • *Inn at Forest Hills,* PO Box 783, Franconia 03580, 823-9550, grand Tudor home, $–$$ CP • *Adair-A Country Inn,* PO Box 850, Bethlehem 03574, ten minutes north of Franconia, 444-2600, $$$–$$$$ CP • *Mittersill Resort,* Mittersill Road, Franconia

03580, 823-5511, rustic chalet-style resort surrounded by Franconia Notch State Park, indoor and outdoor pools, tennis, riding, hiking. Hotel, $, efficiencies, $$, one-bedroom units, $$$, two bedrooms, $$$$ • *Mill House Inn,* Box 696, Lincoln 03251, 745-2245 or (800) 654-6183, rooms, $–$$, suites, $$–$$$$.

DINING *Franconia Inn* (see above), continental menu, highly recommended, $$ • *Lovett's Inn by Lafayette Brook,* Route 18, Franconia, 823-7761, long considered one of the best in the area, $$–$$$ • *Horse & Hound,* 205 Wells Road, off Route 18, 823-5501, another old-time favorite, $$ • *Sugar Hill Inn* (see above), by reservation only, prix fixe, $$$ • *Hilltop Inn* (see above), by reservation only, $$ • *Rosa Flamingo,* Route 302, Bethlehem, 869-3111, Italian, $$ • *Tim-Bir Alley,* Adair-A Country Inn (see above), one of the region's best, $$ • *Clement Room,* Woodstock Inn, Route 3, North Woodstock, 745-3951, formal and informal dining rooms in a Victorian home, $$–$$$; also known for their breakfasts, $ • *Tavern at the Mill,* Main Street, Lincoln, 745-3603, part of the old mill, varied menu, $–$$ • *Common Man,* Route 112 and Pollard Road, Lincoln, 745-3463, old-timer in area, rustic farmhouse setting, basic menu, $–$$. • *Polly's Pancake Parlor,* Route 117, Sugar Hill, 823-5525, is a local legend for home-ground cornmeal and whole-wheat pancakes and waffles with luscious fillings and homemade sausages • Take-out picnic sandwiches are available at the *Cannonball Pizza & Deli,* Route 18, Main Street, Franconia, 823-7478.

SIGHTSEEING *Franconia Notch State Park,* Routes 3/93, Franconia, 823-5563. Hours: daily, late May through mid-October, 9 A.M. to 4:30 P.M., July 4 to Labor Day to 7 P.M. Free admission to park. Major attractions include *The Flume,* 745-8391, adults, $6, ages 6 to 12, $3.50; *Cannon Mountain Tramway,* adults, $9, ages 6 to 12, $4.50 • *New England Ski Museum,* next to Cannon Mountain Tram, PO Box 267, Franconia, 823-7177. Hours: daily except Wednesday, late December to March and late May to mid-October, noon to 5 P.M. Free • *Frost Place,* off Route 116, Franconia, 823-8038. Hours: July to Columbus Day, daily except Tuesday, 1 P.M. to 5 P.M.; June, weekends only. Adults, $3; ages 6 to 15, $1.25 • *Lost River Reservation,* Route 112, Kinsman Notch, 745-8031. Hours: daily, mid-May to mid-October, 9 A.M. to 5 P.M.; summer to 6 P.M. Adults, $6.50; ages 6 to 12, $3.50 • *Loon Mountain Gondola Skyride,* Lincoln, 745-8111. Hours: late May to mid-October, Monday to Saturday, 9 A.M. to 5 P.M., Sunday, 8:30 A.M. to 5 P.M. Adults, $8.50; ages 6 to 16, $3.

INFORMATION Franconia/Easton/Sugar Hill Chamber of Commerce, P.O. Box 780, Franconia, NH 03580, 823-5661 or (800) 237-9007.

Meandering the Mohawk Trail

It was the Pocumtuck Indians who first blazed the trail, invading the lands of the Mohawks in 1663 by creating a footpath from their home in Deerfield, Massachusetts, through the Berkshire Mountains to Mohawk territory in Troy, New York. Later pioneers made this strategic route the first toll-free interstate road, opening the Berkshires to tourists.

Eventually the 63-mile route, still known as the Mohawk Trail, became the first official scenic drive in New England, opened to the public in 1914. It stretches from the Massachusetts–New York border to the Connecticut River Valley just east of Greenfield, an up-and-down route of twists and turns and amazing mountain views. One 42-mile segment connects two beautiful New England towns, Deerfield and Williamstown, as well as providing access to Greylock Mountain, the state's highest peak, with soaring views of fall foliage. There are few more rewarding autumn journeys.

Whether to base yourself at the eastern or western end of the road depends largely on whether you prefer historic homes or mountain scenery. Since the Deerfield Inn is located on one of America's most magnificent Main Streets, it may rate a special recommendation.

Known simply as the Street, Old Deerfield's main avenue is a mile-long row of more than 50 fine Colonial and Federal houses, each one carefully maintained in its original condition. In the dozen buildings open to the public, visitors can see more than 100 rooms filled with china, glassware, silver, pewter, fabrics, and furniture—all testaments to the good taste of our early settlers.

But this is by no means a museum town. The houses on the Street have been continuously occupied over the years, and even the museum homes have apartments in the rear for the faculty of Deerfield Academy, the noted school that has stood on the Street since 1797, giving Deerfield a rare living continuity with the past that is evident the moment you arrive. It is heightened by the fact that no modern intrusions such as telephone wires have been allowed; they are carefully buried to preserve the street's untouched beauty.

It's hard to believe that this peaceful, elm-shaded village was once a frontier outpost, twice besieged by Indian attacks. The stubborn survivors rebuilt their town, worked their farms, and began to prosper, replacing their primitive homes with gracious, weathered clapboard houses in the Connecticut Valley tradition, marked by distinctively carved doorways. Though rustic compared to houses in Boston or Philadelphia, their very simplicity makes them all the lovelier.

Deerfield's farmers used their new wealth to commission the finest furnishings they could find, particularly from the excellent craftsmen and cabinetmakers of their own valley. Fortunately this era of good taste has been preserved, thanks largely to the generosity of Mr. and Mrs. Henry Flynt, who came to Deerfield in the 1930s when their son was enrolled at the academy. The Flynts first bought and restored the white-columned inn at the center of town, which remains a gracious Colonial lodging, and then acquired one of the old houses for themselves. One house led to another until, in 1952, they founded Historic Deerfield, Inc., to care for the properties.

Though Deerfield is only a village, it deserves a full day of touring if you want to savor all it has to offer. A visit to Historic Deerfield includes a walking tour of the village, but you might prefer to start on your own by strolling the Street, with time to savor the town's setting among wooded hills and observing the exteriors of the saltbox houses, with their steep-pitched gambrel roofs, weathered clapboard siding, and carved doorways. Note the Academy buildings, the old Brick Church, and the post office, a replica of a 1696 meetinghouse.

You may want to take a detour onto the Channing Blake Meadow Walk, a half-mile footpath leading from the village into the nearly 1,000 acres of beautiful meadows that surround the western and northern edges of the community. It gives a close-up view of the fields that have been farmed continuously for more than three centuries and brings into focus the critical roles of agriculture in past and present-day rural New England. Then head for the Hall Tavern Information Center, where color photos will help you make the difficult choice of which houses to visit during a limited stay. Each house tour takes 30 minutes.

You can begin with Hall Tavern itself, once a hostelry for travelers. One of its seven rooms is an unusual ballroom with gaily stenciled walls. A must on any tour is Ashley House (circa 1730), the home of Deerfield's Tory minister during the American Revolution. Many may have quarreled with the Reverend Jonathan Ashley's politics, but no one could fault his taste. The north parlor, with blue walls setting off red shell-crowned cupboards, a gold satin settee, and rich oriental rugs, has been called one of the most beautiful rooms in America.

Each of the other houses has its own special attractions and a knowledgeable guide to point them out. Many of the guides are local residents who have family stories to add to the town's history.

The Sheldon-Hawks House (1743), home of the town's historian, contains fine paneling, a display of sewing equipment, and a memorable bedroom with brilliant flame-stitch bed hangings and red moreen curtains and chairs. Behind the austere, Colonial facade of the Wells-Thorn House (1717/1751) are a series of rooms furnished to depict changing periods in Deerfield's history. The Dwight House (1725) has an elegant parlor and a doctor's office behind its weathered exterior.

The Asa Stebbins House (1799), the town's first brick edifice, was built by the wealthiest landowner and decorated with French wallpapers and freehand wall drawings. Like many of Deerfield's homes, this one has an excellent collection of early export china.

Mr. Stebbins also built the town's other brick house for his son, Asa, Junior, in 1824. Now called Wright House, it is distinguished for its exquisite collection of Federal furniture.

Frary House (1720/1768), a home with a double history, is another highly recommended stop. Its location on the town common made it a refuge for the Frary family in pioneer days and a profitable tavern for the Barnards later on. The house contains a ballroom, many examples of country furniture, and a variety of cooking, spinning, and weaving equipment. There is also a "touch it" room where children and adults may handle some of the tools that are off-limits elsewhere.

The newest home on the tour is the Hinsdale and Anna Williams House, opened to the public in 1993 after 12 years of painstaking restoration and research. The furnishings are based on the personal inventory of household property owned by Hinsdale Williams at his death on June 1, 1838.

For a change of pace, step into some of the specialized buildings such as the Henry N. Flynt Silver and Metalware Collection, a farmhouse containing a smith's workshop, a pewter collection, and an outstanding display of American and English silver. The house dates from around 1810. Inside a Victorian barn is the Helen Geier Flynt Textile Collection, a remarkable assemblage of American, English, and European needlework, textiles, quilts, bed hangings, and costumes.

The last weekend of September brings the annual Old Deerfield Crafts Fair on the front lawn of Memorial Hall Museum, a bonus for autumn visitors. The museum also hosts a Living History weekend in October with a military encampment and historical reenactments. The building itself is something of a town attic, with memorabilia that includes doors still bearing gashes from the 1704 massacre.

If you've given Saturday to Deerfield, plan an early start Sunday to allow for the scenery and sights awaiting along the Mohawk Trail. Take I-91 six miles north to Greenfield to connect to the trail (Route 2) and its many vistas heading west. Allow two hours for the 42-mile trip because of the dips and twists and stunning scenery along the way. You can't miss the best views because, sad to say, they've been marked by signs at local souvenir shops and restaurants adjoining scenic lookouts. The first is Whitcomb Summit, the top of the trail, an elevation of over 2,000 feet with views of mountains as far away as Vermont and New Hampshire. The most famous of the lookouts is the Hairpin Turn opening to another soaring mountain vista.

Other than these well-visited spots, much of the trail remains wooded and unblemished, allowing you to enjoy this state's premier autumn panoramas. There are a number of sightseeing stops along the way if you have the time. Among them are the unique Bridge of Flowers in Shelburne Falls, a five-arch concrete span, once an old trolley bridge, now covered with a profusion of shrubs and blossoms, and Salmon Falls just downstream, a historic spot where the Mohawk and Penobscot tribes signed a fishing treaty, now best known as the site of many ancient glacial potholes. New England's only "natural bridge"—a white marble span over Hudson Brook—can be found in North Adams.

By the time you get to North Adams, the Mohawk Trail scenery has given way to commercial establishments. North Adams itself is a little town on the way up, with a spruced-up Main Street and a new attraction, the Western Gateway Heritage State Park, housed in wooden railroad buildings, all on the National Register of Historic Places.

The Visitors' Center in a former freight house traces the history of the region. In an exhibit housed in a tunnel-like setting, you learn about the building of the Hoosac Mountain Tunnel, the longest railway tunnel of its time, which connected Boston to the west. It was considered a marvel back in the 1850s, created by digging 1,000 feet straight down through rock. There are also films of steam train days.

Some of the old freight houses now house the Marketplace, a complex with a general store, shops selling antiques and crafts, plus a restaurant and a bakery and ice cream parlor to feed your sweet tooth.

If funding ever is found to turn plans into reality, North Adams will also become the home of a museum of contemporary art, housed in a former mill. Plans are big, and include a 100-room hotel, but there have been several postponements due to the cost.

If you watch for the signs on Route 2 in North Adams and make a left turn onto Notch Road, you'll be on the road to the 3,491-foot summit of Mt. Greylock, the state's highest peak and the most stunning view of all. The road may seem bumpy at the start, but it gets better as you ascend.

At the summit in Bascom Lodge, you'll find an information center manned by the Appalachian Mountain Club, with maps covering the 35 miles of hiking trails available here for hikers of all abilities. A favorite hiking destination is the Hopper, a wildlife preserve of giant conifers and lush growth where the natural scene is untouched by any human development. By car, follow the signs to Stony Ledge for an outlook over this heavily wooded, brook-coursed canyon.

The famous hiking route, the Appalachian Trail, also passes through Mt. Greylock Reservation, a 10,000-acre preserve around the mountain maintained by the Massachusetts Department of Environmental Management. The state agency and the Appalachian Mountain Club combine to offer many guided tours and talks on the mountain.

You can return to the bottom on Notch Road or on the road that takes you to the Route 7 Information Center in Lanesboro. Either way, your next stop is Williamstown, a classic New England town with a college dating back to 1793 as its center. Williams is so much a part of its hometown that it is hard to tell where the campus stops and town begins, and the campus offers some interesting places to visit, including the collection of rare books at the Chapin Library (closed weekends, unfortunately) and the quite spectacular Williams Art Museum.

Williamstown's best-known art attraction is the Sterling and Francine Clark Art Institute, one of the most impressive small museums in the country. Sterling Clark had the good fortune to be heir to the fortune his grandfather amassed as a partner to Isaac Singer, the sewing-machine king. He began collecting fine art around 1912, starting with works of the Old Masters; but with the encourage-ment of his French-born wife, he shifted emphasis in the 1920s and 1930s to nineteenth-century French painting and to American artists such as Sargent, Remington, and Winslow Homer, who is represented by seven excellent oils. The real heart of the museum is the exceptional display of paintings by Rubens, Monet, Degas, and Renoir.

When the Clarks decided in the 1950s to build a museum to hold their treasures, they chose Williamstown for the beauty of the setting and designed a building to make the most of it. Tall windows in the corridors look out on natural scenery that adds immensely to the pleasures of visiting the building. The galleries are done to drawing-room scale, and many are furnished with antiques, making this museum particularly enjoyable.

While you're in Williamstown, a stroll over to Water Street (Route 43) will bring you to a few interesting shops. The Potter's Wheel, a gallery with picture windows overlooking a brook, has particularly attractive displays of art, glass, sculpture, and jewelry.

Williamstown's most elaborate lodging is The Orchards, contemporary on the outside but elegant Colonial inside, offering oversize rooms and a highly regarded dining room. The Williams Inn, though actually a hotel of recent vintage, has managed to maintain a measure of New England warmth, and there is the advantage of an indoor pool. More charming smaller choices are River Bend Farm, an antique-filled 1770 Georgian home, or you can drive 12 miles from Williamstown to the Mill House Inn, a gemütlich Alpine chalet hideaway just 500 feet across the New York border from Hancock.

Field Farm Guest House is another possibility, the contemporary home of a late art collector now being run by the state's Trustees of Reservations as a B & B. Bedrooms are plain, but with 254 private acres dotted with trails and sculptures and striking views of Mt. Greylock, you may not mind. Yet another possibility is Jiminy Peak, a mountain resort in nearby Hancock, which offers an attractive modern inn or condominium accommodations.

Hard-core hikers may want to consider the spartan but clean accommodations at Bascom Lodge. The rooms and familystyle meals are a real bargain.

Whether you hike, house tour, look at art, or concentrate on the scenery, Deerfield to Williamstown is an end-to-end route that can hardly be bettered. And whether you make a return scenic trip on the

Mohawk Trail or find a speedier route home, you'll be bringing back memories of the New England autumn at its best.

Area Code: 413

DRIVING DIRECTIONS Deerfield can be reached via I-91, Exit 24 northbound or Exit 25 southbound to Route 5, which leads six miles north into town. Williamstown is at the intersection of Route 7 and Route 2 (the Mohawk Trail), reached via I-91, Exit 26, a few miles north of Deerfield. Though the portion designated as the Mohawk Trail stops at Millers Falls, Route 2 continues east to Boston. Deerfield is about 100 miles from Boston, 187 miles from New York, and 77 miles from Hartford.

PUBLIC TRANSPORTATION Peter Pan Bus Service to Deerfield, Bonanza buses to Williamstown. You'll need a car to travel on the Mohawk Trail.

ACCOMMODATIONS *Deerfield Inn,* The Street, Deerfield 01342, 774-5587, $$$ • *The Orchards,* 222 Adams Road, Williamstown 01267, 458-9611, $$$$–$$$$$ (ask about weekend packages) • *Williams Inn,* on the green, Williamstown 01267, 458-9371, $$$–$$$$ • *River Bend Farm,* 643 Simonds Road, Williamstown 01267, 458-3121, $$ CP • *Field Farm Guest House,* 554 Sloan Road, Williamstown 01267, 458-3135, $$ CP • *The House on Main Street,* 1120 Main Street, Williamstown 01267, 458-3031, pleasant home, walking distance to town, $$ • *Goldberry's,* 39 Cold Spring Road (Route 7), Williamstown 01267, 458-3935, attractive 1830 home, also within a walk of town, $$ CP • *Jiminy Peak Mountain Resort,* Corey Road, Hancock 01237, 738-5500; inn building, $$$$, condos with kitchens, $$$$$; less on weekdays and off-season • *Mill House Inn,* Route 43, Stephentown, New York 01268 (518) 733-5606, $$–$$$ CP • *1896 Motel,* Route 7, Williamstown 01267, 458-8125, pleasant motel on lovely grounds, $–$$ CP • *AMC Bascom Lodge,* Mt. Greylock, PO Box 686, Lanesboro 02137, 743-1591, $.

DINING *Deerfield Inn* (see above), $$–$$$ • *Le Jardin Inn,* Route 7 and Cold Spring Road, Williamstown, 458-8032, converted estate, French menu, $$–$$$ • *Savories,* 123 Water Street (Route 43), Williamstown, 458-2175, new American, $$$ • *Le Country,* 101 North Street, Williamstown, 458-4000, relaxed, convenient, $$ • *The Orchards* (see above), $$–$$$$ • *Hobson's Choice,* Water Street, 458-9101, cozy, informal, $$ • *Mill on the Floss,* Route 7, New Ashford, 458-9123, fine French, $$$ • *Freight Yard Restaurant & Pub,* Western Gateway Heritage State Park, North Adams, 663-6547, informal, wide-ranging menu, good prices, $ • *Hancock Inn,* Route 43, Hancock (not far from Williamstown), 738-5873, excellent restaurant in an old home, $$–$$$ • For lunch and light fare almost any time, a best bet is the *Erasmus Café at the College Bookstore,* 76 Spring Street, Williamstown, 458-8071, open Monday to Saturday, 9 A.M. to 10 P.M., $.

SIGHTSEEING *Historic Deerfield,* PO Box 321, Deerfield, MA 10342, 774-5581. Hours: daily, 9:30 A.M. to 4:30 P.M. Adults, $10; children, $5 • *Sterling and Francine Clark Art Institute,* South Street, Williamstown, 458-9545. Hours: daily except Monday, 10 A.M. to 5 P.M. Free • *Williams College Museum of Art,* 1846 Lawrence Hall, 597-2429. Hours: Tuesday to Saturday, 10 A.M. to 5 P.M.; Sunday 1 P.M. to 5 P.M. Free • *Chapin Library,* Stetson Hall, 597-2462. Hours: Monday to Friday, 10 A.M. to noon and 1 P.M. to 5 P.M. Free.

INFORMATION The Mohawk Trail Association, PO Box J, Charlemont, MA 01339, 664-6256.

Breezing Through the Past in Essex

Standing on the docks at Essex, Connecticut, enjoying the sea breeze and admiring the panorama of sleek sailboats in the harbor, you'll find it hard to believe that this placid spot was once the most bustling landing on the Connecticut River.

With its pleasure boats, lanes of picket fences, and handsome white clapboard Colonial and Federal homes, today's Essex is the picture of Early American serenity, a mecca for sailors and strollers.

But for more than 300 eventful years of history, this town has been a major port on the 410-mile river that has served as a main artery for much of New England. There's rich history to be explored as well as some special pleasures of the present, including a cruise on the majestic river, some unusual shops, and several exceptional inns.

Just up the river is a Victorian jewel box of a theater offering classic American musical comedies. Here, too, is Connecticut's answer to those romantic castles on the Rhine, not to mention the chance nearby to ride a puffing, chugging turn-of-the-century steam train, all adding even more incentive to make the trip.

Start your get-acquainted tour of Essex at its most significant site, Steamboat Dock, at the foot of Main Street on the riverfront. Situated in lush countryside just five miles above the spot where the Connecticut

River feeds into the sea, Essex has been inextricably tied to its river from the first days in 1648 when settlers from the shore colony of Old Saybrook decided to form a farming community a bit inland. The first wharf at the site of the present Steamboat Dock was in operation as early as 1656, and trade with the West Indies had begun by the 1660s.

Shipbuilding was soon a major activity as well, and Connecticut's first warship, the *Oliver Cromwell,* was built at the Hayden Yard here in 1776. The British raided and burned the 28 ships in the harbor during the War of 1812. That event is commemorated with a marker at the foot of the harbor, as well as by the Essex Fife and Drum Corps, known as the Sailing Masters of 1812, who parade down Main Street in period dress to mark most national holidays.

Things revived after the war, however, and Essex's ships and sailors were known to nineteenth-century commerce throughout the world. A new era of prominence came with the arrival of steamboat service on the river in 1823; the original Steamboat Dock was built in 1845 to accommodate the growing traffic. It was enlarged and the dockhouse built in the 1860s. The three-story clapboard structure with its graceful cupola became a well-known landmark for river passengers.

The Connecticut River Foundation has restored the exterior of the historic dockhouse and a portion of the interior as it was in its warehouse days. The building also houses a small museum with exhibits telling the story of the waterway and Essex-built ships with tools, navigational instruments, paintings, and scale-model steamboats.

An unusual display is a full-size reproduction of *The Turtle,* America's first submarine, designed in 1776 in nearby Old Sayville. Though the sub fared better in its river trials than it did once it went to war, it is still a fascinating exhibit.

From here, it's on to the rest of the town's sights. You'll certainly want to check out some of the many shops on Main Street and in a little shopping complex just behind it for antiques, handicrafts, gifts, and gewgaws, many with a nautical bent.

For those who want a closer look at the river itself, there are several excursion trips offered nearby, including lunch and dinner cruises. Bushnell Park off Bushnell Street above the boatyards and the Town Park off Main Street are ideal spots for a picnic lunch on land with water views.

The town tour leads past the gracious homes that once belonged to schooner captains and shipbuilders, and past the churches and other historic buildings that tell more about the Essex of yesterday. As you follow along Main to Essex Square and up Methodist Hill to Prospect Street and West Avenue, watch for some of the distinctive fan lights, the handsome doorknobs and knockers, and the unusual brick patterns and chimneys that mark many of the homes in town.

The Pratt House at 20 West Avenue, restored and furnished by the Essex Historical Society, gives a glimpse of life in Essex in the mid-1800s. Inside you'll see fine oak and chestnut beams, burnished paneling, and many rare antiques originally owned by the Pratts, an important early family in town. The Essex Garden Club has planted a fragrant Colonial herb garden around the house.

The 1845 Baptist Church is hard to miss, with its white steeple and gold dome. It is one of only two examples of Egyptian revival architecture in the country.

Walk to the end of Prospect and turn left on North Main and you'll be at the Riverview Cemetery, resting place of the Pratts, Haydens, and other Essex first families. This is a cemetery with a river view—a lovely panorama across the Connecticut River to the Lyme Hills.

The Griswold Inn in Essex should be part of any tour. Even the British troops who invaded in 1814 made a point of staying at "the Gris," which has been open for business on the same spot on Main Street since 1776 and has hardly changed on the outside over the years. You'll have to call early to get one of the much-in-demand rooms here, but a stop is a must, at least for a meal and a visit. The Sunday Hunt Breakfast, a local tradition, includes the inn's 1776 sausages, made from a recipe handed down for eight generations.

If the inn is filled, there are other possibilities in the neighborhood. The Copper Beech Inn in Ivoryton has elegant rooms and a restaurant to match, and The Inn at Chester is a country hotel with an excellent dining room. The Riverwind Inn in Deep River is a true country charmer, and Bishopsgate Inn in East Haddam is an attractive small inn with a special advantage, because it is within walking distance of one of the area's best attractions, the Goodspeed Opera House.

Reserve well ahead for all the choice small inns in this popular region as well as for the Goodspeed Opera House, a highlight of a Connecticut River Valley visit. Musicals of the 1920s and 1930s are served up here in a restored Victorian theater on the river, a playhouse full of frou-frous and charm. There is a newer branch of the Goodspeed in Chester, dedicated to new musicals.

If you've spent Saturday on foot in Essex, you might want to begin Sunday's sightseeing with a drive along River Road, with glimpses of water and many fine houses along the way. Then it's on to a different kind of ride—or two of them, to be exact, by land and by sea. The Valley Railroad, just a couple of miles from the center of town, offers a double dose of nostalgia, a ten-mile excursion into the countryside aboard the same kind of steam train that grandpa might have ridden when he was a boy, then an optional connection to a riverboat for a half-hour cruise up the Connecticut River.

If you haven't taken a ride on the river, don't miss the opportunity. The pristine and beautiful woodland banks are a pleasure to behold anytime and a blaze of color in autumn foliage season. And there are just enough diversions to whip photographers into action—hilltop mansions, the gingerbread facade of the Goodspeed Opera House, or the stone turrets of Gillette Castle.

When you get back to shore, take the three-minute ride across the river from Chester to Hadlyme aboard one of the region's oldest and smallest ferryboats, and on to East Haddam for a close-up view of Gillette Castle, a one-of-a-kind curiosity.

It was built by William Gillette, a somewhat eccentric gentleman who gained fame and fortune by portraying Sherlock Holmes on the stage. The castle cost over a million dollars, quite a sum when it was built in the early 1900s. Complete with turrets and balconies, it was meant to re-create the feel of the castles on the Rhine that Gillette had admired in Europe.

Among Mr. Gillette's eccentricities was a dislike for metal. All the doors are fitted with wooden locks operated by hidden springs, and even the light switches are made of wood. The walls are wooden also, hand carved of oak. There are some 47 different kinds of latching doors and cabinets. To protect all that wood, Gillette had fire hoses and a sprinkler system installed, safety features that were many years ahead of their time. Trick locks and trapdoors fascinate, and children are intrigued by Gillette's love for cats and frogs, evident throughout the house in the form of bookends, salt shakers, and even a wishing well where his frogs used to live.

Whatever you think of the castle, you'll certainly admire the clifftop river view. The grounds are now a state park, and the perfect place for a picnic with a last sweeping perspective on the Connecticut River as it winds its way downstream to Essex and on to the sea.

After the castle, there are plenty of diversions in either direction. A short drive north, in Higganum, is the Sundial Herb Gardens, with formal gardens for touring and a shop selling herbs and tasteful gifts. Teas and tours are offered on many Sunday afternoons.

Downriver a bit, pretty little Chester is a perfect town for browsing. The shops include the Connecticut River Artisans Cooperative, showing work of local artists. Further east, the Great American Trading Company in Deep River is a treasure of toy nostalgia, filled with old-time favorites such as wooden pick-up sticks, marbles, and Chinese checkers.

Heading on toward Old Saybrook, the Essex-Saybrook Antiques Village has a little bit of everything, with 80 dealers under one roof.

In Old Saybrook, where the Connecticut River meets Long Island Sound, you can wind up the weekend with a fine seafood dinner. Whether you pick plain or fancy surroundings, the water view is grand.

Area Code: 203

DRIVING DIRECTIONS   Essex is reached via I-95 or I-91. From either direction, take Route 9 to Exit 3, then Route 153, which becomes Main Street. It is about 133 miles from Boston, 118 miles from New York, and 35 miles from Hartford.

PUBLIC TRANSPORTATION   Amtrak to Old Saybrook, Greyhound to Middletown. Both are just a short drive from Essex. A car is needed to get around the area, however.

ACCOMMODATIONS   *Griswold Inn,* Main Street, Essex 06426, 767-1776, $$–$$$$$ CP • *Copper Beech Inn,* 46 Main Street, Ivoryton 06442, 767-0330, $$$–$$$$$ CP • *Bishopsgate Inn,* Goodspeed Landing, East Haddam 06423, 873-1677, $$–$$$ CP • *The Inn at Chester,* 318 West Main Street, Route 148, Chester 06412, 526-9541, $$–$$$, CP • *Riverwind Inn,* 209 Main Street, Deep River 06147, 526-2014, wonderful country decor, $$–$$$$ CP.

DINING   *Griswold Inn* (see above), dinner, $$–$$$; Sunday hunt breakfast, $$ • *Copper Beech Inn* (see above), $$$–$$$$ • *Oliver's Taverne,* Route 152, Essex, 767-2633, informal, popular, $–$$ • *The Post and Beam,* The Inn at Chester (see above), $$$ • *Restaurant du Village,* 59 Main Street, Chester, 526-5301, country French bistro, $$$–$$$$ • *Fiddler's Seafood Restaurant,* 4 Water Street, Chester, 526-3210, country decor, good food, $$ • *Fine Bouche,* Main Street, Centerbrook, 767-1277, fine French food, $$–$$$ • *Dock and Dine,* Saybrook Point, Old Saybrook, 388-4665, $–$$$ • *Saybrook Fish House,* 99 Essex Road, Old Saybrook, 388-4836, $–$$ • *Saybrook Point Inn,* 2 Bridge Street, Old Saybrook, 395-2000, $$–$$$.

SIGHTSEEING   *Valley Railroad,* Exit 3 off Route 9, Essex, 767-0103. Call for current schedule and rates. • *Connecticut River Museum,* foot of Main Street, Essex, 767-8269. Hours: Tuesday to Sunday, 10 A.M. to 5 P.M. Adults, $3; under 12, $1 • *Pratt House,* West Avenue, Essex, 767-0681. Hours: June to September, Saturday and Sunday, 1 P.M. to 4 P.M. Adults, $2; children, free • *Goodspeed Opera House,* East Haddam, 873-8668, April to November. Phone for current offerings • *Gillette Castle,* Gillette Castle State Park, 67 River Road, East Haddam, 526-2336. Hours: mid-May to mid-October, daily, 10 A.M. to 5 P.M.; October to mid-December, weekends only, 10 A.M. to 4 P.M. Adults, $4; ages 6 to 12, $2. No fee for visiting the park • *Camelot Cruises,* 1 Marine Park, Haddam, 345-8591, phone for current schedules and rates for lunch and dinner cruises • *Deep River Navigation Company,* River Street, Deep River, 526-4954. Phone for information about cruises out of Old Saybrook.

INFORMATION   Connecticut River and Shoreline Visitors Council, 393 Main Street, Middletown, CT 06457, 347-0028 or (800) 486-3346.

Mountains and Sea in Camden

Captain John Smith (of Pocahontas fame) said it well: "Camden lies under the high mountains of the Penobscot against whose feet the sea doth beat."

In less poetic terms, Camden, Maine, is a town where the mountains meet the sea. The deep blue natural harbor fed by rushing falls reflects the wooded slopes of Mt. Battie and Mt. Megunticook in a scenic juxtaposition that has won the admiration of visitors ever since the days of Samuel de Champlain and other early explorers.

It is a winning summer destination that becomes doubly appealing in early fall when the crowds recede and the harbor begins to mirror the myriad autumn colors of the mountain. Middle to late September, before the Camden Windjammer fleet calls it a season, is an ideal time for a visit.

At the turn of the century, Camden's favored location attracted the wealthy, who built elaborate summer homes here and traveled up the coast by steamer to vacation. The homes still grace the town, but today Camden is a tourist magnet for everyone. The well-kept village, festooned with hanging flowerpots on every available lamppost, has good reason for its boast of being "the prettiest town in Maine." The harbor scene has been made even more picturesque by the presence of New England's largest fleet of Windjammers, the many-masted sailing ships patterned after clipper ships of old.

The resulting influx of visitors has transformed quiet Camden into an attractive browsers' town, filled with shops, galleries, and restaurants, and has led to a bumper crop of lodgings that can't be beat anywhere on the Maine coast.

The queen is Norumbega, a virtual castle, with many porches and balconies overlooking the ocean. The elaborate carving, golden oak paneling, and other touches that make this residence so distinctive have been restored to mint condition. The furnishings in the public rooms and seven bedrooms do justice to their formal setting.

Camden also has a number of attractive small bed-and-breakfast inns, most of them on High Street, which is U.S. Route 1 up the hill just north of town. One of the nicest is the Edgecombe-Coles House, right across the street from Norumbega. Set well back from the road, it is one of the early summer homes, furnished with antiques and with a warm country feel. Route 1 can be quite busy, and the Swan House, a small, attractive bed-and-breakfast inn, is appealing for its location, still convenient to town but off the main road.

The rambling Whitehall Inn is the dowager in town, the place where

Edna St. Vincent Millay was discovered by a wealthy patron when she read her poem "Renascence" in the parlor now named for her. Two other options are The High Tide Inn, an unpretentious lodge-and-cottage arrangement right on the water, and the Samoset Resort not far away in Rockland, which provides tennis, golf, and many other amenities in a setting hugging the sea.

Wherever you stay, it's Camden's Public Landing that most people head for first of all, to admire the sleek boats in the harbor and take in the extraordinary view—Camden hills rising on one side, Penobscot Bay opening on the other.

Most of the tall-masted windjammers in the harbor sail off on six-day cruises on Monday, returning on the weekend in a regal display of furling sails. While some of these "tall ships" were built exclusively for the tourist trade, others have intriguing histories as Grand Banks fishing schooners or pilot ships before they were converted to passenger vessels.

The local tourist office is behind the parking lot at the landing, and is well stocked with information, including a walking-tour map. You can't miss all the shops on Bay View Avenue, at the landing, and on Main Street. The town tour proceeds from the landing left past the shops to the Yacht Club, a fixture on the docks since 1906, and along the water to the Camden Harbour Inn, which has a specially nice harbor view from the front porch.

Turn right on Limerock past the inn, then right again on Chestnut to see some of the town's finest homes. Number 77 is Thayercroft, a distinguished 1821 house that was a setting for the movie *Peyton Place*. This entire block is lined with historic homes from the late 1700s and early 1800s, including the Hathaway-Cushing-Millay house at number 31, which belonged to members of the family of Edna St. Vincent Millay.

Past the Baptist church, you'll be back at the village green, where you can bear left to Elm and Wood and Pleasant to see more homes, or take a stroll down Main Street to see some more interesting nineteenth-century town architecture while you check out the shops. You'll no doubt want to return to the many other shops around the landing as well.

Like many Maine towns that attract tourists, Camden has become a showcase for talented state artisans, and you'll be able to find anything from hand-thrown pottery to handmade fisherman's sweaters. The Patchwork Barn offers the work of many Maine craftspeople, and Once A Tree displays fine woodworking. Among the many shops on Bayview, Unique 1 specializes in Maine woolen sweaters plus ceramics, and Ducktrap Bay Trading Company near the Public Landing has decoys and other nautical carvings. Back on Main, you'll be offered complimentary coffee or tea on a balcony overlooking the harbor at the Smiling Cow, a crafts and gift store that has been run by the same family on the same spot since 1940. The Admiral's Buttons is one of many clothing stores in town that sell chic and practical boating attire.

For a change of pace, visit Camden's Center for Creative Imaging, where students learn a relatively new skill, how to create digital computer images. The center offers tours, demonstrations, weekend programs, and computer classes, and includes an art gallery and café.

If you're ready for a lunch break, two other good choices are Cappy's Chowder House on Main or the Waterfront, with a deck on the harbor. Or you might choose to pick up a lunch and picnic on the grassy slopes of Camden Amphitheater behind the library, a pleasant place to gaze at the harbor view. Another possibility is the shoreside picnic area at Camden Hills State Park on Route 1, just north of town.

Lunch or not, take the park toll road to the top of Mt. Battie for an exceptional view of the town and harbor below. A short, steep hiking trail from Megunticook Street in Camden will also bring you to the top.

Some of Maine's most scenic hiking, in fact, is in this park. The top of Mt. Megunticook, the second highest point on the Atlantic seaboard, can be reached in a one-hour hike from park headquarters on Route 1 that includes a stop at a natural grotto. Megunticook Lake and Megunticook River separate the several peaks in the park's 5,000 acres from the Camden hills, making for views on all sides. In winter, Mt. Battie and Camden Snow Bowl are among the rare places where you can see the sea as you ski.

If you prefer your water views from the side of a boat, you'll find several going out on excursions from the landing into Penobscot Bay through mid-to-late September. All year round you can drive north to Lincolnville and board the ferry for the 25-minute crossing to Isleboro or go south to Rockland for the ferry rides to Vinalhaven or North Ferry Islands, an hour and a half and an hour and ten minutes away, respectively. Boats to Monhegan Island leave from Port Clyde.

Vinalhaven is the biggest of the islands, with shops and an art gallery, and Monhegan is by far the most scenic, with dramatic clifftop vistas of the sea. Isleboro offers a state park, a Sailor's Memorial Museum, a gallery, beaches, and the Dark Harbor House, if you want to get away from it all. These are pleasant outings on a fine fall day. There's also a good chance of spotting seals cavorting in the water along the way and even dolphins and whales if you are lucky. Some of the ferries do not operate on Sunday, so check current schedules before you plan a trip. Excursions go out of Rockland harbor as well; inquire at the Public Landing.

A highly recommended Sunday activity is the six-mile drive to Rockport village, a tiny and totally charming fishing and shipbuilding village dating back to the early 1770s. The entire village was made a Historic District in the mid-1970s, and there are some 127 buildings listed in the inventory.

In Marine Park, overlooking the harbor, you'll find a statue of Andre the Seal, a late local hero who used to swim up from Boston to spend the summer every year. Smart seal.

Rockport has become very much an artist's town, home of the Maine Coast Artists Gallery in a strikingly renovated old livery station-cum-firehouse and also host of the respected summer Maine Photography Workshops. The restored Town Hall–Opera House at the entrance to Marine Park is known for its acoustics and is home to summer Bay Chamber Concerts, theater, and other cultural events.

What to do in Rockport? Visit the Artists Gallery, check for a last exhibition at the Photography Workshop Gallery, and wander through the handful of galleries and shops on Main Street. Look in on the Artisans School, where the art of building traditional wooden boats is taught; visitors are welcome.

Then, admire the many fine historic homes on almost any village street, and drive out to Vesper Hill, known as the Children's Chapel, a gift to the community by a former resident, for a quiet and beautiful spot overlooking the sea. You'll understand why this is a favorite locale for marriages. The Sail Loft is the place if you want to have Sunday brunch or dinner overlooking the harbor. If you fall in love with the town, as many visitors do, you may be able to arrange for rooms in a couple of small inns right on the harbor.

To finish off the day, drive a few miles farther south into Rockland, not the most scenic town you've seen but home of the Farnsworth Art Museum, a superior regional museum of paintings and sculpture. Among the Maine collections are works by all three generations of Wyeths. The handsome Farnsworth Homestead, the home of the museum's benefactress, adjoins the museum.

Or you may choose to return to Camden for more hiking or shopping—or simply a last look at that incomparable harbor scene where the mountains meet the sea.

Area Code: 207

DRIVING DIRECTIONS Camden is about halfway between Portland and Bar Harbor on U.S. Route 1 on the Maine coast. From the Maine Turnpike, take Route 17 east to Route 90 to Route 1. It is about 200 miles from Boston, 400 miles from New York, and 290 miles from Hartford.

PUBLIC TRANSPORTATION Greyhound bus service to Camden; air service to Bangor, 50 miles away; Portland, 85 miles away; or Rockland, 8 miles away. You can manage easily without a car if you stay in town; get to the park by hike or bike.

ACCOMMODATIONS All Camden addresses are zip code 04843. *Norumbega,* 61 High Street, 236-4646, exceptional, $$$$$ CP • *Edgecombe-Coles House,* 64 High Street, 236-2336, $$–$$$$ CP • *Whitehall Inn,* Box 558, Camden, 236-3391, tennis, boating, $$$–$$$$ MAP • *Camden Harbour Inn,* 83 Bayview Street, 236-4200, $$$–$$$$ CP • *Swan House,* 49 Mountain Street, 236-8275 or (800) 207-8275, $–$$$ CP • **Many pleasant B & B inns are found on one block:** *Maine Stay,* 22 High Street, 236-9636, 1803 Colonial, $$–$$$ CP; *Hawthorn Inn,* 9 High Street, 236-8842, 1894 Victorian B & B, $$–$$$$ CP; *Mansard Manor,* 5 High Street, 236-3291, antiques, folk art, $$–$$$ CP; *Windward House,* 6 High Street, Greek Revival home circa 1854, $$–$$$ CP • *Highland Mill Inn,* Mechanic and Washington streets, Camden, 236-1057 or (800) 841-5590, refurbished mill on the river, some decks, $$–$$$$ CP • *Rockport Harbor House,* 11 Mechanic Street, Rockport 04856, 236-2422, all rooms with balconies or terraces on the harbor, $$–$$$$ CP • *Mary Helen Amsbury House,* 25 Amsbury Street, Rockport 04856, 236-4653, more harbor views, $$–$$$ CP • *The High Tide Inn,* Route 1 North, Camden, 236-3724, motel on the water north of town, $$–$$$ • *Samoset Resort,* Rockland 04856, 594-2511 or (800) 341-1650, tennis, golf, indoor and outdoor pool, gym, $$$$–$$$$$ CP.

DINING *Belmont,* 6 Belmont Avenue, 236-8053, long considered best in town, $$–$$$ • *The Waterfront,* Bayview Street, Harbor Square, 236-3747, informal, on the harbor, good for lunch or dinner, $–$$ • *Peter Ott's,* 16 Bayview Street, 236-4032, reliable old-timer, varied menu, $–$$ • *O'Neil's,* 21 Bayview Street, 236-3272, casual, brick oven pizza, $–$$ • *Reunion Grill,* 49 Mechanic Street, 236-1090, renovated mill on the river, grill specialties, $$ • *Cassoulet,* 31 Elm Street, 236-6304, Italian menu in the house or the garden, $$ • *Marcel's,* Samoset Resort (see above), recommended both for cuisine and setting, $$–$$$ • *The Sail Loft,* Public Landing, Rockport, 236-2330, seafood and harbor views, $$–$$$ • **Informal fare:** *Cappy's Chowder House,* 1 Main Street, Camden, 236-2254, open 7:30 A.M. to midnight, try the chowder, $–$$ • *Sea Dog Brewing Company,* 43 Mechanic Street, 236-6863, brew-pub, tavern menu, $–$$; brewery tours daily June through October at 11 A.M. and 4 P.M., rest of year on Saturday at 3 P.M. • **For lobster:** *Lobster Pound Restaurant,* Route 1, Lincolnville Beach (next town after Camden), 789-5550, open 11:30 A.M. to 9 P.M. in summer, after Labor Day best to check hours, closes Columbus Day; *Capt. Andy's,* High Street, 236-6155, or Upper Washington Street, 236-2312, take-out lobsters, steamers, great place for picnics to go; *Young's Lobster Pound,* Mitchell Avenue (follow signs from Route 1), Belfast, 469-3963, classic by-the-sea setting for those who are driving north from Camden.

SIGHTSEEING   *Camden Hills State Park,* Route 1 North, Camden, 236-3109. Free except toll road to top of Mt. Battie. Shore area open May to November, small fee. Hiking trail maps available at Information Center on Route 1 • *Cruises,* Public Landing, June to September, many options; inquire at Camden Information Booth for current schedules and rates • *Maine State Ferry Service,* Route 1, Lincolnville Beach, 780-5611, and 517A Main Street, Rockland, 596-2202; inquire for current schedules • *Maine Coast Artists Gallery,* Russell Avenue, Rockport, 236-2875. Hours: June through October, daily, 10 A.M. to 5 P.M. Donation • *Farnsworth Museum,* off Route 1, Rockland, 596-6457. Hours: June to September, Monday to Saturday, 10 A.M. to 5 P.M., Sunday from 1 P.M. Closed Mondays from October. Adults, $5, under 18, $3; winter rates, adults, $3, under 18, $1. Admission includes Farnsworth Homestead, open June to September • *Windjammer Cruise Information:* Maine Windjammer Association, Box 617CC, Camden, ME 04843, 236-2938.

INFORMATION   Rockport-Camden-Lincolnville Chamber of Commerce, PO Box 919, Camden, ME 04843, 236-4404. Information booth at Public Landing parking lot.

A Bewitching Halloween in Salem

It stands to reason. Since Salem, Massachusetts, is known for the long-ago days when witch fever swept the town, it seems only natural that Halloween is a cause for celebration here.

Not that Salem today bears much resemblance to the town that was notorious for its witch hunting. These days visitors will see a pleasant New England maritime center dating back to 1626, now in the process of sprucing up its historic waterfront, and a town as much a literary shrine for its "House of Seven Gables" complex as a reminder of witch-trial terror. For a relatively small town, Salem has a large share of sights, including an exceptional museum and some handsome old sea captains' mansions.

But there's no question that Salem is a great place to be at Halloween, when the whole town gets into the spirit of the holiday. On the weekend before the big day, there are eerie events such as haunted houses for touring, ghost-story telling, a spooky treasure hunt at the Peabody Essex Museum, broom-flying classes for children who come in witch costumes, costume balls, a costume parade on the common—even a gathering of psychics ready to read your fortune. And you can join a spooky "Witch Trial Trail" walk by candlelight, or take a candlelit tour of the House of Seven Gables. Latter-day witches wearing "Ask a Witch" buttons are posted throughout town to give factual answers about Halloween customs and practices, Salem history, and the state of witchcraft today.

The events change slightly from year to year as more activities are continually added to the roster. The agenda offers more that can be fit into one day, so you'll have to pick and choose your activities, saving some of the sights for Sunday.

With or without kids, do take time for the Children's Costume Parade, usually at 2:00 P.M. on Saturday, a procession of several dozen Salem children of all sizes in Halloween finery. It's guaranteed to bring smiles and some adorable souvenir snapshots.

For fun, visit Crow Haven Corner, a tiny shop in the historic district run by a self-proclaimed witch who sells crystal balls, magic wands, and how-to books for casting a spell.

A highlight for most people is the Salem Witch Museum, a spooky stone building on Washington Square, across from the Salem Common. It is crowded during Halloween weekends, so an early or late visit is a good idea. The excellent presentation here puts you in the center of a darkened room and uses spotlights to showcase the life-size reenactments of the shameful 1692 hysteria.

Salem's was not the only witchcraft trial in New England, but it was by far the worst. The only thing to be said for the debacle was that the revulsion it caused finally put an end to sentencing so-called witches to death. To mark the 300th anniversary of the trials in 1992, the town erected a simple stone memorial as a reminder of the need for tolerance.

The Witch House in Salem turns out to be the restored home of Jonathan Corwin, judge of the original witchcraft court. Preliminary examinations of the accused were held here, but the residence is actually of far more interest as one of the oldest dwellings in the United States. Built in the early seventeenth century, it is filled with a fine collection of furniture and household items from that period. A number of other handsome historic houses have been preserved with period furnishings and opened to the public in Salem.

Several of these are maintained and operated by the Peabody Essex Museum, a recent merging of one of the oldest historical societies in the country and the oldest continuously operating museum.

This Essex Street portion of the two-building complex contains the art and artifacts of Salem's Essex County since its beginnings, including displays of furniture, clocks, china, silver, paintings, and military memorabilia. It is attractively laid out on two floors around a Federal-period garden.

The Liberty Street building across the square holds treasures brought back by Salem mariners who had navigated the seas near or beyond the Cape of Good Hope or Cape Horn. In those days, Salem was one of the busiest seaports on the East Coast, and her ships were found in all the world's waters. The "curiosities" garnered by the ships' captains formed the basis of the original Peabody Museum. The holdings were augmented when the Peabody merged with the China Trade Museum of Milton, Massachusetts, in 1984. An $11 million wing was added a few years ago to house the permanent collection of some 12,000 pieces of Asian export art, paintings, and decorative works. It also holds some fascinating nautical exhibits of scrimshaw, figureheads, old fishing implements, and navigational instruments. There's even a full-size reconstruction of the master's saloon of *Cleopatra's Barge,* built in 1816 as America's first oceangoing vessel.

The 1992 merging of the two institutions created one of New England's largest museums. Together they feature nearly a half million objects, including important art and artifacts from Japan, China, the Pacific Islands, Southeast Asia, and Africa. One of the superb research libraries, the Phillips Library, contains the original court documents of the 1692 witch trials, along with original manuscripts by Nathaniel Hawthorne and rare ships' logs from early voyages to China.

Doing justice to all of this can take up a worthwhile afternoon of your time. It's probably best to schedule one museum per day to get the most of each—but even then you won't have exhausted the most important sights of Salem.

The Salem Maritime National Historic Site, overseen by the National Park Service, is playing a growing role, evidenced by the information center that opened in 1994 near the museum in the heart of the town's central pedestrians-only mall.

The Park Service is in the midst of a project that should be completed by 1996—restoring Salem's historic wharves. At the height of Salem's boom years, there were 50 wharves in the harbor. Derby Wharf, stretching half a mile into Salem Harbor, is one of the few surviving pre-Revolutionary port facilities. When it is fully restored, it will include replicas of the warehouses that once stood beside it and a reproduction of a 120-foot, three-masted square-rigger will be permanently docked and open for touring.

On land, the Salem National Maritime Historic Site already includes the original Customs House of 1819, with offices furnished just as they were in the old days when Nathaniel Hawthorne worked there as a clerk, as well as several historic houses, the old Scale House where weighing and measuring equipment was kept, and the West India Goods Store, built to sell cargoes brought from Africa and the West Indies and now a gift shop for the site.

Across the street is the House of Seven Gables, made immortal by Nathaniel Hawthorne's novel. It was actually the 1668 home of ship captain John Turner. The house with its secret stairway is a charmer, and it is easy to see why it captured Hawthorne's imagination when he came to visit his cousin, Susan Ingersoll, whose family later lived here. The Turner house is part of a small historic complex of early homes, including Hawthorne's own birthplace, an antique-filled, gambrel-roofed seventeenth-century residence that was moved to this appropriate site in 1958. An outdoor café here is set amid lovely perennial gardens.

A more modern addition to the waterfront is nearby Pickering Wharf, a replica of a commercial wharf lined with shops and restaurants.

Another addition to the scene is Salem Marketplace, a former open-air fruit and vegetable market that has been converted into brick stalls housing a variety of galleries and antique shops.

Also of interest, especially if you've brought children along, is the Pioneer Village, a living history museum re-creating the Salem of 1630, with thatched cottages, workshops, wigwams, gardens, and animals of the period. Guides in period costumes tell about the people, conditions, and politics of the era, and demonstrate period skills and chores.

As if it weren't difficult enough to fit all of Salem's sights into a weekend, there's the lure of Marblehead, one of the shore's most picturesque seaside communities, beckoning just four miles away. When George Washington visited here, he noted that Marblehead certainly had "the look of antiquity." Some 200 years later you can walk the same twisting streets and see the same mix of merchants' mansions and steep-gabled fishermen's cottages that mark this village's 350-year existence as a seaport. The harbor is a veritable forest of sailboat masts.

A ride along the steep shoreline past the homes crowded pell-mell along the winding lanes is exceptional and shouldn't be missed. The area's loveliest inn, the Harbor Light Inn, is in Marblehead, as well. If you can't stay a while, at least stop for fried clams and chowder at The Barnacle, the best place in town for boat-watching, and give yourself time for a drive. The biggest houses are across the causeway at Marblehead Neck, the hilly peninsula that shelters the harbor from the open sea.

Better yet, enjoy the spooky hijinks of Halloween and then think about a return visit to Marblehead in the spring. After the goblins have gone, you can concentrate on the rest of the sights of these two intriguing neighbors by the sea.

Area Code: 508

DRIVING DIRECTIONS   Salem is located on the Massachusetts shore 16 miles north of Boston at Exit 25E off Route 128. It is 238 miles from New York and 128 miles from Hartford.

PUBLIC TRANSPORTATION   MBTA bus and North Station train service from Boston. Information, 722-3200. North Shore Shuttle Service connects to Logan Airport (800) 649-8660.

ACCOMMODATIONS   All Salem zip codes are 01970. *Haw-thorne Hotel,* 18 Washington Square West, Salem, 744-4080, Federal-style, nicely renovated 1920s landmark in the town center, $$–$$$ • *Salem Inn,* 7 Summer Street, Salem, 741-0680 or (800) 446-2995, brick 1834 sea captain's home, pleasant rooms, $$–$$$ CP • *Suzannah Flint House,* 98 Essex Street, Salem, 744-5281 or (800) 752-5281, modest bed-and-breakfast inn, central location, $–$$ CP • *The Stepping Stone Inn,* 19 Washington Square North, 745-2156, bed-and-breakfast home on the green, $$$ CP • *The Inn at 7 Winter Street,* 7 Winter Street, Salem, 745-9520, Victorian bed-and-breakfast inn, $$–$$$$ CP • *Amelia Payson Guest House,* 16 Winter Street, Salem, 744-8304, small, nicely decorated, $$ CP • *Harbor Light Inn,* 58 Washington Street, Marblehead 01945, 631-2186, special, beams and four-posters, pool, $$–$$$$ CP • *Spray Cliff,* 25 Spray Avenue, Marblehead 01945, 744-8924 or (800) 626-1530, English Tudor with grand ocean views, $$$–$$$$ CP • *Pleasant Manor Inn,* 264 Pleasant Street, Marblehead 01945, 631-5843, Victorian inn with a tennis court, $–$$ CP.

DINING   *The Lyceum,* 43 Church Street, 745-7665, historic building, long-time local favorite, $$ • *The Grapevine,* 26 Congress Street, 745-9335, eclectic menu, bright setting, $$ • *Nathaniel's,* Hawthorne Hotel (see above), elegant dining room, American menu, $$–$$$ • *Grand Turk Tavern,* 110 Derby Street, 745-7727, seafood in a sea captain's home, $$ • *Roosevelt's,* 300 Derby Street, Salem, 745-9608, fun Teddy Roosevelt decor, $$ • *Stromberg's,* 2 Bridge Street, 744-1863, informal, good chowder, seafood, outdoor deck with harbor view, $–$$ • *J. Anthony's,* Salem Inn (see above), Italian, $–$$ • *Mike Purcell's,* 90 Washington Street, 745-1633, American menu, moderate prices, $–$$ • *The Barnacle,* Front Street, Marblehead, 631-4236, basic seafood and the best view in town, $–$$.

SIGHTSEEING   *Salem Halloween Happenings,* write to Chamber of Commerce for complete current schedule • *Salem Witch Museum,* 19 Washington Square North, 744-1692. Hours: daily, 10 A.M. to 5 P.M.; July and August to 7 P.M.; during Halloween weekends to midnight. Adults, $4; ages 6 to 14, $2.50 • *Peabody Essex Museum,* East India Square, 745-9500. Hours: Monday to Saturday, 10 A.M. to 5 P.M., Thursdays to 8 P.M., Sunday noon to 5 P.M. Adults, $6; ages 6 to 18, $3.50; admission including historic houses, adults, $10; children, $6; family rate, $25 • *Salem Maritime National Historic Site,* 178 Derby Street, 745-1470. Hours: daily, 9 A.M. to 4:30 P.M. Free • *House of Seven Gables,* 54 Turner Street, 744-0991, guided tours, July to Labor Day, daily, 9:30 A.M. to 5:30 P.M.; rest of year, daily 10 A.M. to 4:30 P.M. Adults, $6.50; ages 13 to 17, $4; children 6 to 12, $3 • *Pioneer Village, Salem 1630,* Forest River Park, Routes 114/1A and

West Street, Salem, 745-0525. Hours: June to October, Monday to Saturday, 10 A.M. to 5 P.M., Sunday and holidays, noon to 5 P.M. Adults, $4; ages 13 to 17, $3.50; ages 6 to 12, $2.50.

INFORMATION Salem Chamber of Commerce, Old Town Hall, 32 Derby Square, Salem, MA 01970, 744-0004. National Park Visitor Information Service, Essex Street, Museum Place Mall; entering the city, follow information signs for nearby parking.

A Peak Experience at Killington

Back in 1739, Reverend Samuel Peters stood atop the 4,241-foot peak of Killington Mountain, surveyed the land around him, and christened the land "Verd-Mont," ever after to be known as the Green Mountain state.

It's probably fortunate that the good reverend made the climb in the "verd" of summer, for had he come to the top of Killington in autumn, Vermont might have gone nameless. The four-state panorama of mountains and valleys cloaked in crimson, gold, and orange has left more than one viewer at a total loss for words.

The good news is that nowadays you don't even have to climb for the view. The Killington Gondola, one of the longest ski lifts in America, is in service in the fall to bring leaf watchers to the highest point reached by aerial lift in New England.

The ride alone is good reason to plan an early October weekend near Killington, but the area has more than its share of lures all year long. In addition to being the largest ski complex in the East, with six mountains to choose from, this is prime hiking territory, offering both the Appalachian and Long trails, which converge on Route 4 at a point near Pico, Killington's smaller ski mountain neighbor. Tennis and golf facilities are plentiful, and you'll search far to find more scenic backroading via bike, horseback, or car. Mountain-biking enthusiasts take their bikes up on the Killington Chairlift and enjoy panoramic views coming down on 37 miles of trails. The interesting sights to be seen nearby make a visit all the more rewarding.

The same rugged terrain that makes the area so attractive also prevents it from having a central village. Rutland is nearby to the west on Route 4, and Woodstock is within easy reach to the east on the same road. But other than the ski-lodge motels on the access road, accommodations near Killington are scattered. They run the gamut from motel to condominium to cozy inn to full-scale resort, and where you stay may well depend on just how much activity you have in mind, as well as on your budget.

One major advantage to a popular ski area with over 100 lodgings in the vicinity is that even at the height of the foliage season, when all the country inns have been booked up for months, some of those motels on the access road or Route 4 may still have vacancy signs. And the Killington Lodging Bureau is available to help you find a place with just one phone call.

If you plan ahead, two of the prime inn candidates are in Chittenden, a small village with an attractive reservoir, tucked away from it all in the woods on a back road about six miles from Route 4. For a secluded, homey country inn where meals are served family style and guests get a chance to know one another, Tulip Tree Inn is the place. This is just what many people imagine a country inn should be—tastefully done but simple, comfortable, and warm.

Not far away is Mountain Top Inn, a resort with a spectacular 500-acre site high above a lake surrounded by mountains. The views from the inn terrace and dining rooms are unbeatable. There's everything to do here: sailing, canoeing, or fishing on the lake, tennis, horseback riding, golf, and indoor exercise and recreation rooms plus sauna and whirlpool. If the tab is within your budget, you won't go wrong.

Red Clover Inn, a former 1840 summer estate, offers a gracious stay out in the country in Mendon. Vermont Inn, just off Route 4, is homey and more reasonably priced, and though it has a motel layout, the Cortina Inn is quite elegant, with tennis courts, an indoor pool and health club, entertainment, and student chefs from the Vermont Culinary Institute who show off their talents in the attractive Oak Room.

If you want to drive about 15 minutes west of Rutland to Fair Haven, you can stay in style at the Vermont Marble Inn, a marble mansion, circa 1860, which also has a highly regarded dining room.

The Inn of the Six Mountains, located on the Killington access road, is a somewhat citified hotel but has nicely furnished rooms, indoor and outdoor pools, exercise and game rooms. The Villages at Killington will suit those who like spacious condominium accommodations. It is a mountainside community with tennis, golf, lakes, and ponds. Guests at the reasonably priced Villager Motel, part of the complex, have use of all the recreational facilities.

One last luxurious possibility is Hawk Inn and Mountain Resort, not far from Killington on Route 100 in Plymouth. There's a well-appointed modern inn, but for views and privacy, opt for the fieldstone and wood condos and homes high on the mountainside. There are picture windows to bring in the view and big stone fireplaces to warm those cool Vermont evenings. Tennis, riding, boating, hiking trails, an indoor pool, and a health spa are all available on the grounds.

If you choose more modest accommodations, take note that you can still have access to the stables at Mountain Top and Hawk, and tennis courts can be rented at Cortina Inn, Killington Resorts, Summit Lodge, and the Vermont Inn. You can also take advantage of the many health spas offering whirlpool, massage, and other nice things. These include the Pico Health Center and the Mountain Green Health Club. Bikes can also be rented at the First Stop Ski & Bike Shop at the junction of Routes 4 and 100 south.

Having settled in, you can plan your activities. If hiking is on the agenda, a popular short trek is Deer Leap Trail, which takes about half an hour up a steep winding path ending on a cliff with a panoramic view from 2,490 feet up. All the skiing trails on Killington and Pico become hiking trails off-season. The recently opened Merrell Hiking Center located at the Killington base lodge can provide both guided hikes and an educational trail map for self-guided tours in the area.

The Long Trail Hiking Path, part of the well-known Footpath in the Wilderness, runs from Killington Mountain to Pico and then down to Sherburne Pass on Route 4. If you start at the top by taking the gondola to the summit, average time down is about three hours.

Hike or not, that gondola ride is quite something. There is a small nature trail at the top, a cafeteria, and a deck where you can have drinks with an unforgettable view: The Green, White, Berkshire, and Adirondack Mountains spread out around you.

There's no real competition for this view, though the outlook at the top of Killington chair lift, which is slightly less expensive, is clearly not to be sniffed at. There is another scenic ride in store if you take the chair lift up to the Alpine Slide at Pico and come down the trails some 3,410 feet on a sled. The sled has a control stick, so you needn't worry about descending at breakneck speed; you set your own pace.

Most people choose a more earthbound kind of ride, doing the back roads by car. It's usually most pleasant to plan a route with sightseeing stops along the way, and that's easy to do in this area.

Heading north, you might want to begin by following Route 4 through Rutland and then north on Route 3 to Proctor, a town where everything is made of marble, from the schools and churches to the sidewalks and the bridge spanning Otter Creek.

Proctor is the heart of the Vermont marble industry and the largest marble production center in the country. A film at the Vermont Marble Exhibit briefly explains how the marble quarried from the Green Mountains is processed into the handsome polished slabs that mark many of the nation's best-known buildings. From the visitor's gallery you can watch huge slabs weighing up to ten tons swing through the air to the diamond-blade coping saws that slice them right before your eyes.

A sculptor is in residence to show how marble can be polished and carved into works of art, and the hall of presidents displays the heads of 40 former chief executives, carved from purest white marble, a

20-year project for one of Vermont's finest sculptors. There are slabs and seconds for sale at the marble market outside, in case you want to take home a tabletop as a souvenir, and many smaller marble items are available inside at the gift shop.

There's another sight in little Proctor: Wilson Castle, a nineteenth-century mansion on a 115-acre estate. It is quite a place, with 84 stained-glass windows, hand-painted ceilings, and priceless Oriental and European antiques as well as fine art and sculpture.

Having had your fill of finery, head north from Proctor to Route 7 and Pittsford, where you can learn about another backbone Vermont industry, maple sugaring, at the New England Maple Museum. This small museum doesn't look too promising at first glance, but it turns out to be quite interesting. Watch the slide show to find out how sap is turned to syrup, then inspect the tools involved—in this case, one of the largest collections of antique sugaring equipment ever assembled. The history of maple sugaring is shown in over 100 feet of murals painted by artist Grace Brigham. There's also a simulation of modern techniques, complete with sap dripping from a tree into a bucket, with the wonderful smell of boiling syrup at the end of the process permeating everything. Needless to say, there is a gift shop waiting, filled with you-know-what.

A little farther north is Brandon, a pleasant village with some 200 historic buildings around two village greens. Among them is the Stephen Douglas Homestead, the home of the famous orator who debated Abraham Lincoln. The Brandon Antiques Center on Route 7 is a recommended stop for treasure hunters.

For views, the best bets are the roads that cut across the mountains. Brandon Gap, running from Route 7 to Route 100, is unexcelled. If you want to do a giant scenic loop back, follow Route 100 five miles north to Hancock, with a detour there to Route 125 to see the cascades at the Texas Falls Recreation Area.

Then make the drive from Route 100 back to Route 7 across the Middlebury Gap, also known as the Robert Frost Memorial Drive. Frost's home was in Ripton, a town along the gap road. Youll come out in East Middlebury, just four miles from the attractive college town with its excellent Vermont State Crafts Center at Frog Hollow. Middlebury also has many shops that make for pleasant browsing.

An alternative return route is to go back to Brandon and then south on Route 30 to Lake Bomoseen in Castleton or Lake St. Catherine in Poultney, both in attractive state parks and ideal for picnicking.

You can easily fill a weekend admiring nature via gondola, slide, hiking boots, or automobile, but if you want indoor diversions, Rutland offers the Chaffee Art Gallery, with continuous exhibits, and the Norman Rockwell Museum on Route 4 east of town, which has more than 1,000 pictures, including his famous Four Freedoms and Boy

Scouts series, Rockwell memorabilia, and all 326 of his *Saturday Evening Post* covers.

The first weekend in October brings the Foliage Craft Show at Killington's Sunrise Mountain, at Route 100 South and Route 4 East.

For attractive shops, drive farther east on Route 4 to the lovely town of Woodstock. Or, for a final dose of both scenery and history, make the 11-mile drive south on Route 100 to the Plymouth Notch Historic District, and enjoy the view that made Calvin Coolidge decide he'd rather be in Vermont than be President.

Area Code: 802

DRIVING DIRECTIONS   Killington Mountain is on U.S. Route 4 near the junction with Route 100. Killington is 158 miles from Boston, 250 miles from New York, and 166 miles from Hartford.

PUBLIC TRANSPORTATION   Air service to Burlington, Vermont, or Lebanon, New Hampshire. Vermont Transit buses to Sherburne (Killington), Rutland, or Woodstock.

ACCOMMODATIONS   Lower rates usually apply on weekdays and off-season; expect highest rates in autumn. *Tulip Tree Inn,* Chittenden Dam Road, Chittenden 05737, 483-6213 or (800) 707-0017, $$$–$$$$ MAP • *Mountain Top Inn,* Mountain Top Road, Chittenden 05737, 483-2311 or (800) 445-2100, $$$–$$$$$ MAP • *Red Clover Inn,* Woodward Road, Mendon 05701, 775-2290 or (800) 752-0571, $$$–$$$$$ MAP • *Vermont Inn,* U.S. Route 4, Killington 05751, 775-0708 or (800) 541-7795, $$–$$$ CP, $$–$$$$ MAP • *Cortina Inn,* Route 4, Killington 05751, 773-3331 or (800) 451-6108, $$$–$$$$ • *The Inn of the Six Mountains,* Killington Road, Killington 05751, 422-4302 or (800) 225-0888, $$–$$$$ CP • *Vermont Marble Inn,* on the green, Fair Haven, 265-8383, $$$$–$$$$$ MAP • *The Villages at Killington and Villager Motel,* 718 Killington Road, Killington 05751, 422-3101 or (800) 343-0762, condominium units, $$–$$$$$; motel, $$ CP • *Hawk Inn and Mountain Resort,* Route 100, Plymouth 05056, 672-3811 or (800) 451-4109, inn rooms, $$$–$$$$; town houses and homes, expensive but well worth it, $$$$$ • *Mountain Meadows Lodge,* Thundering Brook Road, Killington 05751, 775-1010 or (800) 370-4567, familystyle lodge, comfortable, no frills, reasonable, $$$ MAP • For information on last-minute vacancies and free area reservations, contact Killington Travel Service, 67 Merchant Row, Rutland 05701, 773-0755 or (800) 372-2007.

DINING   *Hemingway's,* Route 4 east of Route 100, 422-3886, continental, the area's best, prix fixe, $$$$$ • *Cortina Inn* (see above),

$$–$$$ • *Claude's,* Killington Road, Killington, 422-4030, elegant continental menu, $$–$$$, or casual dining at *Choices,* $–$$ • *Mountain Top Inn* (see above), unbeatable view, $$–$$$ • *Vermont Inn* (see above), $$ • *Red Clover Inn* (see above), $$–$$$ • *Jason's at the Red Rob Inn,* Killington Road, Killington, 422-3303, informal Italian restaurant, $–$$ • *Ernie's Grill at Royal's Hearthside,* 37 North Main Street, Rutland, 775-0856, New England specialties, $–$$ • *Countryman's Pleasure,* Townline Road (off Route 4), Mendon, 773-7141, fine dining in a country home, $–$$$ • *Vermont Marble Inn* (see above), $$–$$$ • For casual dining, try *Casey's Caboose,* Killington Road, 422-3795, $–$$, and *Wobbly Barn,* Killington Road, 422-3392, $–$$. Also see Woodstock, page 7.

SIGHTSEEING *Killington Gondola,* Route 4, one mile west of Route 100 South, 422-3333. Hours: daily, mid-September to mid-October, 10 A.M. to 4 P.M. Adults, $15 round trip, $10 one way; children, $8 round-trip, $5 one way • *Killington Chairlift,* Killington Road, five miles from junction of Routes 4 and 100. Hours: daily, mid-June to mid-October, 10 A.M. to 4 P.M. Adults, $10; children, $5 • *Pico Alpine Slide,* Route 4, Pico, 775-4346. Hours: late June to early September, daily (weather permitting), 10 A.M. to 6 P.M., hours vary after Labor Day—best to check. Adults, $4; children, $3 • *Vermont Marble Exhibit,* 62 Main Street, Proctor, 459-3311. Hours: mid-May to October, daily, 9 A.M. to 5:30 P.M.; rest of year, Monday to Saturday, 9 A.M. to 4 P.M. Adults, $3.50; teens, $2.50; ages 6 to 12, $1 • *Wilson Castle,* West Proctor Road (off Route 4), Proctor, 773-3284. Hours: late May to mid-October, daily, 9 A.M. to 6 P.M. Adults, $6; ages 6 to 12, $2 • *New England Maple Museum and Gift Shop,* U.S. Route 7, Pittsford, 483-9414. Hours: Memorial Day through October, daily, 8:30 A.M. to 5:30 P.M.; rest of year, 10 A.M. to 4 P.M.; closed January and February. Adults, $1.50; children, $0.50 • *Chaffee Art Gallery,* U.S. Route 7, Rutland, 775-0356. Hours: June to October, daily except Tuesday, 10 A.M. to 5 P.M.; November to May, 11 A.M. to 4 P.M. Free • *Norman Rockwell Museum,* Route 4 East, Rutland, 773-6095. Hours: daily, 9 A.M. to 6 P.M. Adults, $2.50; ages 8 to 16, $0.75 • *Plymouth Notch Historic District,* Route 100, Plymouth, 672-3773. Hours: late May to mid-October, daily, 9:30 A.M. to 5:30 P.M. Adults, $4; under 14, free.

INFORMATION Killington Association, Box 114, Killington, VT 05751, 775-7070; Rutland Chamber of Commerce, 7 Court Square, PO Box 67, Rutland, VT 05701, 773-2747.

Bringing the Kids to Boston

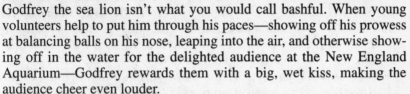

Godfrey the sea lion isn't what you would call bashful. When young volunteers help to put him through his paces—showing off his prowess at balancing balls on his nose, leaping into the air, and otherwise showing off in the water for the delighted audience at the New England Aquarium—Godfrey rewards them with a big, wet kiss, making the audience cheer even louder.

Godfrey and his equally flamboyant flippered friends are perennial favorites, but their antics are just one of many things children can cheer about in Boston. From the playful sea lions at the Aquarium to wonderfully creative museums to the Boston Tea Party ship, where visitors take a turn at tossing chests of tea overboard, this is a town filled with family activities that are as much fun for grown-ups as for the youngsters. It's hard to imagine a better joint outing for either generation. The fact that much of the fun is also educational is just icing on the cake.

Making things even nicer is a welcome from city hotels who have joined to offer "family friendly" packages. They run the gamut from video games and fun packs at Howard Johnson to miniature bathrobes, teddy bears, a reasonable children's menu, and nightly milk and cookies at the Four Seasons. The visitors bureau has published a special children's guide to the city. It features a sculpture tour that includes grasshoppers, dolphins, lions, horses, and a giant 12-foot bronze teddy bear outside the local F A O Schwarz on Boylston Street.

The New England Aquarium is literally guaranteed to start things off with a splash. The exhibits of more than 2,000 exotic fish and aquatic animals from around the world are exceptional, particularly the 80-foot-high central tank simulating a coral reef in all its dazzling colors and shapes. A spiraling ramp lets you see huge sea turtles, inquisitive sharks, technicolor fish, and sleek moray eels from every angle. Everyone is entranced when deep-sea divers plunge into the giant tank to feed its residents. Two other exhibits guaranteed to please are the colony of penguins on the ground level, and the "Edge of the Sea" exhibit, a replica of a Maine tidal pool that allows visitors to actually touch tidepool creatures such as sea urchins and starfish.

In the show held in a boat theater next door, the performing sea lions not only entertain the kids but teach them a lot about sea mammals, ecology, and conservation.

Countless groups of schoolchildren have gotten a lively lesson in American history by following the three-mile, red-brick line of Boston's Freedom Trail. It's a good idea to make the trail your introduction to the city first thing Saturday, while everyone is still fresh. It takes from two to three hours if you do the whole thing, strolling three centuries of American history. You can begin anywhere along the clearly marked lines, and any city information booth has brochures to tell you about the sights. But the best place to start is at the National Park Service Information Center across from the Old State House, which officially maintains the major structures as Boston National Historical Park. They have guides to both the Freedom Trail and a Harbor Walk and also offer free guided tours.

Boston by Foot, an organization that sponsors walking tours of the city, also has a special tour, "Boston by Little Feet," designed for six- to twelve-year-olds (accompanied by adults).

If you don't think little ones can make it all on foot, there are trolleys with narration; some allow you to get on and off as often as you like all day.

From the information center, the Freedom Trail runs roughly in a figure eight with a tail leading into the North End. In one loop are Boston Common, the land set aside for common use in 1634 that was a training ground for Revolutionary soldiers and is now the nation's oldest public park; the golden-domed State House, designed by Charles Bulfinch for the newly independent Commonwealth of Massachusetts; Park Street Church, where the song "America" was first sung publicly; and the Granary Burying Ground, where Paul Revere, Samuel Adams, John Hancock, James Otis, and other patriots are buried.

While you are at Boston Common, you may want to stroll over to the more formal Public Garden next door and take a ride on the famous Swan Boats, which have been a fixture here since 1877. A statue honors Mrs. Mallard and her brood, who were immortalized in Robert McCloskey's classic children's tale set in the Public Garden, *Make Way for Ducklings.*

Sights on the second loop include the 1749 Kings Chapel, the first Anglican church in the United States and later the first for the Unitarian faith; the Kings Chapel Burying Ground, established in 1630; The Old State House, where James Otis roused his countrymen in 1761 when he proclaimed, "Taxation without representation is tyranny"; and the Old Corner Book Store, a 1712 home that later became a meeting place for such authors as Longfellow, Hawthorne, Emerson, Holmes, Stowe, and Whittier.

Ahead is Faneuil Hall, nicknamed "The Cradle of Liberty" by John Adams for its fiery and eloquent town meetings of Colonial patriots. Beyond, just as the younger tour members may be getting restless, is the perfect place to take a pause from history for some good food and fun—the historic world of food at Quincy Market. There's pizza, barbecue, Chinese food, shish kabob, gyros, Polish sausage, and just about everything in between in the market stalls. Deciding which of the luscious displays to patronize is half the fun. Unless you choose to pass up the stalls to dine at one of the cafés around the market, you'll take your selection to benches outside, where there is often entertainment by street musicians to go with your meal.

After lunch, continue along the trail to the North End to see Paul Revere's home and the Old North Church where he got the signal to begin his fateful ride to warn the Colonists at Lexington and Concord that "The British are coming."

The Freedom Trail ends beyond the North End in Charlestown, with two historic sites that are usually favorites of young people. In Charlestown, you can board the USS *Constitution,* the oldest commissioned ship in the U.S. Navy, nicknamed "Old Ironsides" for its strong oak planking. And you can climb Bunker Hill, with its 330-foot obelisk commemorating the famous battle of June 17, 1775. A film, "Whites of Their Eyes," is shown at the Bunker Hill Pavilion and tells the story of the historic battle. A trip up the spiral stairway to the top of the monument is rewarded with a fabulous view of the city.

If you've spent the afternoon in this part of town, dinner in one of the many North End Italian restaurants is a perfect way to end the day. At the least, stop for a cannoli.

At night, one of the exciting things to do in Boston is to get a skyscraper-high view of the glimmering city from the fiftieth floor of the Prudential Tower or the top of the John Hancock Tower.

On Sunday, head for the Children's Museum and the Computer Museum, two outstanding institutions sharing a restored warehouse on the waterfront at Museum Wharf.

The participatory displays at the Children's Museum are designed to exercise mind and muscles, teach about other cultures, introduce a bit of science—and much more. Kids in this four-story educational playland may visit a life-size Japanese home or sit in a wigwam, experiment with gravity by playing with balls on a series of giant ramps or by blowing five-foot bubbles, scale a two-story puzzle maze or clamber through a castle. A circle-view aquarium allows room for watching life on the bottom of the sea. Exhibits may have changed by the time you visit, but you can depend on imagination and fun, along with a variety of activities, from crafts workshops to games from other countries.

The one-of-a-kind Computer Museum is found on the top two floors of the building. It is guaranteed to intrigue. Take a walk through the world's only two-story model of a personal computer and learn what really makes these machines tick. Kids love climbing on a giant mouse and rolling the trackball or standing on a larger-than-life keyboard, then walking inside to watch lights flash, drives spin, and information flow.

You can walk through time tunnels tracing today's personal computers back to their giant ancestors of the 1940s and 1950s, or take a turn at over 35 interactive stations that invite you to explore all the amazing things you can do with a personal computer, from experiencing virtual reality to starring in a video commercial. There are equally exciting changing exhibits allowing visitors to experience the latest computer developments.

The Computer Museum takes you to the future; at the other end of the street is a bit of the past, the Boston Tea Party Ship and Museum, which includes the full-scale replica tea ship, the *Brig Beaver II.* The small museum located beside the ship features exhibits and video presentations explaining what the famous tea party of Revolutionary days was all about. The big attraction is the reenactment, where you can join the Colonial guides, tossing your own case of tea overboard into the harbor, just like the protesting patriots of 1773.

The historic Harbor Walk, marked out in blue lines along the rejuvenated Boston waterfront, traces the maritime history of the city and takes you to the handsome waterfront park beyond the Marriott Hotel at Long Wharf.

If you haven't already been, you can end your day with the Aquarium; it's right in front of the Marriott. If time allows, there are also harbor cruises from the Long Wharf, a treat for young seafarers.

For older children, Boston's Museum of Science is a fascinating place, with everything from dinosaur bones to an explanation of how a telephone works. This museum also has many sophisticated participatory exhibits, as well as an OMNI theater and its own fine planetarium shows. Since it is open late on Friday night, this museum can be a good warm-up for the weekend.

Nor will you find a better introduction to art than the Museum of Fine Arts, one of the country's premier art museums. It is even more spectacular now with the addition of the skylighted West Wing designed by I. M. Pei.

You can also introduce your youngsters to first-class ballet in Boston, or attend the symphony—or show them how American cities looked almost 200 years ago on Beacon Hill—or step back to the re-created world of the Kennedy presidency at the New Museum at the John F. Kennedy Library. Or just forget about history and culture and go down to the Esplanade by the Charles River to watch the skaters and joggers in action on land and the sailboats on the water. There are several play areas to channel youthful energy with swings, slides, animal climb ons, and jungle gyms, or you can rent a sailboat or windsurfer at Community Boating and join the boats on the river.

Boston is a city loaded with pleasures of all kinds for all ages. It's almost guaranteed that if you come once with your family, everyone will want a second helping.

Area Code: 617

DIRECTIONS AND TRANSPORTATION   See page 74.

ACCOMMODATIONS See medium-priced possibilities on pages 74–75. Ask the visitors bureau for a copy of the family-friendly hotel package brochure.

DINING **A few inexpensive family recommendations:** *Bristol,* Four Seasons Hotel, 200 Boylston Street, 338-4400, well-behaved youngsters get a menu coloring book, featuring kids' favorites for pint-size prices; adults, $$ • *California Pizza Kitchen,* Prudential Center, 800 Boylston Street, 247-2352, children's menu, $ • *Hard Rock Café,* 131 Clarendon Street, 542-2255, kids love it, $–$$ • *Durgin Park,* North Market, Street Level, 227-2038, shared tables, an only-in-Boston experience, $ • *Faneuil Hall,* pick any of the informal cafés or patronize the stands and eat outside watching the street performers, $–$$ • *The Old Spaghetti Factory,* 44 Pittsburgh Street, 737-8757, near the Children's Museum, $ • *Fuddruckers,* 8 Park Place, 723-3833, good hamburgers, children's menu, $ • *Jimbo's Fish Shanty,* 245 Northern Avenue, 542-5600, on the pier, seafood in an informal setting, $–$$ • *Bennigan's,* 191 Stuart Street, 227-3754, predictable chain menu, reasonable, $–$$ • *Dakota's,* 101 Arch Street, 737-1777, popular business lunch spot is quieter at night, has children's menu, $$ • For additional family dining, see lower-priced choices on pages 76–77.

SIGHTSEEING *Boston National Historical Park Visitors Center,* 15 State Street, 242-5642. Hours: daily, June to August, Monday to Friday, 8 A.M. to 6 P.M., Saturday and Sunday, 9 A.M. to 6 P.M.; rest of year to 5 P.M. Maps and information on the Freedom Trail; free ranger-led, 90-minute walking tours offered regularly. Check for current schedules • *New England Aquarium,* Central Wharf, 973-5200. Hours: early September to June 30, Monday to Wednesday and Friday, 9 A.M. to 5 P.M., Thursday 9 A.M. to 8 P.M., Saturday, Sunday, and holidays, 9 A.M. to 6 P.M.; July 1 to Labor Day, Monday, Tuesday, and Friday, 9 A.M. to 6 P.M., Wednesday and Thursday, 9 A.M. to 8 P.M., Saturday, Sunday, and holidays, 9 A.M. to 7 P.M. Adults $8.50; ages 3 to 11, $4.50.; $1 discount for all Wednesday and Thursday after 4 P.M. • *Children's Museum of Boston,* Museum Wharf, 300 Congress Street, 426-6500. Hours: July 1 to Labor Day, daily, 10 A.M. to 5 P.M., Friday to 9 P.M.; rest of year closed Monday unless a holiday. Adults, $7; ages 2 to 15, $6; one-year-olds, $1; $1 for all Friday, 5 P.M. to 9 P.M. • *Computer Museum,* Museum Wharf, 300 Congress Street, 423-6758. Hours: Tuesday to Sunday, 10 A.M. to 5 P.M., summer hours to 6 P.M. Adults, $7; students, $5; under 5 free. Half price on Sunday after 3 P.M. • *USS Boston Tea Party Ship and Museum,* Congress Street Bridge near Museum Wharf, 338-1773. Hours: daily, March through November, 9 A.M. to 5 P.M., summer hours to 6 P.M. Adults, $6; children, $3 • *Museum of Science,* Science Park, 723-2500. Hours: daily, 9 A.M. to 7

P.M., Friday to 9 P.M. Adults, $7; ages 3 to 14, $5. Planetarium or laser show, adults, $6; children, $4. Omnimax theater, adults, $7; children, $5. Museum and one attraction, adults, $11; children, $8. Museum and both attractions, adults, $15; children, $11. Free on Wednesday, 1 P.M. to 5 P.M. • *Swan Boat Rides,* Public Garden, 522-1966. Hours: late June to Labor Day, daily, 10 A.M. to 5 P.M., weather permitting; April to June and Labor Day to mid-September, weekdays, noon to 4 P.M., weekends, 10 A.M. to 4 P.M. Adults, $1.50; under 12, $0.95 • **Walking tours:** *"Boston by Little Feet,"* for ages 6 to 12 (accompanied by a parent), phone Boston by Foot, 367-2345, for current information. For all other city attractions, see pages 77–78.

INFORMATION Boston Common Visitor Information Booth, Tremont Street, and Prudential Center Visitor Center, 9 A.M. to 5 P.M. daily. National Park Service Visitor Center, 15 State Street, Monday to Friday, 8 A.M. to 5 P.M., Saturday and Sunday, 9 A.M. to 5 P.M., June through August to 6 P.M. For written information, Greater Boston Convention and Visitors Bureau, Prudential Plaza, Box 490, Boston, MA 02199, 536-4100 or (800) 888-5515. Send $3.95 for a copy of the city guide for children, "Kids Love Boston."

Winter

Overleaf: *Old Sturbridge Village, Massachusetts.*

Merry Days at Mystic

Seaman John Blood was puzzled. Here it was, Christmas Eve, 1885. His boat had overcome rough seas to dock in the evening, barely in time to get him home for Christmas. And just as he was hurrying home, he was being asked to take time out to show a group of strangers through the town. An unlikely lot they were at that, wearing odd clothes like none he had ever seen before.

But it was, after all, the holiday season, so Blood decided not to leave the strangers stranded. He took up his lantern and led the way, lighting the paths of town for his charges as they wended their way to see how Christmas was celebrated a hundred years ago in seaside towns like Mystic, Connecticut.

Lantern Light Tours at Mystic Seaport have become a treasured tradition in southeastern Connecticut, the way that many families choose to mark the official start of the holiday season.

The seaport staff and local volunteers love the custom, too, and they enjoy getting into the spirit of Christmas past, taking the part of characters who might have lived in Mystic a century ago. The hour-long tours, usually held nightly for about three weeks before Christmas, are a little different every year, but take you into a variety of homes and places such as the local tavern, store, and chapel, as well as aboard the tall ship *Charles W. Morgan,* where the occupants are in the midst of celebrating the season. The dates span the century, showing how Christmas customs changed through the 1800s.

At the Buckinghams' house, for example, the time is the early nineteenth century, and a Puritan mother is complaining that she has no use for frivolity on a serious religious holiday.

There's plenty of merriment down at the tavern, however, and visitors are cordially invited to join in dancing to the tune of the fiddle. By the mid-1850s, families like the Burrows decorated and baked for the holidays almost the way we do today. But this Christmas Eve, Mrs. Burrows is far from happy. Her seafaring son is overdue, and she is fearful. Blood and his group have arrived just in time to see him slip in the back door to surprise his overjoyed mother.

At a stop aboard ship, the captain reminisces about Christmases spent at sea, and in the village store the shopkeeper shows the kinds of toys children will be finding under their trees tomorrow morning.

Then, as everyone pauses at the window to admire the tree in the Edmondsons' house, who should appear in the living room but St. Nicholas himself, filling stockings with toys for the little ones who are sleeping upstairs. At the final stop, the Thomas Greenman home, a prosperous Victorian family is celebrating the holiday.

Lantern Light Tours at Mystic Seaport are a little bit educational and a lot sentimental, and when followed by a glass of hot cider or a roast goose dinner at the Seamen's Inne next door to the seaport, they lend a cheerful start to a family holiday excursion.

For those who cannot make the evening tours, there are also guided Yuletide tours by day that repeat the evening itinerary, though without the good-humored dramatics.

Though Mystic Seaport is usually thought of as a warm-weather destination, it has a special charm in the winter chill, especially if a dusting of snow has covered the village green. Christmas trees are tied atop the masts of the tall ships to herald the season.

The Northeast's premier maritime exhibit is more than just a collection of ships, however. It is a complete 17-acre re-creation of a nineteenth-century waterfront village, and all the exhibit buildings as well as the ships themselves remain open for winter visitors.

Mystic's history as a nautical center dates back to the 1600s, when the real Thomas Greenman headed a major shipbuilding company on this same site, a yard that produced some of the fastest clipper ships on the seas. In 1929, three local residents got together to form a marine historical association to preserve some of this maritime heritage, and the project steadily gained support from sea-minded friends all over the country. To date, the museum has grown to encompass 60 historic buildings, four major vessels, and more than 400 smaller boats, important collections of maritime artifacts and paintings, and a planetarium to teach the secrets of celestial navigation. The Christmas show focuses on the skies in winter. Visitors can attend before or after the Lantern Light Tours, as well as during the day.

There are additional special programs for children and for adults, before and after Christmas. Like the Lantern Light Tours, those requiring reservations are filled quickly, so it's best to get in touch with the Mystic Seaport office well in advance to get the schedule.

Boarding the ships remains the best part of Mystic Seaport for most people, and December or no, you're still able to walk the decks, examine the intricate rigging and enormous masts, and go below to see the cramped quarters where the captain and crew lived.

In winter you're likely to spend more time at the indoor exhibits that sometimes get short shrift on warmer days. In the village shops the warmth of coal stoves and wood fires welcomes guests, and the ship carver, shipsmith, chandler, and all the local craftspeople find time for an extra chat.

There are several fine galleries on the grounds displaying maritime art, ship's models, and scrimshaw, and tracing the development of the maritime and fishing industries from the seventeenth to the nineteenth centuries. One of the most delightful exhibits is the collection of ships' figureheads and wood carvings in the Wendell Building.

And don't think the sights of Mystic are finished when you leave the seaport. The Mystic Marinelife Aquarium, with its dolphins, seals, and penguin pavilion, is almost as popular with youngsters as the Mystic Seaport itself.

The town of Mystic is also appealing, with many fine old homes lining its streets, and plenty of shops to explore. Olde Mystick Village, a pseudo-Colonial shopping mall, has dozens of stores; there are discount outlets nearby, and shops in town sell just about everything, including antiques. Don't overlook the Mystic Seaport stores, where there is a tremendous selection to choose from, everything from stick candy and fresh-baked goods to Christmas ornaments, books, paintings, and many tasteful gift ideas with a nautical theme.

You can shop. You can sightsee. You can relive the old-fashioned holiday traditions of yesterday. A Mystic weekend is a special way to bring back Christmas past—and to get everyone into the spirit of Christmas present.

Area Code: 203

DRIVING DIRECTIONS Mystic Seaport is located on Route 27, one mile south of Interstate 95 at Exit 90. Mystic is about 95 miles from Boston, 127 miles from New York, and 55 miles from Hartford.

PUBLIC TRANSPORTATION Mystic is served by Greyhound buses and Amtrak.

ACCOMMODATIONS *Steamboat Inn,* 73 Steamboat Wharf, Mystic 06355, 536-8300, romantic quarters on the river, $$$–$$$$ CP • *Whaler's Inn,* 20 East Main Street, Mystic 06355, 536-1506, convenient in-town location, $$–$$$ • *Red Brook Inn,* 2750 Gold Star Highway, Box 237, Old Mystic 06372, 572-0349, bed and breakfast in two historic houses, charming, $$$–$$$$ CP • *The Old Mystic Inn,* 52 Main Street, Old Mystic 06372, 572-9422, nicely furnished B & B home, $$–$$$ CP • *Applewood Farms Inn,* 528 Colonel Ledyard Highway, Ledyard 06339, 536-2022, country charmer ten minutes from Mystic, $$$ CP • *The Inn at Mystic* (motel and real inn), Route 1 at Route 27, Mystic 06355, 536-9604 or (800) 237-2415, $$$–$$$$$ • *Mystic Hilton,* Coogan Boulevard, Mystic 06355, 572-0731, $$–$$$$$ • *Howard Johnson,* Route 27 at I-95, Mystic 06355, 536-2654, $$–$$$ • *Days Inn,* off I-95, Mystic 06355, 572-0574, $–$$$ • *Ramada Inn,* Route 27, off I-95, Mystic 06355, 536-4281, $–$$.

DINING *Seamen's Inne,* Greenmanville Avenue, 536-9649, seafood specialties, lunch, $; dinner, $$–$$$ • *Floodtide,* The Inn at Mystic (see above), 536-8140, continental, $$–$$$ • *The Mooring,* Mystic Hilton (see above), $$–$$$ • *J. P. Daniels,* Route 184, 572-9564, $$$ • *Captain Daniel Packer Inne,* 32 Water Street, Mystic, 536-3555, $$ • *Anthony J's,* 6 Holmes Street, Mystic, 536-0448, Italian, $–$$ •

Drawbridge Inne, 34 West Main Street, 536-9654, casual, steaks and seafood, $$ • *Randall's Ordinary,* Route 2, North Stonington, 599-4540, authentic Colonial open-hearth cooking in an eighteenth-century farmhouse, prix fixe, $$$$ • In warm weather, visit *Abbott's Lobster in the Rough,* 117 Pearl Street, Noank, 536-7719, for outdoor service with a water view, $–$$.

SIGHTSEEING *Mystic Seaport Museum,* 75 Greenmanville Avenue (Route 27), Mystic, 572-5315. Hours: daily except Christmas, April to October, 10 A.M. to 4 P.M.; April to mid-June, September to October, 9 A.M. to 5 P.M.; mid-June to September, 9 A.M. to 8 P.M. Adults, $15; children 6 to 12, $7.50; under 5, free. *Lantern Light Tours,* Hours: daily, 5 P.M. to 9 P.M., about three weeks in December. Check for current dates and fees. • *Mystic Marinelife Aquarium,* 55 Coogan Boulevard, Mystic, 536-3323. Hours: daily, 9 A.M. to 4:30 P.M., to 5:30 P.M. in summer. Adults, $9; children, $5.50.

INFORMATION Southeastern Connecticut Tourism District, PO Box 89, 27 Masonic Street, New London, CT 06320, 444-2206.

Christmas Card Country in Hanover

No doubt about it. This is Christmas card country.

Cradled in the beautiful upper Connecticut River Valley between the White Mountains of New Hampshire and the Green Mountains across the state line in Vermont, Hanover and its heart, the picture-perfect Dartmouth College campus, make an idyllic scene any time of year. Sprinkle a cover of snow on the combination campus green and town center, add a tall, twinkling Christmas tree, and you'll have to look far to find a more magical holiday setting.

With that kind of inspiration, it's no wonder the season is celebrated in a big way here. With the annual Christmas Revels—entertainment that literally has folks dancing in the aisles—and Christmas festivities at the Hanover Inn that rival home for their warmth and tradition, Hanover is just the place to spend a memorable December weekend.

It's impossible to talk about Hanover without talking about Dartmouth because, even more than most college towns, this little community of 6,800 was shaped from the start by the school. The town was founded in 1761 by a venturesome band of Connecticut families ready to carve a new frontier in what was then wilderness. Just eight years later Dartmouth was established beside the new settlement, a dream that many thought would be impossible to achieve.

Eleazar Wheelock, a Connecticut missionary with a vision of civilizing the wilderness, chose this unlikely site for his "grand design" precisely because it was on the frontier of the northern colonies and near the Indians, in whose education he had a special interest. Against all odds, Dartmouth survived to become one of the nation's great names in higher education, with an unbroken succession of graduating classes since the first enrolled in 1771.

A walking tour of the campus with its original Colonial buildings and many handsome later additions is a first order of business on a Hanover visit. Student-guided tours leave from the Admissions Office in McNutt Hall off North Main Street—check for current schedules—or you can stroll on your own. Ask at the Hanover Inn for a walking guide.

Especially notable are the four classic Federal and Georgian buildings around the green known as Dartmouth Row, the oldest dating to 1784. Be sure to go into the Baker Memorial Library, the imposing spired building on the green, to see the 3,000-square-foot fresco by the great Mexican muralist José Clemente Orozco, found downstairs on the basement level.

When you see this lovely school, you may better understand Daniel Webster's sentiments 150 years ago when he defended the independence of his young alma mater in a famed case before the U.S. Supreme Court: "It is, as I have said, sir, a small college, but there are those who love it."

The history of the Hanover Inn, across the green from the college, parallels that of the school. Eleven years after Dartmouth's founding, one General Ebenezer Brewster arrived as college steward and redesigned his home on the present inn site to serve as a tavern, no doubt to supplement his academic earnings. One historian noted that the enterprise was "not altogether . . . to the gratification of the College authorities," but the business flourished—so much so that Brewster's son had the tavern moved to another site and put up a larger building in its place, naming it the Dartmouth Hotel.

When that structure burned in 1887, a new hotel, the Wheelock, was built, and in 1901 the college undertook remodeling and renamed the building the Hanover Inn. With many additions and modernizations, that building still stands, and it is as gracious a hostelry as you could wish for. The furnishings are on the formal side—wing chairs, Queen Anne tables, canopied beds—as is the dining room, with its fireplaces and chandeliers. But the perennial presence of young Dartmouth men and women keeps things from becoming stuffy.

At Christmas time the inn is at its best. Two giant trees go up, covered with brightly decorated cookies, one in the dining room and the other in the front window. Since the decorations are all but irresistible, the trees bear a sign pleading, "Please don't eat the cookies."

Hanover Inn is the only place to stay right in Hanover, but Stonecrest

Farm is a very attractive bed-and-breakfast inn just 3½ miles away in Wilder, Vermont. This tastefully decorated 180-year-old residence on two acres is a favorite with Dartmouth visitors. And just one mile from the campus in Norwich, Vermont, the old-fashioned Norwich Inn has redecorated its modest rooms and offers reasonable rates.

If children are along, you'll definitely want to pay a visit to Norwich for the Montshire Museum of Science. This creative $4 million science museum was designed for young children, and is filled with lively hands-on exhibits that fascinate while they educate. It makes for a wonderful family outing. Norwich also boasts one of the best restaurants in the region, a French café called La Poule a Dents.

Fine dining, in fact, is one of the attractions of the Hanover area. The Hanover Inn is reliably excellent, and there are a couple of highly touted gourmet havens in nearby smaller towns, Home Hill in Plainfield and D'Artagnan in Lyme.

For location, you can't beat the Hanover Inn. It is connected by a covered walkway to the Hood Museum and the Hopkins Center, both sources of culture and entertainment for the whole community as well as for the campus. The Hood Museum's rotating art exhibits are always worth a look. The most treasured local holiday tradition, the Christmas Revels, takes place at Hopkins Center, usually on the second weekend of December each year.

The revels are a combination hometown musicale and salute to the season. Though the look and the direction is professional, the actors are locals and the costumes are made by volunteers. Each year the cast salutes the customs of another culture. The production is unusual, lively, and full of color and music, with a minimum of the expected caroling. Just about everybody in town turns out for one of the performances, which are perennial sellouts. So faithfully do they come that the audiences seem to know in unison exactly when the moment has arrived to join the cast in song and dance. If you're not prepared, you may be shocked when your neighbor all but leaps over you to get to the merriment in the aisles. The revels are guaranteed to lift your spirits.

And you won't find a pleasanter place to do a bit of Christmas shopping. Hanover shops are on the traditional side, but the Dartmouth Co-op has a wide range of merchandise and you may be able to pick up some one-of-a-kind treasures from the League of New Hampshire Craftsmen's store at 13 Lebanon Street. Just down the block at 3 Lebanon is Hanover Park, a small shopping complex where you'll find attractive country furniture and accessories at Pompanoosuc Mills and homemade candies at the Chocolate Shop.

There's more shopping to be found about 20 minutes away in the many shops of Woodstock, Vermont. Make a detour off Route 4 into Queechee to see glassblower Simon Pearce's studio in a restored mill. Besides his exquisite glassware, pottery, Irish sweaters and woolens, and antiques are for sale.

If you'd rather enjoy the outdoors than the shops, there's every opportunity around Hanover. You can set off cross-country skiing within a few blocks of Main Street. There's downhill skiing at the Dartmouth Skiway 13 miles away or at the smaller Oak Hill area on the edge of town, and ice skating is excellent at Occum Pond adjacent to the Dartmouth Outing Club. The pond is lighted for night skating. There's indoor skating at Thompson Arena and Davis Rink, in case you don't want to brave the winter weather. Both offer rental skates.

The final special holiday observance each year takes place around Christmas Eve at the Hanover Inn, a celebration so special it may change your mind about spending the holiday at home. The festivities include caroling, storytelling around the Hanover Inn tree, and learning from the inn's chef how to make holiday favorites such as "stained-glass" cookies and clove oranges, right in his own kitchen.

Things start off on December 23 with the multicourse "groaning board" buffet, served up home-style right in the cheerily decorated kitchen. Celebrate Christmas Eve sleigh riding, skating, and tobogganing at the Dartmouth Outing Club, with blazing fires in the clubhouse to warm frosty noses and lots of tea and hot chocolate, for all.

The Christmas Eve candlelight dinner is served family style so that friends old and new can share the evening. You wake on Christmas morning to find that Santa has left a little something outside your door, and following the afternoon dinner of turkey plus the trimmings, there's a "second-time-round" buffet starting at 6:00 P.M., when the turkeys and other goodies reappear so you can make sandwiches and nibble on the stuffing, just like at home.

Whether you come to celebrate Christmas or to get into the spirit of things in advance, you may agree that there's no place like Hanover as a second home for the holidays.

Area Code: 603

DRIVING DIRECTIONS   Hanover can be reached off I-89 at Exit 18, Lebanon, New Hampshire, or I-91 at Exit 13, Norwich, Vermont. It is 135 miles from Boston, 270 miles from New York, and 150 miles from Hartford.

PUBLIC TRANSPORTATION   Vermont Transit bus service to Hanover and Amtrak service to White River Junction, Vermont. Air service to Lebanon, New Hampshire, ten miles away. Airport shuttle service to Hanover from Manchester, New Hampshire, and Boston airports.

ACCOMMODATIONS   *Hanover Inn,* at Dartmouth College Green, Hanover, NH 03755, 643-4300, $$$$–$$$$$, write for special Christmas brochure and prices • *Stonecrest Farm Bed & Breakfast,* 119

Christian Street, Wilder, VT 05088 (802) 295-2425, $$–$$$ CP • *Norwich Inn,* Main Street, Norwich, VT 05055 (802) 649-1143, $$.

DINING *Ivy Grill,* Hanover Inn (see above), innovative bistro menu, $–$$ • *Daniel Webster Room,* Hanover Inn (see above), formal dining room, $$–$$$ • *La Poule a Dents,* Main Street, Norwich (802) 649-2922, pleasant setting, French menu, extensive wine cellar, $$–$$$ • *Norwich Inn* (see above), standard menu, $$; very popular for Sunday brunch, $ • *Home Hill,* River Road, Plainfield, 675-6165, highly regarded French chef-owner, prix fixe, $$$$ • *D'Artagnan,* 13 Dartmouth College Highway, Route 10, Lyme, 795-2137, French, nouvelle, prix fixe, $$$$$ • *Cafe Buon Gustaio,* 72 South Main Street, Hanover, 643-5711, Italian, $–$$ • *Molly's Balloon,* 45 South Main Street, 643-2570, casual, cheerful, wide menu, $–$$ • *Bentley's,* South Main Street, 643-4075, campus favorite, dancing on weekends, jazz and folk music Thursday and Sunday nights, $–$$ • *Peter Christian's Tavern,* 39 Main Street, Hanover, 643-2345, informal, good for families, $–$$ • *Panda House,* 3 Lebanon Street, 643-1290, Chinese, Szechuan specialties, $ • *Lou's Restaurant and Main Street Bakery,* 30 South Main Street, Hanover, 643-3321, a budget standby for all three meals, dinners, $. Also see Queechee, page 83, and Woodstock, page 7.

SIGHTSEEING *Christmas Revels,* contact Hopkins Center, Hanover, NH 03755, 646-2422, for current dates and prices • *Hood Museum of Art,* south side of the green, Hanover, 646-2900. Hours: Tuesday to Friday, 11 A.M. to 5 P.M., Saturday and Sunday, 9:30 A.M. to 5 P.M. Free • *Dartmouth College information:* 646-2900 • *Montshire Museum of Science,* Montshire Road (just west of Hanover, right off I-91 Exit 13), Norwich, VT (802) 649-2200. Hours: daily, 10 A.M. to 5 P.M. Adults, $5; ages 3 to 17, $3.

INFORMATION Hanover Chamber of Commerce, PO Box A-105, Hanover, NH 03755, 643-3115.

Holiday Cheer in Hartford

Some might say it was gilding an already flamboyant lily to add Christmas trimmings to the elaborate home of Mark Twain in Hartford, Connecticut. But Twain, a consummate showman who loved decorating and entertaining for the holidays, would no doubt be pleased to know that each year his home is set up as it was when he and his family were getting ready to receive guests.

For that matter, Twain would likely approve of several of the special Christmas scenes in his onetime hometown, for Hartford is a city that makes the most of the holidays. Though Connecticut's capital city isn't generally thought of as a weekend getaway, during December you'll find the city aglow with festivities sure to kindle your holiday spirit, and neighboring towns like Farmington and Wethersfield will add a touch of Colonial charm to the trip.

At Constitution Plaza in the city's center, the Festival of Lights transforms the plaza into a glittery scene of sculptured reindeer, trumpeting angels, and thousands of tiny twinkling lights. The 38-story City Place lights up with some 2,000 lights forming red and green wreaths around the building, and the top of the Hartford Insurance Group Tower becomes a twinkling tree of lights.

The Wadsworth Atheneum, the city's fine art museum, displays dozens of trees lavishly decorated by local garden clubs and other organizations, all for sale to benefit the museum. At the Old State House, the yearly gathering of work by Connecticut craftspeople is a perfect place to find unusual Christmas gifts. Add the annual performances of *The Nutcracker* by the Hartford Ballet and the traditional holiday ice show at the Civic Center, and you have a capital weekend, indeed.

Downtown Hartford has its share of hotels, but better yet, stay in Colonial Wethersfield or the Farmington Valley, both picture-perfect New England scenes as well as places where you can add unique shopping to the agenda.

Wherever you stay, spend Saturday seeing the many sights in the center of Hartford. A traditional old-fashioned scene in town is the Butler-McCook homestead, a 1782 house that has managed to survive right in the middle of downtown. The tree is adorned with antique ornaments, gingerbread animals, and garlands of popcorn and cranberries. In the kitchen, paper cornucopias are filled with fruits, nuts, and candies, just as they were when the family of Reverend McCook used to distribute these gifts to neighborhood children.

Since the family was a large one, there are lots of leftover Victorian toys to see, including sleds, cannons, a steamboat, toy soldiers, and china dolls. The house, which until 1971 was occupied by one family for four generations, is particularly interesting for the continuity of life within its walls.

The other historic building that has remained in the heart of Hartford is the 1796 Old State House, a masterpiece of Federal-style architecture designed by Charles Bulfinch. Fresh from a major restoration that brought its courtroom, senate, and office chambers back to their original splendor and installed a museum underground, the building now serves as an exhibit and concert hall for the community. The gift shop is always an excellent place to look for folk art and handicrafts, and the Christmas show and sale is an ideal place to find original jewelry, pewter, quilts, and all kinds of collectibles.

Some other interesting stops for shoppers (and diners) are in the Richardson Mall, an 1875 department store converted to shops and a food court; the shopping pavilion near the Old State House; and the Civic Center Mall, bedecked with finery to get you into the proper holiday mood.

Save plenty of time for the outstanding Wadsworth Atheneum. America's first public art museum has benefited over the years from wealthy patrons such as J. P. Morgan, who once lived in Hartford and donated money as well as his private collection of paintings and some 3,000 pieces of priceless porcelain. The total complex consists of five buildings and a court featuring sculpture, and contains works from every period. More than 45,000 paintings and objects are part of the museum collections.

A strong point is American decorative arts, including the Wallace Nutting Collection, the largest and best-known collection of early Colonial furniture, with over 1,000 examples from the "Pilgrim century," 1630 to 1730. Two fully restored period rooms have been removed from their original sites and installed in the museum. The noted Philip H. Hammerslough Collection of more than 600 items made by the finest Early American silversmiths is also displayed.

American painting is an important part of the collection as well, including many fine landscapes from the nineteenth-century Hudson River School, which included Thomas Cole and Hartford-born artist Frederick Church. Costume and textile galleries, European Old Masters, Impressionist paintings, and African-American and twentieth-century art are also part of the museum's extensive holdings.

The Atheneum Gift Shop is a treasure trove of gift ideas, and the tree collection is guaranteed to inspire if not tempt you to somehow take one home.

If you still have time and energy and the weather is cooperative, when you've seen the indoor sights, pick up a walking tour at the Old State House and take in the unusual mix of old and new that marks downtown Hartford. You'll see, for example, the white steeple of Center Church, circa 1788, reflected in the gold-mirrored walls of the Bushnell Tower, designed by I. M. Pei in 1969. Stroll over to Bushnell Park to see the ornate state capitol with its gold dome, then to Constitution Plaza to view what is considered one of the earliest successful urban renewal efforts. You'll want to come back at night for the light show, which includes a cascading fountain of lights.

On Sunday, sleep late, have a hearty Sunday brunch, and head for Mr. Twain's masterpiece, a home that he described as part steamboat, part medieval stronghold, and part cuckoo clock. Nook Farm, the literary colony that housed the homes of both Mark Twain and his neighbor, Harriet Beecher Stowe, is a prime Christmas attraction.

The house that Twain built cost $130,000, a whopping sum back in 1874, and includes decorations by artisans such as Louis Comfort

Tiffany. It is filled with lavish touches—patterned ceilings, carved doors, massive fireplaces, stenciling, elaborate wallpaper that looks like tooled leather—and the last word in High Victorian furnishings.

For the holidays the staircases and mantels are festooned with greenery, and a glittering Victorian Christmas tree stands tall in the library. Gifts in all stages of wrapping are set about in the Mahogany Room, where the Twains used to hide the presents from curious young eyes. Upstairs in the schoolroom, Christmas stockings hang as though waiting to be discovered by the three young daughters of the household.

Scheduled to be completed by 1995 is the newly restored room of Twain's butler, believed to be the inspiration for the character of Jim in *Huckleberry Finn*.

The scene is simpler in the cottage of Harriet Beecher Stowe, where the author of *Uncle Tom's Cabin* lived from 1873 until her death in 1896, but the Christmas spirit is no less. A replica of the Stowe family Christmas tree stands in the rear parlor, along with a number of Victorian pieces owned by Mrs. Stowe. The dining room table is set for a Yuletide feast, with ribbons descending from the chandelier to each place setting, where a tiny gift is set for each guest. Period Christmas trees also adorn the mantel and tables in the living room.

After your tours, stop in each gift shop, where you may be able to buy a copy of *Tom Sawyer* or *Uncle Tom's Cabin* as well as charming Victorian geegaws, Christmas tree ornaments, and reproductions of period jewelry. There are even Mark Twain and Harriet Beecher Stowe T-shirts for sale, if you want to surprise a literary friend.

From here, there are several choices. To see some of Hartford's historic surroundings, drive just a few miles south to Old Wethersfield, a gem of a town, dating to 1634 and with more than 150 remaining homes built before 1850. The Buttolph-Williams House is one of the oldest. It dates to the turn of the eighteenth century and is furnished in the style of the early Pilgrims. The three main attractions in town, the eighteenth-century Webb-Deane-Stevens homes, are part of one excellent historic tour.

The first two weekends in December are filled with seasonal fun: old-fashioned decorations and costumed interpreters describe holiday observances from the past in the historic houses; candlelight strolls; a Victorian Christmas Open House at the Francis House, decorated for the occasion by the Wethersfield Historical Society; and Christmas concerts in the town's venerable New England churches.

There's interesting shopping here, as well at Old Wethersfield Shops on Main Street, offering everything from embroidery to dolls and toys and a host of decorations at the Red Barn Christmas Shop. Comstock, Ferre & Co., the nation's oldest seed company, has been at the same stand on Main Street since 1820, and offers a host of gifts for the home and garden in atmospheric surroundings.

If you continue west from Nook Farm, you'll come to West Hartford and two more attractions. The Museum of American Political Life features the trappings of our nation's political campaigns. It is one-of-a-kind and fascinating, spanning politics from the days of torchlight parades to TV clips of the Kennedy-Nixon debates. If you are interested, note that you must find time on Saturday; the museum is closed Sundays.

On Main Street in West Hartford is another bit of the past, the salt-box home of an important early Hartford citizen, Noah Webster. It's a simple homestead, but interesting to tour nevertheless, to see Mr. Webster's first volumes and realize how he changed our language by insisting that Americans needed their own dictionary. A festive old-fashioned Christmas tree heralds the season.

Beyond, in the beautiful Colonial village of Farmington, you can tour the Hill-Stead Museum, a mansion-museum with its original furnishings intact and with a wealth of Impressionist art on the walls— paintings by Manet, Degas, and Monet, to name a few.

If you are thinking of buying art or crafts, head for nearby Avon, where the Farmington Valley Arts Center off Route 44 includes the working studios of 20 artists and artisans. The annual Christmas show and sale from late November until Christmas offers the chance to choose among the works of dozens of talented craftsmen in addition to the artists in residence, original and beautiful ways to check off your Christmas shopping list.

Area Code: 203

DRIVING DIRECTIONS   Hartford can be reached via I-91 and I-84. It is 100 miles from Boston and 110 miles from New York.

PUBLIC TRANSPORTATION   Hartford is served by Greyhound, Peter Pan/Trailways, and Bonanza bus lines, Amtrak, and many major airlines.

ACCOMMODATIONS   Center-city hotels all have bargain weekend packages: *Goodwin Hotel,* 1 Haynes Street, Hartford 06103, 246-7500, Hartford's only small luxury hotel, in a historic building, $$$–$$$$ • *Ramada Inn-Capitol Hill,* 440 Asylum Street, Hartford 06103, only fair, 246-6591, $$ • *Holiday Inn-Downtown,* 50 Morgan Street, Hartford 06120, 549-2400, $$–$$$ • *Sheraton Hartford,* Trumbull Street at Civic Center Plaza (connected to Civic Center), Hartford 06103, 728-5151, $$$ • *Susse Chalet Motel,* 185 Brainard Road (I-91 exit 27), Hartford 06114, 525-9306, $ • *Centennial Inn of Farmington,* 5 Spring Lane, Farmington 06032, 677-4647, all suite hotel, $$$–$$$$ CP • *Barney House,* 11 Mountain Spring Road, Farmington 06032, 677-9735, handsome old home, $$ CP • *Farmington Inn,* 827 Farmington Avenue, Farmington 06032, 677-2821, elegantly refurbished motor inn, $$–$$$ CP • *Chester Bulkley House,* 184 Main Street, Wethersfield 06109, 563-4236, 1830 Greek Revival B & B home, $$ CP.

DINING *Carbone's Restaurant,* 588 Franklin Avenue, 249-9646, Italian restaurant popular with politicos, $$–$$$ • *Gaetano's,* 1 Civic Center Plaza, second level, 249-1629, excellent French and Italian, $$–$$$; *Bistro Café,* $ • *Peppercorns Grill,* 357 Main Street, 547-1714, Italian dishes and more, $$ • *Pierpont's,* Goodwin Hotel (see above), attractive setting for fine dining, $$–$$$ • *Capitol Fish House,* 391 Main Street, 724-3370, in a restored nineteenth-century hotel, $$–$$$ • *Max on Main,* 205 Main Street, 522-2530, sophisticated bistro, very popular, $$ • *Hot Tomato's,* 1 Union Place, 249-5100, lotsa pasta, $–$$ • *Congress Rotisserie,* 7 Maple Avenue, 560-1965, grill specialties, $$ • *Costa Del Sol,* 901 Wethersfield Avenue, 296-1714, Spanish charm, good food, $$–$$$ • *Truc Orient Express,* 735 Wethersfield Avenue, 296-2618, first-rate Vietnamese food, $ • *Brown Thompson & Company,* 942 Main Street, 525-1600, light fare and the city's most congenial bar, $ • *Hartford Brewery Ltd.,* 35 Pearl Street, 246-BEER, sandwiches, salads, and home brew, $ • *Apricots,* 1593 Farmington Avenue, Farmington, 673-5405, French, longtime favorite, $$–$$$$ • *The Whitman,* 1125 Farmington Avenue, Farmington, 678-9217, attractive, interesting menu, music on weekends, $$–$$$ • *Standish House,* 222 Main Street, Wethersfield, 721-1113, lovely 1790 home, varied menu, $$–$$$.

SIGHTSEEING *Wadsworth Atheneum,* 600 Main Street, 278-2670. Hours: Tuesday to Sunday, 11 A.M. to 5 P.M. Adults, $5; students, $2; under 13, free. Note: Free to all on Saturday, 11 A.M. to 1 P.M., and all day Thursday • *Old State House,* 800 Main Street, 522-6766. Hours: Monday to Saturday, 10 A.M. to 6 P.M. Free • *State Capitol,* 210 Capitol Avenue, 240-0222. Hours: Monday to Friday, 9 A.M. to 3 P.M.; free tours, 9:15 A.M. to 1:15 P.M. Saturday tours, April through October, 10:15 A.M. to 2:15 P.M. Free • *Museum of Connecticut History,* 231 Capitol Avenue, 566-3056. Hours: Monday to Friday, 9 A.M. to 4:45 P.M. Free • *Butler-McCook Homestead,* 396 Main Street, 522-1806. Hours: May 15 to October 15, Tuesday, Thursday, and Sunday, noon to 4 P.M. Special Christmas displays in December. Adults, $3; children, $1 • *Mark Twain Memorial,* 351 Farmington Avenue (I-84, Exit 46), 247-0998. Tours: Monday, Wednesday to Saturday, 9:30 A.M. to 5 P.M., Sunday, noon to 5 P.M. Also open Tuesdays Memorial Day to Columbus Day and in December. Adults, $6.50; under 16, $2.75 • *Harriet Beecher Stowe House, Nook Farm,* 77 Forest Street, 525-9317. Hours: Tuesday to Saturday, 9:30 A.M. to 4 P.M.; Sunday, noon to 4 P.M. Adults, $6.50;

under 16, $2.75 • *Hill-Stead Museum,* 35 Mountain Road, Farmington, 677-9064. Hours: April to October, Tuesday to Sunday, 10 A.M. to 5 P.M.; November to March, Tuesday to Sunday, 11 A.M. to 5 P.M. Closed mid-January to mid-February. Adults, $6; ages 6 to 12, $3 • *Museum of American Political Life,* Harry Jack Gray Center, University of Hartford, 200 Bloomfield Avenue, West Hartford, 768-4090. Hours: Tuesday to Friday, 11 A.M. to 4 P.M.; Saturday and Sunday, noon to 4 P.M. Donation • *Noah Webster House/West Hartford Historical Museum,* 227 South Main Street, West Hartford, 521-5362. Hours: October to mid-June, daily except Wednesday, 1 P.M. to 4 P.M.; June 15 to September 30, weekdays except Wednesday, 10 A.M. to 4 P.M., Saturday and Sunday, 1 P.M. to 4 P.M. Adults, $3; children, $1 • *Stanley Whitman House,* 37 High Street off Route 4, 677-9222. Hours: March, April, November, and December, Sunday, noon to 4 P.M.; May to October, Wednesday to Sunday, noon to 4 P.M.; closed January and February. Adults, $3; ages 6 to 14, $2 • *Webb-Deane-Stevens Museum,* 211 Main Street, Wethersfield, 529-0612. Hours: May to October, Wednesday to Monday, 10 A.M. to 4 P.M.; rest of year, Saturday and Sunday only; last tour begins 3 P.M. Adults, $6; students, $4; children, $1. • For information on Christmas events, contact Olde Towne Tourism District, 105 Marsh Street, Wethersfield, CT 06109, 257-9299.

INFORMATION Greater Hartford Convention and Visitors' Bureau, 1 Civic Center Plaza, Hartford, CT 06103, 728-6789.

Shopping by the Sea in Portsmouth

"Have yourself a merry little Christmas," caroled the speaker in one of the shops in Portsmouth, New Hampshire. We were doing just that.

Portsmouth is a lovely old seafaring town, with a wide harbor, handsome sea captains' homes, and a long, proud history. In summer it is filled with tourists—and therefore it is a town filled with shops.

Come December, the crowds are gone but the many shops remain, offering choice selections for shoppers in pic-turesque surroundings. There's a bonus, too, since New Hampshire has no sales tax.

Things are made even more inviting with gala decorations and music. Little Prescott Park sets the waterfront aglow with tiny twinkling lights on every tree. Portsmouth also offers an event that is absolutely guaranteed to imbue even Ebenezer Scrooge with Christmas spirit—the annual Candlelight Stroll at Strawbery Banke.

When the first settlers arrived in Portsmouth, they found the area covered with luscious wild strawberries, inspiring them to name their new home "Strawbery Banke." It became the third settlement in the New World, preceded only by Plymouth and Jamestown.

Though the town name changed in 1653, Strawbery Banke lives on today in the form of 30 original buildings in various stages of restoration, a village representing 350 years of the town's history. Many of the homes were continuously occupied until the 1950s. Preservationists stepped in when there was a proposal to raze the decaying neighborhood. Rather than following other restorations that re-create only the early settlement, they chose to portray life as it has changed over the years, a fascinating approach. For more about seeing the village in season when the houses are open for daytime touring, see page 243.

On the first and second weekends of December, Strawbery Banke becomes a haven of holiday cheer. The streets are lit by candleglow and music fills the air with a melodious salute to the season. For the annual Candlelight Stroll, a tradition for more than a decade, each home is bedecked with period holiday decorations. When you enter, each one holds its own delightful musical surprise—professional musicians playing early Christmas airs. A harpsichord and early winds consort may greet you in one, a flutist in another, perhaps a chorus in yet a third.

The village uses some of its historic houses as places for local artisans to live and work, displaying their skills and selling their wares. A potter, cooper, or resident artist is usually present for the evening festivities, offering you a chance to pick up handmade one-of-a-kind gifts for special names on your Christmas list as you stroll.

More gifts are to be found at the Dunaway Store, the old-fashioned country store, and at a second gift shop, both good bets for tasteful presents. The Dunaway Store has a wonderful selection of books.

It's an unbeatable evening in a town that makes gift shopping a true pleasure. Market Square is the center of town. Market Street, which runs out from the square paralleling the Piscataqua River, and curving Bow Street, which intersects Market, offer just about anything you could ask for—wooden ware, art glass, Southwestern jewelry, candles, mugs, clothing, you name it. Handmade crafts are plentiful, from leather goods to hand-forged iron pieces to jewelry.

There are plenty of antiques shops if you want to splurge for someone special—including yourself. M. S. Carter, at number 175 near the foot of Market, is one of the nicest of the antiquers' stops, packed with furniture, folk art, hooked rugs, antique decoys, and antique Christmas lights. Old Port Artisans, across the street at number 206, will delight fans of folk art. Among the offerings are charming hand-painted pieces by owner-artist Lisa Carpenter.

Lovers of old books will find two treasure troves a few doors apart on State Street, a block with more antiques and other shops with a funkier feel.

If you want to take a break and warm up a bit, you'll find that Portsmouth is brimming with coffee shops such as Breaking New Grounds on Market Street.

For bargains, drive just across the bridge to Kittery, Maine, and you'll find discount shopping galore, including outlet stores for Dansk, Mikasa, Lenox, Waterford, Wedgwood, Hathaway, Bass, Timberland, and just about any brand label you can name, all in a series of outlet centers along Route 1.

Remember, too, that prices at the state-run liquor stores in New Hampshire are excellent. The nearest one, at the Portsmouth Traffic Circle on I-95, is the biggest in the state.

Portsmouth has an increasingly varied selection of good restaurants, and though it is technically off-season, many young professionals are moving to town permanently, meaning that there are places to go at night for jazz or other live music. Ask your innkeeper who is playing where.

Though the Candlelight Stroll and special Christmas tour hours enable December visitors to get inside Strawbery Banke's homes, you'll have to return in summer to do full justice to the complex and its beautiful gardens, and to go into the historic showplace mansions on "The Portsmouth Trail." But you can have a look at some of them, and at many other fine homes as well, by making your own compact driving tour. Be sure to see the Wentworth-Gardner House at 141 Mechanic Street, the Moffatt-Ladd House at 154 Market, the Rundlet-May House at 364 Middle Street, the Warner House at the corner of Daniel and Chapel, the Governor John Langdon House at 143 Pleasant Street, and finally, the most historic of all, the John Paul Jones House at Middle and State. This is the place where the admiral oversaw fittings for his new command, the *Ranger,* which sailed out of Portsmouth Harbor on November 1, 1777, bearing the first American flag to be flown at sea.

The Portsmouth Tourist Information Office is not usually open on winter weekends, but you can write in advance for material to guide you on your tour.

Portsmouth has much to offer in the summer when the houses are open, the gardens are in bloom at Strawbery Banke and Prescott Park, and the sightseeing cruise boats are out in the harbor or heading for the Shoals Islands. But there's nothing to match the town on a frosty December night, when Strawbery Banke is aglow with candlelight and music. And when it comes to Christmas shopping, you won't find a snugger port anywhere.

Area Code: 603

DRIVING DIRECTIONS   Portsmouth is on I-95, 60 miles north of Boston, 268 miles from New York, and 158 miles from Hartford.

PUBLIC TRANSPORTATION   Air and Greyhound bus service.

ACCOMMODATIONS   All Portsmouth zip codes are 03801. *Sise Inn,* 40 Court Street, Portsmouth, 433-1200, handsome Victorian ambience, hotel services, $$–$$$ CP • *Governor's House,* 32 Miller Avenue, Portsmouth, 431-6546, gracious, spacious, tennis court, best of the B & Bs, $$–$$$$ CP • *Martin Hill Inn,* 404 Islington, Portsmouth, 436-2287, cozy, pretty decor, hearty breakfasts, $$–$$$ CP • *The Inn at Christian Shore,* 335 Maplewood, Portsmouth, 431-6770, Federal house with period furnishings, more big breakfasts, $$ CP • *Gundalow Inn,* 6 Water Street, Kittery, ME 03904 (207) 439-4040, snug Victorian just across the river on Portsmouth harbor, fabulous four-course breakfasts, $$–$$$ CP • *Leighton Inn,* 69 Richards Avenue, Portsmouth, 433-2188, Federal home on a residential block, $$ CP • Also see York, page 103.

DINING   *The Blue Strawberry,* 29 Ceres Street, 431-6420, one seating, reservations essential, old-timer that some call superb—others call it overpriced, prix fixe, $$$$$ • Two restored warehouses with great atmosphere and seafood specialties, perennial favorites: *The Oar House,* 55 Ceres Street, 436-4205, $$, and *The Dolphin Striker,* 15 Bow Street, 431-5222, $$ • *The Metro,* 20 High Street, 436-0521, brasserie, stained glass, gaslights, varied American menu, known for chowder, $$ • *The Library,* 401 State Street, 431-5202, book-lined walls and a varied menu, $$ • *Porto Bello,* 67 Bow Street (upstairs), 431-2989, much-praised Italian, $–$$ • *Stockpot,* 53 Bow Street, 431-1851, Mediterranean and Middle Eastern dishes, on the water, $–$$ • *Café Mirabelle,* 64 Bridge Street, 430-9301, attractive French café, $–$$, or prix fixe, $$$$ • *Portsmouth Brewery,* 56 Market Street, 431-1115, brew-pub, lively, $–$$.

SIGHTSEEING   *Strawbery Banke,* Hancock and Marcy streets, 436-1100. Candlelight Stroll, first and second weekends in December, Friday and Saturday evenings, 3:30 P.M. to 8:30 P.M. Adults, $10; children, $7; under 6, free. Regular hours: May 1 to October 31, daily, 10 A.M. to 5 P.M. Adults, $10; ages 7 to 17, $7; family rate, $25.

INFORMATION   Greater Portsmouth Chamber of Commerce, 500 Market Street, PO Box 239, Portsmouth, NH 03801, 436-1118.

Winter Carnival at Stowe

"Stowe Is King," proclaimed the ice sculptures at a recent Winter Carnival in Stowe, Vermont.

Three generations of skiers would agree. But you don't have to be a skier to love the hometown of Mt. Mansfield, Vermont's highest mountain peak.

Stowe blends the charm of a New England village nestled in a stunning mountain setting with sophisticated food and lodgings that few ski resorts can match. Come Winter Carnival week, with fanciful ice carvings, dog-sled racing, parades, ski racing, and other gala events added to the agenda, it's a stellar winter destination for all.

The mountain scenery has been attracting visitors since the 1840s, when the first inn was built under the mountain and another, Mansfield House, arose in Stowe village to house 600 guests. The Dartmouth College team was skiing the Toll Road as early as 1914, but it was in 1933, just as agriculture was declining as a source of revenue, that the Civilian Conservation Corps cut a four-mile trail down the mountain and serious skiing began. The next year Mt. Mansfield Ski Club was formed, setting up lodging in a former logging camp at the bottom of the trail, and by 1937 the first rope tow was in place. Those who are used to paying well over $35 a day to ski might like to know that use of that first lift cost 50 cents a day, $5 for the season.

Winter recreation saved the town of Stowe from the hard times that the demise of small farming brought to many other Vermont communities. Mt. Mansfield emerged as the Eastern skier's supreme test, with the steep trails known as the "Front Four," including "Starr" and "Goat," becoming legendary for their challenge. And while it has competition from emerging giants such as Killington, now Vermont's biggest mountain, Stowe's special cachet remains unmatched. The proliferation of fine facilities that grew up around skiing now makes it a prime year-round resort destination.

The first Winter Carnival, held in 1921, consisted of ski jumping and tobogganing on a hill in the village. The tradition was abandoned for a time but was reborn in 1974 as an antidote to the mid-January doldrums common to ski areas. Today Stowe hosts a ten-day "king of carnivals," offering something for everyone, sports enthusiast and spectator alike.

Each year's theme is spelled out in an ice sculpture contest, with the fanciful carvings appearing in front of almost every inn and restaurant. It's a feast for photographers. Popeye, King Kong, and the *Star Wars* crew are just a few of the elaborate sculptures seen in recent years.

The kick-off carnival event, known as Village Night, is a small-town affair with lights and balloons festooning Main Street and a parade of locals in storybook costumes, traditionally followed by fireworks. Carnival sporting competitions are both serious and silly, with top contenders on hand for ski races and all invited to join the "Anyone Can Do It" cross-country race, as well as to Game Night, which includes a trivia contest. There are also snow-golf tournaments with prizes for wacky costumes, and snowboard, mountain bike, and telemark skiing competitions.

Almost everyone turns out to watch the excitement of sled dogs streaking down the track with their drivers standing on the sleds at the rear, urging the racers onward.

Evening carnival festivities include Tyrolean Night, with Alpine entertainment; Las Vegas Night, the chance to try your luck at gaming tables; and hearty homemade church suppers. Whatever is slated over your weekend visit, you can count on a spirited schedule.

When it comes to choosing a place to stay at Stowe, the possibilities are enormous. At the top of the scale, Topnotch is just that. You can skate here, go sledding or sleigh riding, use the on-premises Cross-Country Ski Center, take advantage of the extensive indoor tennis facilities, swim at an indoor pool with a waterfall, or luxuriate at a multimillion-dollar spa. Equally pleasant is sitting in front of the giant fireplace and looking out the 12-foot windows at snow-covered Mt. Mansfield in a living room that is a tasteful blend of rustic fieldstone and country antiques.

Skiers may appreciate the convenience of the Mount Mansfield Resort. Decor is basic; the big advantage is direct access to the mountain from their own double chairlift. There's a choice of hotel or condo accommodations.

Ten Acres Lodge is the definite choice for those who enjoy a more traditional antique-filled Colonial-style New England inn. The Alpine-style Trapp Family Lodge is big and busy, but may appeal to cross-country skiers for its excellent Ski Touring Center and extensive trails. Edson Hill Manor, with a secluded location and a pleasant rustic feel, also offers ski touring as well as a riding center on its 500 acres.

On a more modest scale, The Siebeness Inn is a delightful, sunny, and welcoming small inn decorated with country charm and with a hot tub for sore muscles, while the congenial, old-fashioned Gables welcomes you home each afternoon with hot soup and hors d'oeuvres on the house. Brass Lantern is a pleasant B & B just north of town, and Timberholm Inn is tucked away on a quiet wooded hillside away from traffic, but just one block from the mountain road.

For the budget-minded, there's the warm and cozy Golden Kitz Lodge and Motel, a happily cluttered establishment that offers not only hot soup, but wine and cheese as antidotes to wintry afternoons, and a family resort, Golden Eagle, has more moderate rates than most resorts and includes an indoor pool and health club, sleigh rides, ice skating, and children's programs. Those who stay at the adjacent Alpine Motor Inn also get to use these facilities.

There are dozens of other lodgings—over 60 at last count. Contact the Stowe Area Association for further information and free reservation service.

When it comes to food, Stowe offers some of the best dining in ski country, with some 45 restaurants to choose from. Top recommendations include fine dining at Edson Hill Manor and Ten Acres Lodge, Italian at Trattoria La Festa, and creative American menus at the Blue Moon, a small café that wins raves in town.

Popular for après ski are The Shed, and for a change of pace, Mr. Pickwick's Pub for a pub menu accompanied by British folk songs and a pint of ale. The prize breakfast in town is at The Gables Inn and Motel, where you can choose from the extensive menu until noon.

Even without the Winter Carnival, you can stay busy at Stowe with a dozen different activities, beginning but not ending with the 350 miles of alpine skiing terrain and over 100 miles of cross-country trails. Besides the tough stuff for the experts, the 6,400-foot Toll House Chairlift opens many trails for novices on Spruce Peak. The original Toll Road is now a four-mile run from the top that is one of the most scenic novice trails to be found. In recent years, Stowe has added one of the world's fastest eight-passenger gondola lifts and night skiing on the longest lighted trail in northern New England.

If you don't ski, you can choose from ice skating at the indoor Jackson Arena in the village or outdoor and indoor fun open to the public at some of the area resorts: a sleigh ride for two at Stowehof Inn or in a wagon for 20 at the Trapp Family Lodge; indoor tennis lessons from the pros at Topnotch, horseback riding at Edson Hill Manor, or exercise at the Golden Eagle Resort Spa. Guided outings on snowshoes are offered by two local outfitters, Umiak and Bedside Turners. Several inns offer their indoor pools to nonguests for a fee.

If your favorite sport is shopping, you've still come to the right place. There are plenty of possibilities in town and all along Route 108, the road to the mountain. A recommended stop at the beginning of the mountain road is the Stowe Crafts Gallery, a converted old red mill with excellent woodenware, including handcrafted ski and tennis racks, as well as attractive pottery, glass, and jewelry. Right across the parking lot, the Game Shop offers unique games and puzzles and handmade wooden game boards. In town, the old Depot building features handsome reproduction country furniture, crafts, and a big bookstore, and Prints and Patches across the street has everything quilted, from king-size spreads to bibs and eyeglass cases, as well as hand-hooked rugs. Quilts can be ordered in your own color scheme. On the edge of town are Harrington's for cob-smoked hams and Vermont cheese and Orvis for outerwear. And don't overlook Everything Cows, a "bovine boutique" featuring that famous Vermont black-and-white-cow motif on anything you can think of. Try Green Mountain, Stowe Antique Center, and English Country at Stowe for collectibles, and Shaw's General Store for almost anything.

If you want a tour of the Ben and Jerry's Ice Cream Factory, from whence comes Vermont's best-known sweet treat, you'll find them on Route 100 in Waterbury, just ten miles away. On the way, you'll pass the Cold Hollow Cider Mill, where you can see cider making year-round, and get free samples, to boot.

In fact, there's not much of anything you can't find around Stowe, a town that richly deserves its title as king—carnival or not.

Area Code: 802

DRIVING DIRECTIONS Stowe is in northern Vermont on Route 100, ten minutes north from Exit 10, Route I-89. It is about 185 miles from Boston, 325 miles from New York, and 200 miles from Hartford.

PUBLIC TRANSPORTATION Air service connects to Burlington, 45 minutes away; shuttle service is available to Stowe from the airport, as well as many car rentals offering special ski packages. Vermont Transit, Greyhound bus service, and Amtrak rail provide service to Waterbury, which is ten miles away, and taxis are available for the rest of the route. Regular shuttle-bus service from the village to the slopes makes it easy to get around without a car during the day, and many restaurants are within walking distance of lodgings.

ACCOMMODATIONS All Stowe zip codes are 05672. **Free reservation service:** Stowe Area Association, Box 1320 Stowe (800) 24-STOWE • *Topnotch at Stowe,* Mountain Road, Stowe, 253-8585 or (800) 451-8686, $$$$–$$$$$ • *Stowehof Inn,* Edson Hill Road, Stowe, 253-9722 or (800) 422-9922, luxury accommodations, $$$$$ MAP • *Mount Mansfield Resort,* Mountain Road, Stowe, 253-8610; Inn at the Mountain, $$$$–$$$$$ MAP; condominiums, $$$$$ • *Ten Acres Lodge,* Luce Hill, Stowe, 253-7638, $$–$$$ CP; Hill House rooms with fireplace, $$$–$$$$$ • *Trapp Family Lodge,* Luce Hill Road, Stowe, 253-8511 or (800) 826-7000, $$$$$ MAP • *Edson Hill Manor,* Edson Hill Road, Stowe, 253-7371, $$$–$$$$ MAP • *The Siebeness Inn,* 3681 Mountain Road, Stowe, 253-8942 or (800) 426-9001, $$ CP • *Green Mountain Inn,* Main Street, Stowe, 253-7301, village landmark, $$–$$$ • *Timberholm Inn,* Cottage Club Road, Stowe, 253-7603, $–$$$ CP • *The Gables Inn and Motel,* Stowe, 253-7730, $$$–$$$$ MAP • *Brass Lantern,* Route 100 North, Stowe, 253-2229, $$–$$$$ CP • *Golden Kitz Lodge and Motel,* Mountain Road,

Stowe, 253-4217, $–$$ • *Golden Eagle Resort,* Mountain Road, Stowe, $$$ • *Alpine Motor Inn,* PO Box 1090, Stowe (800) 626-1010, $$–$$$, includes Golden Eagle facilities. All are less on weekdays; also ask about weekend or ski packages.

DINING   *Blue Moon Café,* 35 School Street, 253-7006, innovative chef, $$ • *Edson Hill Manor* (see above), $$–$$$ • *Ten Acres Lodge* (see above), eclectic menu, $$; also tavern menu, $ • *Topnotch* (see above), menu includes spa choices, $$–$$$ • *Stubbs,* Mountain Road, 253-7110, interesting dishes, $$; also lighter fare in the lounge, $ • *Trattoria La Festa,* Mountain Road, 253-8480, Italian favorite, $–$$ • *Partridge Inn,* Mountain Road, 253-8000, seafood specialties, $$ • *The Siebeness Inn* (see above), home-cooked meals by reservation, prix fixe, $$ • *Whiskers,* Mountain Road, 253-8996, prime ribs, steak, salad bar, $$ • **Less formal fare and lunch:** *The Shed,* Mountain Road, 253-4364, $–$$; *Gracie's,* Main Street, 253-8741, $–$$; *Restaurant Swisspot,* Main Street, 253-4622, a tiny charmer noted for fondue and quiche, $–$$; *Depot Street Malt Shop,* Depot Street, 253-4269. For breakfast: *The Gables Inn and Motel* (above), *The Siebeness Inn* (above), or *Green Mountain Inn,* Main Street, 253-7301 • **Apres ski:** *Mr. Pickwick's Pub Ye Olde New England Inn,* Mountain Road, 253-7558 and *The Shed* (see above).

SIGHTSEEING   *Stowe Winter Carnival,* 10 days in mid- to late January, dates and schedule of events from Stowe Area Association (see above) • **Ski information:** Mount Mansfield, 253-7311; Snowphone, 253-2222 • **Sleigh rides:** *Pristine Meadows,* 253-9877; *Stowehof Inn,* 253-9722; *Edson Hill Manor,* 253-7371; *Trapp Family Lodge,* 253-8511 • **Ice skating:** *Jackson Arena,* 253-6148 • **Cross-country skiing:** *Edson Hill Manor,* 253-8954; *Mt. Mansfield Resort,* 253-7311; *Topnotch,* 253-8585; *Trapp Family Lodge,* 253-8511 • **Snowshoeing:** *Bedside Tuners,* 253-7222; *Umiak,* 253-2317 • *Ben & Jerry's Ice Cream Factory Tours,* Route 100, Waterbury. Hours: year-round, Monday to Saturday, 9 A.M. to 4 P.M. Admission donation goes to charity; under 12, free.

INFORMATION   Stowe Area Association, Box 1320, Stowe, VT 05672, 253-7321 or (800) 24-STOWE, for lodging and general Stowe information.

Stirring Things Up at Sturbridge

The soup kettle was simmering and the spit was being turned, searing the joint of beef to a crispy brown and sending heavenly smells through the kitchen. Several guests were busy preparing potatoes, carrots, and onions to be browned in the drippings, the men as involved with the chores as the women.

Another group was filling a pottery dish with whole-wheat pie crust, ready to receive chicken and gravy and vegetables, then be baked into a savory pie in the cast-iron Dutch oven heating in the hot coals. Meanwhile, some were busy forming wafers fresh from the wafer iron into cone shapes that would hold sweet fillings for dessert.

It's one thing to visit the kitchen of an early New England home. It's a lot more fun to roll up your sleeves and pitch in when preparing dinner on the open hearth, just the way it was done 150 years ago. That's just what you can do if you sign up for "Dinner in a Country Village," a cooking-and-dining program held each Saturday night during the winter months at Old Sturbridge Village in Massachusetts.

New England's largest historical restoration, Old Sturbridge Village is a lively re-creation of a rural New England village of the early nineteenth century, with "villagers" in authentic dress demonstrating what work and daily life were like in early America. The 200-acre property includes more than 40 New England homes, mills, churches, craft shops, and a fully operating period farm.

But for the lucky 14 who snag a place at Saturday dinner, the real fun begins when the gates close and everyone else heads home. That's when the kitchen of the white saltbox Parsonage on the Village Common swings into action.

Dinner guests are escorted into the 1748 home, which has been restored to reflect the fashions and furnishings of a clergyman's family in the 1830s, and greeted by members of the village staff who are well versed in the art of fireplace cooking. Everyone helps in the preparation of a full-course meal that might have been served in a home like this one, using historical kitchen utensils reproduced from the Sturbridge Village collections.

With the group limited in number, everyone really gets a chance to participate, and while dinner cooks there is time to socialize and learn to play some early nineteenth-century parlor games.

It's a delicious way to relive a bit of the past, something you can also do by day at Old Sturbridge Village. In this quieter time of year, Old Sturbridge is a perfect destination for families, providing a chance for all ages to step back in time, actually performing some of the skills that were necessary long ago.

Winter weekend activities include a host of workshops teaching how to do everything from woodworking and candle making to stenciling, toy making, and more opportunities to cook on the open hearth. Each of these workshops produces something useful to take home. Many are designed for families working together, a chance for parent and child to share the fun and satisfaction of mastering a new skill. There are activities for children as young as six, for teens, and every age in between. Special workshops during holiday periods are the perfect answer for parents looking for something to do with the kids during school vacation.

Visiting the village in winter is also a special treat. A coat of winter white only makes everything more beautiful, and gives you a chance to ride in a horse-drawn sleigh. A cold-weather visit also allows you to see the special activities of the peaceful winter season. Outdoors, you might find farmers hauling logs with a team of oxen to make repairs in the split-rail fences or provide material for the sawmill. Indoors you can join country artisans in front of a cheery fireplace or cast-iron stove, a mighty welcome invention in early America.

The usual crafts demonstrations—weaving, printing, tinsmithing, and the like—still take place in the winter, and the artisans have more time to chat and answer questions. The schoolteacher will give you a colorful introduction to education as it was in the 1830s, guaranteed to fascinate all ages.

And you finally may have time to take a look at some of the indoor exhibits that usually are forgotten in the summer. There are seven galleries to be seen, filled with firearms, lighting devices, folk art, textiles, blown and molded glass, mirrors, scientific instruments, hand-sewn and knitted garments, weaving, quilts, and much more. The Clock Gallery adjoining the Visitor Center is a standout.

There's a real village of Sturbridge to be explored as well, an authentic New England town with its original green and many historic buildings intact and a host of enticing shops. Two shops on Main Street across the driveway from the Publick House Inn are of special note, the Green Apple for its excellent stock of antiques, folk art, and country furnishings and Sadie Green's Curiosity Shop, whose name does not do justice to the enormous selection of original design jewelry made with luminous antique glass.

The Seraph has fine reproductions of Early American furniture, and the Shaker Shop features Shaker furniture designs. There's surely a basket for everyone among the hundreds for sale at Basketville, and the Marketplace, a restored mill, has a little of everything, including a whole top floor of handcrafts.

Antiquers will find dozens of lures. Some of the larger selections are available at the Antique Center of Sturbridge, a collective of several dealers, and Sturbridge Antiques to the east on Route 20 with 25 dealers under one roof.

When it comes to choosing lodging for the night, the most attractive Sturbridge inn by far is the 1771 Publick House, a longtime New England standby that is full of Colonial charm, and its equally attractive, cozier, and quieter adjunct, the Colonel Ebenezer Crafts Inn. The Publick House runs a series of very pleasant "Yankee Winter Weekends," featuring lots of hearty fare and visits to Sturbridge Village. However, the package includes dinner, something of a waste if you plan to take part in cooking at the village. Old Sturbridge Village has a motor lodge adjoining the grounds, as well as the Oliver Wight House, a handsome, restored Early American home that is a very fitting lodging for the weekend. The Wildwood Inn in Ware, about 20 miles away, is an alternative, another charmer, a Victorian home with very reasonable prices.

On Sunday you have a choice of destinations, depending on whether you want indoor or outdoor activity. For starters, you might follow Route 20 a few miles east to Auburn for the year-round antiques fair and flea market held on Route 12. Clock fanciers should take the Mass Pike east a few miles to Grafton for the Willard House and Clock Museum, the birthplace of the famous Willard clock makers. Featured are many fine early clocks, including some prize tall clocks, as well as eighteenth-century furnishings.

Worcester, Massachusetts's second largest city, is just 20 miles from Sturbridge via Routes 90 and 290. Here's a city that is a sleeper, still thought of by many as primarily a factory town, but actually much more. In addition to a Colonial heritage dating back to 1673, an attractively hilly terrain, and lovely residential areas, Worcester is the home of 12 college campuses and two fine small museums.

The New England Science Center is unique and worth a visit, a fine complex on 60 acres with participatory science exhibits, a solar/lunar observatory and planetarium, and an indoor-outdoor zoo. In winter, the stars of the outdoor show are the polar bears. A special window lets you watch them swimming underwater.

The Worcester Art Museum, a handsome traditional stone building, may surprise you as well, with a collection of paintings that tell the story of art through 50 centuries of development. Rembrandts, Goyas, Matisses, and Picassos are among the treasures here, and one particularly fine exhibit is a thirteenth-century French chapel rebuilt here stone by stone.

The museums are easy to find, as signs are posted pointing the way no matter where you enter the city. And when you're done with gallery hopping, you'll find that some of those dull factories in the city have been converted into very lively places for food and drink. Maxwell Silverman's Tool House on Union is a prime example.

Another conversion in town is Exchange Place, at Exchange and Walden, just across from Worcester's civic center, the Centrum.

Exchange Place is but a transformed police station/firehouse complex, which now holds restaurants and stores, including a branch of Boston's well-known Legal Sea Foods. There's some fine dining to be found in Worcester, as well, at Stendahl's and the Struck Café.

If you prefer ski slopes to city, follow Route 20 east to Route 31 north and turn off on Route 62 in Princeton for Wachusett Mountain, a small, friendly ski area with good snow-making facilities and a most attractive lodge.

Wherever you spend the afternoon, you may want to drive to West Brookfield, northwest of Sturbridge, for dinner at the Salem Cross Inn, a fine restaurant in a beamed and beautiful Colonial home that is listed in the National Register of Historic Places. Meats are sometimes roasted here in the giant 42-foot fireplace, and now that you're an amateur expert, you can test their mettle.

Area Code: 508

DRIVING DIRECTIONS   Sturbridge is located on Route 20 in south-central Massachusetts, Exit 9 on I-90, the Massachusetts Turnpike. It is 55 miles from Boston, 160 miles from New York, and 40 miles from Hartford.

PUBLIC TRANSPORTATION   Sturbridge can be reached by Amtrak to Worcester, Springfield, or Boston; or by Peter Pan bus lines from Boston, New York, or Hartford. Airport transport service is also available from Boston, Worcester, and Hartford-Springfield's Bradley International Airport.

ACCOMMODATIONS   The lower rates listed are generally available in the winter. *The Publick House,* Main Street (Route 131), Sturbridge 01566, 347-3313, a charming 1771 inn, $$–$$$ • If you like smaller inns, ask for the *Colonel Ebenezer Crafts Inn,* a restored 1786 home under Publick House management • *Country Motor Lodge,* also run by Publick House, $$ • *Old Sturbridge Village Lodges,* Route 20 west, Sturbridge 01566, 347-3327 (motel adjacent to the village itself), $$–$$$ • *Oliver Wight House,* 1789 home-turned-inn, part of Village Lodges above, $$–$$$ • *Quality Inn Colonial,* Route 20, Sturbridge 01566, motel, tennis, pool, $–$$ • *Sturbridge Host Hotel and Conference Center,* Route 20, Sturbridge 01566, 347-7393, indoor pool, tennis, $$$–$$$$ • *Wildwood Inn,* 121 Church Street, Ware 01082 (413) 967-7798, 20 minutes from Sturbridge and a bargain, $ CP.

DINING   *The Publick House* (see above), very pleasant dining room, $$–$$$; tavern for informal meals, $ • *Whistling Swan,* 502 Main Street, Sturbridge, 347-2321, 1855 home and barn, continental, excellent, $$–$$$; *Ugly Duckling,* loft for casual dining, $ • *Salem Cross Inn,* West Brookfield (north of Sturbridge), 867-2345, $$ • *Le Bearn Restaurant Français,* 12 Cedar Street, Sturbridge, 347-5800, French cuisine in a Cape Cod house, $$–$$$ • *Crabapple's,* Haynes Street, Sturbridge, 347-5559, informal, good for families, $ • *Piccadilly Pub,* 362 Main Street, Sturbridge, 347-8189, pub fare, popular lounge, $ • *Stendahl's,* 8 Austin Street, Worcester, 752-0600, continental, excellent, $$$–$$$$ • *Maxwell Silverman's Tool House,* 25 Union Street, Worcester, 755-1200, $$–$$$ • *Struck Café,* 415 Chandler Street, Worcester, 757-1670, top reviews for this tiny café, $$$ • *Arturo's Ristorante,* 411 Chandler Street, Worcester, 755-5640, tops in town for Italian, $$ • *El Morocco,* 100 Wall Street, Worcester, 756-7117, Lebanese fare and live jazz, $$ • *Legal Sea Foods,* One Exchange Place, Worcester, 792-1600, $$–$$$$.

SIGHTSEEING *Old Sturbridge Village,* Route 20, Sturbridge 01566, 347-3362. "Dinner in a Country Village," Saturday nights at 5 P.M. December through March, limited to 14 people, minimum age 14, reservations required, approximately $50 per person. Daytime hours: November to April, Tuesday to Sunday and Monday holidays, 10 A.M. to 4 P.M.; rest of year, daily 9 A.M. to 5 P.M. Adults, $15; ages 6 to 15, $7.50; under 6, free; tickets are good for two days' admission • *Willard House and Clock Museum, Inc.,* 11 Willard Street, Grafton, 839-3500. Hours: Tuesday to Saturday, 10 A.M. to 4 P.M.; Sunday, 1 P.M. to 5 P.M. Adults, $3; under 12, $1 • *Worcester Art Museum,* 55 Salisbury Street, 799-4406. Hours: Tuesday to Friday, 11 A.M. to 4 P.M.; Saturday, 10 A.M. to 5 P.M.; Sunday, 1 P.M. to 5 P.M. Adults, $5; students, $3; under 14, free • *New England Science Center,* 222 Harrington Way, Worcester, 791-9211. Hours: Monday to Saturday, 10 A.M. to 5 P.M.; Sunday 12 P.M. to 5 P.M. Adults, $6; ages 3 to 16, $4 • *Wachusett Mountain State Reservation,* Princeton, 464-2712; phone for ski conditions and current rates.

INFORMATION Sturbridge Area Tourist Association, PO Box 66, Route 20, Sturbridge, MA 01566, 347-7594; Central Massachusetts Tourist Council, Inc., 850 Mechanics Tower, Worcester, MA 01608, 753-2920.

Happy Landings in Salisbury

They fly through the air with the greatest of ease, those graceful ski jumpers in Salisbury, Connecticut.

Ever since 1926 the best of these daring young people, including many of our top Olympic contenders, have shown off their style each year in early February at the United States Eastern Ski Jump Championships, held at Salisbury's Satre Hill.

Even the most sedentary spectator will appreciate the extraordinary coordination and skill required to make a 55-meter jump with a happy landing. Sports enthusiasts and firesiders alike will also appreciate the many cozy inns and other attractions of this particularly charming corner of the state.

Northwest Connecticut is Currier and Ives country, set in the rolling foothills of the Berkshire Mountains and blessed with a string of picture-pretty Colonial towns. It has long attracted writers and artists, but though the area now has also been well discovered by wealthy New Yorkers looking for vacation homes, it has escaped any obvious kind of commercialization. Except for inflated real estate prices and the appearance of such items as gourmet pasta and cheese in local grocery stores, villages such as Salisbury, Sharon, and Lakeville retain the unspoiled air that attracted the newcomers in the first place.

This is also ideal country for anyone who wants to learn to ski, either downhill or cross-country, with low-key Mohawk Mountain a few miles south in Cornwall offering excellent facilities without the hassles found at the bigger areas farther north. This area is so civilized that the ski lodge even hangs up potted plants and provides a library of books for nonskiers. There are extensive snowmaking facilities to help ensure the necessary white stuff on the slopes, as well as miles of cross-country trails in the adjacent state forest.

The Ski Jump Championship, a one-of-a-kind event in the East, is held both Saturday and Sunday from 11:00 A.M. Saturday's jump is the annual Salisbury Invitational, Sunday's, the official Eastern competition. The old 217-foot record may already have been bettered by this time.

In their slick, skin-tight jumpsuits, with special light boots, bindings, and skis, the jumpers are a thrilling sight as they leap off into space. All it takes is some watching to begin to understand the standards that go into making a champion. In addition to the length of the jump, the bend of the body, the position of the skis, the spring of the takeoff, and the grace of the landing are all calculated by the judges before each competitor is given a score.

Even with the coffee or hot chocolate served at a convenient stand, a

couple of hours in the cold is enough for most viewers, so there is
plenty of time to explore Salisbury and some of the surrounding towns.

Don't expect rows of shops, however. The lack of such touristy
sights is one of this area's chief delights. There is just enough to keep
you occupied for a pleasant hour in town and to give you an excuse to
tour some of the nearby territory.

Right in the village, you'll find the Salisbury Antiques Center on
Library Street, just off Route 44, with an interesting and eclectic
selection. Serious antiquers should proceed north on Route 7 across
the Massachusetts state line to Sheffield, where every other house on
the main street seems to have blossomed into an antiques shop.

Other stops in Salisbury are Garlande Limited, where selection of
heirloom Christmas tree decorations is the specialty of a store "where
every day is Christmas," and Lauray, on Undermoun-tain Road, a top
source for cacti and succulent plants, in person or by mail. Chaiwalla
is the place to sample exotic teas, then buy your own to take home.
You can also have a delicious light lunch in the tea room.

For more fine teas, walk directly across the street from Chaiwalla
to the real estate office, and in the front room you'll find a surprise:
a selection of teas from Harney & Sons, Ltd., who supply some of
the finest restaurants in the country. The teas are brewed right in the
back room.

Go back on Route 41 and take Route 44 west to Lakeville, home
of the prestigious Hotchkiss School and a few upscale shops. Or you
can follow Route 44 east into East Canaan for the Connecticut
Woodcarvers' Gallery, a shop featuring hand-carved birds, animals,
clocks, frames, and other objects done by some 14 professional
wood-carvers. If you don't see what you want, they'll carve it to
order for you.

Drive farther east on Route 44 into Norfolk to discover one of the
prettiest towns around, complete with village green, church steeples,
shuttered Colonial houses, and a mansion in the middle of town that
serves as summer quarters for the Yale School of Music. When snow is
on the ground, there are ten miles of groomed cross-country ski trails
at the Blackberry River Inn. No snow? Check out the current art
exhibit in the handsome 1889 library building here, and then mark
Norfolk down as a place to return for summer concerts.

Continue east to Winsted if you want to visit Folkcraft Instruments,
which features handcrafted harps, dulcimers, and psalteries. The
owners claim they'll teach you to play the dulcimer in ten minutes—
15 for slow learners. There are interesting records and books here also
in this folk music center.

Then take Route 20 north and you'll arrive in Riverton, once known
as Hitchcockville for the factory that opened here in 1826, where
Lambert Hitchcock produced the famous painted and stenciled chairs
that bear his name. A collection of the originals can be seen in the

Hitchcock Museum in an old church in the center of town, open April through December. Chairs are still made in the factory, using many of the original hand procedures, and new models of the old patterns are for sale at the showroom and shop adjoining the factory.

Riverton offers some other interesting shopping as well. Antiques and Herbs of Riverton offers old and new baskets, bears, antiques, and herbs. Handcrafts in pewter, pottery, porcelain, glass, wood, and fiber are to be found at the Contemporary Crafts Gallery. You'll also find a Seth Thomas factory outlet here, where you can get good buys on mantel, wall, and grandfather clocks from America's oldest clock maker.

Riverton is home to one of Connecticut's oldest inns, as well, a good bet for a meal or an overnight stay. Other traditional inn lodgings are to be found in Salisbury and Norfolk, and Lakeville's Interlaken Inn is a mini-resort, often with attractive packages for skiers at Mohawk Mountain and at the Catamount ski area just across the state line. If your idea of a winter weekend means cuddling by the fire, most of the inns can oblige you with the proper setting.

If you have more touring time after the ski-jump competitions on Sunday, drive south about 25 miles from Salisbury on Route 7 and then Route 63 to Litchfield, a town that is invariably high on the list of most beautiful Main Streets in New England. You'll probably recognize the Congregational Church on the green, since it shows up in countless magazine photos of New England scenes. Next door is the 1787 parsonage where Harriet Beecher Stowe was born. The extraordinarily fine homes here are still occupied, some by descendants of the original occupants. Take a walk or a slow drive on North and South streets to see the handsome early architecture, and make special note of the little house on South where Tapping Reeve opened the nation's first law school in 1773, with his brother-in-law, Aaron Burr, as his first pupil. The fine collections of the Litchfield Historical Society are closed in winter, but there are many art galleries that make for pleasant browsing. The West Street Grill on the green is one of the best in the state, highly recommended for a lunch or dinner stop.

Litchfield's White Memorial Foundation offers 35 miles of cross-country skiing trails for those who want to make the most of the wintry weather. Ski rentals are available at the Wilderness Shop on Route 202, about a mile from the foundation property.

Or follow Route 202 west out of Litchfield to Bantam Lake to end your winter outing by watching yet another speedy sport, for this is the home course for the Connecticut Ice Yachting Club. Up to 30 boats gather here every weekend for this unusual activity, which requires just the kind of winter conditions most of us try to avoid—high winds and frigid temperatures. The hardy competitors seem to find the thrills and speed ample compensation, however, and when conditions are right, it's not unusual to see a DN-60 or Skeeter-class boat skimming along at up to 100 miles an hour. It's great fun to watch—just be sure to dress for the weather.

Area Code: 203

DRIVING DIRECTIONS Salisbury is on Route 44, reached via Route 7 from the east and Route 22 from the west. Salisbury is about 150 miles from Boston, 103 miles from New York, and 65 miles from Hartford.

PUBLIC TRANSPORTATION Bonanza bus service to Canaan, Connecticut, a few miles from Salisbury.

ACCOMMODATIONS Ask about weekend and ski packages. *Under Mountain Inn,* Undermountain Road (Route 41), Salisbury 06068, 435-0242, attractive 1700s home, warm hosts, $$$$ MAP • *The White Hart,* Village Green, Salisbury 06968, 435-0030, longtime local landmark and gathering place, $$–$$$$ • *Yesterday's Yankee,* Route 44, Salisbury 06068, 435-9539, Cape Cod cottage B & B, $–$$ CP • *Interlaken Inn,* Route 122, Lakeville 06039, 435-9878, modern resort with Victorian inn lodgings also on grounds, indoor sauna and Jacuzzi, ice skating nearby, $$–$$$ • *Wake Robin Inn,* Route 41, Lakeville 06039, 435-2515, $$$$ CP, former private school turned-inn, nicely furnished but some rooms are quite small, ask for a large room, $$ CP • *Mountain View Inn,* Route 272, Norfolk 06058, 542-6991, homey Victorian, $–$$$ CP • *Manor House,* PO Box 701, Maple Avenue, Norfolk 06058, 542-5690, showplace Victorian, $$$–$$$$ CP • *Greenwoods Gate,* Greenwoods Road East, Norfolk 06058, 542-5439, stylishly furnished Colonial, $$$$–$$$$$ CP • *Old Riverton Inn,* Route 20, Riverton 06065, 379-8678 or (800) EST-1796, atmospheric 1796 Colonial, $–$$ CP • *Tollgate Hill,* Route 202, Litchfield 06759, 482-6116, attractive decor in 1700s Colonial, $$$–$$$$.

DINING *Under Mountain Inn* (see above), British specialties, $$–$$$ • *The White Hart* (see above), cozy ambience $$$; Tap Room, informal meals, $$ • *Savarin,* Wake Robin Inn (see above), good reviews, $$$ • *The Pub and Restaurant,* Station Place, Norfolk, 542-5716, informal, $–$$ • *Woodlands,* Route 41, Lakeville, 435-0578, casual, popular locally, good bet for Sunday brunch, $–$$ • *Cannery Café,* 85 Main Street, Route 44, Canaan, 824-7333, decorated with canning jars, Cajun and other good things on the menu, $–$$$ • *Mountain View Inn* (see above), $$–$$$ • *Old Riverton Inn* (see above), $$ • *West Street Grill,* 43 West Street, Litchfield, 567-3885, $$–$$$ • *Tollgate Hill* (see above), Colonial ambience, traditional menu, $$–$$$.

SIGHTSEEING   *U.S. Eastern Ski Jumping Championships,* two days, usually first weekend in February, single tickets or combination for both days. Write to Salisbury Winter Sports Association, Salisbury, CT 06068, for current dates and ticket prices, or contact Chamber of Commerce • **Skiing:** *Mohawk Mountain Ski Area,* Route 4, Cornwall, 672-6464.

INFORMATION   Litchfield Hills Travel Council, PO Box 968, Litchfield, CT 06759, 567-4506.

Wintering in the White Mountains

Winter is the magic season in the White Mountains of New Hampshire.

Well-paved roads lead through mountain passes beneath imposing peaks that are all the more beautiful under winter coats of white. The snow adds its crowning softness to the tall pines and maples in the pristine national forests that surround the mountains and to the rooftops and greens in tiny roadside villages where skaters on the ponds make living Grandma Moses scenes.

The stupendous scenery, unmatched in the East, plus the great variety of activities and facilities available in the White Mountains, make New England's highest peaks the peak choice for couples or families who have differing abilities or enthusiasm for the ski slopes.

Whatever your winter pleasure, you'll find it here. Skiers can take their turns at more than half a dozen nearby slopes for all abilities; ski tourers have miles and miles of exquisite cross-country trails from which to choose. There's also ample opportunity for such pastimes as sledding, tobogganing, snowshoeing, and ice skating. And for indoor challenge, the North Conway bargains await—a whopping total of some 150 discount outlets in the general area.

The unsurpassed setting makes many people content to spend a weekend just driving the scenic highways, riding the mountain cable cars for the views, or simply settling in before the fireplace at a cozy inn and enjoying the view from a picture window.

For those who do come to ski, White Mountain loyalists claim that the sport here still has an old-fashioned, no-frills flavor that is missing in the slicker, newer areas. Tradition is strong, after all, and northeastern skiing was born in these mountains. Norwegian immigrants were skiing here as early as the 1870s, and the first American Alpine ski school, started in the 1920s by Austrian champion Sig Buchmayr, made Franconia the Northeast's first great winter resort.

The boom continued when the first aerial tramway was built at Cannon Mountain in 1938, and prospered even further when Austrian Hannes Schneider came to North Conway in 1939 and built the first skimobile, which is still on display at Mount Cranmore. It adds a certain quirky charm to the scene, and is a treasured sight for families who are into a third generation of skiing here, enjoying modern amenities such as night skiing and a triple chair to the summit. Cranmore is homey, has 100 percent snow-making coverage, and is within walking distance of North Conway, all good reasons why it still appeals to families.

There are many other ski areas in the White Mountains, with something for just about everyone. In the North Conway–Jackson area, Wildcat, located near Mount Washington and legendary for its howling winds, is a challenging mountain. Though known for its long trails and views, it also has a separate beginner area with its own triple chairlift, a real bargain since the skiing here is free. A recent third-floor addition to the base lodge offers sit-down dining and spectacular views of Tuckerman's Ravine and the Presidential Range.

Bretton Woods is small but growing, gentler than Wildcat, and also prides itself on spectacular views. A "super chair" high-speed quad lift was recently installed, with a restaurant at the top with spectacular vistas. Black Mountain, another family area, has its own bit of history— the first overhead cable tow in America, built in 1935. Half of the mountain is teaching or novice terrain.

Newer Attitash offers 28 trails with extensive snowmaking and grooming operations. Purchased in 1994 by Sunday River, the area is undergoing major expansion.

Across the mountains in Franconia, Cannon Mountain, owned by the state, is the largest ski resort in the area with 35 trails, nine of them for experts but plenty left for everyone else, and 50 miles of nearby ski-touring trails past scenery that may tempt you to trade your ski poles for a paintbrush. The mountain boasts New Hampshire's only aerial tramway. Cannon remains an unspoiled world of white—no condos or commercial development in sight.

The New England Ski Museum at Cannon features audiovisual exhibits showing some early skiers in action, and displays of the wooden skis belonging to Sig Buchmayr and other adventurers such as Lowell Thomas. Other displays include the progression of skis and ski clothing from the nineteenth century to today, plus ski art and photos.

To the south are two newer complexes that don't quite fit the old-fashioned mold. The Mountain Club on Loon has the distinction of being the only ski resort with an operating steam train; it shuttles skiers between two base complexes. Loon also boasts a high-speed gondola, good intermediate slopes, and a resort complex with its own lodge.

Waterville Valley, with two mountains and trails for all abilities, is a chic resort that is a village in itself, with hundreds of condominiums, a sports center, restaurants, and some very choice inns. Waterville is a convenient choice for families, since a bus makes the rounds from village accommodations to the slopes regularly, allowing parents to sleep in while their kids get to be first on the trails. Sleigh rides and ice skating add to the fun. Waterville recently added snow-making to a cross-country loop, guaranteeing good conditions.

For cross-country skiing, Cannon and Bretton Woods take the prize for mountain scenery, but Jackson, one of the prettiest of the White Mountain villages, offers the largest ski-touring complex in the East, run by the Jackson Ski Touring Foundation and offering lessons and 150 kilometers of trails for all abilities. Experts can try their mettle on the Wildcat Valley Trail, which begins at the top of Wildcat Mountain and then swoops down 3,400 feet to meet the rest of the trail system. At Bretton Woods, cross-country skiers can take the quad chairlift for lunch at the Top O'Quad restaurant and a five-mile intermediate descent on the Mountain Road trail.

The Mount Washington Valley Ski Touring Foundation in Intervale, north of North Conway, also offers 60 kilometers of trails that link nine small inns to Mt. Cranmore.

The accommodations are as extensive as the skiing choices, ranging from lodges on the slopes to resorts to secluded country inns.

When you're settled in and the skiers are happily challenging the slopes, nonskiers will want to take the "scenic tour." From North Conway, the recommended route is the drive along Route 16 north to Pinkham Notch, then down to Conway and west on the magnificent 32-mile Kancamagus Highway, through the White Mountain National Forest from Cannon to Lincoln. At Lincoln, take Route 3 north to Franconia Notch State Park.

Franconia Notch is a natural mountain pass between the towering peaks of the Kinsman and Franconia ranges, with some of the most spectacular scenery in the White Mountains. Here's where you'll meet the symbol of New Hampshire, the "Old Man of the Mountain," that famous face carved in granite on the mountainside by some celestial sculptor.

The views and picture-book villages continue north on Route 18 to Sugar Hill, then back down and west on Route 3 to connect with Route 302 at Twin Mountain for the drive back to North Conway, past Bretton Woods and Crawford Notch.

Shopping is the thing in North Conway. If you need ski equipment or outdoor clothing, you won't do better than the Jack Frost, Eastern Mountain Sports, and International Mountain Equipment and Ragged Mountain Equipment stores here. There are good buys at outlet stores for Patagonia outdoor wear, for down jackets, and at the L.L. Bean, Banana Republic, and Eddie Bauer clothing stores, plus well-stocked shops at each ski area.

Check the Scottish Lion for a fine selection of wares and choice sweaters from Scotland, Ireland, England, and Wales. You'll also find casual clothing, country collectibles, and a few art galleries and antiques shops to explore on Main Street (Route 16). Among the larger antiques shops are the Antiques & Collectibles Barn and North Conway Antiques & Collectibles, both group shops featuring a variety of dealers. The League of New Hampshire Craftsmen Shop in North Conway is always worth a look for their fine selection of work by state artisans.

For bargains, there are outlet stores galore in North Conway, including Anne Klein, Calvin Klein, Barbizon, Cole-Hahn, Corning, Danskin, Donna Karan, Levi's, London Fog, Oshkosh, Gorham, J. Crew, Liz Claiborne, Polo/Ralph Lauren, Seiko, and Timberland. And just a few miles farther in Conway, Hathaway, Bass, Cannon Mills, Lenox, White Stag, and other outlet stores await.

Between skiing, scenery, and shopping, the days fly by. Come dinner hour, there are more fine choices than can ever be fit into one weekend.

For après ski, try the Wildcat Tavern in Jackson Village, the Red Parka Pub in Glen, or in North Conway, the Up Country Saloon, Horsefeathers, or Barnaby's.

Day or night, about the only thing you may find lacking in the White Mountains is time to do justice to the cornucopia of winter pleasures.

Area Code: 603

DRIVING DIRECTIONS North Conway and Jackson in the Mount Washington Valley are reached via Route 16 or 302, connecting from I-95. Franconia is on Route I-93/3; Waterville Valley is reached via I-93 to Exit 28, then 11 miles to Route 49 to the valley. North Conway is 145 miles from Boston, 335 miles from New York, and 245 miles from Hartford; Franconia and Waterville are roughly 15 miles closer.

PUBLIC TRANSPORTATION Concord Trailways has bus service to Conway and Jackson, air service to Portsmouth (1½ hours) or Manchester (2 hours), New Hampshire, or Portland, Maine, 1½ hours.

ACCOMMODATIONS In addition to inns listed for Mt. Washington Valley on pages 97–98, and Franconia on pages 190–191, the following are convenient for ski areas; ask about weekend and ski week packages. *Bretton Woods Area,* Bretton Woods 03575, 278-1000 or (800) 258-0330, includes: *The Bretton Woods Motor Inn,* indoor pool, sauna, Jacuzzi, $$; *Bretton Woods* condos, $$$$–$$$$$; and *Bretton Arms,* a bed-and-breakfast inn, $$–$$$ CP • *Attitash Mountain Village,* Bartlett 03812, 374-6501, indoor pool, game room, ice skating, snowmobiling; slopeside motel, $–$$, condos, $$–$$$ • *Whitney's Inn at Black Mountain,* Jackson 03846, 383-8916, ice skating, convenient to the mountain, $$–$$$$ CP; $$$$ MAP • *The Mill House Inn,* Route 112, Lincoln 03251, 745-6261 or (800) 654-6183, attractive hotel, indoor pool, exercise room, free shuttle to the mountain, rooms, $–$$, suites, $$–$$$; also part of The Mill development, with similar rates and free ski shuttles, are the *Rivergreen Resort Hotel,* with in-room Jacuzzis and suites with kitchens, 745-2450 or (800) 654-6183, and the *Lodge at Lincoln Station,* with an indoor pool, 745-3441 or (800) 654-6188 • *The Mountain Club on Loon,* Kancamagus Highway, Lincoln 03251, 745-8111 or (800) 229-STAY, whirlpool, exercise equipment, squash, racquetball; rooms, $$$; studios, $$$$; suites and condos on the mountain, $$$$–$$$$$ • *Waterville Valley Lodging Bureau,* Waterville Valley 03215, 236-8311 or (800) GO-VALLEY, upscale condos or modern inns with indoor pools, saunas, Jacuzzis, etc., ice skating, sleigh rides, sports club; excellent package rates, kids free; condos, $$–$$$$; *Snowy Owl Inn,* $$–$$$$; *Black Bear Lodge,* suites, $$$–$$$$; *Golden Eagle Lodge,* $$$–$$$$; and *Valley Inn,* $$$–$$$$ (MAP in winter) • *Mittersill Alpine Resort,* Mittersill Road, Franconia 03580, 823-5511, chalet-style resort one mile from Cannon, indoor pool, sleigh rides, tobogganing; hotel, $; efficiencies, $$; one-bedroom units, $$$; two bedrooms, $$$$ • The homey *Cranmore Mt. Lodge,* Kearsarge Road, North Conway 03860, 356-2044, $–$$ CP; the classic New England *Franconia Inn,* Easton Road (Route 116), Franconia 03580, 823-5542 or (800) 473-5299; $$–$$$ CP; and the elegant Victorian *Nestlenook Inn,* PO Box Q, Dinsmore Road, Jackson 03846, 383-8071, $$$$–$$$$$ CP, have their own ski-touring trails as well as ice skating. Franconia Inn and Nestlenook offer sleigh rides as well. Free reservation service for the Mt. Washington Valley: (800) 367-3364.

DINING   See Mt. Washington Valley, page 98; and Franconia, page 191.

SIGHTSEEING   *New England Ski Museum,* next to Cannon Mountain Tram, PO Box 267, Franconia, 823-7177. Hours: daily except Wednesday, late December through March and late May to mid-October, noon to 5 P.M. Free • **Ski areas (write for trail maps and current rates):** *Attitash,* Route 302, Bartlett 03812, 374-2368 or (800) 223-SNOW for lodging; *Black Mountain,* Jackson 03846, 383-4490 or (800) 677-5737; *Mt. Cranmore,* off Route 302/16, North Conway 03860, 356-5543 or (800) SUN-N-SKI; *Wildcat,* Route 16, Jackson/

Pinkham Notch, 466-3326 or (800) 255-6439; *Bretton Woods,* Route 302, Bretton Woods 03575, 278-5000 or (800) 258-0330 in the Northeast; *Loon Mountain,* Lincoln, 745-8111 or (800) 229-STAY; *Cannon Mountain,* Route 3, Franconia, 823-7771 or (800) 227-4191; *Waterville Valley,* Waterville Valley 03215, 236-8371 or (800) 468-2553 • **Cross-country skiing:** *Jackson Ski Touring Foundation,* Jackson, 383-9355 or (800) XC-SNOWS; *Mt. Washington Valley Ski Touring Foundation,* Route 16A, Intervale 03845, 356-9920; *Inn-to-Inn Cross Country Touring* (800) 448-3534.

INFORMATION Mount Washington Valley Chamber of Commerce, Route 16, PO Box 2300, North Conway, NH 03860, 356-31711 or (800) 367-3364; Franconia-Sugar Hill Chamber of Commerce, Franconia, NH 03580, 823-5661 or (800) 237-9007. For New Hampshire ski information, and free regional guide: Ski New Hampshire, PO Box 10, North Woodstock, NH 03262, 745-9396 or (800) 88-SKI-NH.

Back to Nature in Bethel

When a noted Cleveland surgeon, Dr. John Gehring, suffered a nervous breakdown in 1887, he came to the peaceful New England village of Bethel, Maine, to recover.

The cure worked so well that Gehring opened a pioneering clinic in Bethel, and it soon became famous. Many prominent people came to regain their health and good spirits with a program that combined outdoor activities such as planting crops and cutting wood with contemplating the beauty of the surrounding forests and mountains.

The formula still works. Visitors these days are more likely to get their exercise hiking or skiing, but for a restorative weekend close to nature, it's hard to beat this beautiful corner of western Maine.

For skiers, the excellent snowmaking and vast variety of trails at Sunday River, New England's fastest growing ski resort, may prove to be a rejuvenating experience in themselves. The resort recently launched the first ski train in the East, the Sunday River Bullet Ski Express between Portland and Bethel, a boon for those who don't like driving in winter weather. A new train station goes up in 1995, and a major new shopping complex including a hotel is projected to follow, extending the classic New England center of Bethel.

The history of this handsome Colonial town of 2,500 goes back much farther than Dr. Gehring's day, and much of it can be revisited on a walk through the old town. Bethel was founded in 1774 as Sudbury, Canada, after the original grantees from Sudbury, Massachusetts, all of whom had fought in the campaign to conquer Canada. The early sawmills and farms along the Androscoggin River prospered after the Revolutionary War, and in 1796 the town was incorporated as Bethel, a biblical name meaning "House of God."

With the arrival of the railway, wood products became (and remain) an important factor in the town's economy. The trains also brought the first summer visitors to enjoy the town's extraordinary setting in the White Mountain foothills.

The 1836 founding of Gould Academy, one of Maine's oldest prep schools, brought notice to the town. Later, the residency of William Rogers Chapman, an outstanding musician who attracted many of the nation's music greats to visit, and the 1947 arrival of the National Training Laboratories with their experimental human relations and leadership programs, further helped give Bethel a prominence beyond its size.

Much of the center of Bethel is now a National Historic District marking the early landmarks. Stroll down to the end of the aptly named Broad Street and you can see Dr. Gehring's original clinic, an 1896 Queen Anne home that is presently the headquarters of the National Training Laboratories.

It was Dr. Gehring and one of his patients, William Bingham II, who in 1913 built the Bethel Inn on the choice spot facing the long town common. The inn presently consists of the old main building and a series of surrounding 1800s residences bought up over the years for additional lodging space. It isn't as formal or as elegant as it once was, but it is still attractive, with big warming fireplaces and picture windows in the dining room and main lounges that look out on an evergreen-rimmed golf course and the White Mountains beyond. In winter, the course is a perfect place for cross-country skiers. The inn offers 22 miles of trails connecting to some of the many other touring trails in the area, plus a sauna to ease aching muscles when tired skiers come home. It also hosts a touring center with rental and instruction open to all. And if you stay at the inn, you can splash around in an out-door pool heated to 91 degrees, a treat when the world around you is covered with snow.

Everyone is invited to enjoy ice skating on the community pond just off the common.

Around the common are some classic clapboard mansions such as the 1848 Greek Revival Major Gideon Hastings House, built by the founder of one of western Maine's timberland and lumbering dynasties, and the Moses Mason House, the circa 1813, Federal-style home of one of the town's leading early residents. The Mason House is now a museum of eight period rooms restored by the Bethel Historical Society. Though it is generally open in winter only by appointment, during the annual February Heritage Day celebration the house hosts special tours and demonstrations of old-time crafts.

One of the other attractive homes on the common is the Hammons House, now an appealing bed-and-breakfast inn.

The handsome Gould Academy campus at the other end of town includes the James B. Owen Art Gallery, which is open from nine to three on weekdays and on weekend afternoons. The white-spired West Parish Congregational Church near the school housed the congregation led by Reverend Daniel Gould, a teacher and pastor, for whom the academy was named.

Having seen the sights of Bethel, skiers will want to make haste north on Route 26 to Sunday River. From its beginnings as a community ski area, Sunday River has grown to include six peaks, 101 trails, 14 lifts including five triple and seven quad chairs, and more than 570 acres of skiing, with 90 percent snowmaking coverage. These days, you need never leave the mountain for lodging or dining variety. Among many recent additions are a slopeside condominium hotel, more condos, and the Spruce Peak lodge with food service at the summit between North and Spruce Peaks. Après-ski fun and food ranges from Bumps!, a sports pub, to a variety of fine dining.

In addition to Sunday River's welcoming youngsters with special attention on the slopes, après-ski on weekends and holidays also includes the kids, who can enjoy sledding, games, ski movies, and more at Camp Sunday River (for ages seven and up). Teens have their own supervised club, MVP's (Music, Video, and Pizza) with a pizza bar and a live deejay. Getting around the complex is easy, with trolley service that covers the parking areas, base lodges, and most condo complexes. Special family evenings each week include activities such as ice skating by a bonfire, horse-drawn sleigh rides, and fireworks.

Yet even as it grows, Sunday River is careful to maintain the reputation that made its success—friendly spirit and quick and efficient lift lines. Any wait over seven minutes brings a cash rebate on your next ticket.

Cross-country ski enthusiasts will also find a center on the Sunday River access road with 40 kilometers of trails.

South of Bethel are Mount Abram, five miles from town on Route 26, and Shawnee Peak, a bit farther in Bridgton, both low-key family areas with very reasonable rates.

There's some interesting shopping on Bethel's Main Street. Bonnema Potters produces stoneware and porcelain in rich multi-colors. If you drop in at a shop called Mt. Mann, gemologist Jim Mann will show off some of the treasures from nearby quarries that make the Bethel area a summer favorite with rock hounds. Maine Line Products has everything from birdhouses to pine furniture made in the state, and True North is the place to pick up outdoor apparel and travel gear. Mountain Side Country Crafts on the Sunday River access road specializes in Maine-made handcrafts.

A tour of other towns in the area will bring you to more small shops and some lovely winter scenery. Bridgton, Harrison, and Naples offer tempting stops for antiquers, and Bridgton has several fine crafts galleries as well. There's a dazzling gem display at Perham's in West Paris, with quarries nearby that can be visited.

If your travels take you to Lynchville, south of Bethel on Route 35, you can photograph the famous road sign leading to such faraway places as Norway, Paris, Denmark, Naples, Poland, Peru, and China, all of them nearby villages in Maine.

While you are driving, be sure to include the perfect little Colonial hamlet of Waterford in your travels, another good prospect for lodging with three exceptional small inns to choose from.

Generally, all is peaceful in these little towns, but there's a bit of excitement during Western Maine Winter Wonderland Week held in late January or early February, highlighted by daily hot air balloon lifts from the Sunday River ski area (weather permitting, of course). Whether you ride the balloons or just watch them soar, it's a beautiful experience.

Area Code: 207

DRIVING DIRECTIONS   Bethel is about 70 miles northwest of Portland and its airport. It can be reached via Route 26 from the Gray exit of the Maine Turnpike or from the west via Route 2, which connects to I-91 at St. Johnsbury, Vermont. It is 175 miles from Boston, 385 miles from New York, and 275 miles from Hartford.

PUBLIC TRANSPORTATION   Closest air service is Portland, 70 miles away. Sunday River has been trying out a ski train from Portland.

ACCOMMODATIONS   *Bethel Inn & Country Club,* Bethel 04217, 824-2175, $$$$–$$$$$ MAP; ask about weekend packages • *Hammons House,* Broad Street, PO Box 16, Bethel 04217, 824-3170, sunny, spacious 1859 home on the common, $–$$ CP • *L'Auberge,* PO Box 21, Bethel 04217, 824-2774, simple secluded village inn, $$ CP • *Sudbury Inn,* PO Box 521, Bethel 04217, 824-2174, unpretentious, reasonable village inn with a good dining room, $–$$$ CP • *Holidae House,* Main Street, Bethel 04217, 824-3400, Victorian, filled with antiques for sale, $–$$$ CP • *Chapman Inn,* on the common, Bethel 04217, 824-2657, 1865 home, informal, $$ CP; dorm for skiers, $ CP • *Sunday River Ski Resort,* Sunday River 04217, 824-2187 or (800) 543-2SKI, includes: *Summit Hotel,* luxury slopeside condo-hotel, heated outdoor pool, rooms and studios, $$$–$$$$; *Sunday River Condominiums,* family-pleasing units offering heated indoor pools, game rooms, and laundry facilities, include Fall Line, Cascades, and Sunrise, one-bedroom units sleeping four, $$$–$$$$$; *Snow Cap Ski Dorm,* budget-priced five- and eight-person bunkrooms with private baths, $ • *Sunday River Inn,* RFD 2, Box 1688, Bethel 04217, 824-2410, ski lodge and dorm at cross-country ski center, $$$ MAP (including skiing); dormitory bunks, $ CP • *Philbrook Farm Inn,* off Route 2, Shelburne, NH 03581 (603) 466-3831, cozy farmhouse not far from Bethel, on 100 acres with its own cross-country trails, $$$ MAP • Waterford accommodations, see page 176 • **Bethel Area Reservation Service:** For all lodgings (800) 442-5826.

DINING *Bethel Inn & Country Club* (see above), $$ • *Mother's,* Upper Main Street, Bethel, 824-2589, cozy ambience and good food in a village home, $–$$ • *Sudbury Inn* (see above), restaurant, $$, and *Suds Pub,* $ • *L'Auberge* (see above), Italian, $$ • *Center Lovell Inn,* Route 5, Center Lovell, 925-1575, northern Italian specialties, $$ • *Maurice,* Main Street (Route 26), South Paris, 743-2532, continental menu, $$ • *Olde Rowley Inn,* Route 35, North Waterford, 583-4143, charming former 1790 stagecoach station, French cuisine, $–$$ • *Moose's Tale at Sunday River Brewing Company,* Route 2 and Sunday River Road, 824-4ALE, brew-pub and restaurant serving steak to pizza, $–$$ • **Sunday River Ski Area restaurants:** *Legends,* 824-3500, fine dining, $$; *Walsh and Hill Trading Company and Restaurant,* 824-3000, steaks, lobster, $–$$; *Rosetto's Ristorante,* Italian fare and steak, $–$$; *Saturday's Tavern,* informal, $; for après-ski: *Bumps! Pub,* entertainment, informal menu, $ • Also see Waterford and Bridgton dining, page 176.

SKI AREAS All have both downhill and cross-country: *Sunday River Ski Resort,* Route 26, six miles north of Bethel, 824-2187 or (800) 543-2SKI • *Sunday River Cross-Country Ski Center,* Sunday River Access Road, RFD #2, Box 1688, Bethel 04217, 824-3181 • *Mount Abram Ski Slopes,* Route 26, Locke Mills (five miles south of Bethel), 875-2601 • *Shawnee Peak Ski Area* at Pleasant Mountain, Mountain Road off Route 302, Bridgton, 647-8444.

INFORMATION Greater Bethel Chamber of Commerce, PO Box 121, Bethel, ME 04217, 824-2282.

Beyond the Mansions in Newport

Newport, Rhode Island, is a town with multiple personalities.

There's the opulent Newport, summer bastion of the superwealthy, evidenced by some of the grandest mansions in the country.

There's the nautical Newport, easy to discern in summer by the dozens of yachts in the harbor and enough visitors clad in Top-Siders to sink a ship. The old wharfs have bloomed anew with restaurants and shops to accommodate all the sailors plus the army of landlubbers who join them on warm-weather weekends, giving rise to the touristy Newport.

And then there is the Newport that tends to get lost in all the tourist activity—a town of rare scenic beauty. It is seen best on the spectacular ten-mile Ocean Drive along a clifftop overlooking the sea and on the Cliff Walk along the bluffs.

And don't forget Colonial Newport, a town of enormous charm whose narrow old streets have undergone one of the most impressive restorations in the country.

In the quiet off-season when the harbor is still, it is these last and sometimes neglected aspects of Newport that shine through. And with the mansions and many other attractions still open for sightseeing and the shops and restaurants still very much in business, there's plenty of activity when you want it. Add the drama of wintry winds that send waves dashing against the cliffs and you have a winning winter getaway.

In fact, there's more reason to come out of season every year, because Newport is changing. You can see it as soon as you enter town to be greeted by the big Gateway Transportation and Visitors Center, with a 16-screen multimedia presentation and space to handle the thousands who jam the picturesque streets in summer. There's enough room in back for a fleet of tour buses. Winter is really the only time you can appreciate the wonderful old charm that attracted so many in the first place. It's also a chance to enjoy fine dining without waiting in long lines. To make things even nicer, lodging rates go way down.

The town has made things livelier in its slow season with a February Winter Festival that grows larger by the year. Horse-drawn hayrides, snow sculptures, an ice-carving competition, and a scavenger hunt through town are among over 100 events. One of the tastiest sides of this festival is food. A festival ticket entitles you to visit restaurants all around town who cooperate with samplings of their specialties from Southwestern ribs to New England clam chowder. Restaurants also feature dinner specials during festival week, including progressive dinners. Come evening, jazz concerts and candlelight tours of historic homes are on the agenda.

If Newport today seems to have more than its share of personalities, it may be because of the town's unusual past. It was founded in 1639 by settlers seeking religious freedom but soon prospered as a major seaport of the infamous "Triangle Trade"—actually an extension of the slave trade using African slaves to obtain West Indian sugar and molasses to be made into Newport rum. The pineapple, Newport's hospitality symbol, was first brought to town by sea captains returning from the West Indies, who placed the exotic fruit in front of the house to tell neighbors they were home safely and welcoming visitors.

Newport's era of prominence as a port ended when the British burned the harbor, once during the Revolutionary War and again during the War of 1812. Later it became a haunt of artists and writers taken with its natural beauty. They were followed in the late 1800s by the wealthy who put up the opulent palaces they called "cottages" to be used for a feverish six-week season that became the nation's most elaborate social scene.

Though many wealthy summer people remain, Newport's Gilded Age died out with changing times. The mansions survive as tourist attractions. The seven homes operated by the Newport Preservation Society currently draw a million visitors a year.

The building of a bridge connecting Newport to Jamestown in 1969 made it far more accessible for travelers; and the Newport Jazz Festival, born in the same period, brought even more crowds. Newport had gone public, and in 1973 when the Navy moved out of the base that had helped support the town economy, the city fathers began to encourage the trend further. The waterfront was restored, and shops and restaurants opened, attracting a seasonal flood of tourists.

During all this activity, a part-time resident, the late Doris Duke had begun to take interest in the many fine early eighteenth-century buildings that had been allowed to decay. She set up a foundation that renovated some six dozen of the houses, renting them at reasonable rates to residents who would appreciate and protect their heritage. Others followed suit, spreading the restoration area.

If you want to start your Newport tour chronologically, a stroll up the cobbled streets leading uphill from the town center and along the waterfront on Washington Street—the area known as The Point—will show you early Newport in a series of some 400 pastel-hued town houses that are perhaps the nation's most extensive collection of authentic Colonial dwellings. Washington Street has some particularly fine homes. You can rent a taped driving or walking tour at the Chamber of Commerce if you want to know more about the history of this area, as well as about the rest of the town.

Next, a tour on the well-marked Ocean Drive past the mansions and out on the bluffs will show you the views that attracted all those millionaires to Newport. If the weather is kind, stop off along Bellevue Avenue, bundle up, and follow some of the Cliff Walk, a $3^1/_2$-mile path along the top that gives you a rare perspective of lawns and mansions on one side and an eagle's-eye ocean view on the other.

By now you'll probably be dying to see the inside of the houses. If you think we had no royalty in America, you may well change your mind when you see the massive scale, the marble floors and chandeliers, and the priceless brocades of the summer palaces of America's upper crust.

Three of the finest of the houses remain open weekends for touring all year: Marble House, designed by Richard Morris Hunt for William K. Vanderbilt and named for the many colors of marble used in its construction and decorations; The Elms, a summer residence of Philadelphia coal magnate Edward Berwind, modeled after the Château d'Asnieres near Paris; and Château-sur-Mer, one of the most lavish examples of Victorian architecture and the site of Newport's first ballroom.

There are other mansions to be toured as well. Mrs. Astor's Beechwood takes you back to 1891, when Caroline Astor ruled as queen of American society, bringing the Gilded Age to life with lavish theatrical performances.

Back in town, everything centers on the harbor, where the first American navy was established in 1775 to provide protection against the British fleet. Along the restored wooden wharves, in old warehouses and new structures with Colonial-modern lines, is the touristy Newport with the usual assortment of shops to be found wherever visitors congregate.

At Bowen and Bannister wharves, right on the waterfront, there are clothes from the Greek Isles or Ireland, original gold and silver jewelry designs, handcrafted leather, children's clothing and toys, and a candy store noted for its homemade fudge. Across the street at the Brick Market Place, a cobbled maze of condominiums and shops, there is even more variety.

If antiquing is your goal, you'll find shops on lower Thames and on parallel Spring Street, as well as the side streets in between, particularly Franklin Street. Newport shop hours are irregular in the winter, so check the times for the stores that interest you or call for an appointment.

When it comes to lodgings, the town is now chock-a-block with choices. The coziest accommodations are the inns. Top choice for a romantic outlook is The Inn at Castle Hill on Ocean Drive. The rambling Victorian mansion has spacious rooms, an unmatched view of rocky coast, and a crackling fire downstairs to ward off winter chills.

There are many appealing smaller guest houses in the historic district. Among the best choices are the three "Admirals." My favorite is the modest Admiral Farragut Inn on Clarke Street, a quiet block that is just a stroll from all the action in town. The inn is filled with hand-made Shaker-style furniture, painted chests, hand-glazed walls, and whimsical original folk art murals. The Admiral Benbow, now an old-timer in rapidly changing Newport, still has loyal fans for its pretty rooms. The newer Admiral Fitzroy also has lots of hand-painted touches, this time in a Victorian mood.

The Francis Malbone House, a neighbor of the Fitzroy on Thames Street, is one of the most elegant lodgings, a 1760 mansion beautifully furnished in Federal style and with a lovely garden out back, a rarity in crowded Newport. One of the most authentic restorations is the 1751 John Banister House, filled with fine antiques and with a fireplace in every room. A delightful choice closer to the beach is Elm Tree Cottage, done in elegant country style by the artistic young innkeepers.

In The Point, the Sanford-Covell Villa Marina is a grand 1870s Victorian right on the water and with dazzling views. The Stella Maris Inn, a fine residence circa 1853, and the more intimate 1871 Sarah Kendall House are across the street but with their own views from the front bedrooms.

Excellent restaurants are plentiful. Some of the better ones are a bit on the formal side, so males should be prepared with jacket and tie.

If Saturday was filled with mansions and scenery, Sunday brings another set of Newport sights, mostly clustered around Touro Street and Bellevue Avenue. From the grand days, there is the Tennis Hall of Fame, located on Bellevue in the Old Newport Casino building, designed by Stanford White. Pass through the arch to see the fashionable resort that once was the epitome of recreation for the "cottage set," with lawn games, tennis and racket courts, and bowling alleys. You can try your hand at tennis here at the Casino Indoor Racquet Club or in summer on those gorgeous grass courts.

Touro Synagogue, a National Historic Site, is the oldest Jewish house of worship in the country, a sign of the religious freedom of the early Rhode Island colony. The building, dedicated in 1763, is a beautiful edifice designed by Peter Harrison, the nation's first architect, in Colonial style that has been carefully preserved. It is worth a visit for anyone interested in early American architecture.

In Queen Anne Square on Spring Street you can see Trinity Church, the first Anglican parish in the state, with Tiffany windows, an organ tested by Handel, and the silver service and bell dating from its dedication in 1726. The Second Congregational Church on Clarke Street is another early building, commissioned in 1735 and attended by many prominent Colonial citizens. St. Mary's Church on Spring Street is of interest as the place where John Kennedy married Jacqueline Bouvier, who summered in Newport at her mother's home, Hammersmith Farm, which is now open to the public in summer. Another lavish mansion to be toured in summer is Belcourt Castle, an 1891 Hunt estate designed in the style of Versailles.

More? The Newport Historical Society on Touro Street has Colonial art, prize Newport silver and china, and early American glass and furniture. Changing exhibits are featured at the Newport Art Association on Bellevue Avenue, a Beaux Arts building dating back to 1862, and the Museum of Yachting on Ocean Drive is open to fans in winter by appointment. Even the Redwood Library on Bellevue is historic; it is the oldest library building in the country in continuous use. Among those who used it were painter Gilbert Stuart, and writers William and Henry James and Edith Wharton.

Mansion or not, almost every building in Newport seems to have a history worth noting, and this is a town where you could spend hours tracing the past. That is, unless you'd rather forget it all to head back to the Cliff Walk and gaze a little longer at that mesmerizing winter seascape. It's the side of Newport that many people like best of all.

Area Code: 401

DRIVING DIRECTIONS   From the south, I-95 leads to Route 138 and the Newport Bridge; from the north, follow I-195 to Route 114 south; from Boston take Route 128 south to Route 24 south via the Sakonnet River Bridge to Route 114 or 138 into town. Newport is about 75 miles from Boston, 185 miles from New York, and 75 miles from Hartford.

PUBLIC TRANSPORTATION   Amtrak (800-523-8720) runs from New York and Boston to Providence, with bus connections from the station to Newport. Major airlines serve T. F. Green Airport in Providence, with limo connections from the airport. Much of the town is walkable.

ACCOMMODATIONS   Rates listed are for high season; all are considerably lower in winter, some as much as 50 percent. Ask about special rates, and send for the hotel package brochure printed by the Convention and Visitors' Bureau. All zip codes are 02840. **Inns and guest houses (be sure inns provide parking space):** *The Inn at Castle Hill,* Ocean Drive, 849-3800, $$–$$$$$ CP • *The Admirals* (reservations for all at 846-4256 or toll-free (800) 343-2863 outside Rhode Island): *Admiral Farragut Inn,* 31 Clarke Street, $$–$$$$ CP; *Admiral Fitzroy,* 398 Thames Street, $$$–$$$$$ CP; *Admiral Benbow,* 93 Pelham Street, $$–$$$$ CP • *Francis Malbone House,* 392 Thames Street, 846-0392, $$$$–$$$$$ CP • *Elm Tree Cottage,* 336 Gibbs Avenue, 849-1610, $$$–$$$$$ CP • *Sanford-Covell Villa Marina,* 72 Washington Avenue, 847-0206, $$–$$$$$ CP • *Sarah Kendall House,* 47 Washington Street, 846-7976, $$$–$$$$ CP • *Stella Maris Inn,* 91 Washington Street, 849-2862, $$$ CP • *The Jailhouse Inn,* 13 Marlborough Street, 847-4638, offbeat choice, the renovated 1772 Newport jail, $$–$$$ CP • *The Inntowne,* 6 Mary Street, 846-9200, hotel comforts in an inn setting, $$$–$$$$ CP • *John Banister House,* Pelham and Spring streets, 846-0050, $$$–$$$$ CP • **Some other appealing small guest houses:** *The Inn at Old Beach,* 19 Old Beach Road, 849-3479, elegant Victorian, $$–$$$ CP • *The Victorian Ladies,* 63 Memorial Boulevard, 849-9960, nicely decorated, $$–$$$$ CP • *Melville House,* 39 Clarke Street, 847-0640, small and cozy (closed January and February), $$–$$$ CP • *Brinley Victorian,* 23 Brinley Street, modest, cheerful, $$–$$$$ CP • *Wayside,* Bellevue Avenue, 847-0302, imposing home on mansion row, $$–$$$ CP • *Cliffside Inn,* 2 Seaview Avenue, 847-1811, breezy Victorian near the beach and the Cliff Walk, $$$–$$$$$ CP. If you come back in season, consider *The Willows,* 8 Willow Street, The Point, 846-5486, open April to October, where the hostess specializes in romantic weekends, serves breakfast in bed, $$–$$$ CP • **Resorts and larger hotels:** *Doubletree Islander Resort,* Goat Island, 849-2600, on a private island, $$$$–$$$$$ • *Newport Harbor Hotel and Marina,* America's Cup Avenue, 847-9000, on the harbor, $$$–$$$$$ • *Newport Marriott,* 25 America's Cup Avenue, 849-1000, also on the harbor, $$$$–$$$$$ • *Inn on the Harbor,* 359 Thames Street, 849-6789 or (800) 225-3522, modern 58-suite hotel with mini-kitchens, $$$–$$$$$.

DINING　**Top of the line:** *La Petite Auberge,* 19 Charles Street, 849-6669, renowned French chef, $$–$$$ • *Le Bistro,* 250 Thames Street, 849-7778, French café, one flight up, $$–$$$ • *Clark Cooke House,* Bannister's Wharf, 849-2900, elegant eighteenth-century dining room, $$–$$$ • *Black Pearl,* Bannister's Wharf, 846-5264, converted wharf warehouse, $$–$$$ • *White Horse Tavern,* Marlborough and Farewell streets, 849-3600, nation's oldest continuously operating tavern, $$$ • *Inn at Castle Hill* (see above), $$$ • *Canfield House,* 5 Memorial Boulevard, 847-0416, gracious 1841 home, $$–$$$ • *Rhumbline,* 62 Bridge Street, 849-6950, snug Colonial home, $$ • **Other good choices:** *La Forge Casino,* 186 Bellevue Avenue, 847-0418, French and American, overlooking tennis courts, $$–$$$ • *Yesterday's,* 28 Washington Square, 847-0116, fine dining, $$–$$$; or *The Place,* informal wine bar and grill, $–$$ • *Pronto,* 464 Thames Street, 847-5251, Italian, $–$$ • *Elizabeth's,* Brown and Howard Wharf, Lower Thames Street, 846-6862, attractive decor, varied menu includes Welsh and English specialties, $$–$$$ • *Sardella's,* 30 Memorial Boulevard, 849-6312, traditional Italian, popular, $$–$$$ • *Puerini's,* 24 Memorial Boulevard, 847-5506, tiny, reasonable, always crowded Italian, BYOB, $–$$ • *The Pier,* W. Howard Wharf off Lower Thames Street, 847-3645, overlooking the harbor, entertainment on weekends, busy, $–$$$ • *Sea Fare's American Café,* Brick Market at Thames, 849-9188, pizza to full meals, regional American, $$ • **For seafood:**

Scales and Shells, 527 Thames Street, 846-3474, $–$$ • *Anthony's Shore Dinner Hall,* Waites Wharf (off Lower Thames Street), 848-5058, totally informal, counter service, $–$$ • **For light and reasonable fare:** Both the *Black Pearl* (see above) and *Clark Cooke House* (see above) have café adjuncts; also try *Brick Alley Pub,* 140 Thames, 849-6334 or *Salvation Café,* 140 Broadway, 847-2620. For brunch with a smashing view, *The Inn at Castle Hill* (see above) can't be beat.

SIGHTSEEING *Newport Mansions,* Preservation Society of Newport County, 424 Bellevue Avenue, 847-1000. Hours: Marble House, The Elms, and Château-sur-Mer: November to March, Saturday, Sunday, and Monday holidays, 10 A.M. to 4 P.M.; except December, open daily early December until Christmas week and December 26 to 30. Other mansions have varying weekend and daily schedules from late March to April; all are open daily May to October, 10 A.M. to 5 P.M., later hours in summer. Admission: $6.50 to $8 at each house. Two houses: adults, $12, children, $4; three houses, adults $17.50, children, $5 • *International Tennis Hall of Fame and Tennis Museum,* Newport Casino, Bellevue Avenue, 846-4567. Hours: November to April, daily, 11 A.M. to 4 P.M.; rest of year, daily, 10 A.M. to 5 P.M. Adults, $6; children, $3 • *Touro Synagogue,* 72 Touro Street, 847-4794. Hours: October to May, Sunday only, 1 P.M. to 3 P.M. Rest of year, daily except Saturday, 10 A.M. to 5 P.M., except Friday, to 3 P.M. Free • *Trinity Church,* Church and Spring streets, 846-0660. Hours: October to May, Monday to Friday, 10 A.M. to 1 P.M.; rest of year, Monday to Saturday, 10 A.M. to 4 P.M., on Sunday, after services, to 4 P.M. Free • *Newport Art Museum,* 76 Bellevue Avenue, 848-8200. Hours: Labor Day to Memorial Day, Tuesday to Saturday, 10 A.M. to 4 P.M., Sunday 1 P.M. to 4 P.M.; summer, daily, 10 A.M. to 5 P.M. Adults, $4; under 13, free • *Belcourt Castle,* Bellevue Avenue, 846-0669. Hours: December to April, daily, 10 A.M. to 3 P.M.; Memorial Day to October 15, daily, 9 A.M. to 5 P.M.; April to Memorial Day and mid-October through November, 10 A.M. to 5 P.M. Adults, $6.50; students, $4; ages 6 to 12, $2.50 • *Astor's Beechwood,* Bellevue Avenue, 846-3772. Hours: May to November, daily, 10 A.M. to 5 P.M.; November to mid-December, 10 A.M. to 4 P.M.; rest of year, hours vary—best to phone. Adults, $7.75; children, $6 • *Hammersmith Farm,* Ocean Drive, 846-0420. Hours: daily, April to November, 10 A.M. to 5 P.M. Adults, $6.50; ages 6 to 12, $3 • *Newport Winter Festival,* usually first week of February; write to visitors' bureau for current schedule.

INFORMATION Newport Convention and Visitors' Bureau, 23 America's Cup Avenue, Newport, RI 02840, 849-8098 or (800) 326-6030.

Boning Up on Cambridge

Without its colleges, Cambridge, Massachusetts, might be just another town on the perimeter of Boston. But two prominent residents, Harvard, the nation's oldest and proudest university, and MIT, considered by many to be the birthplace of modern technology, make Cambridge as rightful an attraction for U.S. visitors as Oxford or the original Cambridge University are for travelers to Britain.

Since a visit to Boston seldom leaves enough time to do justice to the town across the Charles River, a weekend in Cambridge can give you a chance to tour the famous universities, explore the many bookstores and shops, join the crowds in the coffee houses, enjoy the fine films and theater in the area, savor finè dining, and generally bone up on a fascinating community.

To begin with, know that Cambridge is not a typical college town. A city of 95,000 that is in many ways a microcosm of a metropolis, it is more than its universities, and more than a suburb. A large part of the population is working class and represents a wide mix of nationalities.

Another part of the mix is intellectual and creative, people ranging from John Kenneth Galbraith to author John Irving to TV chef Julia Child, who live in the handsome and historic residential neighborhoods that mark a city that is now more than 350 years old.

It is almost impossible to separate the history of Cambridge from that of Harvard, the institution that shaped it. The town was founded in 1630 as Newtowne; the college came along just six years later. It was named for local minister John Harvard, who died in 1638, leaving his fortune and library to the institution.

As Harvard grew to greatness, Cambridge flowered as well. Great universities tend to collect impressive architecture, famous people, and fine museums, and Cambridge has them all. Students and visitors usually attract good restaurants, shops, and attractive lodging, and Cambridge offers all of these in abundance as well.

There is so much, in fact, that at first glance academic Cambridge is a jumble of impressions. Busy Harvard Square, the hub of activity, seems to be in perpetual motion, filled with people and traffic. The big out-of-town newspaper stand, the sprawling Harvard Coop, the string of stores and sandwich shops and banks say little about the past, yet the square opens directly into the gate to Harvard Yard, a tranquil, ivied repository of history. The information booth in the square has maps to make it easier to get your bearings.

Since the university is the major lure for most visitors, you'll likely want to spend Saturday getting to know that campus and its rich variety of sights, beginning with the Yard. Harvard has its own information center on the plaza at Holyoke Center, 1350 Massachusetts Avenue, where you can pick up a free map that identifies every Harvard-owned building and all the streets in the immediate area. Student-guided tours of the campus also leave from this point.

If you prefer to tour on your own, cross the street and enter Harvard Yard through the Quincy Gate to see the oldest part of the campus. Massachusetts Hall, where the university president has his office, has stood on this spot since 1720. Holden Chapel, dating from 1744, is a gem of Georgian architecture. Untold numbers of students and visitors to the campus have had their picture taken with the seated statue of John Harvard that stands in front of University Hall, the gray stone building designed in 1815 by Charles Bulfinch.

The quadrangle in back of University Hall is dominated by the bulk of Widener Library, the largest university library in the world. Behind Widener's Corinthian portico are ten stories holding the equivalent of 50 miles of books, some three million volumes. Walk inside to see panoramic scale models of Harvard and Cambridge, old and new.

Across the quadrangle is the steepled 1932 Memorial Chapel and Sever Hall, an 1880 classroom building designed by H. H. Richardson, the late-nineteenth-century master architect, two more of Harvard's many architectural treasures.

Straight on to Robinson Hall, then left past Emerson Hall and onto Quincy Street will bring you to the Fogg Art Museum, whose collections include almost every significant period of Western art. The Wertheim Collection of Impressionist and post-Impressionist art is world class, and there are important works by Picasso, Ingres, Whistler, and many others. The Fogg is a training ground for curators the world over.

Adjoining the building is the Busch-Reisinger Museum, one of the few museums in this country specializing in the art of North and Central Europe. The collection of German expressionist paintings is particularly outstanding.

Next door to the Fogg is the Carpenter Center for the Visual Arts, a sweep of glass and concrete that is the only Le Corbusier building in North America.

Exit the Fogg Museum on Quincy, turn right, and cross the street to Broadway and the Arthur M. Sackler Museum, the newest campus art repository. The ancient Islamic and Oriental art here includes the world's richest collection of Chinese jades.

Continuing on Quincy, on the left is Memorial Hall, a massive cathedral-like brick building with a tiled roof. It houses the Sanders Theater, where many of the area's music and dance groups often perform.

Back on Kirkland, turn right on Oxford and you'll come to the Harvard University Museum building, four museums under one roof that include everything from dinosaurs to rare jewels. The garden of Blaschka glass flowers in the Botanical Museum is world renowned—bigger than life and absolutely true to nature.

In addition to the interesting museum displays of North, Central, and South American cultures, the gift shop in the Peabody Museum of Archaeology and Ethnology is worth a visit. It is filled with the finest in Indian baskets, Eskimo carvings, beadwork, and fine Navajo jewelry, among many other unique handcrafts.

The printed guide will lead you to more Harvard, Radcliffe, and Cambridge sights. In addition to the museums, you can see the fine residence houses of the campus between Harvard Square and the Charles River. Dunster, Lowell, and Elliot Houses are the three domes you see standing out. The huge, modern complex off of Massachusetts Avenue is the new Science Center. A campus map will show you where other schools are located.

Outside the campus, Cambridge history merges with that of the college. At the edge of Harvard Yard is the Wadsworth House, a 1726 frame house that was for 100 years the residence of Harvard presidents and was also the site of George Washington's militia offices in 1775. It now houses the Harvard alumni office.

Across the square from the Yard is the 1631 Ancient Burying Ground, where both Harvard presidents and important Revolutionary leaders are buried. It is beside the nineteenth-century wooden Gothic building of the First Parish Unitarian Church. Next to the Burying Ground on Garden Street opposite the common is Christ Church, the town's oldest, worth a look inside for its handsome Georgian interior. The church became a barracks during the American Revolution, but was restored to its intended use by George Washington, who worshiped here in 1775 and 1776.

Historic Cambridge Common, the starting place for many events that led to our nation's freedom, is where the Massachusetts Bay Colony held its elections in the seventeenth century, where French militia trained for the French and Indian Wars, and where Washington took command of the First Continental Army. Today it is crowded by twentieth-century buildings, including the Harvard Law School.

Having seen the sights, go back to Harvard Square to explore the mix of bookstores, cafés, and shops that are a hub not only for Harvard but for all the thousands of students at Boston's many colleges. You certainly needn't be a student to enjoy Harvard Square, however. The Harvard Coop is all but overwhelming—a sort of intellectual department store occupying several buildings, selling clothing and almost everything else you can think of, including a stock of books and art prints that is nothing short of extraordinary.

All of Cambridge, in fact, is an extraordinary place for book lovers. Words Worth on Brattle Street is a discount bookstore, Pangloss on Mt. Auburn Street has an impressive collection of rare and out-of-print volumes, Shoenhof's has foreign books, and the Grolier and Harvard bookstores add to the incredible variety of volumes available in this small area, more than 20 at last count, including a host of used bookstores packed with dusty treasures.

What else is around the square? Jeans and fine tailoring, stationery and wares from Greece, herbs and incense, Russian wooden dolls, fringed shawls, and exotic earrings, pricey women's clothing and inexpensive cottons from India, posters and housewares for the home, traditional Ivy League dress at J. Press. You'll see the shops as you walk Mt. Auburn, Dunster, and the other narrow streets off Harvard Square and in small complexes such as the Garage on Dunster or the Mall at 99 Mt. Auburn.

A good street for browsing is Brattle, where the Brattle Street Theater has old film fare to delight buffs. Radcliffe Yard, another lovely academic complex, is on Brattle across from the Loeb Drama Center, the home of the excellent productions of the American Repertory Theatre.

Brattle was once known as Tory Row, and you'll see why if you continue walking past the impressive homes on the street. The Longfellow House at 105 is a National Historic Site, the place where the poet lived and wrote many of his poems while he taught at Harvard.

The Blacksmith House nearby is the present home of the Cambridge Center for Adult Education, where you'll find many interesting evening programs. It was at one time the home of the "village smithy" made famous by Longfellow's poem.

Cambridge is still home to creative minds producing a prodigious number of books, poems, plays, theories, music, art, and ideas. The feeling of creativity is almost tangible, particularly in the coffee houses and cafés, where Cambridge literati often seem to arrive with works in progress. The Algiers Coffee House and Au Bon Pain, the French bakery café, are popular spots. The outdoor café in front of the latter is a gathering spot for chatters and chess players on all but the most frigid days.

The restaurants in Cambridge reflect the community's cosmopolitan makeup. You'll find everything from haute cuisine to inexpensive ethnic, something for every taste and budget. The trendy spots come and go quickly here, but a few seem to stand the test of time. These include the long-established Harvest, the romantic Upstairs at the Pudding (above the famous Hasty Pudding Club), and old-timers such as Legal Sea Foods. Newer favorites include Anago Bistro, the East Coast Grill, the Cottonwood Café, and the Rialto at the Charles Hotel, where well-known chef Michela Larson took over in 1994.

There is a range of hotels as well, with the stylish Charles near Harvard Square at the top of the list. There's a first-class spa and indoor pool here, and the Regatta Bar is a favorite gathering place to hear jazz. Another luxury choice is the Inn at Harvard, on the eastern edge of the square. There are motels with lower rates, including one almost directly on Harvard Square.

The Hyatt Regency affords the best view of the Charles and the Boston skyline from its revolving rooftop restaurant and has an indoor pool and health club, while the Royal Sonesta offers excellent weekend packages, but both are far from the action around Harvard Square.

This is also a particularly good town for bed-and-breakfast accommodations, since they may put you in one of the very private neighborhoods of lovely old homes.

Having given Saturday to Harvard and Harvard Square, fortify yourself with Sunday brunch and move on to the impressive campus of MIT on the Charles River. Instead of ivied red-brick halls, you'll find stately stone neoclassic buildings and stunning modern architecture. Many of the newer buildings are significant contributions by contemporary architectural greats such as Eero Saarinen, who designed the Kresge Auditorium and the MIT Chapel.

As you might expect, the major MIT museums trace the development of science and technology. The Hart Nautical Galleries concentrate on marine engineering. All is not science, however. Contemporary art may be seen at the List Visual Arts Center, and the entire MIT campus is a museum of outdoor sculpture by Calder, Moore, Picasso, and other masters.

From MIT you can drive directly across the Massachusetts Avenue Bridge over the Charles River and be in Boston in two minutes. An eight-minute ride on the "T" from Harvard Square will also put you in the heart of the city. Assuming that this is a winter weekend, it may be just the chance to catch up on some of the indoor Boston attractions you may have missed in warmer weather—the treasure-filled Museum of Fine Arts, perhaps, or the Museum of Science or the John F. Kennedy Library.

But though easy access to Boston has always been a plus for Cambridge, this exceptional small city really needs no added incentive to make it a prime destination. Wherever you go in Cambridge, whether sightseeing at Harvard and MIT, shopping in the Coop, or sipping espresso in a café, you know that you are in the company of people and ideas that not only shaped America's past but are molders of its future.

Area Code: 617

DRIVING DIRECTIONS   Cambridge is on the northwest bank of the Charles River, four miles east of Boston and connected to the city by many bridges over the Charles as well as via the "T," the local subway system. See Boston directions on page 74.

ACCOMMODATIONS   Most hotels have weekend package rates much lower than the daily rates given here; ask for them. _Charles Hotel,_ One Bennett Street at Eliot Street, 02138, 864-1200, $$$$ • _Inn_ *at Harvard,* 1201 Massachusetts Avenue, 02138, 491-2222 or (800) 222-8733, $$$–$$$$ • *Sheraton Commander,* 16 Garden Street, opposite the common, 02138, 547-4800, $$$$–$$$$$ • *Hyatt Regency Hotel,* 575 Memorial Drive, 02139, 492-1234, $$$$–$$$$$ • *Royal Sonesta Hotel,* 5 Cambridge Parkway, 02142, 491-3600, $$$$$ • *Howard Johnson,* 777 Memorial Drive, 02139, 492-7777, $$–$$$$ • *Quality Inn,* 1651 Massachusetts Avenue, 02138, 491-1000 or (800) 228-5151, $$–$$$ • *Harvard Manor House,* 110 Mt. Auburn Street, 02138, 864-5200, motel, $$$ CP • *Mary Prentiss Inn,* 6 Prentiss Street, 661-2929, charming small bed-and-breakfast inn, 1843 Greek Revival home, located just off Massachusetts Avenue near Porter Square, a ten minutes' walk from Harvard Square, $$–$$$ CP • **A budget possibility:** *Irving House,* 24 Irving Street, 547-4600, restored small inn, $ CP.

DINING *Anago Bistro,* 798 Main, 876-8444, excellent reviews, $$–$$$ • *Harvest Restaurant,* 44 Brattle Street, 492-1115, perennial favorite, American and continental, $$$–$$$$; *Harvest Café,* $–$$ • *Upstairs at the Pudding,* 10 Holyoke Street, 864-1933, elegant northern Italian, $$–$$$ • *Rialto,* Charles Hotel (see above), new headquarters for well-known chef Michela Larson, $$–$$$ • *Legal Sea Foods,* 5 Cambridge Center, Kendall Square, 864-3400, a local institution, $–$$$ • *The Blue Room,* 1 Kendall Square, 494-9034, Mediterranean and French, good reports, $$ • *East Coast Grill,* 1271 Cambridge Street, 491-6568, spicy ribs, Tex-Mex, and more, $$ • *Cottonwood Café,* Porter Exchange, 1815 Massachusetts Avenue, 661-7440, interesting Southwestern fare, $$ • *Peacock,* 5 Craigie Circle, 661-4073, cozy, continental, $$ • *Jae's Café & Grill,* 1281 Cambridge Street, 497-8380, Asian cuisines, bigger version of a Boston favorite, $–$$ • *Changsho,* 1712 Massachusetts Avenue, 547-6565, attractive setting for well-prepared Chinese food, $$ • *Daddy-O's Bohemian Café,* 134 Hampshire Street, 354-8371, funky, Mediterranean-Jewish, $–$$ • **Good and cheap ethnic choices:** *Tandoor House,* 991 Massachusetts Avenue, 661-9001, Indian, $–$$; *Trattoria Il Panino,* 1100 Massachusetts Avenue, 547-5818, Italian, $; *Border Café,* 32 Church Street, 861-6400, Mexican, $–$$; *Skewers,* 92 Mt. Auburn Street, 491-3079, Middle Eastern, $; *Bertucci's,* 21 Brattle Street, 864-4748, pizza, $; *Iruna,* 56 John F. Kennedy Street, 868-5633, Spanish, $; *Singha House,* 1105 Massachusetts Avenue, 864-5154, Thai, $ • Highly recommended is brunch at the *House of Blues,* 96 Winthrop Street, 491-2583, a Southern-style buffet accompanied by live gospel music, $$. This is one of several good jazz clubs in Cambridge; others include the *Regatta Bar* in the Charles Hotel and *Ryles,* 212 Hampshire Street, 547-4600.

SIGHTSEEING Harvard University, Information Center, 1350 Massachusetts Avenue, 495-1573, Monday through Saturday, 9 A.M. to

4:45 P.M.; check current schedule for free guided campus tours. *Harvard Art Museums,* 495-9400: Hours for all: daily, 10 A.M. to 5 P.M. Admission includes all three museums; Adults, $5; students, $3; under 18, free. *Fogg Art Museum,* 32 Quincy Street; *Arthur M. Sackler Museum,* 485 Broadway; *Busch-Reisinger Museum,* enter through Fogg Art Museum. *Harvard University Museums of Cultural and Natural History,* 26 Oxford Street, 495-1910. Hours: Monday to Saturday, 9 A.M. to 4:30 P.M., Sunday, 1 P.M. to 4:30 P.M. Adults, $4; students, $3; under 13, $1. All Harvard museums are free to all on Saturday, 10 A.M. to noon • *Massachusetts Institute of Technology,* Information Center, 77 Massachusetts Avenue, 253-1000. Hours: weekdays only, 9 A.M. to 5 P.M.; free campus tours weekdays, 10 A.M. and 2 P.M. *MIT Museum,* 265 Massachusetts Avenue, 253-4444. Hours: Tuesday to Friday, 9 A.M. to 5 P.M., Saturday and Sunday, noon to 5 P.M. Adults, $3; children, $1. • *Hart Nautical Galleries,* 77 Massachusetts Avenue, 253-4444. Hours: daily, 9 A.M. to 8 P.M. Free • *List Visual Arts Center,* Wiesner Building, 20 Ames Street, 253-4680. Hours: September to June, Monday to Friday, noon to 5 P.M.; Saturday and Sunday, 1 P.M. to 5 P.M. Free. • *Longfellow National Historic Site,* 105 Brattle Street, 876-4491. Hours: daily, 10 A.M. to 4:30 P.M. Adults, $2; under 17 with adult, free • *American Repertory Theater,* 64 Brattle Street, 547-8300. Check for current offerings.

INFORMATION Cambridge Chamber of Commerce, 859 Massachusetts Avenue, Cambridge, MA 02139, 876-4100.

Sugaring Off in Grafton

Maples and Vermont are all but synonymous. So it is not surprising that maple sugaring—a major state industry and a livelihood for hundreds of Vermont farmers—is a cause for local celebration. After a long winter, sugaring is the first sure sign of spring, despite the layers of snow that may still be on the ground.

Seeing how the sugaring is done and getting in on a traditional "sugar on snow" party with fresh syrup hardened into candy in the snow is good reason for a late winter visit. Dozens of Vermont sugarmakers welcome visitors, though most appreciate a call for an appointment first. A list of sugarmaking farms is available free from the state Department of Agriculture.

It takes cold nights and warm days to make the sap rise, so the timing of the sugaring season is entirely in the hands of Mother Nature. Usually, early to mid-March is the peak in the southern part of the state; it takes a little longer up north.

The state's official Maple Festival is held in late April way up north in St. Albans, but since the most interesting sight for most visitors is a visit to a farm, you needn't journey quite so far or wait so long. Farms all over the state carry on the traditional tapping of the trees and gathering of the buckets, a task that still is often accomplished best by horse and sled despite all the modern improvements in methods.

One excellent southern home base for viewing this century-old operation is Grafton, a town with a wonderful inn and a special ambience that will add much to your stay. Grafton's own Plummer's Sugar House is open for tours, and the town is located within easy reach of farms in Chester, Ludlow, Marlboro, Putney, and several other locations.

Remember that unusual weather can speed or slow the season, so be sure to phone and check before you set off on a trip. For example, in one recent year Thomas Eldridge and his sons had fired up the first kettles in their Baltimore, Vermont, sugar house by February 23.

The Eldridges have a large operation, with some 2,000 taps to tend. The syrup they produce and sell has been ordered and shipped to customers as far away as New Guinea. They use tractors to pick up buckets from the trees nearest to the road, but in late afternoon you can usually see a team of horses setting out into the woods to gather the buckets from more remote areas, just the way it has been done for a hundred years or more.

You can enjoy a horse-drawn sleigh ride through the "sugar bush," the area where sap is running, at the Putney farm of Donald and Madeline Harlow. They also set up a treat booth during sugaring season where you can buy homemade goodies such as maple-coated apples, corn fritters with fresh syrup, and the traditional "sugar on snow" treat. The Harlows have assembled a small exhibit of old-time sugaring methods, with photos of the oxen-drawn sleds that were used to gather the buckets and displays of old kettles and other utensils. A film about the Vermont maple sugaring industry is shown regularly in their little gift shop, where you can buy syrup and maple candy year-round.

If you've never seen how maple syrup is made, you may be surprised to learn that the sweet sap running into the buckets is as thin and clear as water. When the buckets are full, they are taken to the sugar house, where the sap is emptied into an evaporator to simmer slowly over the fire until it thickens into a golden, gooey, and delicious syrup. On hillsides all over Vermont, you can see the clouds of smoke day and night, marking a sugar house in action.

A good tree will produce 40 quarts of sap drip by drip, which must be hauled down day by day to the evaporator. You may understand better why the syrup is so costly when you learn that it takes 40 gallons of sap to produce one gallon of syrup. To provide enough heat to boil down that much sap requires a log as big as a man, split, sawed, and dried.

The finished syrup comes in grades, fancy for the lightest and sweetest; medium-amber Grade A for general use on pancakes and French toast; dark Grade B, a robust caramel flavor used in cooking; and grade C, an even stronger flavor also used for cooking. Some people find the richer flavor of the B and C grades more to their liking than the more costly A syrups.

The picture-perfect village of Grafton is an ideal destination for any season. The town still looks much the way it did in its 1800s prime, and that is no accident. It is a town that had the good fortune to be "adopted" by the Windham Foundation, which was founded by millionaire Dean Mathey, former chairman of the Bank of New York.

Mathey had no children, so most of his fortune went to the foundation after his death in 1962. The trustees looked for a project he would have approved, and decided there was no more appropriate idea than the salvation of the tiny town of Grafton, a place that Mathey loved. He had his own summer home right on Main Street, and many of his family members were longtime residents as well.

Once a prosperous mill and agricultural center, Grafton, like many such towns, had declined by the early twentieth century. The population had dwindled to less than 500, and many of the old buildings had been left to deteriorate, though their original charm could still be seen.

In the 1960s, the Windham Foundation, named for Grafton's home county, set out to bring the town back to its former self. The first project was a practical one. The old grocery store was in sad shape, and the townspeople found themselves having to travel elsewhere for food and other daily necessities. So the derelict building was shored up, sagging floors were leveled, warped walls were straightened, and pretty soon the store was looking much the way it had when it was finished back in 1841, at least on the outside. Inside it became a complete modern market.

One by one the village houses were also purchased and refurbished. At the same time the Windham Foundation took on the renewal of The Old Tavern, once a noted stopping place when Grafton was a trading center. The old guest books list such notables as Rudyard Kipling, Ulysses S. Grant, Daniel Webster, Oliver Wendell Holmes, Theodore Roosevelt, and Ralph Waldo Emerson.

With the restoration the tavern became one of New England's most elegant little inns. People now come to Grafton from around the country and around the world. Early reservations are a must.

If the inn is filled, a delightful alternative is The Inn at Woodchuck Hill Farm, an antique-filled 1790 farmhouse on 200 acres just outside town. The property is on a hilltop with soaring views. Rooms are in the main house or the quaint restored barn. Recently, small bed-and-breakfast inns have provided more options in town.

What to do in Grafton? Very little, which is very much part of this town's charm. If there is snow, you can downhill-ski at Stratton Mountain nearby, or make tracks through the woods at the Grafton Ponds Cross-Country Ski Center, which is run by The Old Tavern. If the spring thaw has set in, or if you don't ski, paddle tennis is available at the inn, or you can simply stroll through Grafton's picturesque streets or take a bike ride or a hike on the walking trails that abound around town. The inn will give you a folder of trails that will show you the Grafton of old. If you hike the more wooded trails, be forewarned that spring is known as "mud season" in Vermont, so wear proper footgear.

Cheese is still made at the restored cheese factory in Grafton, and visitors are welcome to come by to see how it is done. The Grafton Village Apple Company has apples and cider in season, maple syrup in the spring, and Grafton Goodjam offers jams and chutneys made with maple syrup and organically grown fruit. There are a couple of gift shops for browsing in town, and the Gallery North Star features art work by regional artists.

More diversions can be found about 14 miles south in Newfane. The Newfane Country Store is chock-a-block with New England quilts, and a choice place to shop for handicrafts, homemade baked goods, and old-fashioned penny candy as well. There's an art gallery upstairs. Schommer Antiques across the street has a diverse and interesting stock, and there is an antique cooperative a couple of miles east of town. If you come back from May to October, you can look for treasures at the big flea market held weekends on Route 30, the oldest and largest open air market in Vermont.

Newfane is another particularly lovely Vermont town; bring a camera to capture the columned buildings around its perfect village green. Plan to stay for dinner, too, for the local inns, The Four Columns Inn and the Old Newfane Inn have renowned dining rooms. These are also happy alternatives for lodging as well; The Four Columns Inn, is first choice.

For those who prefer a more rustic farmhouse setting and the chance for horseback riding (a nice way to see the countryside this time of year), the West River Lodge provides homey and comfortable surroundings and very congenial hosts. Two lovely inns in the general vicinity are the Windham Hill Inn, set on a secluded 160-acre hilltop in West Townshend, and Rowell's Inn, an 1820 stagecoach stop filled with atmosphere, antiques, and informal warmth. Townshend, a few, miles west of Newfane on Route 30, is another town with a beautiful two-acre village green. It offers a few more stops for antiquers.

One final possibility is The Governor's Inn in Ludlow, north of

Grafton, a small inn that has gained renown for its lavish six-course dinners served by waitresses in Victorian costume.

This is a weekend that will take you back to the tranquility of another time—a visit to the farm, a stroll through peaceful country towns and village shops. At day's end there's lots of time to savor a drink in front of a roaring fire and dinner in a cozy, beamed dining room.

To make it even better, there's that delicious maple syrup to bring home as a sweet souvenir of the trip.

Area Code: 802

DRIVING DIRECTIONS   From I-91, Exit 5 (North Westminster and Bellows Falls), take Route 121 west to Grafton. Alternate route: From I-91, Exit 2, Brattleboro, follow Route 30 west to Newfane, then Route 35 north to Grafton. Call each farm for specific driving directions. Grafton is 152 miles from Boston, 221 miles from New York, and 111 miles from Hartford.

PUBLIC TRANSPORTATION   Vermont Transit has bus service to Bellows Falls.

ACCOMMODATIONS   *The Old Tavern at Grafton,* Grafton 05146, 843-2231, main building and annex, $$–$$$$ CP • *The Inn at Woodchuck Hill Farm,* Middletown Road, Grafton 05146, 843-2398, delightful country hideaway, $$–$$$$ CP • *The Hayes House,* Bear Hill Road, Grafton 05146, 843-2461, bed-and-breakfast home, $$ CP • *The Four Columns Inn,* Route 30, Newfane 05345, 365-7713, $$$–$$$$ CP • *Old Newfane Inn,* Route 30, Newfane 05345, 365-4427, $$$ • *West River Lodge,* Hill Road, PO Box 693, Newfane 05345, 365-7745, $–$$ CP; $$$ MAP • *Windham Hill Inn,* Windham Hill Road, RR 1, Box 44, West Townshend 05359, 874-4080, $$$$–$$$$$ MAP • *Rowell's Inn,* RR#1, Box 269, Simonsville 05143, 875-3658, $$$ MAP • *The Governor's Inn,* 86 Main Street, Ludlow 05149, 228-8830, $$$$–$$$$$ MAP.

DINING   *The Old Tavern at Grafton* (see above), $$ • *The Four Columns Inn* (see above), $$$ • *Old Newfane Inn* (see above), $$–$$$ • *Three Mountain Inn,* Route 30, Jamaica (west of Newfane), 874-4140, $$ • *The Governor's Inn* (see above), prix fixe, $$$$$.

SIGHTSEEING   Farm visits to watch maple sugaring are free, but you must call ahead to make sure the weather is right and syrup is being made. Ask for driving directions as well. The Vermont Department of

Agriculture prints a complete listing of farms in the state that invite visitors. Write to them at 116 State Street, Drawer 20, Montpelier, VT 05602, 828-2416. Farms mentioned here are: *Thomas C. Eldridge & Sons,* Baltimore Road, Route 4, Box 336, Chester (though the post office is Chester, the location is actually in Baltimore), 263-5680 (evenings are the best time to reach Mr. Eldridge) • *Harlow's Sugar House,* Route 5, RD 1, Box 395, Putney, 387-5852 • *Plummer's Sugarhouse,* Townshend Road, PO Box 85, Grafton, 843-2207.

INFORMATION   Vermont Travel Division, Agency of Development and Community Affairs, Montpelier, VT 05602, 828-3236; Vermont Chamber of Commerce, Box 37, Montpelier, VT 05601, 223-3443.

Maps

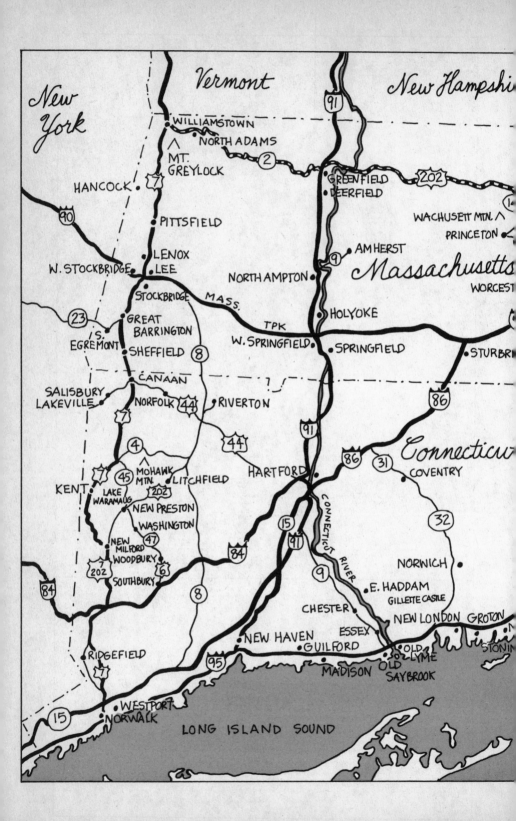

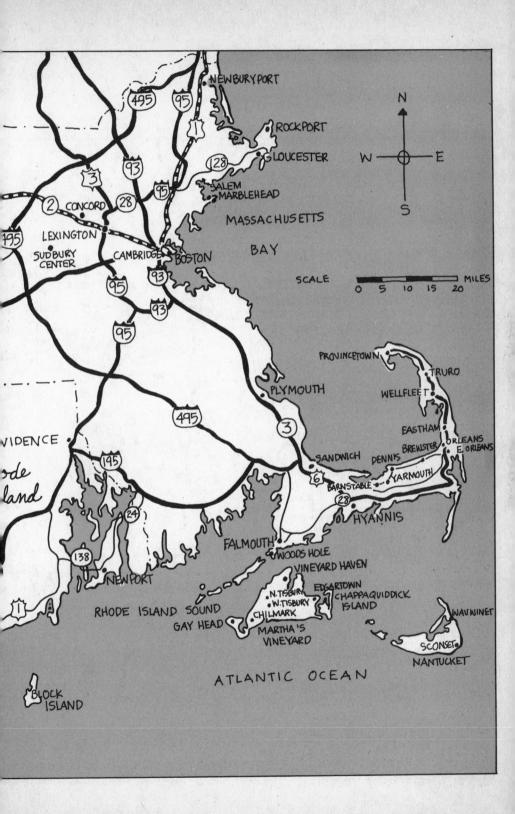

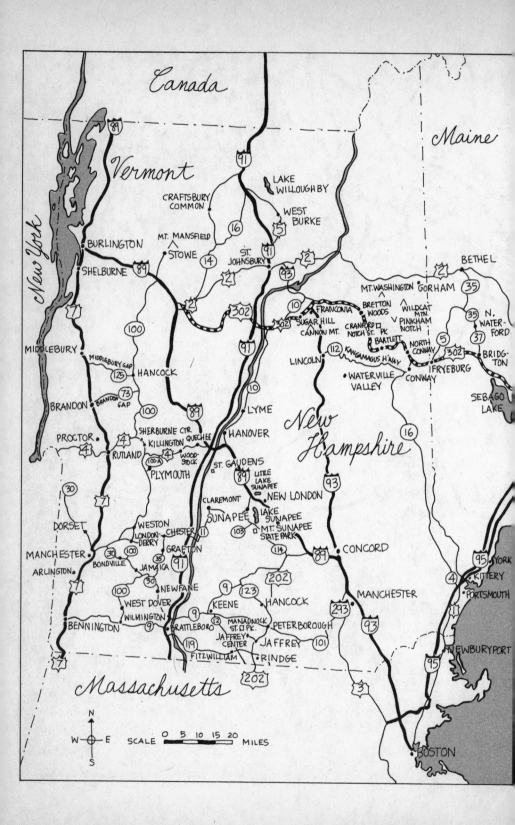

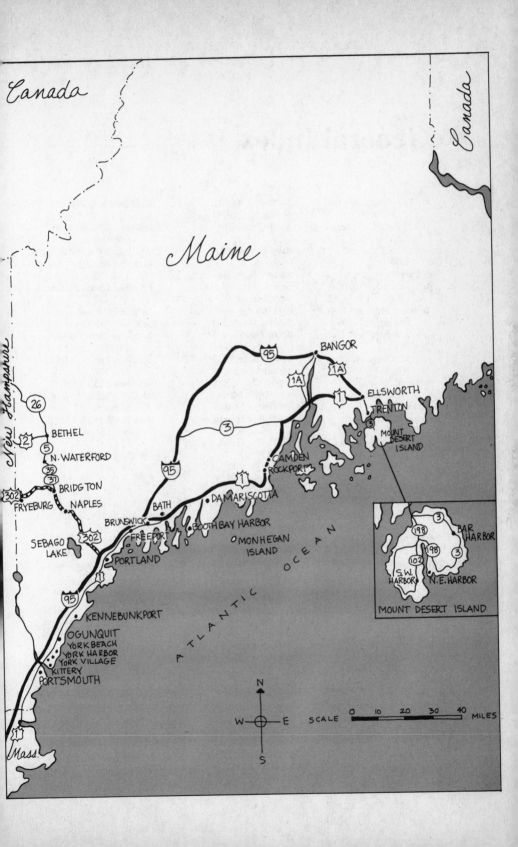

Canada

Canada

Maine

New Hampshire

BANGOR

95

1A

1A

1

ELLSWORTH

TRENTON

26

BETHEL

3

MOUNT DESERT ISLAND

2

5

N. WATERFORD

3

35

37

CAMDEN

ROCKPORT

95

BRIDGTON

1

302

FRYEBURG

NAPLES

DAMARISCOTTA

BATH

BRUNSWICK

3

BAR HARBOR

198

302

FREEPORT

BOOTHBAY HARBOR

198

3

SEBAGO LAKE

PORTLAND

MONHEGAN ISLAND

102

S.W. HARBOR

N.E. HARBOR

1

MOUNT DESERT ISLAND

95

KENNEBUNKPORT

A T L A N T I C   O C E A N

OGUNQUIT

YORK BEACH

YORK HARBOR

YORK VILLAGE

KITTERY

PORTSMOUTH

N

W — E

S

SCALE

0   10   20   30   40   MILES

1

Mass.

General Index

Mt. Chocorua, 191
Mt. Cranmore, 262
Mt. Desert, Maine, 125
Mt. Desert Festival, 127
Mt. Desert Oceanarium, 127, 130
Mt. Greylock, 134, 192, 195
Mt. Greylock Reservation, 195
Mt. Holyoke College, 60
Mt. Hor, 179
Mt. Kearsarge, 140
Mt. Liberty, 188
Mt. Mansfield, 244
Mt. Megunticook, 205
Mt. Monadnock, 108–13
Mt. Monadnock State Park, 110, 113
Mt. Pisgah, 179
Mt. Snow, 163
Mt. Snow Craft Show, 164
Mt. Sunapee II, 139, 142–43
Mt. Sunapee ski gondola, 139
Mt. Sunapee State Park, 138
Mt. Sunapee State Park Beach, 142
Mt. Washington, 93–99
Mt. Washington Auto Road, 98
Mt. Washington Cog Railway, 95, 98
Mt. Washington Valley Ski Touring Foundation, 260, 263
Mt. Washington Valley Theater Company, 96
Museum of American Political Life, 238, 240
Museum of Art (Northhampton), 60
Museum of Connecticut History, 239
Museum of Fine Arts (Boston), 69, 71, 74, 77, 222, 279
Museum of Fine Arts (Springfield), 59
Museum of Rhode Island History, 28
Museum of Science, 74, 223–24, 279
Museum of Yachting, 272
Music at King Ridge, 141
Mystic, Conn., 227–30
Mystic Marinelife Aquarium, 65, 69, 228–29, 230
Mystic Seaport, 63, 69, 227–28
Mystic Seaport Museum, 65, 230

Nantucket, 19–25, 148–51
Nantucket Historical Association, 21
Nantucket Village, 150
Naples, Maine, 172, 266
Narramissic Farm, 175
Nathan Hale Schoolhouse, 64, 68
Nathaniel Macy House, 21
National Training Laboratories, 264
Nature Center for Environmental Activities, 88, 89–90
Naumkeag Museum and Gardens, 135, 137
Nauset Beach, 167, 171
Nautilus, 68
New England Aquarium, 73, 219, 222, 223
New England Brewing Company, 86
New England Center for Contemporary Art, 16
New England Maple Museum, 216, 218
New England Marionette Opera, 108–9, 113
New England Science Center, 251, 253
New England Ski Museum, 189, 191, 259, 262
Newfane, Vt., 284
Newfield, Maine, 175
New Hampshire State Parks, 109, 113
New Harbor, 106
New London, Conn., 63–65
New London, N.H., 138, 139
New London Barn Players, 139, 141
New Marlborough, Mass., 131, 134
Newport, N.H., 139
Newport, R.I., 268–74
Newport Art Association, 272
Newport Art Museum, 274
Newport Historical Society Museum, 272
Newport Jazz Festival, 269
Newport Mansions, 274
Newport Winter Festival, 274
New Preston, Conn., 44
Niantic, Conn., 65
Nichols House, 70, 77
Nightingale-Brown House, 27
Noah Webster House, 240
Noank, Conn., 65
Nook Farm, 236–37, 239–40
Norfolk, Conn., 255

Norman Rockwell Exhibition (Arlington), 166
Norman Rockwell Museum (Rutland), 216–17, 218
Norman Rockwell Museum (Stockbridge), 133, 137
North Adams, Mass., 195
Northampton, Mass., 60–61
North Bridge, 9, 10
North Conway, N.H., 95, 96, 258
Northeastern College, 71
Northeast Harbor, Maine, 125, 126
Northeast Kingdom, 177–82
North Ferry Islands, 205
North Light lighthouse, 105
North Shore Art Association, 33, 35–36
North Sutton, N.H., 139, 140
Norwalk, Conn., 84–90
Norwich, Mass., 16–17
Norwich, Vt., 232
Nubanusit River, 110
Nubble Light, 100

Oak Bluffs, Mass., 115, 116
Occum Pond, 233
Oceanarium Lobster Hatchery, 128, 130
Ocean Beach Park, 68
Ocean Drive, 269–70
Ocean Point, 144
Ogunquit, Maine, 90–93
Ogunquit Museum of American Art, 91, 93
Ogunquit Playhouse, 90
Old Bennington, Vt., 162
Old Burying Ground (Concord), 9
Old Burying Ground (York Village), 100
Old Cemetery Point, 49
Old Corner Bookstore, 73, 220
Old Customs House, 39
Old Deerfield Crafts Fair, 194
Old Fort House, 146
Old Gaol (Nantucket), 20
Old Gaol (York Village), 100
Old Harbor, 104, 105, 106
Old Jail (Concord), 10–11
Old Lyme, Conn., 63, 66
Old Lyme Art Association, 67
Old Man of the Mountain, 96, 187, 188, 260
Old Manse, The, 10, 11, 13
Old Mill, 20, 25

Category Index